SECRETS OF A MASTER MODERATOR™
THIRD EDITION

By: Naomi R. Henderson

Secrets of a Master Moderator™
By: Naomi R. Henderson

©2011, 2015 Naomi R. Henderson

All rights reserved. No part of this publication may be reproduced or transmitted in any form or by any means, electronic or mechanical, including photocopying and recording, or by any information storage and retrieval system, without permission in writing from the publisher.

Cover design by Brian Harris
Edited by Monique Kittka Donlon (Edition III)
        Eleanor Bourg Nicholson (Edition I & II)
Typeset by Janice K. Stallings (Edition I, II & III)
Typeset by Kelley DuBois (Edition III)

ISBN: 978-0-9836739-2-7

Published in the United States by
VISAR Corporation
1700 Rockville Pike
Suite 260
Rockville, MD 20852

Visit us at www.RIVAinc.com

Manufactured in the United States of America

Books are available in quantity for promotional or premium use. Write to Director of SOMM Special Sales, VISAR Corporation, 1700 Rockville Pike, Suite 260, Rockville, MD 20852, for information on discounts and terms or call (301) 770-6456 ext. 101.

The information contained in this book is not a substitute for the experiential learning available via courses, seminars, and workshops. Moderating is a "hands-on" experience. Reading about a tool or technique will not transfer that experience to the reader. For information about RIVA courses log on to www.RIVAinc.com/training/.

Notes from the Editor

Portions of the articles contained here have been published previously in a variety of publications. The sources include *Quirk's Marketing Research Review, Qualitative Health Research, The American Market Association Journal* (a quarterly column entitled *Qualitative Reflections*), and *Alert,* the *Journal of Marketing Research.*

Additionally, some segments have been adapted from RIVA webinars, course curriculum materials, custom courses, speaking engagements, and presentations.

All of the ideas and methodologies presented here have been tested and implemented in research projects, reports, class sessions, client meetings, and presentations over the past thirty years. The author makes no claim that her way is *"the way,"* rather she states boldly: *"This is what has worked for me and I am happy to pass on what I have learned."*

Dedication

For Luc:
Thanks for reminding me
that I can talk about life
or I can live life.
For all you taught me,
I am thankful.

SECRETS OF A MASTER MODERATOR™

THIRD EDITION

CONTENTS

A key logo beside the title of an article indicates new content for the Third Edtion.

- **Preface** I
- About the Author III
- Foreword V
- **Acknowledgments** XI
- How to Use this Book XV

PART I: THE WORLD OF QUALITATIVE RESEARCH

SECTION I: QUALITATIVE RESEARCH

- The Players in the Qualitative Market Research Game 5
  - Figure 1: *Who Talks to Whom in the Research Game* 7
- Qualities of a Master Moderator™ 9
- Anatomy of a Qualitative Research Project 17
- Qualitative Research Projects: A Twelve-Step Process 19
  - Figure 2: *The Twelve-Step Qualitative Market Research Process* 25
- Embracing the Qualitative Quadrangle 27
- Qualitative Research Lessons from *Gone With The Wind* 33
- Qualitative Research Techniques: Taking the Best of the Past Into the Future 37
- Secrets of Our Success: Leading Groups Effectively 55
- What Counts in Life Cannot Be Counted 61

SECTION II: THE ROLE OF A MODERATOR

So You Want to Be a Moderator.. 67
Best Practices for Vested Moderators 71
Magical Thinking: Are Moderators Magicians? 81
The Art of Moderating: A Blend of Basic Skills & Qualities...................... 85
Benefits of Matching Moderators to Cultural Groups 91
Briefcase as Carnival Wagon.. 99
Trained Moderators Boost the Value of Qualitative Research 103
Staying on Top of the Moderator Game 115
Managing Moderator Stress: Take a Deep Breath. You Can Do This 121

SECTION III: DEMYSTIFYING FOCUS GROUPS

What a Moderator Needs to Know About Leading Focus Groups 129
Same Frame, New Game 141
Focus Groups: A Four-Course Meal 147
One Secret to Successful Focus Groups: Holding Context 151
The Magic of Eight 157
Turning Red Lights Green... 163
Problems & Solutions in Focus Groups: Three Tigers to Be Tamed 169
The Invisible Focus Groups in a Qualitative Research Project................. 175

PART II: FOCUS GROUPS: TOOLS, TIPS, & TECHNIQUES

SECTION I: WORKING EFFECTIVELY WITH RESPONDENTS

Let Respondents Be Stars 185
Diving Below Top-of-Mind 189
    Figure 3: *Circle of Communication* 192
Best Practices for Testing Ads.. 195
The BRUM Test: Going Beyond Likes/Dislikes When Testing Advertising .. 199
Do Not Ask Me Why... 207
Cross the Bridge—Enter the Respondent's World 213

SECTION II: TOOLBOX: "POWER TOOLS"

Powerful Guide Development: Seven Protocols 221
The Power of Rapport 227
The Power of a True Question 233
The Power of Probing 239
The Power of Silence 243
Creating Powerful Focus Group Questions 249
Power Up In-Depth Interviews 255

SECTION III: ANALZYING QUALITATIVE DATA & REPORTING RESULTS

"Hot Notes:" Capture What Shouts Loudest 269
A Practical Approach to Analyzing & Reporting Focus
   Group Studies: Lessons from Qualitative Market Research 275
Tools, Tips, & Techniques for Qualitative Report Writing 289
   Figure 4: *Twelve Key Factors in QLMR Reports* *294*
Qualitative Report Writing: Is Faster Better? 295
Adding Value When Reporting Qualitative Data to Clients 301

SECTION IV: THE CLIENT'S ROLE

Choosing a Moderator: How Do You Find the Right Mach for Your
   Project? 309
Enjoy the View: Client Ground Rules for Observing Focus Groups 315
How Clients Can Get the Most From Qualitative Market Research 321
How Clients & Researchers Listen Differently to Focus Group
   Comments 325
Minimizing Client Problems on Focus Group Projects 329
Asking the Right Questions of Clients Will Create the Best Questions
   for Respondents 337

PART III: CONCLUSION: MASTER MODERATOR™ MUSINGS

New Is Not Always Better: The Value of Tried & True QLMR Techniques 347
Figure 5: *Stages of a Standard Two-Hour Focus Group: Timing & Procedures* 351
Two Maxims for Moderators 355
What If? 359
Never Too Late to Learn a Good Lesson 363

GLOSSARY

Glossary 371

APPENDIX

Appendix A: Moderator Maxims: "Naomisms" 402
Appendix B: Supplements
    Boiler Plate Of A Guide 406
    Ten Client Guidelines for Observing Qualitative Research Events 409
    Research Guidelines For Focus Groups 411
    Example of Hot Notes 412
Appendix C: Suggested Reading 414
Appendix D: Industry Resources 418

INDEX

Index 424

Preface

Welcome to the third edition of *Secrets of a Master Moderator*™, updated, expanded, and filled with supportive tools to make it an exceptional **resource document on the inner world of moderating and qualitative research.** The elements presented here have been honed in the fires of experiences and sharpened with actual projects spanning more than three decades.

This book is not an academic treatise on the best way to do anything. It is a document based on working with hundreds of clients and thousands of respondents. There is no attempt to promise "the only way" or "a proprietary design" to be followed like scripture. Rather **it is what has worked for one moderator, often working alone, in hundreds of one way mirrored facilities**, night after night across a landscape of topics that ranged from presidential misconduct to bioterrorism after 9/11. Lessons learned were shaped by projects for companies who wanted insights before changing icons, logos, product lines, and packaging.

It shares the laughter from respondents who brought pictures of their dogs, so they could provide the dog's "viewpoint" on an idea for a new dog food. It honors the tears of widows who lost their husbands suddenly, and received one lump sum insurance check, without advice about how to manage a life alone.

Readers will find a **newly designed table of contents** that facilitates "browsing" to find topics of interest without having to read the entire book in order. The **glossary** has definitions of industry terms as well as RIVA terms that have become part of the qualitative market research industry. An **index** has been added to make this a useful resource book for novice and seasoned market researchers alike. **Sample documents, along with charts and graphs,** bring key points to life and allow the reader to adapt proven methods to their own work.

This book is meant to be a legacy in support of the idea of leaving the industry better by being one of its chief supporters who believes: "***What counts cannot be counted.***"

About the Author

Naomi Henderson has been in research since she was fourteen years old. Her first project took the form of a survey, counting the number of girls in her high school who were wearing Nineteens, a popular flat shoe with an open back from the 1950s. She told her father: *"Everyone is wearing them, and I want a pair!"* Her father quirked an eyebrow and said, *"Everyone?—Well, let's go check."*

They sat outside Roosevelt High School in Washington, D.C., for thirty minutes one morning before school started. The tally of one hundred sightings: twenty-six wore Nineteens and the balance wore some other kind of shoe. The power of research made the case, and she didn't get a pair.

Naomi never forgot the lesson. Now, as CEO of RIVA Market Research and Training Institute, she conducts research for Fortune 500 clients across many industries, bringing the same rigor she had as a teenager—committed to proving a hypothesis.

In addition to being a Master Moderator™, she is also a Master Trainer and Master Coach. She holds certificates of completion in NeuroLinguistic Programming and Synectics, two discipline areas that enhance her work as a qualitative researcher. She has led over six thousand focus groups and interviewed more than fifty thousand individuals in her career spanning multiple decades. She holds both an M Ed. and a BA from American University in Washington, D.C. and she has been a lecturer and/or adjunct professor at Georgetown University, George Washington University, The University of Maryland, and Hood College. She has written over ten thousand pages of core and custom curriculum documents to support the myriad courses that RIVA offers to researchers in the qualitative arena.

To date, the RIVA Training Institute has trained thousands of researchers in the last three decades both in the U.S. and in Canada, in addition to classes and courses in Africa, Asia, Europe, and New Zealand.

As she nears the half-century mark as a researcher, she is taking time to step back and reflect on what she has learned since the 1950s. *Secrets of a Master Moderator*™ is her first qualitative market research industry book.

Foreword

For years, many people—inside and outside the profession—have misunderstood the proper role and purpose of qualitative research. This can be blamed both on those commissioning the research as well as on practitioners too eager to acquiesce to client insecurity about using qualitative methods. Similarly, confusion about the process or dynamics inherent in the group encounter can be a source of disappointment. Typically, interpreters of group discussions miss the valuable resource it can bring to analysis.

The proper qualifications and backgrounds of practitioners in the field are also drawn into the debate. Often, leading an effective focus group discussion, like figure skating or sky diving, seems so deceptively simple that many commonly believe that virtually anyone can lead a session as long as they are armed with a manageable discussion guide. In fact, Master Moderator™s have extensive training in conducting, interpreting, and drawing high-level insights from focus groups.

Furthermore, as a result of cost pressures across the entire business culture, the actual work of conducting group discussions managers occasionally channel downward within the organization, giving a preference to unqualified junior personnel, even interns, rather than to skilled and experienced consultants and seasoned veterans.

The discussion guide, in turn, has become an instrument of control—so extensive, detailed, and managed that little opportunity is left for the creativity, improvisation, or surprises that fuel marketing insights.

Perhaps the common usage of the term "moderator" to describe the role of the principal convener and analyst of the group discussion contributes to the misunderstanding of the process. "Moderator" has grown to imply an event manager rather than a thought partner; an order-taker rather than a skilled and provocative virtuoso.

The nature and conduct of analysis also has been drawn into the debate over the future of qualitative research. What I call "the tyranny of the transcript" often trumps conceptual analysis and insight generation. Naïve clients expect their launch strategies to be based only on one homemaker's comments in Houston. I once had a client quite pointedly declare: "Your job is to get the respondents to say things that we can use in our advertising copy." He was not pleased when I protested that perhaps he was over-estimating my skills as a prestidigitator and ventriloquist.

That is just the start of the problem. Many unsophisticated users of qualitative research fail to appreciate insights drawn from direct involvement with discussion group participants and attention to the nuances of their body language. They devalue our understanding of societal trends and demographic shifts and how these may be getting represented in the discussion. They discourage our application of theoretical models including such well accepted principles as Barney Glaser and Anselm Strauss' injunctions about "grounded theory," Robert Merton's concept of "latent and manifest functions," and Abraham Maslow's "hierarchy of needs." Say "cognitive dissonance" to some clients and their eyes start to glaze over.

Readers of Naomi Henderson's prescriptions for best practices in *Secrets of a Master Moderator*™ will learn to avoid making any of these obvious errors of judgment or inferences about qualitative research shortcomings.

Naomi Henderson's personality, writing, and indeed her entire career are the antidote to the malaise that has infected qualitative research. This volume, which reproduces her output of articles and essays over three decades, remains timely and essential. Naomi has always been generous and authoritative in sharing her command of research tools and techniques with other practitioners and marketers. Her writing is deceptively simple and uncomplicated. Bulleted lists and aphorisms are far more prominent than footnotes and academic fog.

What comes through clearest in her work is Naomi's vast experience as a Master Moderator™, consultant, educator, and presenter. This book distills the advice and wisdom from countless hours on the front lines of practice, deep in the trenches among consumers and clients.

With complete admiration for Naomi's rhetorical devices, please let me introduce the ten facts about qualitative research and human nature you ought to know before reading *Secrets of a Master Moderator*™:

1. Qualitative research refers to a set of tools for understanding the grounds, conditions, and linkages behind people's beliefs and behavior. The fundamental tools for producing qualitative research knowledge include compiling and interpreting materials drawn from one or a combination of several data sources: intensive interviews of individuals and groups, direct observa-

tions of behavior, and documents or artifacts either existing in people's natural environment or created during imaginative exercises. The key word here is interpretation. Qualitative data rarely speaks for itself. Just like any other form of information gathered to represent social reality, the analysts need to make compelling and supportable arguments to defend their conclusions.

2. Qualitative tools are best applied for exploratory and explanatory purposes. As such, they are well adapted to promoting innovation and creativity. Focus groups and ethnography are not strictly tests, even though when the appropriate understanding of consumer meanings, choices, and intentions are achieved, we gain insights into reasons an ad campaign or a new product initiative might or might not work. Qualitative research should not be used to settle internal political disputes or to pick winners without validation.

3. Consumers are inherently conservative and skeptical about new ideas. Upon first hearing they tend to be disdainful and unconvinced by persuasive communications. Most new product concepts leave them cold. Special qualitative research procedures are necessary to go beyond this initial hesitation. Furthermore, voiced skepticism is a variable cultural trait. For example, the Chinese will often repress critical voices in order to avoid causing another to "lose face." In contrast, New Yorkers pride themselves for their hypercritical nature. That's where the expression "fuhgettabouddit" will often appear in transcripts.

4. People are notoriously poor at self-reflection. We have too many defense mechanisms that keep us ignorant of our own motivations and out of touch with our true feelings. We often seek the solace of an authority figure—"the cool kids" or "the thought leader." We tend toward defensiveness and project our own negative thoughts onto others. Consequently, asking consumers direct questions about such issues as what products they need is a notoriously unreliable business that often prompts responses that are trivial and unproductive. Even though qualitative research is always trying to understand the "why" behind people's choices, it is not advisable to ask that question directly. Similarly, asking respondents for an instant evaluation of how much they like or dislike something and counting the "yeas" and "nays" is unlikely to yield very useful or valid results.

5. Most of our decision making is emotionally based; however, many boardroom deliberators are given to overly rationalistic assumptions about how consumers use their products and why they commit to purchasing them. Consumers are primarily driven by fear, passion, vanity, shame, and similar feeling states rather than rational arguments about product superiority. Qualitative research is a strong resource for sensing how people's emotional drivers align with assertions about product benefits and characteristics.

6. Qualitative research gains from sensitive application of a certain amount of indirect questioning. Good researchers are also skilled at applying a full

range of projective and elicitation techniques. These are not "tricks," but rather a scientifically validated strategy for getting study participants to reveal things about themselves that they might be reluctant to share. They also help people verbalize inherent feelings about products with low salience. Consumers are never as involved with categories and brands as much as the clients behind the one-way mirror. Projective and elicitation techniques help to magnify unexpressed feelings and thoughts.

7. Focus groups are often overly ritualistic; their duration is too short and they do not allow for the kind of deliberation and reflection that optimize productivity. Sometimes, consumers simply need more time to engage with an idea. This can be advanced through such procedures as pre-tasking exercises completed in advance of the session, lengthier sessions (discussion groups lasting up to three or four hours are more popular in Europe than in the United States), and keeping the discussion alive through bulletin board discussion groups conducted online. A spirit of experimentation and an acceptance of trial and error enhance qualitative research.

8. The way to validate qualitative research findings is by triangulating, which in a research context refers to examining the same question in a variety of ways and through a succession of techniques (alternately called "bricolage" or "hybrid methods" by some.) Holding multiple sessions and applying different tools, employing a mixture of individual and group interviewing, or collecting both observational and verbal data are examples of ways that we can triangulate. Sometimes, managers are simply too impatient for results to allow valid conclusions and insights to emerge.

9. Group influence within research sessions is a valuable resource for understanding how real-world patterns of persuasion are likely to play out. There seems to be an excessive concern with so-called "dominators" and, consequently, the results of many group sessions are unfairly dismissed or discussions are too rigidly controlled to have much value. True dominators are egotistical bullies, and they differ from influencers, who, by virtue of enhanced knowledge or personal qualities, are capable of explaining their point of view to others. We learn a great deal from these influencers about arguments that may have to be advanced or defeated during product rollouts.

10. Master Moderator™s are a valuable resource that can simultaneously negotiate group dynamics, draw from their own marketing savvy and experience with a range of brands and categories, leverage a broad palette of tools and techniques, and creatively develop insights to build brands. They are there to do much more than read a script. They are social scientists and humanists, committed to ethics and professionalism, who are capable of delivering massive value to businesses and agencies that are responsible for understanding and persuading their publics.

Do you want to learn how to become a Master Moderator™, determine how you can best cooperate with clients and participants to gain valuable benefits for your organization, learn about how to overcome problems, and turn the tedium of research into pleasure? A good place to start is a careful reading of Naomi Henderson's lifetime of insights contained in *Secrets of a Master Moderator*™.

Hy Mariampolski, PhD.
QualiData Research Inc.
hy@qualidataresearch.com

Acknowledgments

This book is the culmination of more than three decades of work in qualitative research and the contents come from a variety of sources: curricula designed and taught, projects completed, reports written, speeches given, staff meetings led, conference presentations, and so much more. On this long journey, it is nice to pause and thank many of the people who have traveled with me from inception to completion of *Secrets of a Master Moderator*™.

To Family

Without the love and support of my family, there would be no context for this book. Thanks to my parents, Anna and Joseph Hairston, who taught me that it is far better to do what is right, not what is easy. Thanks to my birth sisters: Jo Ann Hairston and Victoria Hairston, who remind me to laugh early and often—especially when things are not going all that well! A special thank you goes to my Circles of Light family, who are my wellspring of support in all areas of my life.

Thanks to my spirit sisters and best friends, Romaine Bailey and Dr. Pamela Peeke, who love me, no matter what I am doing. Romaine, your unconditional love for me, reaching back more than thirty years, has been a touchstone for keeping me sane and focused in life. Pam, you have been my doctor and now my friend. You are a perfect demonstration that the written word has power and impact. Because of your publications, I see what a difference a book can make in the lives of readers.

Loving thanks to my godmother and spiritual teacher, Dr. Carolyne J. Fuqua, who is a constant reminder to keep in mind who I say I am. To my goddaughter, Lauren Mobley for her unwavering love to a sister Capricorn. To my brother-in-law, Mujahid Aleem, who has held me in his heart since we met in the seventh grade. Very special thanks to Brian Harris, my nephew, for his work on the cover. Brian, you have created the graphic that fits my idea of leaving a legacy.

To Staff

RIVA Market Research & Training Institute, founded in 1981, is the basis for much of the material in this book. The current staff has not only worked with me on the book itself, but on the framework for the courses that RIVA offers to students and the contracts we fulfill to serve research clients. To all the staff—I could not have come this far without your support: thanks to Monique Kittka Donlon for lovingly supporting me in the actual process of bringing the book from an idea to a finished book; your attention to detail has made all the difference to the quality of this book. Thanks to Amber Tedesco for always being the best "other eyes" in the business and for doing whatever is needed and wanted to keep RIVA moving forward. To Tina Pant and Bonnie Heiserman, my thanks for all your support on both the grand and the small things that are needed to keep a small company functioning smoothly; to Jo Ann Hairston for her steadfast support of RIVA in her role as a staff member, trainer, coach, and listener for more than thirty years; and finally to Romaine Bailey for the day-to-day support of the training classes and for making sure that the way RIVA operates is consistent with the standards we have set. Also a special thanks to Tas Coroneos who has served as RIVA's lawyer and business advisor for more than thirty years. Tas, you always know exactly the right questions to ask. Finally, a special thank you to all the RIVETTES and RIVALOS who worked with me for more than three decades as staff, consultants, and RIVA Alliance members.

To Research Colleagues

The RIVA Training Institute is fortunate to have a cadre of trainers on hand who have a wealth of skills across many disciplines. My thanks to these trainers for their support of the RIVA mission and for their contributions to the course materials: Jean Bystedt, Merlene Cummins, Becky Day, Suzette deVogelaere, Grace Fuller, Barbara Gassaway, Ellen Good, Jo Ann Hairston, Kevin Kimbell, Sandra Kluttz, Siri Lynn, Maureen Quinn Olsen, Dorrie Paynter, Deborah Potts, Cathy Prewitt, Marilyn Rausch, Alice Rodgers, Kristin Schwitzer, Vivian Thonger, and Jeff Walkowski.

A special thank you goes to Dr. Hy Mariampolski, a longtime colleague and friend who has always supported me and what RIVA stands for.

There are a number of people in the category of research partners, joining with RIVA on specific projects and activities. These individuals contributed both to RIVA's growth and expansion, including Isabel Aneyba of Comarka, Clarence

Brewer at John Deere; Norman Goldberg of Goldberg-Marchesano Advertising; Kim Leintz at KCC; Mary Lowden at Boston Scientific; Terence Mandable at Booz Allen; Carole Marchesano of Goldberg-Marchesano Advertising; Maritza Matheus with Matheus Marketing; Heather Moyer at Walt Disney; Angela Mickalide at Safe Kids; Melody Rappaport, RIVA's official cheerleader in the industry; Diana Rubin at Safe Kids; Mary Etta Burt Schoradt at CQ Press; and Lisa Tinch at the Social Security Administration.

To Research Organizations

As a member of a vibrant community of researchers, there are several organizations and individuals I would like to thank for their friendship, guidance, and resources. This list includes the American Marketing Association; Dr. Chuck Chakrapani; Barbara Gassaway with Observation Baltimore who started out as a RIVA student in the 1980s and graduated to become an effective moderator and businesswoman, and RIVA's unofficial marketing arm—Barbara, your good ideas and listening ear always helps RIVA rise to the next level of excellence; Marianne Polk of Atlanta Out Loud Inc.—Marianne, you have always been in RIVA's corner and I deeply appreciate the years of love and support; the Qualitative Research Consultants Association; the *Quirk's Marketing Review* family: Tom Quirks, Steve Quirks, Dan Quirks, Jim Quirks, Evan Tweed, and Joe Rydholm; Robin McClure of Dallas by Definition who stands as a demonstration of class and dignity, Texas style; Joan Shugoll with Shugoll Research, hosting RIVA focus groups since 1978 and teaching the lesson to laugh early and often; and Diane Trotta with Trotta Associates, a sister moderator and another savvy businesswoman who has taken the time to teach RIVA good lessons in the industry.

To More Than 6,000 Graduates of RIVA Courses

It would take an entire book to list all the names of students who have taken courses at RIVA both in the U.S. and around the world. The opportunity to touch the lives of so many researchers and support them in marrying their innate skills to proven research techniques has been a loving and worthwhile effort. My deep thanks to every student who trusted RIVA to teach them about the art and science of qualitative techniques.

To Friends

Writing is both an art and a science and ultimately, the act of writing is a solo experience. One dedicated teacher, Eunice Scarfe, said to me: *"I cannot teach you how to write, but I can show you where to look inside so the writing comes forward."* Eunice, this book is a testament to that teaching. The Sunday Writers Group

(SWG) has supported me for many years in the art and science of writing, meeting about once a month since 1995. Thanks go to Louise Appell, Brenda Barbour, Constance Beck, Pamera Hairston, Constance Hamilton, Rachel Michaud, Angela Shaw, and Lynne Vance.

For the loving support of these close friends I say, "Thanks for being there:" Dr. Marilee Adams, Carolyne Ellison, Barbara Green, Deborah Harris, Kirsten Keppel, Shaiy Knowles, Johncie Lancaster, and Erica Lodish.

To the Editors and Graphic Designers

No book emerges from the mind of the author to the hands of the reader without many visits from the editors and the graphic designers. A chance conversation with Monique Kittka Donlon led to meeting members of her extended family network who guided the original manuscript to the first editions of this book (earlier versions of what you are now reading). My deep thanks go to Eleanor Bourg Nicholson and Janice K. Stallings for all the long hours of work making this book a legacy for me and a resource for readers.

Thanks are also due to Kelley DuBois for her tireless work on Edition III of this book. Her efforts have crafted a more polished version of Secrets of a Master Moderator, further facilitating the author's goal to provide readers with a definitive resource on qualitative market research.

To Everyone Else

I know I have left out people and organizations that could be included in this list. To those who are not mentioned specifically by name, please know that your contributions fall into the "unsung heroes" category and are not forgotten. I am deeply thankful for all the blessings in my life and for the opportunity to write this book.

How To Use This Book

More than thirty years of insights live in this book. Publication demands a certain plan of organization to successfully navigate the trail inside the forest of information presented here. However, the logic of the author may not match the logic of the reader, so this preface is intended to smooth the path for the reader.

The book is organized into three parts, each with multiple sections; the reader can read them in order or randomly, as each article can stand alone.

At the beginning of the book is a complete table of contents. Within each section is a duplicate table of contents for just that section which includes illustrative blurbs about each article in that section. For example, there is a section on writing reports and another section on the role of a moderator and each one has its own separate table of contents.

Here is a listing of each of the parts and their subsequent sections:

PART I: THE WORLD OF QUALITATIVE RESEARCH
- Section I: Qualitative Research
- Section II: The Role of a Moderator
- Section III: Demystifying Focus Groups

PART II: FOCUS GROUPS: TOOLS, TIPS, & TECHNIQUES
- Section I: Working Effectively with Respondents
- Section II: Toolbox: "Power Tools"
- Section III: Analyzing Qualitative Data & Reporting Results
- Section IV: The Client's Role

PART III: CONCLUSION: MASTER MODERATOR™ MUSINGS
- New Is Not Always Better: The Value of Tried & True QLMR Techniques
- Two Maxims for Moderators
- What If?
- Never Too Late to Learn A Good Lesson

Edition III of this text includes a glossary, updated appendices (including a sample guide, client ground rules, respondent ground rules, an example of "Hot Notes"), as well as an index. This supplemental information is meant to serve as further resources for readers.

Caution: While there are many tools, tips, and techniques outlined in this book that can be useful for a moderator, reading this book will not confer those skills to the reader.

This book is not intended to be a training manual for new or seasoned moderators. Rather, it is a compilation of insights, wisdom, and lessons hard learned over more than three decades. As you read, look for those areas that dovetail with your own experiences. Look for those areas where you disagree with me and form your own understanding and philosophy.

I do not profess to have "the answer" or "the way" when it comes to planning, conducting, or evaluating qualitative research.

What I do have are my experiences and I have written about what I found to be of value based on work in the industry. By writing this book, I am happy to pass that value on.

Key Reasons This Book Was Written

This book is intended to serve as a legacy of my experiences as a moderator, a journey that began in 1978 when I received training as part of my work as a researcher in a national research company. When I left and started a consultancy, I took that learning, married it to additional learning in other disciplines and used my experiences as a moderator, both positive and negative, to build a style of moderating that stood on these principles:

- Do what is right, not what is easy.
- Do my best or don't do it at all.
- Tell the truth, even if I do not look good in the process.

As a result, I have been lucky to lead more than six thousand focus groups over the years and hundreds of one-on-one interviews. I have been the midwife to the birth of new products (such as the Swiffer, gel toothpaste, and the new look of the faces used on Aunt Jemima products and American Express cards). The

Kentucky Fried Chicken phrase "We do chicken right!" came out of an 8:00 p.m. focus group I led in the early 1980s when a sweet lady said: *"What I like about KFC is they don't do burgers, they don't do pizzas or fries—they just do chicken and they get it right every time."* I will bet she has no idea she was the godmother of an advertising campaign that ran for almost twenty years!

I have enjoyed the process of compiling this book and I look forward to your comments as a reader. Log on to *www.secretsofamastermoderator.com* to share your comments with me via email.

Naomi R. Henderson
Rockville, Maryland
Fall, 2014

A key logo indicates new content for the Third Edition.

PART I: THE WORLD OF QUALITATIVE RESEARCH

SECTION I: QUALITATIVE RESEARCH

The Players in the Qualitative Market Research Game 5

Every game has players and rules; qualitative market research is no exception. The QLMR game includes: clients, the moderator, the moderator's research project manager, the facility staff, and the respondents. Knowing the role of each player, and the rules, keeps everyone in the loop—ensuring every project is a "home run."

Qualities of a Master Moderator™ 9

What are the skills and techniques needed to lead a QRE effectively and report on qualitative research findings? What elements define the difference between an everyday moderator and a master of the industry?

Anatomy of a Qualitative Research Project 17

So what is a QRE? What does it look like? How does it work? Stop here for a quick, straightforward outline of the process from start to finish.

Qualitative Research Projects: A Twelve-Step Process 19

As every Master Moderator™ will tell you, there is a method and rhythm to qualitative research. Here you will find twelve steps outlined in general and the four steps that have changed the most over the years, plus a very important flow chart!

Embracing the Qualitative Quadrangle 27

Here are the four cornerstones for qualitative research events (QREs). Learn the importance of four major elements for your work: perceptions, opinions, beliefs, and attitudes (POBAs). This is the water in which master moderators swim.

Qualitative Research Lessons from *Gone With The Wind* 33

Marketing research isn't about numbers—it is about people, relationships, and listening intently. Learn how to put together an Oscar-worthy QRE. Tools, tips, and techniques are presented in rich metaphor.

Qualitative Research Techniques: Taking the Best of the Past Into the Future..37

The world around us is constantly changing, so the business of qualitative research must change too! Every Master Moderator™ must learn what things to preserve and what things to change. Come here for advice.

Secrets of Our Success: Leading Groups Effectively 55

What do seasoned moderators say about their industry? Read here for insights from several Master Moderators™ about best practices.

What Counts in Life Cannot Be Counted 61

The world of Qualitative Research is not always a peaceful one—good people, as it is said, can certainly disagree. But stand back and watch as a Master Moderator™ takes on a few mistaken ideas about this business!

THE PLAYERS IN THE QUALITATIVE MARKET RESEARCH GAME

> *Every game has players and rules; qualitative market research is no exception. The QLMR game includes: clients, the moderator, the moderator's research project manager, the facility staff, and the respondents. Knowing the role of each player and the rules, keeps everyone in the loop—ensuring every project is a "home run."*

There are five "players" in the qualitative research game:

1. Client/Observer Team
2. Moderator
3. Moderator's Research Project Manager
4. Facility Staff
5. Respondents

All five parties have to be in place for a successful QRE [Qualitative Research Event] project to be completed.

- **The client sets the objectives for the study** and has the need for the outcomes from the QRE.
- **The moderator needs to be clear about the objectives and have creative ways to get information from respondents.**
- **The moderator's research project manager needs to coordinate all activities between the moderator and client as well as the facility staff.**

- **The facility needs to find enough qualified respondents** and create a research environment for the interviews.
- **The respondents need to have clarity** on what the topic of discussion is as well as be provided with a safe environment in which to share their perceptions, opinions, beliefs, and attitudes (POBAs).

The **client** talks only to the moderator. They never speak to the facility staff [except in passing – usually with a request on-site] and never directly to respondents. The client signs off on research design issues and the moderator's guide; as well as sets the expectations for timelines and the reporting of outcomes prior to the QRE.

The **moderator** talks to all parties: moderator's research project manager, clients, respondents, and facility staff. The moderator is the fulcrum, the pivot point of the whole process. They support the crafting of the study purpose statement; create or review screener elements; check daily on recruiting status of participants; craft the guide to be used in the session; and obtain client signoff on both the guide and the desired stimuli to be used with respondents.

The **moderator's research project manager** is the person in charge of making sure all project elements work for all parties and as such, talks to the client, the facility staff, and daily with the moderator, providing updates and project changes. They are responsible for the research proposal, writing the screener, daily monitoring of the recruiting process and meeting the requests of the moderator and the client when they are on-site at the facility.

The **facility staff** talks to the moderator and to the respondents [via recruiting protocols] and only interacts with clients while they are in the facility by attending to requests or asking logistics questions about comfort needs. As well, they talk with the moderator's research project manager to review the screening requirements and provide daily updates on recruiting until the sessions are filled according to project specifications. They are extremely helpful with suggestions on: best ways to reach recruiting objectives, timing issues, and stipend amounts.

The **respondents** see the facility staff when they sign-in and sign-out and have spoken with a recruiter prior to attending the session. They talk with the moderator in great detail during the QRE. However, they never talk to the moderator's research project manager or the client except in special circumstances. For example, a client or client team may want to come in and meet respondents during the last ten minutes of the session to personally thank them or to ask questions beyond the scope of the planned project.

Knowing the players in Qualitative Market Research and their roles should enhance the partnership experience at every level of the research process, therefore increasing the opportunity for successful projects.

Figure 1: *Who Talks to Whom in the Research Game*

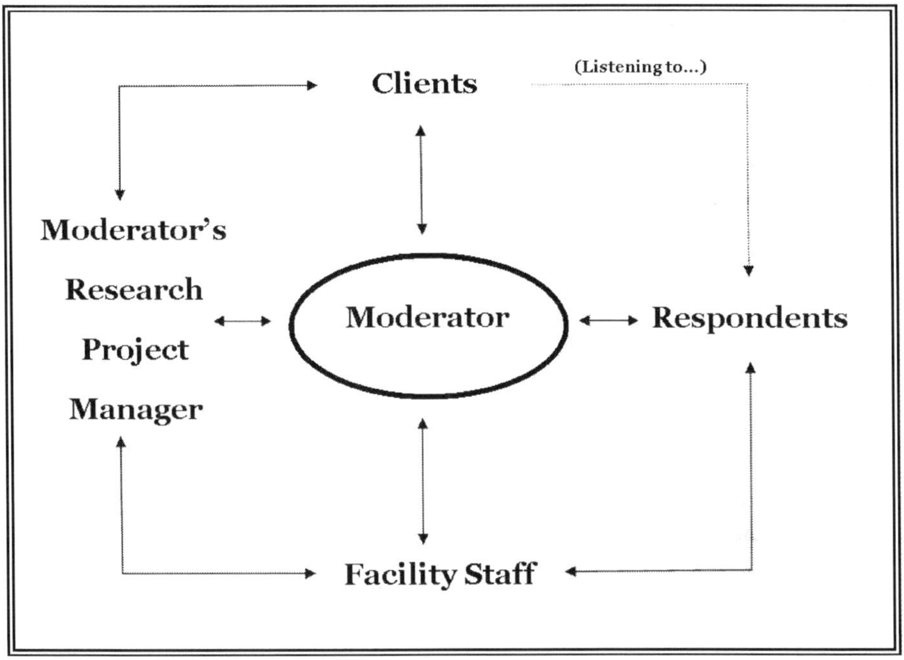

Qualities of a Master Moderator™

> What are the skills and techniques needed to lead a QRE effectively and report on qualitative research findings? What elements define the difference between an everyday moderator and a master of the industry?

As a trainer of moderators, I have observed a variety of moderator styles and experience levels. New moderators frequently give their attention to writing appropriate questions and managing the myriad key elements of group dynamics while probing for important information. Skilled moderators focus more on probing for second and third-level information beyond "top-of-mind" responses as well as finding more creative ways to encourage respondents to deliver behavioral information rather than just conceptual expressions.

This article focuses on the qualities of "Master Moderators™," defined as those who have mastered the key skills and techniques that lead to effective group interactions. Additionally, Master Moderators™ collect and analyze the rich body of oral information, and they report that data in appropriate ways to support the decision making needs of their clients.

General Qualities of a Master Moderator™

There is a phrase among airline pilots that says, "There are bold pilots and there are old pilots, but there are no old, bold pilots."

This maxim **does not** hold true for moderators! A Master Moderator is by nature both bold and old (if not in years, then in number of groups conducted).

However, simply leading hundreds of groups over ten or fifteen years does not automatically qualify one as a Master Moderator™ if one has not acquired and adapted new skills to the ever changing conditions in the world of qualitative research. In general, the following elements make a Master Moderator™:

- Willingness to **take risks and stretch** conventional research boundaries
- Continuous **search for training and learning opportunities** from other related disciplines
- Constant acquisition of **new ways to interact with groups** of individuals in qualitative settings
- Development of **more efficient methods** to collect data in QRE sessions
- Offering clients **variations on classic focus group formats** (e.g. super groups, creativity sessions, piggyback groups, etc.)

Specific Qualities of a Master Moderator™

I have identified twenty-five distinct skills that make a Master Moderator™. This list is by no means complete and I would welcome hearing from senior moderators who have additions. Since the focus group approach is less than a century old and little opportunity exists for moderators to see each other's work, this list is based both on personal experience and on the styles of students observed in RIVA's Moderator Training School since 1981.

Twenty-five Skills of a Master Moderator™

1. ***Understands the foundations/applications of market research.*** The moderator understands clearly the role of qualitative market research and its applications and limitations as well as all of the steps (from client request to final presentation) of classic QRE research projects.
2. ***Markets services appropriately.*** The moderator presents his/her skills and qualifications for a fair price and in a professional manner so that potential clients have a clear understanding of these unique services.
3. ***Manages all project aspects.*** The moderator has equal abilities in managing:
    a) Research tasks (e.g. research design)
    b) Field tasks (e.g. writing screeners, tracking recruiting)
    c) Project tasks (e.g. flow of QRE)
    d) Client tasks (e.g. handling backroom during QRE process)
    e) Analysis tasks (e.g. production of objective reports from subjective data)

4. *Maintains research objectivity.* The moderator has no investment in the outcome of the study beyond doing complete and thorough work and does not have his/her ego tied to the act of moderating or presenting findings.
5. *Establishes research objectives.* The moderator supports and/or directs clients in developing appropriate and attainable research objectives and recommends the appropriate research tools to meet those objectives.
6. *Recommends appropriate methodologies.* The moderator recommends appropriate research methodologies to clients to achieve study purposes and "sticks to his/her guns" to ensure that an appropriate environment can be created with respondents to elicit the fullest range of information. This includes a willingness to recommend against qualitative research when appropriate, even at the loss of personal or corporate revenues.
7. *Creates custom questions and custom guides.* The moderator creates and writes effective questions in an organized guide or outline that follows a logical flow from the perspective of respondents and permits them to answer queries fully and appropriately. This includes reframing questions on the spot, both within the group and between groups.
8. *Practices unconditional positive regard (UPR).* The moderator possesses a superior ability to listen to all comments from respondents and clients that may range from logical to aberrant as long as responses relate to the research topic. This skill includes presenting an empathetic yet neutral face and voice tone while hearing comments and responses that may range from dull to bizarre to exceptional. The moderator recognizes that rich information, creative ideas, or "gold mines" (unexpected, rich comments from respondents) may come from unlikely sources which, on first hearing or observation, would not appear to produce meaningful information.
9. *Maintains good listening skills.* The moderator has an exceptional ability to be attentive to both verbal and non-verbal behaviors and to avoid informing or educating respondents. This skill also encompasses the ability to hear whether the response is a first-, second-, or third-level response (e.g. "top-of-mind" responses versus those from deeper thinking levels).
10. *Remains observant.* The moderator is able to "read" the room on many dimensions. These include the following:
    a) Seeing the room as a group of strangers vying for the approval of the moderator and new "peers."

b) Noting that individuals within a group have a behavior range that runs the gamut from dominant to withdrawn.
c) Seeing when a participant wants to speak before a hand is raised and to read non-verbal clues appropriately.

11. **Practices "invisible leadership" skills.** The moderator possesses the skills necessary to lead a group discussion without falling into the trap of "leading the witness" or letting the room run away with the conversation. This includes the knowledge of when to stay with a topic and probe to allow for new information and when to close down a line of questioning that produces no "pay dirt." The moderator is able to remain in charge without bullying or dominating respondents, is able to create rapport within the first six minutes of a group, and is able to re-create that rapport during the session.

12. **Moderates effectively.** A moderator has the ability to:
    a) Create a safe environment for respondents to deliver their perceptions, opinions, beliefs, and attitudes.
    b) State the purpose of the session and provide clear ground rules for participation.
    c) Relate to respondents without talking "up" or "down" to them.
    d) Terminate topic areas and move on to new ones without the need for long setups or summaries.
    e) Allow for diverse opinions within the group and live with the lack of consensus or closure.
    f) Come down hard when the discussion gets out of hand or off track without losing group affinity.
    g) Avoid serial interviewing but include everyone in the conversation.
    h) Read the room and stay with the participants, not the papers (the moderator's guide).

13. **Handles diverse opinions.** The moderator anticipates and allows for diverse opinions without becoming confrontational, judgmental, evaluative, or threatening and without allowing other respondents to act in these ways toward one another to the detriment of information-gathering opportunities.

14. **Remains flexible.** The moderator has multidimensional abilities to manage the variables contained in the qualitative research interactive process. Some of these abilities include: time management, logic tracking, linking, injecting creative energy for dull groups, asking short questions to get long answers, and shifting unworkable situations into workable ones.

15. *Conducts linking and logic tracking.* The moderator recalls what was said earlier and by whom and links it to current conversation, maintaining a logic path that follows the thinking of respondents and does not slavishly adhere to the pre-developed guide.
16. *Uses a variety of techniques.* The moderator elicits data using various models and/or techniques (e.g. neuro-linguistic programming, projections, devil's advocate, role playing, "board of directors," paper and pencil tasks, etc.) appropriate to the respondents' frames of reference.
17. *Uses interventions.* The moderator utilizes a variety of intervention techniques (from simple to complex) to support the flow of conversation and open new ideas for exploration. Intervention involves any appropriate activity (e.g. paper/pencil activity, dyads, stimuli, etc.) that interrupts the two-way conversation between moderator and respondents for the purpose of enriching the discussion or focusing on a specific issue.
18. *Uses sophisticated naïveté.* The moderator is able to employ a form of "not knowing" to avoid leading respondents or to avoid having the moderator's personal viewpoint embedded in the flow of conversation.
19. *Comfortable with uncertainty.* The moderator can live with surprises, "gold mines," and abrupt changes in research design without losing aplomb.
20. *Thinks rapidly/makes appropriate decisions.* The moderator thinks fast, responds quickly to shifts in conversation, and reacts to endorsement or approval from clients or respondents. This includes an ability to quickly move a project along a foreshortened timeline without sacrificing quality.
21. *Utilizes other paradigms.* A paradigm is a pattern, example, model, or overall concept accepted by most people in an intellectual community as a science because of its effectiveness in explaining a complex process, idea, or set of ideas. The moderator uses skills, techniques, and materials from other paradigms in an appropriate manner and applies them to qualitative research projects to create maximum results for clients.
22. *Allows spontaneity in group process.* The moderator allows spontaneity and bursts of conversation instead of suppressing the natural group process in favor of rigid research formats or oppressive group control measures.
23. *Uses accurate language and paraphrases.* The moderator avoids second-guessing respondents by putting words in their mouths. Instead the moderator provides accurate feedback to respondents using their terms and words, summarizing the discussion from time to time to:

a) Demonstrate that respondents' comments are heard and understood
b) Validate that all comments on target to the discussion are valuable (this includes monitoring his or her own language so that the percentage of moderator words in a group discussion decreases from 80% at the outset of the conversation to 80/20 rule, handing over the reins to the respondents by first quarter of the way through the QRE)

24. ***Analyzes qualitative data.*** The moderator analyzes subjective data with an objective viewpoint, draws trend lines across diverse levels of data, and finds common themes. This includes choosing the right mix of summaries, conclusions, or recommendations to support the client in making the next decision step.

25. ***Remains human, not mechanical.*** The moderator must lead a group as an individual, a researcher, and an expert, but must not act overtly in any of these roles. At no time should the moderator suppress the natural flow of conversation or add any element of artificiality to the discussion. The moderator must be natural rather than contrived and must allow for a full range of personal responses without losing control of the group or appearing to be false or condescending.

Conclusion

While the above list of qualities of a Master Moderator™ is by no means complete, it does encompass many of the factors that make successful moderators effective. Methods to strengthen one's skills and abilities in any of the above areas could include:

- Reading materials from related fields about group dynamics, questioning techniques, right/left brain operations, non-verbal behavior, role playing, etc.
- Observing other moderators and discussing techniques.
- Being coached by a Master Moderator™ (via seminar, workshop, private one-on-one sessions, through review and written critique of submitted video tapes, etc.).
- Taking courses, seminars, or workshops from various disciplines designed to strengthen particular skills.

A Master Moderator™ is made, not born, and in most cases is selfmade. There is no magic number of groups completed that makes a Master Moderator™, just as there is no one course that can deliver all the needed skills to clear up faults overnight.

Continual self-examination, personal stretching of skills and abilities, and a questing nature for better ways to handle individuals in a group setting are some of the steps to becoming a Master Moderator™.

How close are you?

(The author acknowledges contributions from Suzette de Vogelaere, Concepts & Strategies, San Francisco, and Jo Ann Hairston, VARI Market Research, in preparing this article.)

Anatomy of a Qualitative Research Project

> *So what is a QRE? What does it look like? How does it work? Stop here for a quick, straightforward outline of the process from start to finish.*

An executive of a pantyhose manufacturer calls RIVA Marketing Research and asks if Tuesday, Wednesday, and Thursday of the third week in the following month are open for a series of six focus groups in three different cities. The company wants perceptions and attitudes from women ages twenty-one to forty-nine who regularly buy pantyhose in food, drug, or discount stores. RIVA says yes, and provides a cost for the services per group and a request for half of the total project estimate up front as a deposit before work commences. The client agrees, the date is set, and the project begins.

RIVA arranges for the recruiting of nine to ten respondents per group who meet the client's specifications (to ensure that at least six to eight respondents show up for each group). The respondents are invited to attend either a 6:00 or an 8:00 p.m. session on one of the three nights of the study to meet with a moderator and discuss current advertising related to pantyhose.

The group discusses current pantyhose purchasing patterns, looks at a series of print advertisements and chooses the one that most clearly delivers the message about the benefits of a new line of pantyhose. For their time and opinions, the respondents each receive a stipend commensurate with the region of the country and light refreshments. The sessions last between ninety to one hundred and twenty minutes each. The clients (about eight to ten from various departments at the pantyhose firm as well as members of their advertising agency) observe the session through a six-foot by four-foot one-way mirror, and the session is audio recorded with a DVD recording as an option.

When all the groups have been conducted, a RIVA staff member writes a report summarizing the key findings and the consumer reactions to each of the advertisements reviewed. Upon delivery of the final report, RIVA submits the final invoice for the remaining 50% of contract costs and within thirty days, receives the balance of the contract dollars.

Upon receiving RIVA's final report, the client mounts a quantitative study to explore several specific issues raised in the focus groups. Concurrently, plans for an advertising strategy are developed. When the results of the focus groups, the survey, and the advertisement strategy planning are reviewed, a corporate decision is made to follow a particular strategy for advertising the new line of pantyhose. Within that fiscal year, a new print advertisement appears in national magazines.

Conclusion

Every project might not follow this format. Sometimes research vendors request 100% payment up front and sometimes they bill 100% in full within ten days of study completion. Group size might change due to client requests. Not every study has a report, and not every study includes a DVD of proceedings. All the factors described above are negotiable items between the research vendor and the client.

Qualitative Research Projects: A Twelve-Step Process

> *As every Master Moderator™ will tell you, there is a method and rhythm to qualitative research. Here you will find twelve steps outlined in general and the four steps that have changed the most over the years, plus a very important flow chart!*

Qualitative research, by its very nature, is soft and flexible. It centers around POBAs: perceptions, opinions, beliefs, and attitudes. You cannot ask a pet owner what percent of their love is reserved for their children and what percent is given to their pet. Love is not divisible in the qualitative world. However, with qualitative research techniques, you can ask them to tell you how they love their pet and what their pet does to merit that love. Just because the world of qualitative research is "soft," that does not mean it is lacking in rigor. Think about soft things that hold up well under stress:

- Parachutes
- Airbags
- Life preservers
- Pillows
- Mattresses

Everything on the list above is soft by all standards, yet the first three can save a life. The rigor that goes into making parachutes, airbags, and life preservers is remarkable and that same rigor can be applied to the soft world of qualitative research.

In setting up research projects over the last thirty years, I have put some research rigor into those areas that require it, primarily to leave room for those places where the edges are not as firm. I can lock down client purpose, dates for research, and the cities where the study will take place. I can craft a screener to search for the right respondents, and I can schedule a date to complete the final report. However, I cannot plan what the respondents will actually say to me in the groups or IDIs, and I cannot predict how the clients will process the data they hear behind the mirror. That is part of the surprise of qualitative research—one does not really know how it is all going to turn out until the project is over. Yet, the power of knowing who is receiving the emotional energy of a voter before an election can turn the tide of a campaign. Understanding how consumers differentiate between two brands of contact lens solution is the secret to gaining more market share. Altering the image of a formerly well known and previously accepted practice such as drinking and driving came about in part through inspirational advertisements that changed the social environment and raised awareness about the devastating consequences of this behavior.

Recently, I looked at some old files and found a chart I developed back in the early 1980s when I started out as a freelance moderator. As I looked at that original chart (pictured in Figure 2), I laughed. It had exactly twelve steps! Somehow I had managed to fit my research rigor into another twelve-step process. The list that follows includes the steps that I outlined in the 1980s and still use in the twenty-first century:

1. Client makes a request for qualitative research
2. RIVA Market Research determines project purpose
3. RIVA writes a proposal that includes a methodology, timeline, and costs
4. Client reviews proposal and signs off on costs, timeline, and research plan
5. Project logistics are determined: where, when, who, how many
6. Field facilities are located and booked
7. Screener developed, client signs off, recruiting monitored
8. Moderator's guide developed and approved
9. QRE(s) are conducted
10. Recordings are transcribed, analysis begins
11. Report is written
12. Presentation of findings made to client along with final billing

Over the years, a number of these steps have changed in character and emphasis. Not every client wants an in-person presentation of findings, and sometimes a client team handles the fieldwork, only hiring the moderator for steps eight through eleven. This article will address four steps from the above list that have seen the greatest changes in the last twenty years.

Client Requests

In the eighties and nineties, clients would make a request over the phone and seldom sent anything in writing to a qualitative consultant. While that practice still goes on in some industries, these days many researchers often get a document resembling a market research brief that outlines the study purpose, a skeleton research plan, and the framework in which the project occurs along the product or service continuum. As a researcher who likes a little rigor, I love getting one of those documents. I ask better questions on the conference calls and help my client better define the research parameters to get them closer to their objectives. I have also found that when clients are clearer at the research design stage, there are fewer misunderstandings with research suppliers and the projects tend to unfold along a logical path. Client rigor at the front end makes the project more successful and my job a lot more satisfying.

Research Costs for Qualitative Projects

Like the cost of bread, milk, gasoline, and health care, prices for qualitative research have risen steadily over the years. The per-group moderator's fee, the cost of mirrored rooms, expenses for catering food, the cost of finding the "right" respondent, the cost of travel, and respondent stipends have all risen over the years.

In some cases the costs are justified, such as the need to pay more dollars for stipends for an evening session with individuals who give up their personal time to help provide opinions in 2005 versus 1995. But sometimes it feels like other costs are created on a whim and whatever individuals feel the market will bear.

One example comes to mind—the price tag of $100–$200 for a stationary DVD of a QRE where a staff member simply turns on a switch and tapes a two-hour session on a DVD that costs less than five dollars.

Five minutes of staff time, plus the cost of the DVD, does not factor out to a charge of $100–$200 per group. If this cost was applied to two hundred QREs over the course of a year, it would equal $20,000–$40,000—more than enough to pay for the camera, the wiring, and the staff person who pushes the button ten times over.

I used to own and manage a qualitative research facility with two rooms, so concurrent projects could be held at the same time. A location close to a subway made it easy for all kinds of respondents to attend. Those early years as a facility owner have made me sensitive to all elements of the pricing structure for a project, and I am sensitive to costs that are more window dressing than true service.

Some facilities, to their credit, make this a "value-added" feature and make the following offer: "A DVD of your group, using our stationary camera, is free."

Those firms have worked a modest cost into a fair room rental charge since the camera is built into the wall in the pair of rooms that serve as the research venue for a QRE. Everyone enjoys getting something "free," and value-added is the new name of the game in research these days.

Clearly, there are no written rules and regulations about how to charge for services and expenses and since everyone holds their costs close to the chest, it is unlikely that there will ever be any regulations on what is fair to charge. We can all only hope that personal integrity is the key driver for making the decision of what to charge for services and equipment.

Qualitative researchers seldom talk with each other about fees and for sure, they are not talking about their billable rates to a possible competitor. I would like to see a qualitative research project where the respondents were all directors of market research for a variety of companies and organizations. The first client type would be those whose companies had products to sell. Another client type would be those who market services. A third client type would be those who deal with social issues. Those clients who use qualitative research to check on elements related to advertising make up the final group. In fact, keeping to good research design, I would like two groups of each client type making a nice, neat eight-group project so I could compare data across similar groups and between different types of clients.

If I were in the back room for each of these distinct groups of clients, I would want the moderator to ask questions such as the following:

- What is the range of prices clients are quoted in proposals for the same study when they ask for multiple bids?
- What truly makes quotes different? Especially when cost estimates are thirty to fifty percent different?
- What line items drive the variations in prices?
- If price is taken out of the decision, what is the next most important factor clients consider when choosing among several equally qualified research suppliers?
- Which do you prefer: a flat rate charge per group or line item breakdowns?

Now, that would be an interesting focus group study! My primary purpose in wanting data like that from clients would be to get their perspective on a range of consultant pricing options that they receive, because the client is the only one that sees that range. Individual qualitative consultants do not have that particular view and, in truth, they should not— I am sure the Federal Trade Commission would look askance at a group of independent consultants working on "fixing prices."

As an industry, however, I do think that the qualitative market research industry might borrow a page from the health care industry and set some prices for services that are a bit more uniform than the ones we have now. For example, the costs that laboratories charge for a standard blood test are fairly uniform. What if there was a rate sheet for room rentals at facilities with sliding scales based on what is in the room (e.g. rooms with display rails, computer jacks, etc., charge more than rooms that do not have those features)? Such a rate card would go a long way toward weeding out those firms whose costs are out of line with good business practices.

Facility Settings

Twenty years ago, a nice facility was one with a good mirror, decent soundproofing, good audio taping, decent recruiting with no "repeaters," an interesting deli tray, and a fair stipend for respondents. Now, those features are the baseline platform for the facility world and many field houses have stepped up to a level of excellence that includes such items as:

- Remote viewing for clients in another city
- State-of-the-art computer hookups for participants to interact on the Internet and for clients to access data via laptops
- Chefs and stellar catering services
- Ancillary services like the making of DVDs with time stamps and clipping services
- Unique room configurations for a variety of qualitative methodologies
- Trained staff who know how to support qualitative research quirks
- Appropriate recruiting techniques and re-screening procedures
- Serving as team partners with qualitative researchers in order to bring clients a higher level of excellence

So, when a qualitative researcher hires a facility that drops the ball on baseline factors such as recruiting, re-screening, and/or forgetting to record a QRE, these egregious errors blare like the fire truck sirens going to a four-alarm fire. The bar for the research facility has been raised, and woe to the ones that cannot jump that high.

Reports for Clients

Twenty years ago, clients wanted full reports with quotes and deep analysis to help understand the thinking of respondents. Now, the trend seems to be fewer full reports and more "executive summary" or "topline" reports. These types of reports distill the essence of the qualitative experience and target the key insights that relate to the study objectives. Along that dimension, the PowerPoint report is gaining in popularity, and this crisp bullet style format hits all the high notes needed for decision making.

Conclusion

While my twelve-step chart still works like it did in 1981, the emphasis is different. I still go through all twelve stages and at this point in time, I have got a wealth of experience from many successful projects. Therefore I can hold the flag for research rigor so that my clients have every chance for the best possible research for decision making.

Figure 2: *The Twelve-Step Qualitative Market Research Process*

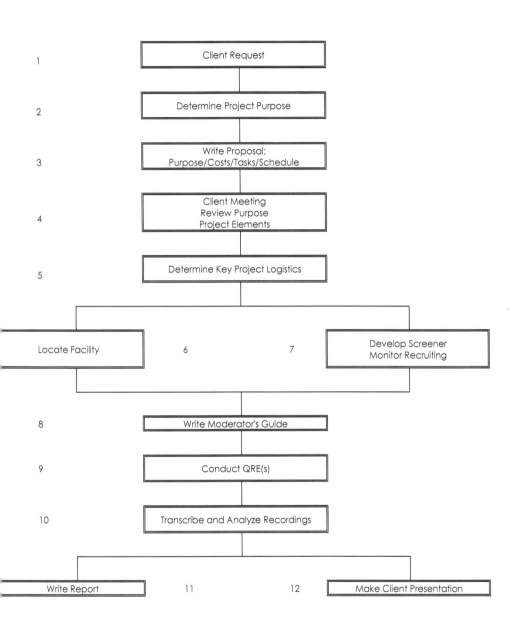

Embracing the Qualitative Research Quadrangle

> *Here are the four cornerstones for qualitative research events (QREs). Learn the importance of four major elements for your work: perceptions, opinions, beliefs, and attitudes (POBAs). This is the water in which Master Moderators™ swim.*

Clients want to know how and what consumers think so they can improve products and services and create new ones. As well, they find it very important to gauge the impact of advertising in order to determine which messages can best reach the intended target market.

The foundation for uncovering consumer opinions in a qualitative environment rests on four cornerstones: perceptions, opinions, beliefs, and attitudes (POBAs). Most qualitative research events (QREs) such as focus groups, focus panels, in-depth interviews, dyads, triads, minigroups, extended groups, mock juries, children's play sessions, and more rest on these four elements. However, the exploration into each element in any one QRE is not always equal or even. The purpose of the research determines the degree to which each POBA is explored.

For example, in a one-hour advertising lab session with consumers in order to get a quick thumbs-up or thumbs-down reaction to a nearly completed advertising campaign, there is minor emphasis on attitudes or beliefs about the product or service being shown. The main focus is on how the advertisement is perceived and what opinions about the product or service are exemplified in the advertisement.

By contrast, in an exploratory round of focus groups to determine how consumers differentiate between the terms "driving while intoxicated" versus "driving under the influence," the emphasis might be more on beliefs, attitudes, and opinions and less on perceptions about those terms.

This article will focus on each of the four corners of the qualitative research quadrangle and provide some key questions that can be used to delve deeper into each of these elements when they arise in QREs.

What Is a Consumer Perception?

The best definition for qualitative research is a mental image or concept of something filtered through the experiences of a consumer. It is their awareness of an element of the physical universe that they recognize through quick and acute cognition, and it is their ability to discern discrete elements among a series of related items.

Questions that help a consumer access this area might include: "Tell me what you think about the ease or difficulty of opening this frozen food package if you choose this item for tonight's dinner."

The probes that might result from the answers received allow the moderator to go deep into what consumers perceive about the physical package (e.g. coated paper, zipper pull, color cues via the red diamond next to the zipper pull, etc.). The line of questions that fit into this corner of the research quadrangle should all address what consumers see in the physical arena and how they filter what they see through previous experiences. It would not be uncommon for a respondent to say in this part of the QRE that they like or dislike zipper pulls or prefer thumb push openings to zipper pulls based on prior experiences with cold plastic coated boxes they have just pulled from the freezer compartment.

What Is a Consumer Opinion?

This corner of the research quadrangle is the one that often receives headliner status and it may be where client attention is often focused. **An opinion is a subjective judgment or appraisal formed in the mind of the consumer and on which he or she bases his or her reasons for feeling one way or another about a product, a service, or an idea.** It can be seen as more than an impression, but less than positive knowledge that can be defended.

Consumers are quick to say a phrase such as "In my opinion, Clinton will not be so well remembered for those long years of economic prosperity as he will be remembered for his dalliance with an intern in the White House." They had some facts on which to base their opinion, but in no way can they say with certainty how history will remember Bill Clinton's presidency.

What is useful for clients is the depth of consumers' opinions, including how long they talk about them, the words they use to defend their position, and the degree to which they work to sway the thoughts of others in the group.

When opinions about a product, service, or idea are mild rather than strong, it is a good indicator for clients to observe the degree of interest something holds for consumers.

When a bank client wants to gauge their image vis-à-vis their key competitor, the opinions of consumers provides valuable insight when the moderator asks a simple association question such as, "What animal do you associate with Framis Bank, and what animal do you associate with Amalgamated Bank?" When answers across four groups indicate that Framis Bank is associated with kittens and puppies and Amalgamated is associated with hippos and elephants, the opinions held about those two banks are very clear.

What Is a Consumer Belief?

This cornerstone of the research quadrangle is a tricky one. **A belief is a state of mind in which trust or confidence is placed in a person or a thing based on evidence.**

What makes this tricky is that consumers believe something without any trouble, but the evidence on which they base it might be faulty. For example, when consumers were asked what data the ten-year census forms collected, they believed there were questions on that form that were in fact, not there! They based their belief on how they felt about what the government might do with the data rather than on what the government actually does. The following quote indicates how a belief becomes "fact" in the mind of a consumer: "I believe that the census forms ask you about how many rooms are in your house, who lives there, what their highest educational level is, and what kinds of magazines they subscribe to." When asked how she knew all those things were "facts," she talked about an article in *Time Magazine* and how census data was used to figure out how to pitch magazine subscription invitations to certain zip codes. It then became clear that she confused the use of zip code cluster analysis with census data collection, and that formed the basis of her beliefs about what data was being collected by the federal government.

Beliefs stand at the core of one's personality and are hard to shake since they are formed early and reinforced on a regular basis. For example, if women believe that girls are not encouraged early to play team sports and to learn some of the leadership lessons that boys receive in that environment, they will translate that belief into how they see women in leadership positions in the workplace. Even when evidence to the contrary is presented, many respondents will say some version of "yeah, but" or "I hear you and I still believe…", since shaking one's beliefs causes the respondent to question long-held values.

It is handy to get a quick scan in a QRE about consumer beliefs so that reactions to products, services, or ideas can be understood in relation to their belief systems. It is necessary that clients understand the ground on which respondents stand if they want to shift how respondents feel about existing or new products or services. No client wants to hear those fatal words: "This product would be great for camping," since the belief would then be "It is not for me on any regular basis."

What Is a Consumer Attitude?

The last area of the qualitative research quadrangle is the concept of consumer attitudes. This is the juiciest area of the whole four-sided game in a QRE. **An attitude is the feeling or emotional or mental position that one holds about a fact or a statement.** Really to delve into attitudes, moderators must engage respondents in lively conversations about the key purpose of a qualitative research study.

When someone feels strongly about something, either positively or negatively, the words that he or she uses to talk about it, the pitch, speed, and pacing of their voices all give clues to their attitude toward it.

A good moderator deftly enters this arena with respondents, not by asking direct, head-on questions, but rather by sliding around the edge of the issue and slipping the camel's head under the back side of the tent. Sample questions about an existing product might be asked in this way:

- What have you seen or heard about pomegranate juice lately? (Set up Question)
- Have you ever tried it? (Baseline Question)
- If so, what did you say to yourself about it? (Attitude Q # 1)
- If no, what keeps you from trying it? (Attitude Q # 2)
- What do you need to know to make purchases of pomegranate juice as frequently as apple juice? (Attitude Q # 3)

What makes this area so interesting for moderators and clients alike (and maybe respondents too) is that it is easy to share an attitude about something without shaking a core belief or value that one holds. It is easy to say, "I never thought about buying pomegranate juice before or doing my banking on-line," without the listener judging the respondent as having limited or poor values. At that point, the rest of the camel's body is under the tent and the clients have a deeper insight into how consumers think.

Conclusion

It is interesting to note that when definitions of the four corners of the research quadrangle are reviewed in a dictionary, the definition of one will often have one or more of the others as synonyms! That makes POBAs as close as siblings in the research family, and a good parent (or moderator), knows that all the children in the family are unique regardless of the fact that they all share the same last name. When moderating, it is good to know in which corner of the quadrangle a line of questions falls so that clients have a clear view of the thinking of respondents. As a bonus, this makes analysis a lot easier too.

Qualitative Research Lessons from *Gone With The Wind*

> *Marketing research isn't about numbers—it is about people, relationships, and listening intently. Learn how to put together an Oscar-worthy QRE. Tools, tips, and techniques are presented in rich metaphor.*

Leading QREs for more than thirty years has provided me with lots of experience and many insights into the art and science of this wonderful research tool. It has also allowed me multiple opportunities to use metaphors for teaching others about qualitative research.

The roles of the key players in the qualitative research game are easy to define when matched up with the elements that go into making a movie to be shown in theaters. The participants are like the actors; the client or end-user is like the producer who provides funds for the movie; the moderator is the director; and the facility is the "set" where the action takes place.

The facility set is dressed with color, art, and provides comfortable and attractive seating. A large one-way mirror for viewing the process is set into one wall. Very often, flowers or plants complete the look of an attractive conference room setting, complete with ledges and tackable walls to allow for the display of advertisements, samples, concepts, prototypes, collages, etc.

QREs have four distinct phases that match the flow and plot of a movie, building from opening scene to the resolution of the story. These phases include:

1. Introduction
2. Rapport and reconnaissance
3. In-depth investigation
4. Closure

To match these elements to a plot line, the introduction phase is where we meet the characters and get a glimpse into the story that will be unfolding. To borrow a scene from *Gone with the Wind*: the movie opens with Scarlett O'Hara dressing for a garden party held at Tara, her father's home. It is before the Civil War, and all Scarlett can think about is whose head she will turn at the party in her pretty and virginal white dress of sprigged cotton. Of particular interest to her is the fiancé of Melanie, her best friend. She believes she loves the scholarly and pale Ashley who is so genteel.

We meet all the key characters (except Rhett Butler) at that party and progress with them throughout the movie as the Civil War and Reconstruction unfolds in Scarlett's life. The underlying theme is Scarlett's belief that Ashley is the man she loves, even when life and circumstances point her in the opposite direction.

In a QRE, we meet the respondents in the introduction phase and tell them the purpose of the session. The underlying theme may sound like this in conversation: *"You are going to discuss some new ideas related to cleaning products,"* or *"You will be discussing two different ways a product can be advertised,"* or *"Tonight's conversation will deal with topics that are in the headlines of this week's news."*

Respondents receive the session ground rules. They then introduce themselves by telling the group their names and some key data about themselves, such as family size or their free-time activities.

In the second portion of a movie, the plot unfolds to show some obstacle the hero/heroine is facing that needs to be resolved before the movie ends. In *Gone with the Wind*, these scenes relate to discussions about the coming war with key characters tossing off the specter of war as "impossible" or "a certainty" via dialogue and action. The red-headed Carlton twins eagerly look forward to what they see as the coming glory of a short war in which they will quickly defeat the Union troops are quickly routed, whereas Ashley sees the war as the end of a glorious era built on the backs of slaves—a way of life he feels must end.

In a QRE, the second phase is rapport and reconnaissance. Early questions are introduced that help set the stage for understanding later sections. It is here where baseline usage and behaviors are discussed and initial POBAs (perceptions, opinions, beliefs, and attitudes) are explored as they relate to the topic.

The primary action takes place in a film's third stage. In *Gone with the Wind*, this includes scenes showing how Scarlett survived the Civil War and the Reconstruction. This includes stealing Frank, her sister's boyfriend, and marrying him for his money, continuing to hopelessly love Ashley to no avail, meeting and marrying Rhett Butler, her third husband, and having his child—all while on her quest to "never be poor or hungry again." In this part of the movie. she makes the famous green dress from the drapes in the old living room at Tara, using her wits and whatever was on hand to forward her goals.

In a QRE, the third stage (in-depth investigation) takes the most time. Nearly two thirds of the two-hour session in a traditional setting is devoted to this stage where, respondents are shown concepts/prototypes, asked to brainstorm ideas, or to react to a series of advertisements/taglines. They may even review package designs, or grapple with thorny issues such as political platforms or whether the government should begin tagging vaccines with microchips to track the spread of disease. In this section, respondents may complete picture sorts, create collages, discuss assigned homework tasks, or work in teams along with traditional Q&A formats. Like Scarlett and the green drapes, respondents use whatever thoughts or feelings they have in response to the stimuli provided to express themselves in a new way.

In this stage of the group discussion, **it is the moderator's job to direct the action of discussion without becoming a part of the discussion.** In the filming of *Gone with the Wind*, the director had the difficult task of getting the actors to say their lines against the backdrop of the Tara mansion, or a flame-lit sky on the night where Scarlet and Mammy flee the Union soldiers after the fall of Atlanta while Rhett decides to join the Confederates. The director had the script, and when he called "action," the actors had to put down their scripts and act a scene that might include handling a team of wild-eyed horses or beating the dust off old velvet curtains.

In a QRE, only the moderator has the script (the moderator's guide) and the respondents are more like characters in an improv show! They are thrown a line (a question) and expected to respond immediately! While the moderator may nod or smile, his or her main job is to throw out questions and probe for more information. No dialogue should draw the moderator into the accumulating pool of data. All the action takes place between the actors on the set and the actors take cues from the director in order to know what to do next.

The moderator should not become a defendant of any one idea or concept or serve as an educator to the group. The moderator allows misinformation to arise when it occurs in the POBA framework and probes to understand how those POBAs were formed in the minds of the respondents. The moderator presents stimuli or tasks for the respondents to explore and helps to round out the type of information needed to reach the study purpose.

The whole time the group is unfolding, the "producer," or client/end-user of the research serves as the audience, listening to understand the topic as expressed through the viewpoints presented in the group discussion. These observers are listening to see if their pre-conceived notions about the respondent viewpoint are true or not and the reasons behind each viewpoint. They are listening for new insights and for the view of the topic through the respondents' life lens. They are looking for new opportunities for products, services, or ideas and they are looking for directional lights that point them in the right direction for future strategy decisions.

In a movie, at about the ninety-minute mark, the key action has occurred and the actors are left to deal with bringing the story to a close. In *Gone with the Wind*, Scarlett and Rhett's little girl, Bonnie, suffers a tragic accident when she is thrown from her pony. Rhett is consumed with grief and does not want his *"baby put in the dark cold ground."* Mammy, whom he had won over earlier with the gift of a red petticoat, finally talks him into letting the child be buried. Hurting from the loss of his beloved Bonnie, Rhett decides to leave Scarlett and their beautiful home and return to his life as a wanderer. The movie closes with the famous scene where Scarlett asks: *"What will I do?"* and Rhett responds, *"Frankly my dear, I do not give a damn."*

QREs do not end quite so dramatically. Instead, the respondents usually leave the facility (the movie set) with the feeling that their comments have made a difference to the moderator as well as the client and that products, services, advertising, or ideas will be improved because the voice of the consumer has been included in the process. Respondents are thanked for their participation and asked to pick up a thank-you that they can spend by seeing the hostess at the front desk, and the session is concluded. In the movies, the credits roll at the end, and in a QRE the client talks with the moderator about insights gleaned from respondents when the groups are over for the evening.

When *Gone with the Wind* aired, it was a great success, earning a number of Academy Awards for acting and direction. What made it a hit was not only the telling of a good story, but believable action from the actors, a stellar set, and good dialogue.

Here are the lessons that qualitative research can take from a movie such as this: have a solid moderator's guide, set a clear purpose and path for the research, pray for a willing client partner/producer, and create a wonderful setting for the research to take place. With all this, every QRE is a candidate for an Oscar!

Qualitative Research Techniques: Taking the Best of the Past into the Future

> *The world around us is constantly changing, so the business of qualitative research must change too! Every Master Moderator™ must learn what things to preserve and what things to change. Come here for advice.*

I. Current Practices

Qualitative market research (QLMR) in the United States was born in the 1930s. Some of the earliest groups on record were completed for soap manufacturers with housewives who were given samples of products in lieu of stipends. These sessions were held in the home of a recruiter with observers in chairs around the edges of a living or a dining room setting.

Focus groups are still the most common form of QLMR, and the term has become commonplace in the language of Americans. Journalists and television reporters now refer to insights from focus groups when reporting on political campaigns. Focus groups are the fodder for laugh tracks on sitcoms such as *Frasier* and *Murphy Brown*. References to focus groups can be found in such movies as *Network*, and mock focus groups are part of the "authentic" look to some current advertising campaigns for the telecommunications and coffee industries. A billboard in England for a high priced luxury car has this headline: *"Rejected by Focus Groups."*

Every day, average Americans are calling into research companies in their area and asking: *"Can you put me in your data bank?"* Qualitative market research has come a long way from focus groups in the homes of recruiters. Fancy facilities, with state-of-the-art equipment for sending focus group pictures via satellite, make it possible for clients to stay in their home city and see the focus group "live." Online focus groups make it possible for everyone involved to stay right in their offices. The only factor missing to date is holographic focus groups, and somebody is probably working on that!

Here are some trends that can be noted in this industry:

- Group size is dropping from ten to eight respondents as clients discover that more is not better and six is fast becoming the new eight.
- Mini-groups (four to six) respondents are on the increase for some types of studies.
- Triads are replacing one-on-ones to maximize research schedules for observers.
- Moderators who work for the client company are on the increase so companies save on freelancer fees.
- Requests for PowerPoint presentations of findings are on the increase as well.
- More trained moderators are in the workplace than ever before.
- Clients asking moderators to elicit more than top-of-mind responses from respondents and to dive into emotional realms.
- Clients are more savvy about QLMR techniques and procedures and ask for more activities in group discussions.
- The range of QLMR methodologies is increasing.
- More and more organizations are adding QLMR studies to their research requirements to fully meet the needs of the target markets they serve.
- Schools and churches are finding QLMR insights useful for short and long-range planning.
- Timing for QLMR projects is no longer limited to evenings. Breakfast groups are common at 7:30 a.m. and groups on Saturdays with either kids or adults are on the rise. Groups at conferences are also increasing in popularity.
- Payments to respondents are increasing and costs for all services in QLMR are increasing.
- Clients expect reports to be more than a reporting of what happened; they want "what does it mean?" insights.
- Demands for "Master Moderators™" are on the increase—moderators with long histories of moderating and familiarity with multiple product or service categories.
- Informed consumers who can talk with knowledge about product erosion and cannibalizing product lines are also desired by clients.

For every hundred qualitative researchers there are a hundred different qualitative research techniques, all aimed at providing insights related to POBAs (perceptions, opinions, beliefs, and attitudes) under a broad umbrella of studying social phenomena. Rossman & Rallis (1998) have identified eight characteristics that fit both qualitative research and the individuals who conduct it:

Qualitative Research

- Takes place in the natural world
- Uses multiple methods that respect the humanity of study respondents
- Honors what emerges—does not seek to match preconceived plan
- Is fundamentally interpretive

The Qualitative Researcher

- Views social phenomenon holistically
- Reflects on his/her own systematic role in the research
- Is sensitive to his/her own biography and how it shapes the research
- Uses complex reasoning that is multifaceted and iterative

If the above eight items provide the frame into which all qualitative research models fit, (e.g. focus groups, ethnographic research, mock juries, taste tests and the like), it is clear that moderators require many research tools to access respondent POBAs. Using the right tools will provide clients with insights that support longand short-range planning efforts. Poor use of qualitative tools and techniques makes the qualitative experience a long and onerous affair.

As a trainer of qualitative researchers for the past three decades, it has become necessary to teach the classic tools of this industry, as well as keep an eye out for new techniques that provide opportunities to get richer answers from consumers and members of target groups. This chapter focuses not only on classic qualitative research techniques but on some innovative solutions to getting more than top-of-mind answers from a variety of respondents.

Stages of a Qualitative Interviewing Event

Qualitative market research or QLMR typically adheres to the following four stages, regardless of whether the session is a traditional two hour focus group, a thirty-minute in-depth interview, or a six-hour extended session. The four stages simply take more or less time according to the time set aside for the event:

1) Introduction
2) Rapport and reconnaissance
3) In-depth investigation
4) Closure

In Stage 1, the researcher's main activity is to create sufficient and appropriate rapport so that respondents feel safe in sharing POBAs with each other and with the researcher. Stage 1 also sets the direction for the discussion, and the moderator demonstrates willingness to listen to diverse points of view without judging.

Stage 2 requires the researcher to provide respondents with a narrowing field of questions that create a floor of understanding about the basic issues being discussed. For example, if the study were about premium dog food and the reasons to buy it over store brand dog food, the Stage 2 discussion would determine such issues as what brands are purchased and for what reasons, as well as the image of specific brands.

Stage 3 starts about one-third of the way into the interview and generally takes up the majority of time set aside for the particular research mode. In traditional two-hour focus groups, this section would start at about the forty-minute mark and last until about the ninety-five minute mark.

Stage 4 is the last portion of the time set aside for the research mode, and when done well, it ties up the key insights gleaned thus far in the group. It allows respondents one last forum for any ideas previously discussed.

Experienced moderators have a fairly large repertoire of interviewing tactics that contribute to successful interviewing events. Chief among them are these qualities:

- Conveying an open, accepting attitude and genuine interest in and respect for each respondent
- Asking more open-ended than closed-ended questions
- Allowing respondents to do most of the talking
- Encouraging all respondents to participate fully
- Encouraging respondents to hold and state own opinions, regardless of what others may believe
- Using exercises appropriately to garner deeper information
- Varying behavior to meet demands of each new interviewing event

Standard Focus Group Elements

QLMR, as it has evolved from related disciplines of cognitive anthropology, sociology, human ethology, ecological psychology, holistic ethnography, and sociolinguistics, now follows a "standard" framework for interviewing selected target populations. Those elements include the following:

- Set timeline (e.g. two hours, or thirty minutes, or six hours)
- Trained interviewer, moderator, or researcher
- Open frame format—loose structure that allows for respondent "gold mines" to emerge
- Fixed number of respondents across a series of interview events
- Respondents share common traits
- In group settings, respondents typically do not know each other
- Respondents have generic study context, not specific context
- Respondents generally receive stipends for participation
- Research setting created in facilities or in the field to accurately document activities and, where possible, provide for observers
- Discussion has a clear purpose and stated desired outcomes
- Four stages for each research interview event
- Allowance for bias of group influence
- Allowance for bias of researcher
- Knowledge that reported behavior may differ from actual behavior

Krueger (1988) provides a detailed description of these elements. Marshall and Rossman (1999) indicate that while the questions in a focus group setting that embrace the above elements may appear "deceptively simple," the goal is to promote participants' expression of their views through the creation of a supportive environment.

QLMR also pulls from other disciplines, such as Neuro-Linguistic Programming (NLP), which is the study of subjective experience. NLP, first developed by Bandler and Grinder in the late 1970s, is defined as the way human beings generalize, distort, or delete their sensory experience and how they act to produce a given result in themselves or others. NLP seeks to define or outline the things we do subconsciously or unconsciously and demystifies the outcomes that are created when we think or act.

NLP techniques serve as good partners to qualitative research techniques by providing tools to access below top-of-mind responses with the support and approval of respondents because, as Chakrapani put it: "NLP, like psychology, encompasses the whole spectrum of human behavior."

Classic Techniques

A number of practitioners of QLMR have written about the industry, but Goldman and McDonald (1987) still offer one of the clearest definitions:

> Qualitative research addresses the nature of structure, attitudes and motivations, rather than their frequency and distribution... the underlying goal is to explore, In-depth, the feelings and beliefs people hold, and to learn how those feelings shape overt behavior.

To explore feelings and beliefs adequately, an environment has to exist in which POBAs can emerge. Five items need to be in place to create that environment:

- Trust between moderator and respondents
- Respect for what respondents have to say
- Steady pace to keep discussion moving along
- Variety of simple activities that keep interest level up
- Methods of asking questions that do not "lead" respondents

Since the goal of QLMR is to explore feelings and beliefs (or POBAs), classic techniques, like those outlined below, are designed to provide platforms so that respondents can share behavioral and rational information concurrently.

Creating Trust

Levels of trust begin the moment the interviewer sees a participant. That first moment of eye contact made by the interviewer should be accompanied by a smile and a sense of welcoming by word and deed. Rapport deepens in the first stages of the interview event when these activities take place:

- State clear purpose
- Provide adequate disclosures about microphones, mirrors, observers
- Provide key ground rules for participation
- Ask easy opening questions

Respecting Respondents

While many observers and some qualitative researchers often make fun of respondents, an attitude of respect is a coin that doubles and triples the investment made. It takes a respondent some measure of courage to come out, alone, to a research session in which questions are asked that reveal motivations and beliefs! A good qualitative researcher knows that when true respect is present throughout the interviewing event, the amount of data increases, and the depth of that information is often deep and rich. When these classic techniques are in place, the information pool is as large as a lake:

- Honor the world where the respondent stands
- Listen actively
- Suspend judgment

Maintain a Steady Pace

The "I ask—you answer" model of qualitative interviewing is interesting for about five minutes, and after that it is more interesting to watch paint dry! When the pace of a qualitative interviewing event is crisp and moves right along, respondents tend to stay interested, and they respect the rigor of planning that means no wasted moments. They learn to answer in headlines rather than novellas, and they tend to be willing to give answers without first over-thinking them. Some ways to establish and maintain a steady pace include:

- Changing activities about every twenty minutes
- Writing and asking good questions and then following up with appropriate probes
- Managing the timeline for the session so respondents work quickly, without rushing

Provide a Variety of Simple Activities to Keep Interest High

Similar to the pacing activities in the preceding paragraph, the inclusion of very simple activities can keep interest high and forward client learning. The following are just a few:

- Ask short questions to get long answers
- Stand and ask questions from different areas in the room from time to time so authority is not rooted in the researcher's chair
- Ask questions that access different models of listening
- Provide written and spoken instructions for all activities
- Find alternatives to charting responses on an easel

- Use manipulatives to forward discussion (e.g. file cards, product sorts, worksheets, etc.)
- Make abstract content more concrete through the use of easel drawings
- Use projective techniques that allow quick access to deeper thinking

Ask Questions That Do Not Lead Respondents

If part of the answer is in the question itself (POAIQ), this is a poor question that tips off the respondent as to what is being asked. Directly leading the respondent to conform to a particular viewpoint is just as risky as the two samples below illustrate:

Poor Q:	You like sports utility vehicles, right?
Better Q:	What do you like about SUVs?

Poor Q:	Why do you grocery shop on the way home? Is that because it is convenient?
Better Q:	When do you usually grocery shop, and what are some reasons for doing so?

Taylor and Bogdan (1984) list these factors as critical to the interviewing process:
- Being nonjudgmental
- Letting people talk
- Paying attention
- Being sensitive
- Probing for clarity
- Using cross checks to get same data in different ways
- Staying in rapport throughout the whole session with respondents

Specific Intervention Techniques to Gain More Than Top-of-Mind Responses

Every qualitative researcher should have a toolbox of techniques that fit their personality and research style. An interview with any set of ten such researchers will probably find some subset of these common tools:

- Product obituaries or eulogies
- Board of Directors

- Sentence completions
- Role play exercises
- Picture sorts
- Product sorts
- Collages
- Custom worksheets
- Debate teams
- Writing stories
- Drawing exercises
- "What if" scenarios
- Product transformations
- Comparisons
- Associations
- Secret pooling
- Personifications
- Balloon drawings
- Easel drawings
- Show/tell items (e.g. concepts)

The preceeding activities can be sorted into two categories: visual interventions and process interventions. An "intervention" is any activity that interrupts the "I ask—you answer" model of interviewing. Simple interventions include listing items on an easel and circling one for deeper discussion. A complicated intervention may require respondents to make a collage that describes the "personality of a brand."

Visual interventions require respondents to look at existing items and make comments. This could include looking at two different taglines for a product or reviewing a brochure that tells the user how to program their new DVD player. Process interventions are those that require respondents to do something and then discuss what they did. It is in the arena of process interventions that most qualitative researchers either create their own techniques or use traditional models, such as those outlined in the preceeding list. Regardless of what type of intervention is used with respondents, their effectiveness tends to stem from adherence to these procedures:

- Plan the intervention.
- Organize materials.
- Write instructions for both researcher and for participants.
- Test the intervention before the QRE, especially if it is new to the researcher.

- Set aside sufficient time for respondents to complete the exercise quickly, without rushing.
- Praise the first person to respond.
- Decide when to use private writing before public disclosure of information by respondents.
- Remain cognizant of order bias.
- Realize that the data comes from the discussion following the intervention, not from the intervention itself.

Innovative Techniques

Sometimes researchers need to create new techniques to meet client needs that range from discussions about preparing for death from AIDS to finding new uses for paper towels. Over the years, the techniques described below have provided useful respondent insights over a variety of service-, product-, or issue-based QLMR projects.

Open Frame

The simplest form of this technique is to draw a rectangle in the middle of the easel paper, about fourteen inches by ten inches. Inside that rectangle, a word or short phrase is placed with ten or so lines radiating out from the edges of the rectangle. Respondents are asked either to provide a definition of the term or phrase or to give an example. This works well when the term or phrase is abstract and has many meanings or definitions. Clients want to see what pops up in the aided conversation or to hear the language of respondents as they provide answers. Some examples of words or phrase tested this way include:

- Diabetic
- Underinsured
- Family values

Once, when a group of teen girls was asked to indicate ways to prevent teen pregnancy, the conversation "bogged down" and then stopped. The moderator drew a face on the easel, in place of the rectangle and gave these instructions:

> This is a fifteen-year-old teen that lives in the next county. She likes hoop earrings (draw hoops on diagram) and she likes headbands (draw headband on the figure). It is your job as an advisory committee to tell her how to avoid getting pregnant. What would you tell her?

The moderator drew lines radiating out from the face and, as fast as the teens talked, key phrases were added to the chart. When the comments (about twenty) trickled to a stop, the moderator circled two of the items (implants and birth control pills) and asked the group to talk more about these two items.

This technique illustrates the need to create simple methods to get respondents to access internal information in a new way. Often, the more simple the technique, the less the emphasis is on the process, and the more the emphasis is on what respondents have to say.

Getting Over the Wall

Many QLMR projects ask respondents to focus on barriers, obstacles or impediments to something. Early questions in this arena—such as *"what prevents you from…,"* *"what gets in the way when you…,"* or *"what are some reasons people have problems with…"*—will promote some conversation, but it can also generate long stories. To quickly access a variety of obstacles across the experience base of participants, the following technique may be useful:

- Draw a line down the middle of an easel paper—a side view of a brick wall.
- On the left side, draw a stick figure facing the line.
- On the left side of line, draw six to ten arrows that touch the line.
- Ask this question: *"How many different barriers or obstacles are there to…"*
- As the first set of comments comes forth, probe with *"what else?"*
- Write the comments on the arrows—working quickly to build a long list fast.
- On the right side of the line, mark three items that the group agrees are key obstacles or barriers, and discuss those in more detail.

Historical Ally

After introductions, ask respondents to write down the name of someone famous from history—someone who is no longer living, but someone whom they admire. Let them know that later on in the group discussion, they will be calling on that person as support to help solve a problem.

At the appropriate time in the discussion, present the problem (e.g. *"How can the state save money on trash pickup services?"* or *"What can be done to lower health care costs?"* or *"What would be a good name for this new product?"*).

Ask respondents to see the problem from the point of view of their historical ally and to provide some comments to the room from that viewpoint.

Sample responses could include comments like these:

- *"Madame Curie would find a way to treat the trash with a chemical wash that will shrink the trash so there would be less to take away."*
- *"Abraham Lincoln would tell us that if each one of us paid more attention to the health of our neighbors, we would all be healthier."*
- *"Salvador Dali would tell us to name the product something provocative so the product would stand out from the competition."*

While the comments may be silly or fanciful, the delivery of such insights opens the door to other comments that are past the range of practical and closer to the arena of creative problem solving. Sometimes a detour can become the shortest route to new information.

II. Current Trends

Widening the Scope of QLMR

As qualitative research enters into another century, traditional focus groups, mini-groups, and in-depth interviews are expanding to include other QLMR models such as:

- Ethnographic research
- Known pairs research
- Extended groups
- Piggyback groups
- Mock juries
- Internet-based QLMR projects
- Ad-labs

Ethnographic Research

There is a flurry of interest in ethnographic research with video cameras, digital cameras, and throwaway cameras used by respondents to record bits of their lives prior to the discussion of products, services, and ideas. Examples include the following:

- A car company asks researchers to visit the homes of owners and non-owners of a certain car to see if there are any differences, asking them to film the environment in which the car plays a role.
- A cereal company asks to visit a family to watch the way the family makes and serves breakfast, taking photographs of the pantry and the refrigerator contents to enhance the discussion with respondents.
- A day in the life of a terminally ill patient is filmed and discussed with family members to see what alternatives might be created to lessen stress.

This QLMR research tool is not used by every qualitative researcher, but the technique is definitely on the rise as more and more companies want to see how consumers and target audiences live—hoping to gain insights that can be turned into better advertising elements or better products.

Guidelines for ethnographic research include:

- Clear study purpose so that field work variables do not overshadow the research plan.
- Team approach—one "interviewer" to talk with respondents and a different researcher to record (audio, video, or notes) insights and comments.
- Sufficient time at the research setting (e.g. someone's kitchen, car test-drives, coffee shop, etc.) to conduct the full interview *and* have sufficient time between interviewing events to allow for travel time, as well as set-up and take-down time.
- Top of the line recording equipment (audio and/or video) since observers will not be present and transcripts or audio and/or video reports will become the data to be analyzed.
- Systematic way to keep materials for one interview together. Many researchers find that large see-through plastic envelopes with string ties allow them to see elements such as recording tapes, disposable cameras, checklists, manipulatives, and stipend checks for respondents. Some researchers use blue envelopes for "users" and yellow envelopes for "non-users" so that more cues are available for the researcher.
- Questionnaire or research guide that avoids leading the respondent through a set of pre-formed ideas. Rather, the guide or research questionnaire should be sufficiently open-ended to promote storytelling so that the respondents can explain and illuminate their lives and their decisions.
    o   Poor ethnographic question: *"What do you like about your car?"*

- o   Better ethnographic question: "*If you sold your car, what features or qualities would you miss most and for what reasons?*"

Known Pairs Research

Friendship pairs, married couples, and mothers with their children are being interviewed to expand on the understanding of how known pairs operate when they are not in a research setting. The interchange between known pairs increases the depth of information about products, services, and ideas. Examples include the following:

- A manufacturer of nail polish products invited girlfriend pairs and girlfriend trios to a set of interviews in a research facility. They were asked to bring their nail polish supplies and "do their nails" while they talked with the moderator. By observing the behavior (e.g. four pads soaked with nail polish remover), the moderator was able to ask reasons for behaviors like using multiple cotton pads, rather than one pad front and back.
- Watching a family play a new board game and talking aloud about how easy or hard the directions were provided game developers with insights missed in the design stage.

A researcher needs to stay alert to "Gold Mines" of information in the interstitial conversations between respondents as well as the respondent replies to the interviewer while resisting the temptation to join the conversation.

Extended Groups

Clients sometimes complain about having insufficient time to delve deeply into respondent POBAs, and if the sessions were longer, then more discussion about and among issues would be possible. To meet those needs, respondents are invited to attend sessions that last two and a half to three hours in some cases and four to six hours in other situations.

In the extended sessions, respondents often complete behavioral tasks, such as collages and storyboards, or engage in creative activities like modeling in clay or drawing stories that access more than top-of-mind experiences. On occasion, they may work in pairs or teams to complete a task.

Sometimes they participate in "field trips" during the research period, such as meeting at a facility and discussing shoe-buying patterns of the past. After that initial thirty-minute discussion, they enter a van and are driven to a nearby mall and given money to shop for shoes at a specific store while observers eavesdrop on the process. On the ride back to the facility, the participants compare shoes purchased and talk about how much money they saved. When the formal discussion resumes, specific questions are asked about elements of the shopping experience and factors about store layout, helpfulness of staff, and pricing.

Another study might invite participants to a large parking lot with instructions to get into nine different cars and rate the ease/difficulty of buckling the seat belt while an interviewer records notes and comments on a checklist form. When all respondents have tested all cars, they convene for a focus group discussion on specific cars with memory aids of photos and seat belt systems.

A toothpaste company asks respondents to meet for a four-hour session and to build two collages. One collage presents images of how they see a specific brand, and the second collage is based on reading a concept statement that positions the brand on a whole new platform.

These longer sessions allow a wide range of topics to be covered in detail without having to rush through a guide to keep to ninety-minute or two-hour deadlines of standard focus group sessions and allow for a fuller creative expression of insights to be gleaned from respondents.

Piggyback Groups

This model is when one group of respondents watches another group and then the groups are interviewed in turn. The "piggyback" research mode relies on current behavioral experiences, rather than reported experiences. For example, a group of dentists in the same practice view a focus group of a set of patients that visited the practice over the last year. The patients are told that their dentists along with others are behind the mirror. Questions about the practice, as a whole, start off the session. Specific comments on "how my dentist does X" are saved until later in the discussion. When the patients leave the research facility, the dentists are then interviewed about what they heard.

A much deeper discussion about patient POBAs is possible when the dentists are talking about the patient group comments, rather than remembering incidents or feelings from the past. To keep patients from being uncomfortable when talking about "my doctor" when they know he/she is behind the mirror, the moderator needs to put in place a clear set of guidelines for participation that encourages a range of comments without devolving into a "bash session."

Mock Juries

In this QLMR process, two sets of "jurors" are convened and each hears a different strategy on the same case points. Then each deliberates, allowing lawyers to be "flies on the wall" in the jury deliberation process to see how case points and strategies affect the final votes.

Typically this process is done on a Saturday or a Sunday, since it can take as long as six hours to hear plaintiff and defendant case points, deliberate on those case points, and reconvene to discuss reasons for voting as they did. A fair amount of role playing is required for this research tool. For example, one lawyer has to play the role of the judge and instruct the jury. Another lawyer has to play a role different from their regular legal function (e.g. a defense firm does not have plaintiff lawyers on staff as a rule, so someone must pretend to be a plaintiff lawyer to make the case points for the mock jurors).

Mock juries typically have a long planning period (e.g. jurors must be found that are similar in most ways to the actual jury that could be seated for the actual trial), and time must be allotted for the legal team to create two distinct strategies for trying the case. In addition, a larger research facility is required since the room is often set up similar to an actual courtroom to give lawyers the practice they need in making case points and to simulate the jury process for the participants. Additional time is also needed to recruit respondents for longer than average sessions.

Mock juries are worth every dollar they cost in cases where a great deal of money rides on the outcome—for example, wrongful death suits where a widow is asking for $9 million in damages from a bus company that ran up on the curb, striking and killing her husband. Mock juries also help in those cases where it is unclear where sympathy might rest for the defendant. A good example is a case where a teenage boy ran into a roof support stanchion in his high school gym during a basketball game and suffered a concussion that later caused his death. The parents sued the school. The lawyer for the school needed to know where the sympathy rested in the case: with the parents for losing their child or with the school that had been in the community for 55 years with no other accidents of this type on record.

When the outcome of a case depends on factors that verge on the emotional response of jurors, rather than clear-cut case points, mock juries are an emerging way to test the waters. Law firms use them to decide before committing to taking on a client or to choose an approach to mount at the actual trial.

Harnessing the Internet for QLMR Projects

Online focus groups, using the power of the Internet to pull respondents from different states and countries into one linked session to report POBAs electronically, provide a modern version of the Delphi technique. Questions are emerging about best uses for this type of research. Early adopters of this research tool are companies that are already using the Internet as a sales opportunity, such as car manufacturers, travel service companies, and companies that market communication products. A rising market for this type of research also includes users of catalog services and education programs. Also, children's research is growing in this field, since computers are so commonplace in homes and schools and an easy medium to reach children. Corporations are exploring ways to reach busy executives and harried decision makers right at their desks.

Problems that have emerged include creating firewalls so that findings and raw data cannot be extracted by non-vested parties and ways to ensure that the respondent recruited is the respondent on the other end of the modem. Some Fortune 500 companies are using this methodology to enhance findings discovered in face-to-face groups. Some recent uses include concept testing, customer service insights, feature testing of new products, web page testing, and package testing.

Another barrier that must be overcome to this technique is the initial poor quality of "virtual qualitative facilities" and the resultant bad press of those early offerings. While second and third-generation technological advances have much improved the services of online focus groups, the initial problems still remain in the minds of some research buyers. As this technique increases in usage, the role of the moderator will change from listener to active participant and a new hybrid researcher will be born.

A variation of this type of research is the bulletin board, where a moderator posts a question and respondents answer within a fixed time limit, such as a twenty-four-hour period. There are choices that must be made as to whether respondents see other responses before posting theirs.

Ad-labs

This is a streamlined focus group where the entire focus is on one aspect of an advertising campaign. It could be the testing of a range of advertising approaches, one campaign with five different taglines, or one approach with four different talent shots. Since the entire focus is on the impact of a campaign and its variations, there is little need for product background questions on product usage or image.

Groups are typically one hour or seventy-five minutes in length, and typically three or four are conducted in one day. All the same tools and techniques of traditional focus groups are in place for this mode of QLMR, and advertising agencies are typically thrilled to have the whole focus on the communications component and not the attitude and usage elements of traditional research.

III. The Future of QLMR Techniques

While the above list does not cover every new methodology, it does outline some of the more common ones and provides some insights into applications. In the last ten to fifteen years, the area of techniques and methods in QLMR has exploded. Moderators developed some of these techniques in response to client needs and some to handle the shifts in technology and communication. Techniques should not be confused with "tricks" or games to play on or with respondents. Appropriate QLMR techniques meet these criteria:

- Has a clear purpose
- Provides a specific outcome related to study objectives
- Allows respondents to participate in a way that does not demean or belittle them or their experiences
- Is conducted by an experienced and trained moderator
- Moves understanding about consumer behavior to a new and deeper level

Some of these new techniques have been borrowed from psychology or NLP. Some have been creatively developed to fit the information needs of specific companies or industries. In the hands of inexperienced moderators, these techniques can "bomb" when they are used without testing. Sometimes moderators feel pressured to show off a technique to entertain clients or create a sense of something proprietary to impress clients. Creative techniques used to "showcase" a moderator are also risky—doubly so when they can be potentially damaging to respondents who are then held up to ridicule by the back room when they fail to understand what is wanted or needed.

In the quest for "new, different, and better," qualitative researchers may erroneously place emphasis on the technique, rather than the outcome produced.

Summary

Qualitative researchers can look to the past and take forward classic techniques such as building rapport and respecting respondents along with standard interventions (such as "Board of Directors"). While new techniques will be added to the classic basics outlined in this chapter, qualitative researchers should always measure the benefits of doing "something new," against the gains it could provide. Remember, **new does not necessarily mean better.** Good baseline QLMR techniques will go a long way in facilitating understanding of the target populations that buy the products and services offered in the marketplace.

Secrets of Our Success: Leading Groups Effectively

> *What do seasoned moderators say about their industry? Read here for insights from several Master Moderators™ about best practices.*

At an annual conference of the Qualitative Research Consultants Association, a group of seasoned moderators was asked to write comments on a variety of topics related to moderating. While every panelist did not comment on every topic area, the compilation of all the comments on all the topics totaled forty-two pages! At the conference, additional questions were posed for a lively interactive session. Below is an excerpt from Section A of the document on leading groups effectively. Panelists' initials are shown in parentheses following their comments. The panel chair was Naomi Henderson (NH); panelists were: Barbara Rosenthal (BR), Lynn Greenburg (LG), Suzette de Vogelaere (SDV), Chris Payne (CP), Pat Sabena (PS), Jean Bystedt (JB), and Judith Langer (JL). These comments are just a sample of the wealth of information from a panel of moderating pros. I was thrilled to be part of such a creative group.

— Naomi R. Henderson

Leading Groups Effectively

1. What are your tips for making every group a great group?

- Do everything I can to ensure my comfort: room temperature, room set-up, no distracting noises, good chair, no sun glare. (LG)
- Generate and transmit energy. Tell them with humor that this may be the most exciting evening, etc., of their lives. They know it is not true, but optimism infects and raises the group's consciousness and rarely actually affects the genuineness of the responses. Recently, an upscale

woman said "I have been to these before, but this was different. You did not BS us." She was educated but emphatic! (CP)
- Listen carefully to what consumers are and ARE NOT saying with regard to addressing the relevant issues. (LG)
- I get twitchy about the term "great group." A great group to me is one in which you get rich information because respondents feel secure enough to spill their guts. I do not necessarily define a great group as dynamic, fast-paced, lively, funny… entertaining to the client. It can be, but not necessarily. A great group can look dull, quiet, maybe even plodding. I believe that excellent listening and observation of the respondents (verbal, non-verbal, and non-vocal communication), skilled probing, a keen understanding of the subject matter, issues, objectives of the study, knowledge of and facility with group dynamics (norms, roles, interaction, leadership functions and styles), interpersonal communication skills, and sensitivity to people, are what moderators do to make a great group. Also flexibility, maturity, and a sense of humor. These are not necessarily "tips," they are core knowledge and skills. (BR)
- Being prepared, energized, and totally present, with warmth, humor, eye contact, sincerity, and totally focused attention. (PS)
- I believe that moderators should develop their own style, based on their personality and skill, and then flex their communication style to that of respondents. For example, I do not have the personality to badger respondents, but other moderators may do that successfully. Knowledge of, and facility with, Myers-Briggs and NLP (neurolinguistic programming) help a moderator to flex communication. (BR)
- Not every group is going to be a great group. Live with it. Things happen; handle them professionally. (BR)
- If I respect the respondents, the group is a "great group," because they will be the way they are and then my only job is to listen to what they have to tell me and the clients in the areas of perception, opinions, beliefs and attitudes. (NH)
- NBF—be nice but firm. (JL)
- Have passion and joy for moderating. (BR)
- Make sure everyone participates and control unruly respondents (kick out if necessary). (LG)
- When I practice UPR (unconditional positive regard) the group tends to share more than top-of-mind answers. When I am "congruent"—what I say and what I do are consistent—they tend to talk more freely and provide more details. (NH)

2. What are some easy techniques that help you quickly build rapport?

- I do not think anything we do is easy. (BR)
- One I learned from Naomi Henderson years ago: asking benign but surprising questions in the introductions, namely: first name, age, and the town where each respondent was born, giving myself as the first example. (PS)
- I use my killer smile and my friendly, winning personality. (BR)
- Welcome respondents as they are walking into the room with small talk, i.e. the weather, weekend activities. Avoid controversial issues, i.e. politics. (LG)
- HUMOR. I used to tell respondents that what they say is private to the study and I do not turn the tapes over to the Special Prosecutor, but that is getting old. (BR)
- Learn and remember names. Throw away the name cards in front of respondents if you dare. The use of a name flatters and confirms you are listening to them and they are not fodder. Get the name wrong, make mistakes, and they will laugh with you. (CP)
- Have kids wave at the people behind the mirror and make faces. Tell adults that is what kids do, and invariably they do it, too. (BR)
- I am in the room when they come in. I start talking with them individually immediately. I do not wait till they are assembled and then make an entrance. (BR)
- Making a ten-second eye contact "bond" with respondents early in the introductions, coupled with a short response to their self intros (e.g. respondent says: "I have three kids, all girls." My response: "Any of them have nicknames?"). (NH)
- I have teens introduce each other to the group with first name, age, school, and one surprising fact. If a group of any age looks mad or dead before I get started, I have them introduce each other, too. (PS)
- Have respondents use colored markers with fruit aromas to create their own place cards with the name they want to be called during the group. (BR)

3. How do you get a group back on focus when they have gone off on a tangent?

- I say, "Well that's for another group, but now we need to focus more specifically on…" (PS)
- Depends on the tangent. If negative, draw a circle on your pad, write in

the issue they are concerned about and underline it to show you have taken notice. Then say we have to move on but I have got this down. If positive but uninteresting, I tend to bring them back with humor. Or simply state the fact that we have to cover a number of things. (CP)
- I say, "This is interesting, now let's get back on subject," and I ask the next question. (BR)
- This is a dicey area because some great data has come out of "tangential stories." However, if the tangent is way off target then my usual technique is to ask: "Can you tell me how what you are saying relates to the question on the table?" If they cannot, then I thank them for their comments and restate the question for the room and ask others to respond. (NH)
- Tell participants they are getting off today's topics and suggest they continue the conversation on their own after the group is over. (LG)

4. What techniques or interventions are your favorites for getting respondents to offer up more than top-of-mind answers?

- I do not let respondents get away with anything. I grill them on their vocabulary, ask what they mean by what they are saying. (BR)
- Mindmapping and laddering often help me to go deeper initially. Psychodrawings, perceptual mapping, and collage are techniques I use frequently. Probes such as, "Tell us more about that," "Go a little deeper on that," and "Dig down deeper on that" help out later. (PS)
- Play on their sympathy by asking them to help me out to understand what they mean. (BR)
- I sometimes use a technique like "open frame" where I draw a box on the easel and lines radiating out from the box. In the box is a statement or a phrase (e.g. recycling effectively). I ask: "What does this term mean for you?" and either write on the lines or just point to them. Making the abstract more concrete via a visual often helps respondents access deeper levels of information. (NH)
- Ask: "Tell me about the last time you…" (LG)
- Probe, probe, probe with insightful, meaningful, relevant, spontaneous questions. Other effective probing techniques: silence, mirroring, active listening, paraphrasing, rephrasing, sentence completion. (BR)
- My favorite projectives (but not appropriate for all groups): picture sorts, drawings, trees (a form of laddering), music. (BR)
- "What do you imagine the creative/designer was trying to achieve?" "What do you imagine the person who had the idea, invented the prod-

uct etc. is like?" This works well to tell you about whether they feel the product idea has relevance to their lives. "Draw the kinds of pictures you imagine would be in the TV or magazine advertising for this." "Imagine you are meeting a friend for a drink or coffee after this group. How would you explain what we have shown you?" (CP)

- Simple projectives (e.g. "What would the people in your zip code think about this new recycling idea?") is one way to get deeper data, shared pairs is another (work in teams of two for two minutes, and create three or more new ways to recycle in your area). Another way is to ask them to act like a board of directors and to come up with ten solutions in ten minutes. (NH)

5. How do you manage the backroom when you are the one leading?

- Spend about ten minutes before the group explaining the value of FGs and FG respondents, objectives of the study, how to observe a group, what they might expect. Explain that we learn a lot from respondents' negative comments. Then hand out an "observational fact sheet." (BR)
- Check with the backroom between groups or during a writing exercise to make sure the client is getting what he/she needs. (LG)
- Ask my colleague to take notes, but listen for issues. Most of the time I ignore the backroom since my work should be front-focused, and they will behave however they wish, no matter what I might desire. The only issue is that sometimes people will worry too much if consumers are critical. I like what you call ethnography, such as in-home interview (not in facilities) and in-store interviews where reality bites and you can feel the honesty and most CEOs or senior clients know the score. They can hear criticism of their product and not die. If they cannot, well… (CP)
- I ask the research director to be my conduit for notes from the back room and, if necessary, I go into the back room during a writing exercise. (PS)
- Providing the backroom with worksheets or tasks (e.g. putting Postits on poster paper with the five key project issues listed one to a page on the backroom walls). I have also asked backroom members to listen for specific words or to make tallies of the number of times "X" or "Y" gets mentioned. (NH)
- Ask one client team member to be the client spokesperson and for all comments and/or requests to go through that person and out to the facility or the moderator. (NH)

- It is hard to handle the backroom when I am not in it and I know that the process of looking through the mirror is a form of sanctioned voyeurism for some clients. I understand the human nature process of putting someone down to make yourself feel more comfortable, and I slip in some kind of comment in the briefing stage along these lines: "I really respect the people who are coming tonight. You couldn't get me out for two hours and $50 to talk about trash... it should be interesting to hear their comments." I know it won't stop the process of putting others down, but I do know that they know I am not going to join them in that process. (NH)
- Handling the backroom when you are videoconferencing can be a challenge. I recommend having one person in the backroom to handle the folks at home, but that is not always feasible. So you do what you have to do. I get myself back there two or three times during the group, while the group is doing some individual activity (e.g. during a picture sort or writing something). (BR)

What Counts in Life Cannot Be Counted
In Response to "When Good Research Goes Bad"
by Alvin A. Achenbaum[1]

> *The world of qualitative research is not always a peaceful one—good people, as it is said, can certainly disagree. But stand back and watch as a Master Moderator™ takes on a few mistaken ideas about this business!*

Alvin Achenbaum makes a number of good points about being careful when using qualitative research. I love the point he makes about going out into the world and hearing real consumer vernacular rather than talking to middle-class colleagues and "affluent and educated spouses," and I concur with a number of key points he makes about qualitative research:

- It can be a useful tool when used appropriately.
- It is great for such tasks as hypothesis formulation.
- It provides an avenue for informal discussions with users about products, services, prices, packaging, and communications as well as a window for decision makers to see the thinking of consumers and hear their language.
- It is an excellent tool for supporting questionnaire development.
- It is misused when clients think that the small sample sizes (e.g. four groups/thirty-two people) constitute a valid cross-section of the buying population.

---

1 Alvin A. Achenbaum's article, "When Good Research Goes Bad," was published in Marketing Research in 2001.

- It is subjective in nature—any number of conclusions and insights can be generated.

I start to disagree with Mr. Achenbaum when he labels, compartmentalizes, and separates research into a category that must be "science-based" to be worthy of the name research. He further argues that qualitative inquiry is a tool of market research and a stimulant to thinking, but outside the realm he defines as "scientific" research because it has:

1. Inadequate samples
2. Inconsistent methods of questioning
3. Subjective analysis
4. Moderator variance

From where I sit (once a "quant jock" myself, and now a qualitative research consultant with more than forty-five years total in the research field), I bring a different viewpoint.

The author states, "It is not my objective to eliminate qualitative exploration. What is done has value. But, I submit, it is not research." It is this statement that spurred me to make a formal written response and provide a counterpoint for consideration.

Starting with recognized dictionary definitions, the word "research" has these meanings:

1. To study thoroughly
2. To engage in or perform research
3. To seek out—to search again

When the word "qualitative" precedes research as a phrase, something interesting happens to Achenbaum's premise. By definition then, qualitative research might have these meanings:

1. To study perceptions, opinions, beliefs, and attitudes thoroughly
2. To engage in or perform qualitative research
3. To seek out—to search again the thinking of different groups of people on issues, products, services, and advertising

I am fully aware that the data from QREs is not projectable to a universe of consumers. I am also keenly aware that QREs have multiple biases including moderator variations, convenience recruiting, payment of stipends, and subjective analysis.

However, I contend that simply because something can be counted (e.g. eighty-one percent of Americans prefer automatic over stick-shift cars) does not make it "better data." Four focus groups with respondents who drive automatic cars and four groups with those who drive stick-shift cars can help car manufacturers a great deal. They will understand what the decision tree is when buying an automatic car, and they can hear the key language cues and performance expectations from those that drive stick shifts. Decision makers, copy writers, and marketing staff in the auto industry can confirm or negate their own thinking as they plan advertising and product strategy in the coming months. For sure, those eight groups are not definitive, and the data is not projectable, but they provide more insight than a cold set of tables depicting that eighty-one percent of Americans prefer automatic cars with no clues as to what drives the high percentage of automatic car purchases! And it sure beats the team at the auto company "imagining" what consumers think!

I fully believe that the things in life that count are things that cannot be counted. There is no way to measure the love of parent for a child or the depth of emotion when a friend stands by you in tough times. There is no way to measure the peace of standing in a field of wildflowers on a sunny day or the soothing quality of waves on a deserted beach. There is no measure of the magic of getting the perfect gift you wanted or replicating the exact taste of your grandmother's peach pie twenty-six years after she died. How do you quantitively measure something like job satisfaction? You can ask about all those things in qualitative research and discover key threads that make up the fabric of society. The science of the heart (emotion) has just as much value as the science of the head (rational thought). For my money, I trust more in the heart!

You may be asking: Who cares about parental love, friendship, inner peace, waves, gift giving, peach pie, or job satisfaction? These companies do: makers of board games, greeting card companies, resorts, shopping malls, frozen pie companies, and the federal government.

I also believe that qualitative research and quantitative research are, respectively, the front and back of a hand. You cannot really tell where one starts and the other ends when you look at the front or back of your own hand. Both are needed to make a complete hand, and both are equally powerful and stand an equal chance of being misused. The same hand that soothes a sick child can also slap that child silly.

Appropriately, Achenbaum points out that quantitative research also can be misused or applied incorrectly. The "manipulated polls" in political elections via biased question wording is just one example. I completely agree with the author that it is not simply a question of quantity being good while quality is bad. Both have issues that should concern thoughtful researchers.

If there is one point I want Achenbaum to consider, it is this: qualitative inquiry is a shiny spear in the panoply of qualitative research. Used well, it can stand alone as a spur to a new thinking or point the way for the more logical and practical quantitative weapons.

SECTION II: THE ROLE OF A MODERATOR

So You Want to Be a Moderator 67

Working as a moderator isn't a walk in the park—it is a hard business and full of challenges. Here are the thoughts of a Master Moderator™ when she hears those fatal words: "I want to do what you do!"

Best Practices for Vested Moderators 71

Thirty years ago, most moderators were non-vested, meaning they were freelancers working for different clients. Now, there is a trend toward using in-house staff as moderators, making them "vested" in the project outcomes in a different way than a freelancer. Due to their unique position in the project process, vested moderators might find it useful to follow a set of standards to ensure that the best possible data is garnered for decision making.

Magical Thinking: Are Moderators Magicians? 81

Does abracadabra work with a QRE? Do you need a top hat to work with a client? Learn why this Master Moderator™ borrows magical metaphors to make her point!

The Art of Moderating: A Blend of Basic Skills & Qualities 85

Moderating is, indeed, an art. There are basic skills and qualities that must be carefully developed by the burgeoning moderator and blended into a seamless event that gets clients key data for decision making.

Benefits of Matching Moderators to Cultural Groups 91

So much of the moderator's world is about relationships—to work well with a QRE, you have to be able to relate. This is why sometimes race and nationality might be critical matching factors.

Briefcase as Carnival Wagon 99

Lessons for the research gypsy! You are on the road much of the time. How can you move effectively through the five business areas to be a successful qualitative researcher?

Trained Moderators Boost the Value of Qualitative Research 103

Learn the true quality of moderator training and how to boost the value of qualitative research by using trained researchers.

Staying on Top of the Moderator Game 115

Competition and change—like most businesses today, qualitative research is beset by both influences. How can you keep in shape and face the constant challenges in the industry? Come here and learn how to stay on top!

Managing Moderator Stress: Take a Deep Breath. You Can Do This!
.... 121

Training! Expenses! Competition! Change! Challenges! How on earth can you do this and remain sane and happy? Here is your vote of confidence and reassurance before you set out to moderate!

So You Want to Be a Moderator

> *Working as a moderator isn't a walk in the park—it is a hard business and full of challenges. Here are the thoughts of a Master Moderator™ when she hears those fatal words: "I want to do what you do!"*

Over the last thirty years I have heard the following phrases a few times: *"I loved the focus group tonight, and I think I would be good at leading a group—I really like talking to people. How hard can it be? You just ask questions and laugh a lot. How can I become a moderator?"*

In the early years of my career as a qualitative researcher, that question would raise my hackles, and the unspoken thoughts that followed sounded like this in my head: *"Do you have any idea of how hard it is to do this night after night, city after city? Do you have any concept of how many times this guide underwent revisions and how I sweated bullets to make sure the specs were right for the recruit? Do you know how hard it is to leave my ego in a suitcase outside the door, ask neutral questions, probe for clarity, manage the timeline, suppress the dominators, and inspire the shy ones to talk while keeping the client's purpose in mind for every question asked? Do you know how hard it is to juggle activities in the session to keep things moving and make sure you get more than top-of-mind responses? And, by the way, do you know what it feels like to be judged by a group of people behind the mirror who want you to move on and get to a key point they are interested in?"*

But, instead of dumping all those thoughts on the respondent who made the comment, I just politely say something like, *"So glad you enjoyed the session, and if you want to know more about the market research industry, be sure to talk with the owner of this facility about ways you can learn about careers in this field."* That usually does the trick, and nothing more needs to be said except, *"Good night and thanks for coming."*

When I hear a respondent talk about wanting to be a moderator, I am reminded of what a duck looks like while floating down river. The duck seems to glide effortlessly but you do not see how furiously he is paddling his feet! I also remember what it is like to watch the Olympic ice skaters glide effortlessly across the ice, smiling, executing jumps and spins. Viewers do not see all the years of practice where the skaters fell down more times than they were upright. Likewise, respondents do not see what it takes to get to the role of being a moderator; they just see the smiles as the moderator lands a research triple axel!

Recently, I asked myself, *"Where does that respondent's comment come from?"* What did he see, hear, feel, or experience that made him voice a statement that implied a desire to lead a focus group? When I see a Western movie, I do not come out of the movie wanting to be a cowboy. After seeing another Cirque de Soleil extravaganza, I do not leave wanting to be an acrobat. When I see Meryl Streep in another stellar role, I do not want to be an actress. However, when I come away from these events, I do take a few moments and savor the beauty, the style, and the quality of what I just witnessed, and then move on in my life. So what happens in a QRE that makes a respondent want to be a moderator?

I believe that when a moderator listens to a respondent and honors his opinions, without judgment, that respondent has an experience that is rare in modern society. Ministers, priests, and rabbis listen, but they often judge. Lawyers listen, and they always judge! Judges listen, and… need I say more? Parents, teachers, and bosses listen (sometimes) and for sure they judge. But good moderators—they listen and do not judge. In fact, they ask for more information!

Respondents attend a group discussion about a product, service, or idea and may see a package design or various elements or prototypes. They may see rough or finished advertising, concepts, or ideas in the planning stage. They are asked for their perceptions, opinions, beliefs, and attitudes (POBAs) about something, and a good moderator listens and probes for clarity but does not judge the response. The moderator praises respondents for having diverse opinions and rewards them with money for their time and for providing insights and comments about a topic.

It must feel great to be able to say whatever you want about the topic and know it is all useful to the moderator who uses it to forward the group discussion. When something is pleasurable, there is a desire to continue to keep feeling those good endorphins created by the experience. What else do respondents like in QREs?

- They like hearing the opinions of others and matching their internal thoughts with those of others.
- They like the chance to think about a topic and then bring their wisdom, experience, and insights to life in a conversation that is valued—

both by affirmations (in word and deed) from the moderator and in cash.
- They like feeling that they are one up on the world, hearing about something before the rest of America sees or hears about it.
- They like being challenged to think about ordinary things in a new way.
- They like looking at the work of creative people at advertising agencies.
- They like looking at the different ways that engineers or researchers create new products or ideas, and they like talking about products, services, ideas, or advertising in such a way as to affect the outcome of what millions of Americans will see in the future.
- They like the chance to play and be creative similar to when they were children, and they like being invited to return to childhood and sometimes to play games such as "let's pretend" and "what if…"
- They like looking at stimuli such as pictures and prototypes, and they like feeling important when they have an insight that is a new thought in the room and further forwards the discussion.

A good moderator sets the tone for the group by providing a welcoming acceptance, ground rules for participation, and a road map for the session so respondents know when the discussion is going to move on. Inside the structure of ground rules and road maps, respondents know the boundaries and limits of the group discussion. Inside these boundaries is the freedom to be themselves, and that is a delicious feeling.

Now, when a respondent says they would like my job, I say something different in response: *"Thanks for letting me know of your interest in the work of market research and moderating. I love my job because I get paid to be nosy and find out what people are thinking. Like all good jobs, this one has a process to go through to be able to lead a session effectively. I have been working for more than thirty years to get to this stage. I am glad you had a good time tonight. I appreciated hearing your thoughts in the discussion."*

I now see that a comment like *"I want to do what you are doing"* is actually a compliment for my work as a moderator. They are really saying, *"I liked gliding down the river with you—it felt effortless, and for a moment I imagined myself in your role."* At the end of a long day that finishes close to 10:30 p.m., that is a nice feeling for me.

Best Practices for Vested Moderators

> *Thirty years ago, most moderators were non-vested, meaning they were freelancers working for different clients. Now, there is a trend toward using in-house staff as moderators, making them "vested" in the project outcomes in a different way than a freelancer. Due to their unique position in the project process, vested moderators might find it useful to follow a set of standards to ensure that the best possible data is garnered for decision making.*

There are situations when a company or organization uses an employee to conduct qualitative research events (QREs). These might include focus groups, in-home interviews, dyads, or any of a myriad number of research methodologies to help understand the perceptions, opinions, beliefs, and attitudes (POBAs) of varied target markets.

In other situations, a company may choose to hire a freelance moderator, who can be a sole practitioner, or an employee of a market research firm or consulting agency.

Many factors impact the decision to use a staff member or a vendor for QREs and this article addresses the impact of either choice.

What Does "Vested" Mean?

Suppose a dog food manufacturer decides they want to conduct research with current dog owners who traditionally buy fifty pound bags of dog food to feed their dogs. The study purpose is to explore perceptions, opinions, beliefs, and attitudes about new coupon and rebate ideas. For a variety of reasons, they choose to use a brand manager of that same line of dog food to conduct the research in three cities. **That moderator is a vested moderator because he/she meets the following criteria:**

   a. He/she receives a salary from the company that makes the product
   b. He/she may have worked on the coupon or rebate ideas that will be addressed by respondents
   c. He/she will be affected by the results of the research when planning short and long term strategies in his/her department

In another scenario at the same dog food company: there is a market research department whose members are charged with tasks to collect both secondary and primary research to help the company with short and long range objectives. The brand manager may contact the market research department and ask one of the qualitative researchers to conduct focus groups with customers about the coupon and rebate ideas generated by the brand manager's team. **That market research department moderator is also vested because:**

   a. He/she works for the company that makes the dog food and receives a salary
   b. It is part of their job assignment to conduct primary research and QREs fall under that umbrella
   c. Their department has a mandate to collect data for other company employee projects

What Does "Non-Vested" Mean?

If a moderator is hired by a company and that moderator is a freelancer or works for a market research or consulting firm that serves a variety of clients, the moderator is deemed to be **"non-vested"** as they:

   a. Do not receive a salary from the manufacturer
   b. Did not work on the stimuli to be shown to respondents
   c. Work in a contractual relationship to collect data with their emphasis being on collecting and analyzing the data to support client decision making

A non-vested moderator is committed to getting the best data from respondents to help client decision makers. They are "vested" in doing a good job, meeting client objectives, and holding the "research flag" for qualitative research. They do not face the same concerns as a vested moderator, so they can focus their full attention on collecting and analyzing data and not on the challenges faced by a vested moderator. The list below outlines those challenges.

Challenges of Being a Vested Moderator

A vested moderator, as a staff member in the company that is deeply entwined in the product or service, is under the spotlight of research and it may take the following forms:

- Staff moderator may feel the **pressure** of work peers and supervisors who observe their work as it relates to job or career performance criteria
- **Job security** issues: *"What if I don't do a good job, or get what the team is looking for...is my job on the line?"*
- Deep concern about **having to implement the results** of the research, no matter the outcome of the research
- **Feels strongly about the direction the company should take** with respect to the product or service being evaluated
- **Subject to temptation** as they may desire a particular outcome, they may subconsciously avoid a line of questions or spend too long "searching" for specific answers rather than keeping the focus on learning what respondents have to say regardless of the impact on future events at the company
- **Runs the risk of being an order taker** rather than a decision maker as they are part of a hierarchical system of boss and subordinate in the company

Benefits/Drawbacks of Vested Moderators

There are some clear reasons to use an "in-house moderator" and there are some clear reasons to hire a freelancer or a market research vendor company to conduct QREs to collect qualitative data needed for client decision making. The chart that follows highlights both sides of the equation with regard to vested moderators.

BENEFITS OF VESTED MODERATORS	DRAWBACKS OF VESTED MODERATORS
• No additional outlay of research consultant funds since **moderator is already on salary as staff member** • **High degree of knowledge** about content of subject matter under discussion • On-site at client office **to handle logistics issues with ease** • Clear knowledge of **where specific research project fits into the "big picture"** for the organization • **Able to provide recommendations based on the research** as they are involved in strategy decisions as well as the research process	• Too close to subject and to target market running the risk of **a myopic viewpoint** • **Hard to remain detached and impersonal** when either positive or negative issues arise in the group • **Hard to continually suppress facial expressions** when respondent comments "strike home" • Increased tendency to **"lead the witness"** either overtly or unconsciously because too knowledgeable about content of the topic • Sometimes **difficult to separate self from "client team"** while serving as an advocate for viewpoints of consumers and remaining objective • Runs the **risk of sacrificing research rigor** due to high degree of product knowledge

Key factors to consider when deciding – to use a vested or non-vested moderator:

- When weighing the pros and cons of vested vs. non-vested moderator for a project, **do not let cost be the prime motivator**
- Make sure **the trade-offs do not affect the quality of the data collected**
- **Do not diminish the impact of peer pressure** on how a vested moderator conducts the session
- Just because a staff member has seen many QREs, that does not take **the place of being trained as a moderator**

How To Be Vested And Still Be A Successful Moderator

Since more and more companies are bringing market research functions back in-house and using staff as moderators, **it would be wise to know how to be vested and still be effective as a moderator.** Below are ten tips on how to work toward successful outcomes.

> *Note: While the list below focuses on what vested moderators should be aware of, the list also serves as a reminder for how to stay sharp as a non-vested moderator as well.

1. When working with "client team," **put everything in writing** to minimize misunderstandings and maximize opportunity to meet expectations.
2. **Give observers "client ground rules"** and treat them the same way you would a client if you were a freelancer.
3. **Avoid going into "collusion" with peers** about what could happen in the research session. Stay professional and detached.
4. **Mentally stay detached** when you are in "moderator mode" – putting all your energy on making your respondents the "star" of the research process and keep the focus away from work peer and supervisor judgments about how and what you are doing.
5. Hold the line on issues such as:
   - Gossiping about participants
   - Including/excluding difficult respondents
   - Changing the guide to stroke an observer's ego
6. **Clear the project methodology** and the moderator's guide with "key clients" well before first QRE is conducted.
7. **Practice UPR** (Unconditional Positive Regard) with respondents and with the "client team."
8. **Practice sophisticated naïveté.** Let respondents tell you what you already know. Avoid looking "smart" in front of colleagues. Instead put your energy on "diving deep" with respondents, even if you do not look so good in the process.
9. On the day of the QREs, **physically distance yourself** from members of the "client team" who have come to observe. Meet them one hour before the start of the first QRE.

10. If the study is "blind" (e.g., respondents do not know the sponsor), **do not lie and say you are a freelancer**. Below are some other descriptors you might consider in place of this falsehood.

BLIND STUDY

1. *I'm on the research team for this study. My job is to ask questions and report findings without using anyone's name.*

2. *I'm under contract to collect research information about the topic of XYZ.*

3. *My team was assigned the wonderful task of talking to consumers about products/services. I'm happy to be the one talking with you this evening.*

If the study is not blind (i.e., they know the sponsor) then these phrases could be useful:

RESPONDENTS KNOW THE SPONSOR OF THE RESEARCH

1. *As you know, I work for _____, but tonight I'm only wearing the hat of a researcher, asking questions about the general topic of _____. I am not able to answer any questions about the project/service you will be discussing.*

2. *The fun part of my job is getting away from my desk and out talking to consumers of this product category. I am an expert on asking questions. I'm expecting you to be an expert on this topic providing your unique insights to the questions I'm posing.*

How Can a Vested Moderator Be Effective?

While a tiger cannot change his stripes and a vested moderator will always have the bias of working at the company that needs the research, they can be trained to uphold some industry standards.

<u>**Sending an untrained moderator with vested interest in to conduct research is like tying together the ankles of a swimmer. He or she can still swim, if they have powerful arm muscles, but a lot of energy is expended, a**</u>

lot of water is displaced, and it takes a lot longer to get from one end of the pool to the other.

> **What a trained moderator can bring to the vested moderator game:**

1. Asks questions from the **logic pattern** of respondents
2. **Paces the discussion** from general to specific questions
3. **Does not "tip their hand"** by saying "we" (referring to self and the company where they work); or letting respondents know the moderator's viewpoint on any issue under discussion
4. **Quickly and naturally creates rapport** as well as a safe environment for a diverse set of answers from respondents
5. **Avoids "why" questions** and does not put respondents on the defensive in their answers
6. **Uses a variety of techniques** to keep the group engaged and highly verbal
7. Is well prepared; **has a sense of "research rigor;"** and follows accepted principles of qualitative research inquiry
8. **Works through the four stages** of qualitative inquiry without shortcutting any steps
9. **Does not analyze or summarize while moderating**, rather the bulk of the inquiry process is spent on asking key questions that lead to achieving the study purpose along with stellar probes to get below top-of-mind answers
10. **Has a variety of techniques** to minimize tendency to "lead the witness"

VESTED MODERATOR TEST

> If you work at a company as an in-house moderator, you are vested. Give yourself the following test to measure how well you did the last time you were a staff moderator.

DID YOU...

1.	Give clear ground rules and disclosures	YES	NO
2.	Tell the truth about your role (freelancer vs. researcher)	YES	NO
3.	Establish rapport and create a safe environment	YES	NO
4.	Avoid POAIQ (Part of Answer in Question)	YES	NO
5.	Keep discussion on purpose without extraneous questions	YES	NO
6.	Probe for clarity and nominalizations	YES	NO
7.	Maintain UPR (Unconditional Positive Regard)	YES	NO
8.	Ask neutral questions	YES	NO
9.	Avoid "do you" or "did you" questions	YES	NO
10.	Ask questions that opened up respondent's ability to answer	YES	NO
11.	Include everyone in the discussion	YES	NO
12.	Avoid "serial interviewing"	YES	NO
13.	Avoid analyzing, summarizing, and paraphrasing	YES	NO
14.	Read the room, maintained eye contact	YES	NO

15.	Attend to non-verbal communications	YES	NO
16.	Use a variety of techniques to promote discussion	YES	NO
17.	Listen rather than inform participants	YES	NO
18.	Change your location/body position during discussion	YES	NO
19.	Give clear instructions	YES	NO
20.	Make sure to follow SQLA (Short Questions/ Long Answers)	YES	NO

Scoring: Review how many "yes" & "no" answers you have circled. If 60-70% are "yes," then you are doing a good job at keeping your inside knowledge and interest in the project in check. If you have more "no" responses than "yes" responses you may want to consider having your skills evaluated.

Summary

It is possible to be "vested" and still be a successful moderator. What it takes is strict adherence to these principles:

I. Commitment to the study purpose
II. Ability to stay objective in a highly subjective environment
III. Able to understand that "bad news" from respondents is not a reflection of moderator skills
IV. Training in effective methods of qualitative inquiry and keeping those skills updated
V. Holding the flag for research rigor and living under the motto: *"Doing what is right, not what is easy."*

A vested moderator has to honor these same principles, but they do not have to do it in the spotlight of work peers and supervisors. If you are a vested moderator and ever in doubt about choosing to conduct research or hire a vendor, trust your instincts and do not let cost be the only factor considered when making the decision.

Magical Thinking: Are Moderators Magicians?

> *Does abracadabra work with a QRE? Do you need a top hat to work with a client? Learn why this Master Moderator™ borrows magical metaphors to make her point!*

Recently, a QRE client observer told the moderator, *"Wow, that was like magic seeing you take that hostile group of respondents and create a forum for them to express their upsets so we could really see what their concerns were."*

I was struck by the use of the word "magic" in relationship to moderating since the act of leading an effective QRE discussion with respondents is more a blend of the art of group dynamics and the rigor of science to probe below top-of-mind to reach perceptions, opinions, beliefs, and attitudes (POBAs). It does not appear as if "magic" has anything to do with the process. However, when the word "magic" is defined, the essence of the above comment emerges. Magic has several meanings including "rites and incantations," "influence from a supernatural source," "something that casts a spell," and finally "the art of producing illusions by sleight of hand."

Incantations and Rites

Early on in a QRE, it is important to set the stage for the group discussion, and that can best be done with a **clear statement of the purpose** of the session and the ground rules for how the session will unfold. Some moderators have worked out a series of statements that clearly and succinctly provide this information, and some make a few comments and dive right into the topic. Either way, those "incantations" are the first phase of creating the environment for the group to provide information on a topic under discussion.

The "rites" portion of this part of the magic process all happens before the group is even seated. There needs to be a clear purpose for the project so the moderator can reach the objectives desired by the client. A written proposal or letter of intent cements that set of objectives and desired outcomes, and a screener is developed to find the right participants. Guide development and revisions are also part of the "rites" of a QRE and that includes understanding what stimuli will be shown and what techniques the moderator will use to obtain key information from consumers.

Influence from a Supernatural Force

While it may be stretching the metaphor a bit, **the only clear supernatural force in the magic of moderating is the client** who is the end-user of the data collected. While every element of how the data will be used is not revealed to the researchers, the end-user of the data usually has a clear understanding of what they want from the QRE participants and some expectation of what they think they are going to hear—either a series of "a-ha!" exclamations or clear confirmation that what they thought was true is borne out in the discussion.

Some clients have to go to extremes to get the funding for their projects, buy-in from management and/or team members, time for travel, time to analyze the insights, and time to weave results into the strategic plans for products, services, advertising, issues, themes, campaigns, etc. That would qualify for superhuman effort, and I will bet more than one client has called upon the "gods" to help them through the process. I would not be surprised to hear that some of them were burning candles and chanting to get the support they need for their projects!

Something that Casts a Spell

Casting a spell is clearly part of the magic of moderating. A complete stranger, often from out of town, shows up in a mirrored room to talk to a group of people who do not know each other. Within two hours that stranger needs to become a "newest best friend" and is expected to create rapport, ask short questions to get detailed answers, hear from two-thirds of the room on most questions, attend to non-verbal as well as verbal communications, and stay on time.

In addition, these "spell-binders" have to invite less verbose participants to chime in and suppress dominators without causing anyone to shut down. They have to handle thought leaders and "me too" types; they have to expose stimuli in a neutral way; they have to refrain from presenting their own opinions either by word (e.g. "I do that too") or deed (expressing shock at comments made).

Moderators have to vary the stems of their questions, find creative ways to get below top-of-mind answers, support respondents in thinking in new ways, and keep their own energy up during a four to six-hour period of time at the end of a day. All this is going on while the rest of the world is heading off to drinks with friends, the gym for a workout, or supper with the family.

While the group discussion is unfolding, the moderator is also regularly checking in mentally to see if he or she is asking questions on point to the purpose of the study, avoiding putting words in the mouths of respondents, maintaining unconditional positive regard (UPR) in all dealings with participants, and keeping respondents totally engaged in the process.

As if all the above is not enough, the moderator is also charged with making eye contact with every respondent and speaking loudly so observers and participants can hear with ease. She must not miss a chance to probe. She needs to link trains of thought that emerge in the discussion and somehow be both flexible and rigorous, accept while directing, and problem-solve quickly when situations emerge.

Moderators have to practice invisible leadership skills, be active and engaged listeners, and express compassion without melting into the sadness of a story or reported incident. They have to be comfortable with uncertainty, turn situations around in a flash, and trust themselves to do what is right, not what is easy. They have to be spontaneous and create authentic spontaneity in participants as well. They need to keep track of what has been said and what still needs to emerge in the discussion—and, like a good poker player, they need to "know when to hold and know when to fold." Moderators need to be authentic to who they are as people, hold the research standard for quality work, maintain a sense of humor, and think analytically.

Magic is very clearly at work in the process of moderating. It takes a magician to juggle all the elements in a QRE and cast a spell over respondents so they feel safe to say whatever is true for them. It takes a magician to create a setting that allows respondents to express a diversity of opinions without judgment from the moderator, and it takes a great deal of magic to hold all the elements in place without looking stressed or pressed for time.

The Art of Producing Illusions by Sleight of Hand

The art of illusion is where moderators really do turn into magicians. Part of the illusion is making the group discussion look like a two-way conversation when, in fact, it is one way: "I ask… you answer."

Another illusionary technique employs the "Teflon method" of responding to questions from respondents who say, "Well, (moderator's name), what is your opinion about making dog food green in color?" The moderator/magician deftly turns that question into another one and shoots it back to the respondent so that nothing sticks to the moderator causing them to have to provide an answer that would add to the data pool in the room. "Good question, Jack... I do have some opinions about green dog food but I would rather hear yours, since you have a dog and I do not—what do you think about your dog eating dog food that is green because of the algae added to increase nutritional value?"

Moderator/magicians also use illusion when they utilize sophisticated naïveté and appear unknowing about elements of the topic, so as not to be seen as an expert or holding a particular viewpoint about the issue under discussion.

Illusion is also used in simple acts such as rotating the order of stimuli shown across a series of groups to prevent first order bias. The simple act of passing out papers, using different colored markers to highlight elements of a concept statement, and using picture or product sorts to get more information are all illusions to help people project feelings outward to reveal innermost thinking.

The very mirror in the room is an illusion. It appears to be a simple reflective mirror, when in fact it is a one-way mirror that allows observers to view the process without being part of the process.

Are moderators magicians? The evidence in this article points to that fact, and I think that top hats, white gloves, canes, and connected silk scarves should be a required uniform for all moderators for their next focus group assignment. Then it will be clear to everyone that a QRE is a magical experience for all concerned: moderator, participants, and observers.

The Art of Moderating:
A Blend of Basic Skills & Qualities

> *Moderating is, indeed, an art. There are basic skills and qualities that must be carefully developed by the burgeoning moderator and blended into a seamless event that gets clients key data for decision making.*

By the time a QRE gets underway, many elements have come together. These elements include research design and the involvement of the four major players: end-users, respondents, facility staff, and the moderator. The purpose of the study has been defined and the respondents recruited. Now it is time to watch the group learn about respondent perceptions, opinions, beliefs, and attitudes (POBAs).

Much of the success of a QRE is in the hands of the moderator. On the surface, the work of a moderator looks transparent. One simply asks questions, and respondents answer them. In fact, the process only looks easy. Effective moderators use a variety of skills and techniques to garner POBAs from a group of eight to ten strangers in a two-hour period.

The purpose of this article is to provide some insight into how individual moderators combine basic skills and individual qualities to provide end-users with appropriate information about target market POBAs. The article also provides a checklist for observers to support an understanding of what moderators do.

What Happens in a Typical QRE?

Before talking about individual moderator skills and qualities, it is necessary to understand the frame in which moderators work. In standard QRE, there are four distinct stages:

- *Introduction.* This typically includes a generic purpose statement for respondents and disclosures about the special research room (mirrors, microphones, observers, taping). During this period, respondents provide self-introductions. The moderator uses part of this time to begin creating a safe space for respondent participation by outlining guidelines for group process.
- *Rapport building and general questions.* This section usually includes easy questions that anyone in the group can answer. Typical questions focus on category usage and knowledge. During this period, the moderator is building trust through eye contact and both verbal and nonverbal feedback. Group norms are established.
- *Specific questions and interventions.* The lion's share of the QRE is spent in this section. The moderator employs a variety of techniques to keep the questions on target to key issues. During this section, the moderator uses interventions (any activity that breaks up the two-way dialogue between the respondents and moderator) to understand the subtle thinking of target market respondents. Other activities can also occur including use of projective techniques, presentation of audiovisual materials, paper and pencil tasks, and/or hands-on team tasks. Throughout this section, deep probing of comments, nominalizations, and consumer statements is conducted to further understand respondent thinking.
- *Closure.* The summary and linking of key insights brought to light in the QRE, along with additional questions requested by the end-user.

What Basic Skills Are Needed to Be a Moderator?

This question is one of interest to many in the research industry. The American Marketing Association (AMA) looks at the whole issue of certification for researchers in general, and that would include moderators. The Qualitative Research Consultants Association (QRCA) holds initial discussions about the same issue. The whole research industry is searching for models to examine from other fields—lawyers, CPAs, teachers, social workers, and others who require certificates or licenses to practice their professions. It is clear that it will be some time before a definitive skill list of what makes a skilled moderator is agreed upon by all.

In the meantime, there are some baseline skill levels that a moderator should manifest:

- **Clarity about project purpose**, strong knowledge base about appropriate research design, and understanding appropriate research tools required
- **Knowledge base about topic area** in sufficient depth to ask questions and probe effectively
- **Effective people skills** and appropriate training in how to manage group dynamics, as well as more than one approach for working with people in group settings
- Ability to **analyze and report qualitative data** in short time frames so that end-users can make effective decisions in a timely fashion

The staff at the RIVA Training Institute have developed a list of qualities that they feel make a good moderator. These are traits and skills that hold true, regardless of the subject matter under discussion or the personal style of the moderator.

- They express warmth and empathy, creating a non-threatening, accepting atmosphere where respondents feel safe to make contributions.
- They appear kind yet firm, enabling a balance between control and permissiveness to exist.
- They are actively involved (while not ego-involved) in the discussion, but do not divulge their own opinion, nor inform or educate the respondent.
- They pay close attention to respondents and are good listeners; they demonstrate this by paraphrasing appropriately, nodding, and verbally acknowledging as well as remembering earlier comments.
- They pursue the understanding of meanings and intents by not assuming positive or negative inflection, by not equating verbalizations with behaviors, by probing and rephrasing to uncover latent and covert intent and by allowing the development of opinions to emerge in non-linear ways.
- They demonstrate unconditional positive regard (UPR), accepting the worth of each participant, respecting individual points of view, and

receiving all divergent viewpoints as relevant to the topic under discussion.
- They link trains of thought and divergent comments into a cohesive whole, help synthesize group meanings and move the conversation forward by providing "signposts" for participants.
- They demonstrate incomplete understanding (sophisticated naïveté) signaling a need for more detailed or in-depth information, while not appearing to be phony or to fake ignorance; they express interest in new ideas, whatever their own level of expertise on the topic.
- They encourage all group members (including shy ones) to participate as fully as they are able, through nonverbal and verbal cues, timing of comments, and voice tones.
- They demonstrate flexibility—the willingness to vary an approach, to not be wedded to the guide, to pursue and capitalize on "gold mines," to mesh optimally with bursts of group enthusiasm, or to refresh the group mood.
- They demonstrate both sensitivity and respect towards participants, including both feelings and experiences, by determining the appropriate depth level of an issue area and by encouraging mutual respect among participants.
- They demonstrate a research orientation, with a constant sense of a project's purpose and direction, enabling them to move beyond simple facilitation.
- They are self-starters and initiators rather than order-takers, and they take full responsibility for all phases of the project, taking risks and making quick decisions as necessary.
- They demonstrate quick thinking, rapidly spotting potential opportunities or problems and finding ways to move toward or away from them.
- They have both physical and mental stamina and have appropriate and effective ways to increase personal energy during the typical duration of qualitative research projects.
- They display a sense of humor and are sensitive to the level of information that can flow forward when laughter is the catalyst.

What Should an Observer Look For in a Moderator?

Just as there are many variables present in the research room, so are there many variables in the back room. Clients are usually intent on finding out what the target market has to say about the topics under discussion and may not have their attention on the processes occurring in the research room. If the end-user is not getting the quality of data desired, the questions listed below may help determine if the problem is moderator driven or due to some other factor.

Did the moderator:

- Give clear ground rules/purpose statement/full disclosure about mirrors/microphones/observers/stipends?
- Establish and maintain rapport, and create a safe place for respondents to share POBAs?
- Flow from point to point without abrupt shifts?
- Keep the discussion on topic and moving along?
- Probe for clarity?
- Maintain UPR?
- Ask questions that open up respondents so they can give full answers?
- Avoid leading the respondents (i.e. putting words in their mouths or inappropriately summarize/paraphrase)?
- Include everyone in the discussion?
- Avoid "serial interviewing?"
- Read the room, stay with the respondents, keep attention off of self and the guide?
- Keep self/ego out of the discussion and avoid talking too much?
- Attend to non-verbal communications?
- Use a variety of techniques to promote discussion?
- Pace/lead respondents?
- Listen rather than inform participants?
- Vary voice tone during process?
- Change location/body position during discussion?
- Give clear instructions/directions to respondents?
- Provide linking and logic tracking for respondents and observers?

Of necessity, the list presented here is made up of observable elements. A good moderator is also doing a number of mental activities that are not observable, including: managing the time line; looking for ways to increase the participation of quiet respondents and limiting the participation of talkative respondents; creating situations that allow for fair airtime for all respondents; physically managing the stimuli used in the group discussion; checking the guide to make sure that all elements planned are covered; listening to what has **not** been said and probing appropriately to get it spoken and on the recording.

Moderating and interviewing skills are based on a science and executed as an art, similar to the work of a medical doctor or musician. This article examined those skills and qualities that moderators need to successfully perform their job and enhance client observation and understanding during the QRE. QREs can be an effective tool for end-users, enabling them to see inside the thinking of a target market.

Moderators and clients alike should pay as much attention to the art of moderating as they do to the data generated through QREs research. Both are critical to effectively serving end-user needs.

Benefits of Matching Moderators to Cultural Groups

> *So much of the moderator's world is about relationships—to work well with a QRE, you have to be able to relate. This is why sometimes race and nationality might be critical matching factors.*

In quantitative market research (QTMR), the survey instrument is the vehicle of data collection, while in qualitative market research (QLMR), the vehicle is the researcher. Qualitative research is both an art and a science, and while there are elements of research rigor in QLMR studies, the actual task of gathering the data is highly dependent on the individual researcher. One primary job of the moderator/researcher is to collect POBAs (perceptions, opinions, beliefs and attitudes) from respondents. The analysis of these elements helps clients understand the thinking of respondents and allows clients to include the voice of the consumer in their strategic planning process.

There are a set of baseline factors that a good qualitative researcher/moderator must have in order to serve as an adequate tool for collecting data about products, services, advertising, or ideas. Those factors include the ability to:

- Create effective research designs to meet client needs
- Understand the study purpose and desired outcomes so questions and probes help meet study objectives
- Create and maintain rapport with respondents and continuously create a safe space for POBAs to emerge
- Provide creative problem solving skills to help get more than top-of-mind answers from respondents
- Hold an understanding of the cultural norms, mores, nuances and insights that a specific ethnic or cultural group (e.g. French-speaking

Canadians) or lifestyle group (e.g. single parents) brings to the research setting
- Manage the logical flow of events in a QLMR session, and keep the discussion on time and on target
- Listen for gold mines and dig out nuggets of information to get deeper into what drives a point of view held by a respondent
- Use linkages from earlier parts of the conversation to later insights and probe discrepancies

One of the areas in the list above relates to "matching" moderators to respondents. Among QLMR colleagues, there have been spirited conversations about the pros and cons of matching moderators to respondents assuming all the other qualities listed above are in place. The possible matches that have come under discussion include:

- *Matching gender*: men lead male groups and women lead female groups.
- *Matching ages*: younger moderators (under age thirty) lead children, youth, teen and young adult groups, while older moderators (thirty-one to sixty-five) lead groups closer to their own ages.
- *Matching race*: Asian moderators talk to Asian groups and Hispanic moderators talk to Hispanic groups, etc.
- *Matching nationalities*: Americans talk to Americans, Europeans talk to Europeans, Africans talk to Africans, Native Americans talk to members of Native American tribes, Japanese talk to Japanese, and so on.
- *Matching content expertise*: this would require that the moderator be an expert in the content arena of the discussion. For example, if the study required talking to doctors, then the mod-erator should be an expert in the field of medicine or, if possible, a medical doctor; if the project required talking to women with children, the moderator should have children too.

It is easy to see that some matches are artificial—a non-mother moderator can talk to a group of mothers about how they shop for groceries and prepare meals without worrying that she'll miss some "mother nuance" because she does not have children. Likewise, a forty-five-year old moderator can talk to a group of teens and elicit just as much data as a thirty-year old moderator, since neither is a teen.

Men can lead women's groups and vice versa as long as the topic matter does not hinge on areas of discomfort (e.g. women talking to men about prostate cancer and men talking to women about hormone replacement therapy for hot flashes)—in these cases, gender matching is a better bet. But a female moderator can talk to a group of male real estate agents about shifting their commission structure, and a male moderator can talk to professional women about financial planning.

The area of content expertise is up for grabs. Some researchers and clients feel that one who is too heavily involved in the baseline content area closes off opportunities to learn nuances because "they already know." Others feel that an expert in the field brings a deeper understanding of key issues. The decision to do matching in this arena is usually a decision made by clients.

However, when it comes to race and nationality, another set of factors comes into play and matching becomes more critical.

Client: National hair care company that makes shampoos and hair coloring products

Study: Gaining reactions to a new line of hair care products for Black women

Respondents: Black women age twenty-five to forty-five

Some Key Questions:

- How do you handle color-treated hair when shampooing only two times per week?
- How does the "kitchen" part of your head act between relaxers?
- When do you color and relax at the same time?

Reasons for Using an Black Moderator:

- Black moderators know why Black women only shampoo one or two times a week, and they know that it is not even worth discussing. If you think it is critical to wash hair every day or every other day, you should not be leading Black groups on hair care!
- Every Black moderator knows exactly what part of the head is the "kitchen" and the reason it is called that!
- Every Black moderator knows that if they ask that question, they will get a lot of laughter, because if you do color and relax at the same time, your hair will fall out!

This example of the hair care study shows the need for knowing the nuances of a culture with respect to hair issues and allows the moderator to step over areas where the obvious is simply the obvious and not "new learning." If a White moderator leads a QRE with Black women on the topic of hair care, there is a risk that the White moderator will get caught up in the sociological nuances of the culture around "hair care practices" rather than keeping the focus on the purpose of the study. A Black moderator talking with Black women who start talking about "handling my edges" and "always fighting with the kitchen part of my head," knows what these phrases mean and does not need to probe the clarity, especially if those issues are not related to the purpose of the study.

One of the most dramatic examples of nationality affecting a corporate decision was the New Coke/Classic Coke controversy at the tail end of the last century. Coke did blind taste tests with New Coke against Pepsi, and the quantitative data showed that New Coke was preferred, even among loyal Pepsi drinkers. On the strength of quantitative data, a corporate decision was made to pull Original Coke off the shelves and replace it with New Coke. When that was done, the hue and cry from Americans was swift and brutal. "Bring back Classic Coke!" became their mantra—"How dare you take away an American icon!"

The architects of the New Coke marketing strategy were long-time, experienced Coca-Cola executives, but they did not grow up in America! One was a VP from South America, and one was a VP from a country bordering the Caspian Sea. Their decision, based on sound quantitative research, lacked one critical element—an understanding of the Coke icon in American history.

Once the Coca-Cola Company realized the error of their ways, they had almost torn the fabric of trust they had spent one hundred years building with the American consumer. They spent millions on the apology to the American consumer and more millions on an advertising campaign to say: "We understand that Original Coke is a classic that should not be retired." Today you will not find New Coke on the shelves of any American store.

It is not a far step to predict the same kind of problem when an American moderator working for an international company is asked to do six groups in the United States on a new package design for cosmetics for women and the same study in three European countries. There are no problems with the groups in the United States, but some real problems emerge with that same project in France, Germany, and Italy. First of all is the very real language problem. It would be hard to find a moderator totally fluent in all four languages. But it would be even harder to find one who has lived long enough on the planet to amass the nuances of the use of cosmetics in four different countries. While they could work with interpreters, much of the dynamics of the interactive session would be sluggish due to the time it takes to translate for clarity in two directions.

The reverse would be true of a French moderator who does the study in France and may be fluent enough to also lead groups in Italy and the United States. While he or she would have solved the language problem, he or she still has not solved the problem of understanding the soft nuances of the differences within and between the various nationalities.

On the surface, it would appear that QLMR is focused on asking qualitative questions and probing for more than top-of-mind answers. While that is true, the questions and probes also come from a set of cultural beliefs held by the moderator!

Perhaps the most dramatic case for the need to match moderators comes from our neighbors across the border in Canada. An American moderator has no idea about the depth of the enmity among Frenchspeaking Canadians and those who do not speak French. Americans do not read the French-language newspapers in Canada that overtly and subtly make a daily case for French-speaking Canadians to secede and start a new country. The QLMR industry in Canada, represented by the PMRS (Professional Market Research Society), has a long history in recommending that moderators do better when matched to the subcultures in Canada (with French Canadians speaking with French Canadians and English-speaking Canadians conducting research with the rest).

The same is true with the very high proportion of Asians living in Toronto. In this case, moderator matching of Asian to Asian is even more fragmented. When respondents are Chinese, it is appropriate that the moderator be someone with roots in China. When respondents are from Thailand, it is appropriate that the moderator be someone with roots in Thailand. It does not matter that both cultures use English as their primary language.

Additionally, it is recommended that Asians from different cultures are not mixed in one group, even if they are second and third-generation and only speak English, because of the wide disparity of purchasing patterns, not to mention the wide differences in culture. Along that same line, Hispanic moderators know that a group will shut down when Puerto Ricans are placed in the same group as Cubans.

It is these subtle but powerful distinctions that make it critical to deeply consider matching when race and nationality are large factors in a QLMR study.

A case study situation illustrating the pitfalls of using cross-cultural researchers follows.

> **Client:** Manufacturer of spirits.
>
> **Study:** To determine occasions for drinking client's brand and to garner reactions to a print advertisement.
>
> **Respondents:** Men aged 25–39, typically called "Players."
>
> **Key Issue:** Client is a European-based company distributing a limited number of barrels of their product in the United States. There is a large study in four countries in Europe and client had four language specific moderators assigned to conduct the study. To avoid getting a United States moderator up to speed on the project for the United States, which had six groups planned, they wanted to send the English (London-based) moderator to the United States to conduct those groups.
>
> **The Problem That Emerged:** When the London based moderator got to the U.S. and began conducting groups with United States "players" (men who frequent clubs and bars and have more than one girlfriend at a time), he heard about behaviors for which he personally had no cultural anchors, and he began to judge the respondents' lifestyle choices and challenge them. In one case he told a respondent that he was lying when the respondent told him that he had won a bet that he could bed three women from the bar at his apartment in the same evening using the client's product as a lure—a mixed drink with a provocative name just coming into popularity.
>
> **Research Solution:** The spirits company decided to repeat the United States portion of the study using an American moderator and collected sufficient data to compare the United States findings against the work done in the four European countries, thus getting an accurate read on the way the product was being used in the different cultures.

In summary, it appears that strict matching is not needed on gender (in most cases, age or content arena), but it is critical in the area of race and nationality and needs to be considered carefully in cases of specific content expertise.

A NOTE OF CAUTION: There are some exceptions to the race factor in the United States in particular. While a White moderator would have a problem conducting a group with Black women on hair care, a Black moderator would not have that problem talking to those same women. The reason: Blacks grow up in a dualistic society, and in order to participate in the American Dream, they are forced to live in and understand the nuances of mainstream America. That duality allows a Black moderator to conduct groups with White women on hair care or health insurance or fire prevention in apartment houses, but it does not allow the reverse—an interesting artifact of the QLMR industry. Conversely, there may be the rare European moderator who may live in France, but grew up in America who could also be a skilled student of American culture and he or she could conduct groups in the United States!

As mentioned earlier, QLMR is both an art and a science and the business of matching moderators to respondents is one that should be carefully considered.

One final note: a Master Moderator™ should be able to lead an effective group regardless of culture, ethnicity, or age. However, there are some cases when matching will increase the likelihood of more than top-of-mind responses. Consider both elements in the process of choosing a moderator.

Briefcase as Carnival Wagon

> *Lessons for the research gypsy! You are on the road much of the time. How can you move effectively through the five business areas to be a successful qualitative researcher?*

The business of being a qualitative researcher operates in five distinct areas, and I have discovered that the speed at which one moves through these areas is the measure of a successful business.

1. Seeking client work
2. Doing client work
3. Juggling client work with personal life
4. Traveling to and from home base to conduct client work
5. All the other administrative tasks it takes to run a successful qualitative research practice so you can serve clients and make a living

Interestingly enough, area five is the one area that usually gets short shrift, since areas one through four take up fifty to one hundred hours in any given week. To make it all work—i.e. running a business and concurrently doing the client work—the travel component becomes critical. A good qualitative researcher learns to segment tasks and get work done no matter where they are. Having the right wagon is key to my success.

My briefcase is the carnival wagon I take on the road as a research gypsy. It has everything I need when I am away from my office. Like a real gypsy, who travels from town to town in a brightly colored wagon with cooking pots, tables, clothes, juggling balls, and tarot cards, I travel with the tools of my trade. When I camp in a different town each night, I have got what I need to ply my trade.

I knew I needed a sturdy briefcase—not some fashion item that looks good swinging on my shoulder, but a good bag that can take the abuse of multiple security checks at airports and possible crushing in overhead compartments or under my airplane seat. It had to be big enough to hold the laptop, the client papers, my water, my energy bars, the alternate makeup bag in case the checked luggage does not make it, pens, markers, and a traveling office packet (with tape, stapler, and clips, but no longer any scissors). It had to hold the charger for the cell phone, the laptop cables and the items for internet access in hotels.

With ease, this briefcase must house the project files for this week and the upcoming weeks. It requires sections to help me organize the stack of administrative tasks I can do in the hotel room, like travel reconciliation forms, contact sheets, reports on leads, updated calendars, thank-you cards, referrals, and the business cards I collect each day. Nifty compartments have to be in place to hold eye drops, mints, keys, a flashlight, stamps, tissues, and my paperback novel.

The bag must roll, just like that gypsy caravan, ready to go at a moment's notice. It must fold into itself so that it can be bigger or smaller as needed, and the handle must be sturdy enough to survive being yanked around by me, the car service, hotel staff, and the security teams at airports. Ideally it should be made of titanium or some other indestructible matter, but that's for scientists, so I looked for the same type of plastic used in the space program. Zippers, flaps and pockets need to appear and disappear as I need them and the color has to be a warm shade of licorice black that goes with everything.

I have had more than twenty briefcases over the years, always looking for "the one." When I found it in a jumbled luggage store in a small mall in Orange County, California, I thought it was just another "almost it." My focus groups were in a facility near Anaheim, and I had flown into John Wayne Airport early enough to do a little shopping before the brief-ing. My plan was to breeze into the luggage store and check out cases or, as a consolation prize, find a new luggage tag for the one I had. I rolled out with the most perfect hard-sided, wheeled briefcase ever made.

The manufacturer is Porter Case—an American company based in Indianapolis, Indiana. Not only does the bag meet the specs listed above, it has another incredible feature: when the handle is fully extended, I can pull two small posts and release the bag from the upright position. At that point, the bag falls forward until it makes an "L" shape. It becomes a miniature version of the two-wheeled luggagedolly that Red Caps have in airports. I can transport one hundred and sixty pounds of luggage on the flatbed of the dolly and my briefcase truly becomes a carnival wagon for my "show on the road." It keeps things moving.

Over the years, I have bought four of them, and three are still in service. From time to time I send one into the factory for reconditioning, like replacing wheels or reinforcing the struts. The customer service lady has become a best buddy on the phone. This briefcase really is my office away from home and it allows me to serve my current clients and future ones, no matter where I am.

I have learned some lessons with this luggage and the business of traveling more than 500,000 air miles every year:

1. Do not let anyone carry your briefcase for you. Act like a federal courier and imagine it is handcuffed to your wrist—it is okay to lose your clothes, but it is not okay to lose anything in this briefcase.
2. Never put it on the luggage cart at the hotel; carry it to your room yourself! A helpful bellman accidentally dropped my case on the marble floor of the lobby, requiring a $2500 repair and data recovery for my computer. It took a long time to get reimbursed from their law firm.
3. Keep it in good repair and always packed like you are a pregnant mother waiting for labor pains to come at any moment so you can go to the hospital without worrying about what is in the suitcase.
4. Constantly seek ways to streamline the contents to avoid carrying items you do not need; every six months, dump the contents onto the floor, and eliminate duplicate items and anything that is past a useful life.
5. Look for the smallest travel size of items that go into the briefcase.
6. Color-code any paper files that are in the briefcase so you can quickly tell one client deck from another or one task area from another.
7. Keep like things together in the briefcase to save time looking for lost items. Use smaller bags to house small things together and to make it easy to repack when departing—colored ones with zippers are a delight and keep one dedicated to pens!
8. Workout in a gym with weights to improve upper body muscles so you can easily lift the bag into the overhead compartments with ease.
9. Always have something in there related to fun, e.g. a crossword puzzle, artistic paperclips or markers, funny stickers, a Luna Bar, etc.
10. Make sure it has two luggage tags on it at all times, and business cards inside.

This is my rolling caravan wagon and like any good gypsy I am always looking for camping sites with good water and plentiful game!

Trained Moderators Boost the Value of Qualitative Research

> *Learn the true quality of moderator training and how to boost the value of qualitative research by using trained researchers!*

Qualitative research is changing, consumers are changing, and end-users want more from qualitative research. Moderators with training and moderators who train themselves through workshops, seminars, and other related courses provide the best value for end-users because they bring dimension to a qualitative research project. They also bring expertise, learning, variety, and creativity. Trained moderators fully support decision makers with the most accurate and detailed in-depth view of how respondents really feel about products, services, issues, and advertising.

These days it costs several hundred dollars to get brakes repaired on an automobile. The person who fixes the brakes must complete a training program that includes working as an apprentice under the guidance of an experienced repair person. In the same vein, a school bus driver in most states must complete a training program, take a test, and be bonded by a licensed agency before being allowed to drive children to and from school. Neither position requires a college degree or even necessarily a high school diploma, but a training program is required to master the key elements essential to proficient job performance.

In the research community, however, any individual with any kind of background or degree can simply declare, "I am a moderator." No training is required, an apprenticeship is not standard procedure, and there is no licensing or bonding agency. Anyone can print business cards and market him or herself as a qualitative researcher. Moderators can charge any fee they want, either in terms of an hourly rate or a flat fee.

One focus group can cost a client thousands of dollars depending on variables such as recruiting specifications, stipends for respondents, and the type of report required. It is ironic that to perform a $200 brake job requires a trained repair person who has served an apprenticeship and to drive a school bus requires a trained and bonded individual. But to obtain qualitative research services, a client could pay more than $10,000 for two focus groups conducted by a moderator who is not required to take a training course, pass a qualifying test, or have any specific credentials at all.

To the credit of many moderators and qualitative researchers, a number of them have taken courses, seminars, and workshops and/or have participated in degree programs that include work in group dynamics, psychology, anthropology, sociology, and other behavioral sciences. Many moderators have been mentored by colleagues who are experts in specific techniques for eliciting qualitative data from a group of strangers meeting for two hours to discuss products, services, issues, or advertising. Others have participated in both formal and informal in-house programs conducted by companies, organizations, and agencies to support staff moderators in learning and using the skills needed to collect qualitative data. Formal external training programs for moderators, however, are a relatively new addition to the research scene.

The following addresses some of the issues related to the value of using a trained moderator for qualitative research. "Trained moderator" is defined here as someone who has done one or more of the following activities:

- Observed more than 100 focus groups led by expert moderators and received coaching from those moderators prior to initiating his or her own project work for clients.
- Participated in an in-house program that included observation, lectures, mock focus group sessions, and feedback from someone considered to be an expert or Master Moderator™.
- Participated in an intensive three to five-day training program conducted by an organization with a training staff qualified in focus group research techniques and skills.
- Obtained a degree in the behavioral sciences and, as part of required work, conducted some type of group work with individuals.

What Happens in a Typical QRE?

As a context for understanding what a moderator does, it is useful to know what typically happens in a QRE. Such groups have four distinct stages: (1) introduction, (2) rapport/reconnaissance, (3) in-depth investigation, and (4) closure.

The introduction stage usually includes a statement by the moderator of the generic purpose of the session: *"You're here today to talk about peanut butter and share your opinions about the brands you buy. You're also going to look at some ideas for advertising a new brand of peanut butter."* The moderator also gives the ground rules for participation and makes ethical disclosure about microphones, observers behind the one-way mirror, and video recording. This stage ends with self-introductions by the respondents.

The next segment is called the "rapport and reconnaissance" stage because the moderator asks easy questions that build trust and uses eye contact and bonding exercises to provide the foundation for subsequent questions. The moderator sees what dynamics are already in place and what dynamics must be encouraged or diminished to create an effective qualitative experience to collect POBAs (perceptions, opinions, beliefs, and attitudes.)

The in-depth investigation stage asks specific questions and uses constructive probing techniques to find out more about respondents' POBAs, as well as to obtain reactions to specific stimuli (e.g. storyboards, concept statements, animatics, packaging deals, etc.)

The final stage of a QRE is closure. Ideally, this is the time to conduct a summary and linking process on all that was learned during the discussion. The QRE ends with a personal acknowledgement from the moderator about the contribution the members have made to better understanding of their POBAs.

The preceding description of what happens in a typical QRE implies a number of skills that are necessary to conduct a QRE and provide a client with qualitative information that will allow for effective decision making. These skills include the following:

- Recasting the research purpose statement in such a way as to involve the respondents without giving away too much information from them.
- Presenting a succinct list of ground rules so that the session works smoothly and efficiently, without adopting the manner of a teacher or parent or setting up a "test-taking" environment.
- Managing the self-introduction so that they are short, illuminating, and serves to bond respondents into a group.
- Writing questions from the logic path or respondents.
- Deciding what kind of general questions precede the necessary specific questions.
- Determining what kind of stimuli will be used and when to introduce those stimuli.

- Observing verbal and nonverbal cues while gathering POBAs.

This list illustrates some of the more subtle elements of moderating the qualities a trained moderator brings to a QRE. These elements require a strong foundation in process techniques and enable a moderator to concentrate on eliciting deeper levels of information from respondents.

What Basic Knowledge Is Needed to Be a Moderator?

As a minimum, anyone claiming to be a moderator—trained or not—should have these four basic kinds of knowledge:

- **Knowledge of market research tools and techniques**: a strong knowledge base about appropriate research designs for a variety of issue areas, and an understanding of and ability to apply appropriate research tools to achieve research objectives
- **Knowledge base about the topic area**: knowledge of the subject matter in sufficient depth to ask useful questions to followup probes
- **Strong knowledge/experience base in group dynamics**: understanding of how to work effectively with people in groups, and knowledge of and ability to use more than one approach and/or solution for problems that emerge in group settings
- **Knowledge of how to analyze and report qualitative data**: the ability to analyze, synthesize, and report key qualitative findings to support needs of decision makers

Abilities a Trained Moderator Brings to Qualitative Research

A trained moderator (someone who has been through a formal external or academic program or a rigorous in-house training procedure) brings a depth and dimension to moderating that someone who has not been trained cannot provide. The following list, though by no means all-inclusive, describes twenty-five key abilities of a trained moderator.

1. Ability to design an appropriate research approach based on experience.
    - Can indicate when focus groups are not the right research tool.
    - Knows when in-depth interviews are needed rather than groups.
    - Knows when focus panels are needed rather than focus groups.
    - Knows about the 17–20 different qualitative variations for collection of QLMR data.
2. Ability to help the client establish appropriate and attainable research objectives.

- Has experience in winnowing myriad objectives into two or three that can be achieved in a qualitative study.
3. Objective, non-vested viewpoint.
    - As an "outsider," the trained moderator brings a fresh perspective to research objectives and their attainment.
4. Mastery of UPR.
    - "Unconditional positive regard" (UPR) is the ability to listen to viewpoints that are widely divergent from the thinking of the moderator and to hold these viewpoints as valid and appropriate because they comprise the belief system of the respondent.
    - UPR is also the ability to let respondents "be exactly the way they are" and to avoid the desire to educate or inform them when they speak in error.
5. Listening rather than "informing" attitude.
    - Allows respondents to *tell* moderator what the moderator needs to know.
    - Is trained to listen to what is **not** being said and to probe appropriately.
6. Ability to attend to various levels of nonverbal communication.
    - Can read the room—"staying with people, not paper."
    - Uses visual cues as anchors for probing (e.g. respondent eyes up after a task = ask: "What picture did you make?")
7. Multiple techniques to handle group dynamics based on working models from different paradigms (e.g. NLP, psychology, sociology, anthropology, etc.).
    - NLP: neuro-linguistic programming tools may include anchoring techniques/eye accessing cues/energy builders.
    - Psychology: effective group dynamic processes.
    - Sociology: knowing how people operate in group settings.
    - Anthropology: collecting data without disturbing belief systems.
8. Multiple skills to handle diverse opinions without becoming judgmental, evaluative, or threatening.
    - Working with hostile or diffident respondents.
    - Handling dominators/"milquetoasts".
    - Suppressing judgments.
    - Avoiding preconceptions.
    - Avoiding "finger-pointing" voice tone.
9. Ability to allow for diverse opinions within the group and accept lack of consensus and closure.
    - Example: Two respondents have very different opinions and polar-

ize the room. A trained moderator knows how to use the polarization as a catalyst for conversation.
10. Ability to handle logic tracking to make sure all key points have been explored and discussed in sufficient depth while staying inside the time frame for data collection.
    - Reads the room like a clock face.
    - Remembers what has been said/not said, as in a poker game.
    - Uses good judgment and knows when to move on in an area so that all key data is collected first.
    - Able to return to previous points, out of order.
    - Uses the energy in the room as a catalyst to discussion rather than following the guide like a survey instrument.
11. Ability to elicit data by using various models/techniques appropriate to the respondents' frame of reference.
    - Treats each group as unique, does not carry over experience from previous groups.
    - Varies approaches to groups on the basis of region, lifestyle, age, and other factors.
12. Ability to design a guide from the logic path of respondents.
    - Writes clear, logical questions that the respondents naturally want to answer.
    - Sees the research from the respondents' point of view, not just the viewpoint of the end-user.
13. Ability to manage the following variables effectively on multiple levels:
    - Research models
    - Client politics
    - Field services
    - Analysis
14. Knowledge of key intervention techniques and ability to present stimuli to support the flow of conversation and open new areas of exploration.
    - Knows five to nine different interventions (e.g. forecasting, "let's pretend," "build your own," "Board of Directors," obituary).
    - Knows quick, efficient, and different set-ups for television spots, marker comps, radio spots, storyboards, etc.
15. Ability to create a safe environment for respondents to deliver POBAs.
    - Can quickly create non-threatening, non-evaluative, non-judgmental settings.
16. Ability to "come down hard" when discussion gets out of hand or off track, without losing group affinity.
    - For example, uses verbal cues ("How does that relate to…") and non-verbal cues ("stop sign" hand gesture).

- Is willing to eject a respondent (if need be) so that others can provide the needed information.
17. Ability to cope with surprises, abrupt changes from group to group, and "gold mines" (unplanned for, but desirable outcomes).
    - Can tolerate a continual state of not knowing—not knowing how things are going to turn out, whether what worked in the last group will work in the next, or what answer might come from a simple question.
    - Can accept lack of closure and realizes that the true findings may not emerge until the analysis stage.
18. Ability to think fast, act independently, react quickly in dynamic situations, and relate to respondents without talking "up" or "down."
    - Knows when to let go and when to hang on (like a terrier with a bone).
    - Learns to act independently of the back room and to be fully responsible for all aspects of the research process.
    - Learns to speak to respondents as life peers, not as a function of their education or ability level.
19. Ability to apply appropriate techniques to create an environment that elicits the fullest range of data from respondents.
    - Can quickly identify the right research tool/technique and apply it when needed.
20. Ability to create an environment that allows spontaneity, creative bursts, and radical points to be as highly valued as conservative points.
    - Can create an environment, a mood, or an atmosphere and shift it when necessary.
21. Ability to encourage group process within pre-established ground rules without resorting to rigid research formats or oppressive group control measures.
    - Within the bounds of the "sanctioned voyeurism" of QREs gives respondents seven to nine ground rules and gently reminds them when a ground rule is broken (e.g. "talk as loud as the moderator," "avoid side conversations," "have the courage of your convictions").
22. Ability to utilize "sophisticated naïveté" to avoid leading respondents or to avoid having the moderator's personal viewpoint imbedded in the flow of discussion.
    - Resists providing verbal or nonverbal evidence of personal points of view.
    - Becomes skillful in seeming like a life peer in the experience of the respondents.

23. Ability to avoid second guessing respondents, provide feedback using the same words/tone as respondents, and pace lead respondents as needed.
24. Ability to analyze subjective data with an objective viewpoint.
25. Ability to draw trend lines across diverse levels of data and find common themes.

Is There a Specific Background That a Moderator Needs to Have?

Although no specific degree or background guarantees a good moderator, trained moderators indicate that they have found it useful to have degrees, course work, or work experience in psychology, sociology, anthropology, research design, marketing, business management, survey research, market research, or a technical background related to client work (e.g. chemistry, engineering, computers, etc.)

More important than a specific degree or work history is a good grounding in group dynamics and a respect for the opinions of others. In addition, a nonjudgmental attitude and a strong foundation in a rigorous research discipline are important qualities of a skilled moderator.

What to Look for When Observing Moderators

By answering the following questions, an observer can determine whether or not a moderator is skilled. For most questions, the right answer is "yes," but for questions 6 and 9 (bolded), the correct answer is "no."

1. Flow from point to point without abrupt shifts?
2. Keep the discussion on topic?
3. Probe for clarity?
4. Maintain UPR?
5. Ask questions that open up respondents so they can give full answers?
6. **Lead the respondents, put words in their mouths, or inappropriately summarize/paraphrase?**
7. Establish and maintain rapport?
8. Include everyone in the discussion?
9. **Conduct serial interviewing?**
10. Read the room, stay with the respondents, and keep attention off of self and the guide?
11. Keep self/ego out of the discussion, and avoid talking too much?
12. Attend to nonverbal communications?
13. Give clear ground rules/purpose statement/full disclosure about mir-

rors/microphones/observers/stipends?
14. Use a variety of research tools/techniques?
15. Pace respondents?
16. Provide linking and logic tracking for respondents and observers?
17. Listen rather than inform participants?
18. Vary voice tone during process?
19. Change location/body position during QREs process?
20. Give clear instructions/directions to respondents/set up and appropriately introduce stimuli?

Where Can Someone Go to Be Trained as a Moderator?

Several organizations have experienced trainers and effective courses that enable novice moderators to learn basic skills and practice them in a hands-on environment:

Burke Marketing Research Seminars	RIVA Training Institute
Seminars are offered several times a month in major cities in the United States. The Burke Institute has established a training program that is well known and respected in the industry.	RIVA's Institute is more than thirty years old and offers fundamental and advanced courses as well as custom courses and seminars. Class size is limited to eight, and part of the course requires students to conduct a portion of an actual focus group with real respondents while being recorded. Private coaching and debriefing sessions with students provide personal feedback for fine tuning skills. The trainer body has led more than 100,000 QREs for a wide variety of clients, nationally and internationally.

Lessons Learned from More Than Thirty Years of Training Moderators

As a trainer for more than thirty years and an observer of the elements that comprise effective qualitative research, I have learned several lessons about moderating:

- There are many nuances in moderator styles—many variables— and the business is often personality-driven; clients like the way certain moderators work and rehire them because of their style or approach.
- There is no one "right" way to moderate. There are lots of good ways to ask questions, and a good moderator is creative and flexible in constructing and posing questions.
- Different topics/issues require different moderating skills. The style needed for a consumer study about peanut butter advertising is not the same as that required for a study with patients in cancer treatment programs.
- Moderating is not "show time" for clients. A good moderator works on becoming an invisible source in the room, putting the emphasis on respondents.
- Being a good researcher is not a guarantee that you will be a good moderator. Research experience with survey design and analysis is not a predictor of success as a moderator.
- It is important to trust your own judgment as a moderator to do the right thing. A good moderator knows instinctively what to do and when to do it.
- The moderator is responsible for clear lines of communication among all four parties involved in qualitative research: end-users, moderator, field, respondents.
- You cannot learn moderating from reading a book. Moderating is an experiential event—watching is not leading, analyzing QRE research is not leading, listening to recordings is not leading. **A person must actually lead QRE to understand the myriad variables present.**
- The "way it is" is not the way it is going to be. The last QRE is not a prologue for the next QRE. Men in Idaho may not respond the same way as men in Montana. The methods used in the last QRE may or may not work in the QRE that follows. A good moderator is a "mental virgin" for every QRE.
- Moderating skills are changing and evolving as more industries and disciplines utilize qualitative research techniques. Being trained once

as a moderator is no longer sufficient. Moderators should continually take courses in related fields to stay abreast of new and improved ways of working with individuals in group settings.
- Moderators must learn to shave seconds in a QRE, and to use time more efficiently as clients demand more activities inside QRE time frames.

Summary

Research is changing, consumers are changing, and end-users want more from qualitative research. Moderators with training and moderators who train themselves through workshops, seminars, and other related courses provide the best value for end-users.

You would not take your car to an unqualified and untrained repair person for a brake job. You would not let a child ride in a school bus driven by an unskilled and unbonded driver. Do not give a qualitative research project to someone who is not trained in the tools, techniques, and procedures for collecting qualitative research from consumers.

Trained moderators bring expertise, learning, variety, and creativity to a qualitative research project. They can support decision makers with the most accurate and detailed in-depth view of how respondents really feel about products, services, and advertising.

Staying on Top of the Moderator Game

> *Competition and change—like most businesses today, qualitative research is beset by both influences. How can you keep in shape and face the constant challenges in the industry? Come here and learn how to stay on top!*

Being in business as a moderator/qualitative researcher means wearing at least two good-sized hats. One hat, with a wide brim, represents getting and keeping clients—while the other hat, which fits more like a baseball cap, relates to services that you provide to those clients.

This article focuses on the services that moderators provide to clients, and offers tips about how to stay on top of the moderating game so that your services are more in demand than those of your competitors.

What Is Unique?

What makes a moderator unique among the thousands of qualitative researchers (QRs) hired to conduct research for a myriad of clients, ranging from advertising agencies to the local zoo? What are the qualities that get one freelancer hired over and over again, while a competitor receives only a fraction of that work?

If you want to stand out among others, consider:

- Offering something nobody else does—perhaps by developing proprietary techniques or skills.
- Giving clients more than they expect, such as extra, non-billable services (perhaps a topline in addition to a full report).
- Getting deliverables in earlier than requested.

- Providing creative solutions to client problems and having a "can do" attitude.
- Being flexible when dealing with clients (acting like a supplier rather than a dictator).
- Establishing yourself as an expert, by writing articles in trade or industry journals, or by speaking at meetings and conventions.
- Offering detailed research plans, proposals, and line item cost estimates—rather than flat fee pricing.

What Are You Really Selling?

Chief among a series of key elements related to being unique is positioning yourself as either a "niche QR" or "general QR." A niche QR works in a limited arena, and all of his or her clients come from within that field. QRs who specialize in areas such as health, finance, or high tech would not dream of doing a project among voters on a bond issue. They would never talk to mothers about the benefits of elastic versus snaps on disposable diapers—and they would run screaming from projects that evaluate label designs for peanut butter or which dog face should go on the can of dog food. That is the province of the general QR.

A niche QR has both an advantage and a handicap when it comes to standing out in a crowd of other freelancers. They have a limited set of client categories in which to target their marketing efforts—but if they have a good reputation, the high referral rates inside that arena can open doorways to new and repeat clients. Of course, if there is a problem on a project that is attributed to the QR, bad-mouthing can derail the best marketing efforts, since the pool is so small.

By contrast, the general QR has a much wider playing field in which to find clients, but also many more competitors trying to gain the attention of the same people. Clients may have difficulty distinguishing one unknown from another. In addition, the general QR will often encounter niche QRs competing for the same projects, which might place the general QR at a perpetual disadvantage in many fields.

There are a few rare QRs who have found a way to have a foot in both camps, and these moderators bring a distinguished set of specialized skills and services to clients. I call these QRs "hybrids." They can niche market not only in specific product or service areas but in the following categories as well:

- Race specifics (Asian, Hispanic, Native American, African American, European cultures).
- Lifestyle preferences (gay and lesbian, nudist, religion).
- Life stage (children, teen, and mature market research).

In addition to offering these types of specific services, they also accept work that any general QR can do—such as advertising and copy testing, package design, or voter issues—which are applicable to both niche and mainstream studies.

So the first thing to establish in the game to stay on top as a moderator is whether you are a niche, general, or hybrid QR. One way to figure it out is to borrow a lesson from Ford. The Ford Motor Company was the first to build cars on an assembly line, and when asked, "What is your mission?" they responded: "We build cars." Later, when their competition surpassed them by building trucks, train cars, tractors, and airplane engines, Ford realized that if they were to grow, they needed to change their baseline premise of "we build cars" to "we are in the transportation industry." Likewise, qualitative researchers need to be clear what business they are in: niche, general, or hybrid.

Reaching Mastery

Once your classification is clear, the next step is to gain an edge on your competition. How do you offer more to clients and keep prices in line? What will help you establish yourself as a unique vendor, rather than just another vendor?

In the "good old days" of the last century, a QR just had to have a decent set of interviewing and analytic skills, and produce good work on time and within budget. When many QRs provided an equivalent baseline set of services, the moderator with the best price often received a project award—and lower-priced QRs sometimes got more work than higher-priced ones.

However, by awarding work on the basis of cost, clients missed a key concept: "You get what you pay for." A QR with two years of general experience, charging "X" per group, may have gotten a particular project because his or her proposal had a low price tag. But what the client really needed was the QR who, although charging "X squared" per group, had ten years of experience talking to the target consumer being interviewed. For example, if a study involved mothers with a disabled child, and the moms started to cry over the frustration they felt, the less expensive, less experienced QR might not know what to do except offer water and apologize for making them cry. That moderator might even shy away from questions which might elicit more tears. The more experienced, higher-priced moderator would be able to cry right along with the respondents, but would never have to back away from asking questions or probing.

But what does it take to become the higher priced, more qualified QR, if you have not already spent ten years in the business?

Multifaceted Is the Name of the Game

In today's market, QRs have to be idea generator experts on Monday, ethnographic researchers on Tuesday, experts in talking to seven-year-olds on Wednesday, and then wrap up a Thursday session as a comfortable conversant with women who are handling stage-four breast cancer. Each client that week wants high-level skills, something extra, and a demonstration of creative problem solving—and all want a topline report the next day!

Where does a QR—niche, general or hybrid—get the skills, experience, and know-how to handle such a variety of client needs? The easy answer: not in one place. The harder answer: anywhere you can. Some of the "anywhere" activities include:

- Reading all the books and articles you can find in the QR field.
- Attending meetings, seminars, workshops, training sessions, and conferences about QR and related topics (such as anthropology, sociology, psychology, and new-age thinking).
- Meeting with like-minded colleagues in pods, groups, and on the internet—both formally and informally.
- Getting peer critiques to hone skills.

Some QRs have also ramped up their skill sets by:

- Returning to universities to take additional degree work in a field (such as anthropology) that allows them to adapt general learning to specific qualitative work.
- Taking a body of courses that leads to a certificate of mastery in a specific discipline (neuro-linguistic programming, creative problem solving, synectics, etc.).
- Creating and branding a proprietary technique which offers clients a proven way to get specific types of data (caution: one should not become so invested in a technique that it becomes a "hammer" to pound every client "nail").
- Entering into "alliances" with QRs of like minds but varied skills—i.e. creating a group that can serve a client's needs. This could be a "tag team," with each person doing a portion of the same study, or could involve passing the baton back and forth from project to project, as needed. For example, a general QR can link with a niche QR in order to offer a client specific expertise in an arena that neither would have

- been able to handle alone, because each lacked resident knowledge in a specific information set.
- Entering into coaching agreements with compatible QRs in order to improve skills. For example, an expert on teen moderating might work with someone experienced in mature markets. By coaching each other in specific techniques, they can both expand their potential client base.
- Using peer critiques to quickly grow new skills. Imagine having a trusted colleague who could watch tapes or live groups to monitor your style. He or she might point out that you only have two probes: "Tell me more about that!" and (the moderator's worst option!) "Why is that?" Via feedback and suggestions, you can quickly develop a new repertoire of approaches to get below top-of-mind responses.
- And watching someone else's tapes may enable you to discover that another moderator can set up and have a group complete a collage in less than fifteen minutes—and talk in detail about what they constructed. You could add to your ability to provide clients with a tool that has always worked, but that took you so much longer! Peer critiques can happen on an informal basis or in the formal settings of workshops and seminars.

QRs are such a valuable resource for clients because they are flexible, independent thinkers who have the ability to respond quickly to requests and to offer creative research designs. However, QRs are often so busy serving clients with current unique abilities that they do not make time to reevaluate, refresh, or learn new skills!

QRs are used to working alone, rather than in teams, groups, or pods. In fact, QRs are so used to figuring it out alone that they generally do not like to ask for help. But QRs need to grow, mature, and finetune skills in order to stay competitive, and they must learn to make the most efficient use of the two hours with participants. This means mastering different models that access the visual, auditory, and kinesthetic. QRs also need to offer unique skills (or repackaged traditional skills) to get to new levels of understanding about how respondents think.

Cannot Coast Any Longer

There is an adage: "If you keep doing what you are doing, you'll keep getting what you got." The application for qualitative researchers is that they cannot coast on the laurels built up in the last decade. QRs have to get out of their comfort zone, and stretch, and learn new skills and techniques if they are to remain at the top of the moderator game.

Managing Moderator Stress: Take a Deep Breath. You Can Do This!

> *Travel! Expenses! Competition! Change! Challenges! How on earth can you do this and remain sane and happy? Here is your vote of confidence and reassurance before you set out to moderate!*

One of the challenges of being a moderator is that the better you are, the easier it looks to others. This leads to comments such as: "How hard can it be— you just ask a few key questions, laugh with respondents, and reel in the data." A good moderator knows that a lot more goes on in the give and take of QREs. Like the duck gliding down the river, no one sees just how fast the feet are paddling.

There are a number of stressors on a moderator, the least being the pressure of doing one's work in a fishbowl (on view to respondents and clients at the same time). It requires the practice of invisible leadership— directing a process while not seeming to do so. The trick is making the group look like a two-way conversation when it is really an elaborate, organized event that guides respondents into a discussion of perceptions, opinions, beliefs, and attitudes (POBAs) about products, services, advertising, or ideas in such a way that they never know the moderator's true stance on any element.

An experienced moderator knows how to balance the stresses of the job (e.g. travel, client requests, etc.) with the demands of being hyper-alert in the actual group discussion without getting lost in the process. The following provides some tips and advice on achieving that balance.

Managing Workload

- **Know your own capacities.** Some people thrive on stress and deadlines; others cannot function well past a certain point. Some early bird moderators love 7:30 a.m. groups and never conduct 8:00 p.m. groups, while night owls thrive on late evening groups and even later debriefings. Depending on needs, an effective moderator works to set a schedule that fits his needs and adapts when client needs override the best of plans.
- Most moderators do two groups on the same day. The time between groups is generally brief, allowing just enough time for a body break or to respond to any changes that observers want made to the guide or the process. Some moderators build in a thirty-minute space to allow for unseen events. Regardless of the timing between groups, **it is a good idea to find a way to have a few minutes of private time to regroup** before starting the next one. Sometimes it will be helpful to go straight from the first group to the bathroom, hallway, or private office for a quick break. Ideally, get a quick breath of fresh air. The goal is to find a way to let go of the first group and prepare for the second. These days, clients are demanding and getting moderators to conduct three groups a day as a standard, and in some cases even four! A whole new level of balance is needed to stay effective in the face of crushing workloads. The clients only see the duck gliding—they do not see the feet! Some moderators like jamming a lot of groups into one day and getting it all over with; others like to stretch things out. Both are negotiating points in client conversations.
- **Expect to work some sixteen-hour days.** It is not uncommon to finish a group at 10:00 p.m., debrief with the client until 11:00 p.m. and race back to finish "hot notes" on your laptop before winding down enough to get to sleep and perhaps wake early for a morning flight to the next city in the rotation. Dehydration, sleep deprivation, and missed meals are common to the stories of the "research gypsies" who traverse the planet in the quest for respondent POBAs. Stamina improves with practice, and experienced moderators have a variety of methods from a lot of caffeine to no-caffeine policies to make it all work. One key item most agree on: **drink a lot of water daily.**

Some moderators have policies that they simply will not allow clients to encroach upon. The following have been heard in shared dialogues with colleagues:

- "*I do not work for clients in July and August.*"
- "*I allow one week a month where I do not travel.*"
- "*I won't sacrifice an important family event for client work.*"
- "*I take any project that comes along and, when I get a break between projects, I reward myself with time off—even though I do not always know when that will be.*"

The key thread in all the comments above is having a policy with regard to personal time and finding a way to carve out time for self in a business environment that is client-driven.

- **Adjust your timetable to allow for quiet time before groups.** Strive to arrive at the facility at least one hour before the first group so you can set up, make sure everything is in place and have time to collect your thoughts before meeting with your client. Remember you're going to be talking and actively listening for the next several hours, and it is good to start that process at something less than a dead run.
- **Do not bring mental baggage into the research room with you.** Avoid rushing from office or client meetings or phone calls to the research room without taking a few minutes of mental preparation. Respondents will notice your stress and focus on it. A quick way to transform that kind of stress into a more peaceful attitude is to take three deep breaths, followed by actively dropping shoulders and humming for thirty seconds. Like magic, you are in a new zone.
- **Put other projects on hold.** It may be difficult to focus when you have several projects running simultaneously. Seek ways to minimize, if not eliminate, phone calls from your office or from other clients during the time allotted to briefing for and conducting groups. Just because you have voice mail, texting, and instant messaging options does not mean you have to attend to them in the moments before a QRE. Those options will still be available to you when the evening is over and you can attend to them in a thoughtful manner. It takes a different kind of discipline to manage yourself—not just your client.
- **Develop a regimen to sustain and nourish you throughout the process.** Moderating is physically and mentally demanding. Imagine treading water for two hours without a break. That is actually easier than moderating! When treading, you only have to focus on one thing—keeping your head above water while moving your feet. At any one point in moderating, you are mentally juggling more than fifty options, such as planning the next question, making sure you have sup-

pressed the dominators and inspired the shy respondents, and drawing responses from at least two-thirds of the respondents before moving on to the next question. You're also remembering what has been said so you can follow productive lines of inquiry and are making sure to insert elements that allow you to get below top-of-mind, all the while asking yourself: "Do I have enough information to analyze this theme in the report?" Metaphors such as a "three-ring circus" come easily to mind when thinking of moderating in these terms.

Managing Your Mindset

View every group as a unique opportunity to learn from respondents' perspectives. The worst thing a moderator can do is pre-judge a group or assume that any one group is like all the others. One of the many paradoxes of moderating groups is that you must be thoroughly familiar with the purpose of the research, fairly well-versed in the basic content area, and proficient in moderating techniques. At the same time, you must remain open-minded, non-judgmental, and even "naïve." One way to do this is to remember that each group is a world unto itself. You will never hear from this group of respondents under the same circumstances again. What an opportunity to learn!

Respect respondents. Unfortunately, disrespect is a common mindset, a kind of gallows humor found among recruiters, observer/clients, and sometimes even among some moderators. Have you ever heard the following types of comments?

- *"What a dud group."*
- *"Did you see that guy with the food stains on his shirt?"*
- *"These women are not creative."*
- *"She never did answer a direct question, did she?"*
- *"With a hairdo like that—no wonder she sounds crazy."*

There are a few alternative ways to shift these kinds of perceptions. First of all, keep in mind that these respondents have done you a tremendous favor. They showed up! Ask yourself how willing you would be to sit in a room full of strangers and talk about feelings and other subjective elements in front of a one-way mirror—always wondering if you'll be made to look foolish or inept. Also, remember that each respondent is a potential goldmine. Every single respondent has the ability to generate essential data and represents hundreds, if not thousands, of consumers.

If the group is a "dud", look to yourself first! Did you get the right people in the room? Was the screener correct? Did you monitor recruitment? Was the purpose clear? Were the questions clear and answerable? Did you establish and maintain rapport? Did you do your best to facilitate discussion and probe effectively? Did you demonstrate active listening? Did you brief your clients on the process of observing a QRE?

Hold no personal opinions in the process of facilitating conversation and gathering data. There is no room for your opinions and attitudes during the two-hour group. At the same time, you must cultivate a healthy ego and hold the courage of your own convictions about doing what is right—not what is easy.

Maintain your researcher neutrality. You are the neutral party, gathering information from those around you. You naturally have opinions on everything: the observers/clients, the facility, the respondents, the product or service, and the project. It is essential that you prevent your personal value judgments from entering into the data gathering process. You should be the model of objectivity and have a genuine interest in the respondents' point of view.

Have courage. It takes a lot of guts to walk into a room full of strangers and get them to talk while clients observe from another room. Remember that most of your clients are too terrified to do what you do, and it has been said that for some public speaking is more scary than dying!

Keep up your own interest. Suppose this is your eighteenth group on plastic freezer wrap. How interested are you going to be? It is fairly obvious that the moderator has to find a way to stay interested. To do this, ask yourself:

- *"Can I laugh at the same joke in this group and sound authentic?"*
- *"How many new things can I learn from this group?"*

Maintain interest in process. Qualitative research extends the privilege of learning about people's lives and behavior to the moderator and to their clients. When moderating gets to be a piece of cake, it may be time to shake things up. Consider refreshing your interest in process by asking yourself:

- *"How many new ways can I probe without using the word 'why'?"*
- *"Is there a better way I can ask this question to get below top-of-mind?"*
- *"Can I find new ways to include everyone in the discussion?"*
- *"What if I gave one of the respondents the guide and let them ask the first five questions in section C while I organize the materials for the product sort?"*

Final Tips for Moderators

Stress has gotten a bad name, often linked to health issues. But consider the alternative: a stress-free life is one that is mundane and boring, a bit like a bowl of oatmeal without any raisins or sweetening. Remember that stress, when managed, can be a tool for creativity and a spur to achievement. Unmanaged, stress enervates and causes problems. To help manage your stress, make use of the following tips.

Schedule down time. RIVA has an established policy to arrive in the key city (if not our hometown) five hours before the start of a planned qualitative research event (QRE). This reduces some of the stress that can result from late or cancelled planes. As well, **RIVA avoids flying on the same plane as the client**, when possible, so that a moderator has some down time to review materials and make notes.

Get refreshed. Some moderators find that washing their hands, brushing their hair or teeth, having a quick beverage, or doing deep breathing helps them unwind and refresh before the next group arrives. Others eat a healthy snack like a banana or rice crackers to recharge.

Restore wonder. A veteran of more than 1,000 groups enthusiastically asks herself before every group, "I wonder who I am going to meet tonight, and I wonder what they can teach me that I do not already know?"

Leave your baggage. As a moderator, envision yourself putting your personal opinions into a suitcase and then leaving it just outside the research room. The moderator's job is to get at respondent POBAs. When a group is going really well, it is almost as if the questions float in from a disembodied voice, and the group is kept on task by invisible reins.

P.S. Make sure to pick up the suitcase on your way out!

SECTION III: DEMYSTIFYING FOCUS GROUPS

What a Moderator Needs to Know About Leading Focus Groups 129

What is a focus group? How is it set up? How is it run? What should you do with troublemakers? What should be you thinking when you run a focus group? Learn the answers to these questions and more right here with your guide to focus group basics!

Same Frame, New Game 141

Focus groups began in the 1930s—almost eighty years later, what are the changes that a Master Moderator™ must face? A history lesson and a healthy diagnosis for the present and the future are worth exploring here!

Focus Groups: A Four-Course Meal 147

Learn all about the four courses of the focus group—introduction, rapport & reconnaissance, in-depth investigation, and closure—and learn how you can put together and enjoy a delicious menu for success!

One Secret to Successful Focus Groups: Holding Context 151

Do not be so distracted with content that you forget about the importance of context. Remember the context is very often invisible, and learn how much of an influence it can have on your focus group—and how you can use context to achieve great success!

The Magic of Eight 157

Not too big, not too small, but just right! This doesn't just apply to Goldilocks and the three bears. Come here to learn more about how you can find the focus group size that is just right!

Turning Red Lights Green 163

Green means GO! Learn as much as you can from the lessons learned from leading over 5,000 focus groups. Avoid the frustrations and the slowing effect of unnecessary red lights on the research highway.

Problems & Solutions in Focus Groups: Three Tigers to Be Tamed 169

There will never be a qualitative research project without glitches. However, a number of traps and pitfalls can be avoided if three of the classic problems are caught early and solved. Like a tiger, these problems can be caged and tamed, so that project energy can be expended in a constructive way.

The Invisible Focus Groups in a Qualitative Research Project 175

There is more to a focus group than the actual focus group! Learn a holistic approach that values the importance of the invisible focus groups that bookmark the process—the focus group is never complete without the pre-focus group and post-focus group!

What a Moderator Needs to Know About Leading Focus Groups

> *What is a focus group? How is it set up? How is it run? What should you do with troublemakers? What should be your thinking when you run a focus group? Learn the answers to these questions and more right here with your guide to focus group basics!*

What is a focus group?

A focus group is a group interview with strangers who meet only one time. The fundamentals of personal interviewing are present:

1. Explain the purpose of the interview
2. Establish rapport
3. Ask questions
4. Record Answers

The primary difference between a focus group and a personal interview is that the interviewer is a moderator, directing the conversation down a channel outlined by a discussion guide. **The moderator presents a question or issue to the group and elicits responses for an interchange among participants, but keeps the conversation centered around the items on the discussion guide.**

Elements of a Focus Group

Focus groups have the following qualities:

- One moderator
- Six to eight participants with name tags/tents
- Special room (one-way mirror and microphones to primary and back-up tape decks/videos/DVD devices)
- One to two-hour session (or longer)
- Payments to participants ($10 to $500 apiece)
- Moderator's guide (covers between one and five topic areas)
- Spontaneous, non-evaluative, non-threatening environment
- Subjective report
- Client (requests the services and observes proceedings)

In a focus group, each person's opinions are considered in the group discussion. Each person is exposed to the ideas and opinions of others. **The interchange among respondents is what makes a focus group effective.**

Role of the Moderator

It is the moderator's responsibility to stimulate group members to interact with each other rather than with the moderator. If individuals direct all their comments to the moderator rather than to one another, a focus group is **not** taking place. This is serial interviewing. The most difficult part of being a moderator is getting out of the role of leader (which is where respondents want you) and into the role of question-asker. The movie industry supplies a working analogy. A director seldom appears in the picture (except Hitchcock!). The scenes take place between actors on sets. The director gets the actors to do what he wants but the actors do all the work. He has a copy of the scripts and he provides the actors with the settings to say their lines. In the case of a focus group, you have the script and the respondents have the lines in their heads (their beliefs, opinions, assumptions, attitudes, feelings, etc.). You give them the cues and they interact. The moderator's role then is:

- Script writer
- Listener
- Director
- Ally
- Confidant

The moderator can and should give words of support and encouragement, however **the moderator should not become a defendant of anyone's ideas or concepts, nor should they be an educator to the group.**

Recruiting

A group is brought together for a discussion because they have something in common. They may not know it, but you do! They may see themselves as ordinary individuals, but you know they use Ivory Snow dishwashing liquid; or are Catholics; or all drive foreign cars that are more than 3 years old. When recruiting of a group takes place, these elements should be remembered:

1. Decide what target elements should be considered:
    a) Sex, race, age
    b) Occupation, income
    c) Place of residence
    d) Common thread
    e) Marital status, number of children
    f) Length of time in area
    g) Use or non-use of client product or service
    h) Previous participation in other groups
2. Over-recruit to ensure minimum number of respondents (e.g. if 6–8 are wanted, recruit 9–12).
3. Tell the respondents as much detail as possible to allay their fears (without compromising the information you want to elicit).
4. Tell respondents how much they will be paid and how long they will be in the session. Tell them of others who are coming (e.g. association members, other people like them, etc.).
5. Avoid being vague. Sound positive. Tell them the purpose of the research effort. Get them on your side. Make them feel the "honor" of the invitation to participate.
6. Give them a number to call you back if they have problems or have questions.
7. Follow up with a confirmation letter stating time, place and purpose, and provide written directions.

Discussion Outline Guide

The script for the session is written by the moderator in conjunction with the client. This is the preferred sequence of events:

1. Initial meeting with client to find out what the client knows, wants to know, and some of the basic assumptions.

2. Obtain information on the target populations, and explore assumptions made about the target populations and their needs.
3. Draft a series of questions or issues that can be explored in a focus group that will meet for between one or two hours—or more.
4. Review questions with the client, and **check all assumptions.**
5. Prepare the topic outline guide. It should contain:
   a) Introduction that covers purpose of the session and ground rules.
   b) Introduction of moderator to the group and group members to one another.
   c) Non-threatening questions asked first to establish rapport.
   d) Content questions on issues to be discussed, with notes to the moderator regarding cues or areas where probing may be needed. (It may be helpful to make notes on intent of some questions to aid in eliciting desired responses.)
   e) Stimuli, prototypes, samples, etc. for "show and tell."

Conducting a Focus Group

Now that you have the respondents in a closed room with recording devices going, what do you do? Your goal is to obtain answers to questions and issues on your discussion outline in an atmosphere that is:

- Spontaneous
- Non-evaluative
- Non-threatening

You have a larger goal in qualitative research, and that is: **question the answers**—probe to find out rationales. Some ways to accomplish this include the following:

1. Prepare nametags ahead of time. Let respondents choose where to sit.
2. If you are in a conference room setting, sit with your back to the mirror so clients can see all respondent faces, and invite participants to address each other rather than you.
3. In introducing members to each other, these techniques are helpful:
   a) Interview each person by asking some general basic questions. For example: *"How long have you lived in this area? Who or what lives with you? What sort of work do you (or did you) do?"*

b) Be sure to tell the respondents something personal about yourself—become as much like a respondent as your role will allow; but do not disclose any product or service information related to the topic.
4. **Your role as a moderator is not to defend a product, service, or concept. Nor is it to educate or evaluate.** Your role is to find out how respondents feel and what **their** opinion is. They may say some thing you know is totally erroneous. Your role is not to correct but to explore why they feel the way they do. These phrases may be helpful:
   a) *"How did you get to that viewpoint?"*
   b) *"I hear you—can anybody support that comment?"*
5. Remember that most respondents will assume you know what you are doing. You have the discussion guide in front of you to review if you get off track. Do not worry about asking stupid questions. You have the script, there are no copies passed out to respondents!
6. Some effective mechanics to facilitate group discussion include the following:
   a) Write name tags with first names in block print, in blue or black ink, one inch high.
   b) Remember to include those sitting next to you in the discussion. The tendency is to relate more strongly to those seated across from you because you have direct eye contact. See the group as a clock face. Be sure you get a report from every "hour."
   c) Remind participants that because the session is recorded, only one person can talk at a time. Make sure the ones sitting next to you do not talk softly because they are next to you. You are the umpire—make the ruling on whose turn it is to talk. The following can be helpful phrases:
      i. *"Ben has the floor."*
      ii. *"One at a time, please. John, would you repeat your comment?"*
      iii. *"Jerry, hold that thought. Sam, can you finish what you were saying?"*
   d) Look for the group catalyst—one who will pick up the ball and run with it in the direction you want the group to go. This often encourages others to participate more, and it minimizes the need for you to participate.
   e) People will wander off the topic track. When that happens, try the following:
      i. Hold up your hands and say: *"Wait, how does that relate to _____?"*

  ii. Say: *"Interesting point. But how about _____?"*
  iii Say: *"That's a side issue. Let's get back to _____"*
f) A moderator walks a fine line between encouraging spontaneity of responses and letting people get carried away to the point where the discussion is not productive.
g) Remember that since respondents do not have a copy of the script, they do not know the order of the questions. **All issues or points do not have to be covered as long as the main points are all covered in the allotted time.**
h) To that end, establish priorities among questions. Know what can be dropped.
i) Encourage shy respondents to speak by calling on them by name and asking:
- *"What do you think, Gary?"*
- *"Has that ever happened to you?"*
- *"What do you do, Martin, when happens?"*

j) Keep the conversation directed toward relevant talk and away from irrelevant chatter unrelated to the client's problems. **Do not let side conversations start.** Ask respondents to share their comments with the group and to talk one at a time and in a voice at least as loud as the moderator.

What to Do About Troublemakers

Watch out for:

- The expert—he intimidates others
- The loud talker—he is garrulous, but his points are not relevant
- The pseudo expert—he wants others to believe he knows it all

Techniques:

- Point out politely that others need to be heard.
- Repeat this once.
- Look annoyed or bored; avoid eye contact.
- Cut him off in mid-phrase.
- Tell him to answer last, after other viewpoints have been heard first.

Sometimes group members will do this for you. However, do not count on it. You may have to assert your control. If it means saving the discussion, do it.

The worst that can happen is that a troublemaker will get mad and leave—and I have never seen that happen in the more than five thousand groups I have conducted.

How to Keep Up the Pace of the Discussion

Sometimes conversation slows down, or the subject is dull. You can:

- Challenge a respondent—put him on the defensive to get the discussion going
- Say something controversial to elicit opinions
- Play devil's advocate
- State an untruth, and have them defend or reject the statement
- Practice a form of "sophisticated naïveté:" *"Oh, I did not know that. Can you tell me more about it?"*

When you are asked for **your** ideas or views by a respondent, remember that you are not there to educate or inform. The client wants respondent views, not yours! Direct the question back to the group by saying:

- *"What do you think?"*
- *"How did you come to feel that way?"*
- *"What would you do?"*
- *"What's your hunch?"*

Avoid alienating respondents. Use some humor. *"Hey, I am not getting paid for my opinion, just to ask the questions!"*

What Should Be Going on in Your Head

As a moderator, you function on several levels at once:

- You should be aware of what is said and what has been said. Very much like tracking what cards have been played in a bridge game.
- You must evaluate whether the information being provided is contributing to answering the client's questions.
- You should know exactly where you want to take the group should it be necessary for you to step into the discussion at any time. This includes:
    o   When to probe and how

- o When to clarify and bring the group to a common level of understanding
- o When to retrace or make a point
- o When and how to move the group onto another topic
- o Linking a comment with a previous statement
- You should be able to determine when **unanticipated** salient or even crucial information is being obtained and be able to weave it into your topic outline. Yes—even the respondents can think of something both you and the client missed!
- You must keep track of time—in terms of the information you need and the data you already have.
- Take off your watch, and put it beside the guide, so you can see the face unobtrusively.
- The best discussion usually comes in the last fifteen minutes of the session.
- A good group discussion usually runs out of time. Keep the recording going even as the sessions break up. People tend to say things to you that may not have been said in front of others. Sometimes it is a good idea to terminate "early" to force discussion. (This is called a "false close.")

Recordings

Here are some hints for producing a good recording:

- Use reliable facilities. Check equipment out before you start each session. **Do not trust the test to others.**
- Make sure the equipment is reliable. A lousy recording makes report writing very hard and does not convey a professional image to the client.
- If you are responsible for your own recordings in the room, keep an eye on the equipment during the session. Time passes when you are having fun!
- **Label recording information** at the end of the session: date, time, place, topic, and recording number, etc.
- **Use high quality equipment.** This recording is your notebook. Otherwise you would be taking notes as well as moderating. You are not a court reporter. Get the best, and save yourself grief!
- Know how to use your equipment.

Being Perfect

Nobody runs a group perfectly. Some are better than others (this includes moderators and groups!). Basically, once you understand the dynamics, it is a matter of practice. Fight the fear of making mistakes. You will make some. Laugh at yourself. **It is all just words.**

- Be prepared—understand the research needs and the intent.
- Do not get rigid—ride easy.
- Do not get defensive—do not inform or educate.
- Do not be an expert—let them tell you what you already know.
- Do not fall into the habit of treating all groups the same way— check out the vibes of each group, and work with that information. Do not let the last group you worked with influence your attitude toward this group.

Preparing a Report

Three kinds of reports can be prepared:

1. An oral report based on your recall of the research sessions
2. A one-page "topline" or executive summary to the client based on your recall of the research sessions along with a copy of the recordings or a digital file
3. An in-depth report based on a review of the recordings by the moderator in one of the following formats:
   a) Written report
   b) PowerPoint
   c) Video or DVD

In every report, the following should be present:

- A copy of the discussion guide complete with any annotations you may have
- Copies of forms filled out by respondents
- Copies of concepts or relevant stimulus materials shown to the participants

Reports tend to follow this format:

- Introduction: purpose and methodology
- Statement of limitations
- Major topic or issue areas with verbatim comments for "VOC" (the "voice of the consumer")
- Summary and recommendations

Cautions

- There is no quantitative data. The ideal report has no numbers except pagination.
- The focus group was biased. People come because they want to. They do not necessarily represent the target population. Do not generalize to any population group. **Focus groups provide insight.**
- Criticism of the product, service, or concept must not be regarded as criticism of the moderator.
- Remember questions were not asked the same way each time, responses are not independent, and some respondents will influence others.

Uses of Focus Groups

Most group requests cover one or more of these areas:

- New product prototype testing
- Package test
- Advertising strategy exploration
- Advertising copy formulation
- Testing the market place for product acceptance
- Taste test
- Idea generation
- Storyboard tests
- Ad-labs
- Pre-quantitative issue and language identification
- Membership issues

Limitations of Focus Groups

Focus group research, a major tool in qualitative research, has several limitations important to note here.

- Non-quantifiable form of data collection.
- Notprojectable to universe of similar respondents.
- Built-in biases (more risk takers participate/non-random selection).
- Sample size small by necessity.
- Non-independent responses.
- Reports are subjective analyses of opinions, beliefs, and assumptions.
- Moderator variations.

The Value of Focus Groups

Given the limitations outlined in the last section, what would make anyone want to spend money on this kind of research? Some of the major reasons include:

- Short timelines—and the need for some research
- To test ideas and concepts in the decision stage
- To serve as a starting point—to generate hypotheses when none are known
- To support other research and confirm hypotheses
- To serve as a "disaster" check when all other research is over
- For security: when a client desires the limited exposure of a new idea
- To allow for client observation of real consumers grappling with issues, products, concepts, services, ideas, etc.
- **Because what counts in life cannot be counted**

Cost of Focus Groups

The following elements go into the cost of a single focus group:

- Research design: planning and meeting time
- Developing recruiting specifications and the moderator's guide
- Recruiting respondents
- Renting appropriate facility
- Conducting groups
- Paying the respondents
- Analyzing the recordings
- Writing the report
- Presenting research results to the client
- Overhead costs (postage, phone, travel, copy/printing, courier)

Depending on the client, product, location, issue, recruiting specifications, moderator fees, and other project specific costs, current costs for one focus group range from the cost of a small motorcycle to the cost of a sedan. Costs are always "custom quoted" depending on project specifications, the expertise of the moderator, the region of the country, and the level of comfort respondents may have when talking about the topic.

Summary

QLMR is a unique field and is not suited for every researcher. However, for those who love this industry, the rewards are wonderful. It gives one the chance to be in on new products and services, the chance to talk to respondents that will never fit into your friendship network, the chance to be an insider in Fortune 500 companies that make products and services used by millions, and the chance to see an idea grow from a quote in a focus group to a product launch. I am happy to be part of this total process.

Same Frame, New Game

> *Focus groups began in the 1930s—almost eighty years later, what are the changes that a Master Moderator™ must face? A history lesson and a healthy diagnosis for the present and the future are worth exploring here!*

As the story goes, the first focus group took place in the late 1930s for Ivory Snow soap, the flagship brand for Procter & Gamble in 1937. Who knows if this story is true? What matters is that somewhere in America in the 1930s, there was a "first" focus group. It would have been part of a pair of daytime groups, with group one starting at 9:30 a.m. with a male moderator (probably a psychologist with an advanced degree) and eight to ten participants (probably women eating donuts and coffee for the morning session and baloney sandwiches on Wonder Bread with mayo for the afternoon group held that same day). Each group would have received payment in the form of coupons, products, or a crisp five-dollar bill.

No one-way mirror existed, nor did any tape recording equipment. The client observers may have been in the room at the time, maybe with a note taker. Maybe the moderator took notes while leading. No doubt it lasted about two hours with introductory questions about the current hit radio show: *Ted Mack's Amateur Hour*. The topics covered probably started with a discussion of how bar soap was used and moved on via an outline list of questions. They probably discussed brands preferred and reactions garnered around either package design or planned advertising in magazines or newspapers. Maybe they even tested the slogan *"Ivory Snow: 99 and 44/100% pure"* in that group!

At the end of the session, the respondents were thanked, paid, and excused, and that first focus group in America was over. The second one probably started after lunch and, after it ended, the moderator and client went out for drinks, dinner, and a debriefing session. They may even have shared cigars over cognac.

Fast-forward decades later to the focus group I led last week. The frame was the same—a two-hour focus group with eight women talking about a product, but in this case it was eye drops. My group in Boston took place in a lovely mirrored facility, with state-of-the-art audio and video equipment, a sophisticated deli platter, and a stipend payment of $75 for each respondent. In the two hours, we discussed package design and the impact of brand name on eye drops choice, along with four other areas. My clients sat behind a one-way mirror and observed a trained moderator leading the session with an opening discussion about the hit show of the season: *American Idol*.

What Is Different?

So what is really different between that first focus group and the more recent one in Boston? The frame is the same but the game is totally different. For starters, most American focus groups these days are not led by male psychologists. Most are led by women researchers who bring a wide variety of skill sets and hold undergraduate and graduate degrees in market research, psychology, sociology, or anthropology. Many have worked on both the client and supplier side and bring experiences from a wide and diverse learning path.

In the late 1930s, the women participants in the group probably met during the day because they did not work away from home. Most groups these days take place in the evening to accommodate the working schedule of most consumers. In Boston, group one started at 6:00 p.m., and group two started at 8:05 p.m.. The client had a hot dinner ordered from a local restaurant, and the moderator had cheese and crackers. The evening ended at 11:00 p.m. after an in-room debriefing of key elements where clients and the moderator discussed insights gleaned over the two sessions. No cigars or cognac were present. While the session in Boston may have started with a light discussion of a popular television show and an introduction of participants, from that point on it was a race to the finish line to get data on six to seven different issue areas in the allotted two hours.

In the 1930s, the session may have lasted two hours, but only three clearly distinct issue areas were covered, and more time was spent delving down deep into motivations, perceptions, and behavioral issues. These days, there is less focus on the drivers of behavior, with more emphasis on getting a quick read on a variety of topics. The chart that follows illustrates that difference.

1930s discussion: Current bar soap usage.	**21st Century discussion: Current eye drops usage.**
• Perceptions about client soap in competitive mix. • Reactions to new package design options.	• Role of ingredients, price, shelf location, store choice, and brand name in eye drops selection. • Review of package designs of client and competitive mix products. • Which message resonates best with women over fifty? • Reactions to sample concept statements. • Reactions to list of thirty new name choices for rebranding of product. • Advice for client as they contemplate re-launch of product category.

The challenge for today's moderator is having the same one hundred and twenty minutes of clock time as moderators in the 1930s, but nearly twice the amount of material to cover in the discussion. Here are some elements I have put into place to make sure I can serve the needs of my twenty-first century clients in the same two-hour time frame:

Streamline the introductory remarks. I would never say: *"Tell me a little bit about yourself,"* as would have been asked in the 1930s. Instead, respondents see a bullet point list of items in the introduction on the easel and hold a set of printed guidelines for participation so that the introductory time is kept to eight minutes or less rather than the twenty minutes allotted in the 1930s.

Avoid using an outline guide. In outline guides, the actual question asked has to be generated *live*. A moderator should use a more detailed universal guide with specific questions and possible probes so he or she can spend time managing the discussion rather than crafting the right question to ask at any particular point. Moreover, a universal guide can ensure that another moderator will be able to step in at any time to lead the session if needed.

Use worksheets. I use these to gather private responses before public disclosure and to focus discussion rather than ranging loosely over a topic like a blind pig looking for an acorn.

Provide clear instructions. This helps ensure that no time is wasted clearing up murky communications about what is wanted. For example, if respondents are reviewing concepts, I have them use a yellow highlighter to mark positive points and a pink one to mark elements they do not like. If I hand them the yellow highlighter first, it is hard for them to do the task incorrectly or to confuse the instruction.

Twenty-first century clients want to conduct more than two groups in a day. It is not unusual for clients to routinely expect a moderator to conduct three two-hour discussions on the same day (and travel to the research site as well). When three groups in a day are coupled with an airplane flight or train ride, it can make for a research day that starts with a 4:00 a.m. wake-up call and does not end until seventeen hours later. Some clients prefer to spend fewer hours and days away from their home offices, so they maximize the use of their time with a request for three groups in a day from qualitative vendors.

Good moderators can make this schedule work, and some like the high level of intensity so they can quickly meet their targets for the month and have more travel-free days "back at the ranch." Some moderators would like more breathing room between groups and trips so they are not sleep-deprived and working solely on adrenaline. In the 1930s, this was not a key issue, since there were few night-time groups, and multiple-city research designs were rare.

Today's Game

Qualitative research, particularly via the medium of focus groups, has a long history of being an effective tool to help include the voice of the consumer in clients' short and long-range decision making. The historical two-hour session has transmogrified to other models including minigroups, extended groups (longer than two hours), task-based groups (doing "homework" before coming to the group), and alternative interview styles (e.g. friendship triads).

Most client requests are for the standard two-hour session with six to eight respondents. So the frame remains the same, but the game inside is definitely different from what happened in the 1930s. It may be another eighty years before we give up the two hour focus group model. In the meantime, the mark of good qualitative research is to rise to the challenge of that timeline and get the best data out of respondents possible. Do not let them see you sweat!

Focus Groups: A Four-Course Meal

Learn all about the four courses of the focus group—introduction, rapport & reconnaissance, in-depth investigation, and closure—and learn how you can put together and enjoy a delicious menu for success!

Focus groups, regardless of how long they take, have four distinct stages: introduction, rapport and reconnaissance, in-depth investigation, and closure. The lion's share of the time is spent on the third stage, indepth investigation, since that is where respondents address the items of importance to the client.

In writing this article I was struck by the similarity between the four stages of a focus group and the four phases of an elegant dinner: appetizers, soup/salad, main course, and dessert. You can count on me to stretch this metaphor to the limit!

Once a client asked me to, *"Cut to the chase—skip all that palaver at the beginning of a group, and get right to the questions."* It took all my good home training to convince him that it was very hard to serve the steak as soon as he sat down, that it would take a while to cook it to his liking. He understood, and we began with appetizers!

When dining out, the right appetizer sets the tone for a meal, and when you make the right selection, the rest of the meal is enhanced from those initial bursts of flavor. In a focus group, **the appetizer covers the initial welcome by the moderator and the self-introductions from respondents.** This is a time for the moderator to calibrate the tone of the group by determining quiet, shy types versus those who talk more. It is also where the ground rules for participation are given.

Having led over 5,000 focus groups and watched hundreds led by other moderators, the way ground rules are handled seems to break down into seven types (the names given here are illustrative of the style of many moderators I have seen and do not refer to any real people):

- *Chatty Cathy/Carl*: A very breezy style of giving the rules, often with preamble that says, *"I have some facts to cover before we start the fun."* This style relies on the warmth of the moderator to impart the key information to keep the group discussion on target.
- *Serious Sue/Sam*: This sounds more like the reading of the charges in a courtroom or instructions to the jury. The tone is more of *"You will_____"* or *"I won't tolerate_____."* This approach can be off-putting to respondents.
- *Warm Wanda/Willy*: This style of ground rules is meant to put respondents at ease and welcome them to the session as well as honor them as individuals. The tone is more inviting with phrases such as: *"It would work best to_____"* or *"I would appreciate it if you would refrain from_____."*
- *Slam Dunk Sally/Stan*: A crisp, but not brusque attitude: *"Let's get down to business"* tone, and usually preceded by this phrase: *"Before we get to the topic at hand, there are a few things you need to know."*
- *Willy-Nilly Betty/Billy*: *"Um—ah—"* is how this moderator begins the group—*"I need you to um, do_____ and then ah… not do___."* This moderator sometimes does not get all the rules delivered because the attention is on the moderator rather than informing the participants what the boundaries are.
- *Careful Cassie/Charley*: This style is often a long laundry list of every conceivable situation that might come up: One might hear phrases such as: *"I may have to cut you off and move on."* Or: *"If the power goes off, please remain calm."* This much preanticipation can sometimes lead to over-orchestrating a session and can drain out the spontaneity of a group.
- *Fast Freida/Freddy*: This type of moderator does not give ground rules, guidelines, or disclosures at all! They may or may not introduce themselves or ask participants to provide a self-introduction. They start the group with the first question, and sometimes they can be pushy, surly or simply adversarial. It sounds similar to this: *"Okay, my time is valuable. Just tell me your reasons for buying Brand X towels."*

The role of ground rules or guidelines is to set some boundaries for the group discussion and to honor the time participants are spending in the research environment. Those boundaries need to be like the ropes on a boxing ring—flexible enough to allow a boxer who has been hit to bounce back into the fray without falling over.

Basic ground rules/guidelines need to cover these requirements:

- Speak up.
- Speak one at a time.
- Honor the opinions of others.
- Excuse self (one at a time) for the restroom or for additional refreshments.
- Have the courage of one's convictions.
- Allow for equal air time for each participant.
- Avoid side conversations.

In times past, there was also a no-smoking rule, but government legislation has removed a need to make that statement in American focus groups.

Some moderators also add ground rules about eating/drinking during the groups, keeping the data discussed confidential, or other elements that are project-specific. The trick is to deliver exactly what respondents need to know to make the most supportive research environment for achieving the research objective without including every possibility that may arise.

The best advice I ever received about delivering ground rules/guidelines is to make them sound fresh and new each time and to keep them short. In the years I have been moderating, I have found it helpful to also pass out the ground rules as a handout so that when one is violated, I can simply say: "Remember guideline number____?" Then respondents check their list and comply quickly.

Some moderators feel they should not offer any guidelines or ground rules at the outset. Rather, they insert them at the time the need arises in a group. For example, if all respondents are talking at once they might say: "Please talk one at a time." I feel that breaks the flow of the discussion. Since it is an inserted ground rule at that specific point in the discussion, respondents may hear it as a one-time admonition instead of a blanket ground rule and continue the behavior at another point, turning the moderator into a finger-pointing teacher rather than a collector of data.

At a restaurant, **after the appetizer comes soup or a salad course. In a focus group this is the rapport and reconnaissance (R/R) stage.** Soup or salad is not the whole dinner, yet it is a complete section of the dinner. When prepared and served well, it sets up the palate for the main course.

R/R is a complete section of the guide with two distinct purposes: to give respondents a chance to answer easy, baseline questions (e.g. product/service usage) and allow the moderator to gauge who talks a lot or a little. In this section, it is important to ask short questions and to probe lightly to get more than top-of-mind answers, and, in the process, "train" respondents to go deeper to provide information. As well respondents are rewarded by comments from the moderator that inspire them to talk freely because none of the answers are judged.

Moving on to the main course at a restaurant requires a change of silverware in most cases. A fresh plate is also presented to the one dining, where meat/fish/fowl is attractively served with a colorful array of vegetables providing color and texture differences. For vegetarians, the main entrée would be an exciting medley of vegetables chosen to complement one another.

In the focus group, the section called "in-depth investigation" is the main course. This section, taking nearly 65% of the time allotted to the group is where the "meat" of the discussion takes place and where consumers help illuminate key areas of interest for the client. Just as the plate for food for the main course must be kept hot so the food is at its most desirable, so must the moderator keep the conversation "hot" and on topic.

The finale to a good restaurant meal is a selection of desserts and chocolate is almost always on the menu. **The ending of a focus group should be soft and sweet, like chocolate mousse, leaving a good taste in the mouths of the respondents and the clients.** A good moderator makes sure that the key hypotheses have been explored in detail and that the research objectives were met. As well, respondents are thoughtfully acknowledged for giving their time and their opinions and, of course, paid a stipend for attending.

If the service is good in a restaurant, a twenty percent tip is considered an appropriate reward for those that waited on the table. In focus groups, the "tip" that moderators expect is to be told something such as: "Good job! We got the data we needed." And it is always nice to hear "thank you."

RIVA believes that good ground rules make for an effective group and the best groups have just the right marriage of good ground rules, effective rapport, and strategic probing to get below top-of-mind. A toolbox brimming with projective techniques acts as garnish to a dinner plate and not only pleases the palate but satisfies the eye.

It was fun to compare a restaurant meal to a focus group, since both come in four parts. I hope the insights provided by stretching this metaphor to the maximum were both interesting and informative.

One Secret to Successful Focus Groups: Holding Context

> *Do not be so distracted with content that you forget about the importance of context. Remember the context is very often invisible, and learn how much of an influence it can have on your focus group—and how you can use context to achieve great success!*

Focus group sessions can be divided into two clear areas: content and context. The topic, questions, processes, activities, discussions, and timelines are some of the elements that compose content. Context, on the other hand, is a very different element, one that can hold the secret to successful focus groups.

Stepping outside qualitative research for a bit, where else can we find context in our society? What is context anyway? I have read about it in newspaper articles or in the op-ed section, or talked about it in discussions among professionals, although I suppose two neighbors living side by side on a condemned property tract might discuss the "context of the new zoning laws" that are going to force them to move to a new location. However, I bet they do not call what they are doing "a contextual conversation."

I contend that context is invisible and it is an experience rather than something strictly tangible. If I look at my friendship network and focus on those who are married, I am looking at them in the context of their marriage. When I do so, I pay attention to the perceptions they have of each other, what they believe about the other partner, the opinions they are willing to share about their relationship in front of me, and the attitudes

I see them strike when the other is in range to be heard or seen or not. Another place I can see context is when attending a convention.

When the conference title, the workshop themes, and the agenda are all congruent, I know the context of the conference has been carefully thought out so that participants like me can keep in mind the reason they came and the objectives they want to reach by attending at the conference.

Context has two definitions in the dictionary. The one that is a perfect fit for qualitative research states that context is the interrelated conditions in which something exists or occurs. One simple way is to think of a bowl of salad. The salad itself is the content, the bowl, the context.

The context of a focus group room can be viewed as a big salad bowl, physically bound by its sides (three walls and one large mirror) and philosophically bound by the focus group purpose statement. The participants, the moderator's guide, the exercises, the discussion, the concept statement, the prototypes, the storyboard, or the product are all like salad elements (such as tomato, olive, onion and feta cheese tucked between the leaves of spinach, romaine, and escarole). Peering into the bowl, trying to understand the thinking of respondents, are observers who very much need to know how a target market consumer thinks so they can serve them better, sell them more, or include the "voice of the consumer" in short and long-range planning.

It is easy to get caught up in the parts of the salad—what's the best kind of olive? Should the feta cheese be authentic Greek or inexpensive American? Which tomato should I use, chopped Roma or tiny grape tomatoes?

Similarly, a researcher can get sidetracked when choosing the "salad dressing," and the client can get fixated on the type of "tongs" to toss the items. But if the bowl is too small to hold the salad, there is a problem and if the bowl is too large, there is a problem. What if the bowl does not present well—is dirty, or chipped, or has a large crack running though the bottom? A good moderator wants to avoid these problems, like having perceptions that poor people are not creative (have you ever seen a low-income mom get creative with store coupons—carefully reading the paper to get the ones that double—if that is not creative, what is?), or believing that doctors would not do a fun projective technique because it is not dignified (when all doctors want to do is break out of their stuffy molds and get a chance to play when they are off duty!).

Some researchers focus primarily on the content and figure any old bowl will do. Some researchers focus so much on the bowl that the contents are skimpy. The best match is the right bowl for the type of salad to be served.

If context is defined as interrelated conditions in which something exists or occurs—then **what are the elements that create context?** *First* among these should be an understanding of the study purpose and objective. *Second* should be the intended use of any results obtained. *Third* might be the assumptions about the target population. Knowing these with precision and clarity can go a long way toward having a delicious salad.

Purpose Statements from Three Points of View

Getting clear on purpose and intended outcomes is a tricky business—part science and part art. A good purpose statement sets the frame for the discussion, covers items that can be discussed in a focus group setting, and points to the desired outcomes that could be achieved if the study purpose is met.

Depending on who has the primary need (manufacturer, advertising agency, or association) the purpose might change, and therefore the discussions and activities among participants in the room will be altered to reflect the change in purpose.

Look at the same baseline topic (sunscreen) and see how the purpose statement changes when the end-user changes.

> Study Context: The client wants to know some POBAs (perceptions/opinions/beliefs/attitudes) about the use of sunscreen products so short and long-range decisions can be made.

- If client is a **manufacturer**: to determine consumer attitudes and opinions about and use of major sunscreen brands and un-derstand beliefs about efficacy with respect to reducing the risk of skin cancer.
- If client is an **advertising agency**: to determine consumer reaction to new communication approaches about sunscreens, which focus on reducing the risk of skin cancer.
- If client is the **American Cancer Society (ACS)**: to determine the degree to which Americans understand the risk of getting skin cancer and the role they feel that sunscreens play in reducing that risk.

Notice how dramatically the purpose statement (context for the study) changes the mood or direction of the study, thereby making the content (e.g. issues and questions) shift to different levels of emphasis. This means that in one case the bowl (context) might be glass, while in another context that same bowl might be olive wood. While both may hold the same kind of salad, the overall view from the observer's point of view is very different.

It is possible that behind the mirror, all three parties listed above could be present and then it would be the job of the moderator to determine who is the "senior client" with the greatest needs to be served while at the same time honoring the viewpoints of the "junior clients" behind the mirror.

It would be nearly impossible to write a purpose statement that serves all viewpoints equally. However, if one of the organizations is the senior client, the other two can have some issue areas dedicated to their needs/interests without undermining the main purpose. All needs can be served, just not at the same level. For example, if the ACS were the senior client, the focus groups would be prioritized as shown below. Note the time devoted to each set of issues.

Baseline information about sun and skin damage (50 min.):

    A. POBAs about how a tan makes one look "healthy" (20 min.)
    B. POBAs about the role of the sun in some skin cancers (30 min.)

Role of sunscreens in protecting the skin (30 min.):

    A. Are all sunscreens equally effective? (15 min.)
    B. Reactions to three new print advertisements for sunscreens (15 min.)

Total time: 80 min.

If the manufacturer of sunscreens were the senior client, the focus of the group discussion and minutes assigned to topics would change. The order of discussion would change, too.

    A. What do you enjoy doing outside in the sun?—baseline info (10 min.)
    B. Products you use on your skin—sunscreen and what else? (15 min.)
    C. POBAs about sunscreen—what's good/what's not? (30 min.)
    D. Baseline information about sun and skin damage (20 min.)
    E. POBAs about the role of the sun in some skin cancers (20 min.)
    F. Role of sunscreen in protecting the skin: are all sunscreen equally effective? (10 min.)
    G. Reactions to three new print advertisements for sunscreens (15 min.)

Total time: 120 min.

Viewing the two different directions outlined above—it seems that what gets discussed in each focus group is very different at least as far as emphasis, order, effect, and the amount of time dedicated to each of the topics outlined above.

For example, in the ACS client driven guide the emphasis is more on the "philosophy of sun tanning" rather than on efficacy of suntan products, while in the manufacturer focus groups there is just a baseline discussion on "being in the sun," and the majority of time is spent on sunscreen products.

That means what the two separate groups discuss is quite different. Interventions and projective techniques would also shift. Harking back to our metaphor, it is the moderator's job to keep both the type of bowl in mind and what it takes to fill the bowl in addition to decide how much dressing is needed to toss the salad or if the dressing is served on the side. Dressing can be seen as the degree to which the moderator's presence is inserted into the process to reach the desired objectives. Most people who have ever been on a diet know the best way to use salad dressing is to ask for it "on the side" and use just what you need.

When teaching students at RIVA's Training Institute we tell them to focus on both information and process while moderating. That means attending to the kinds of questions and activities that they are executing and to the impact of those elements on participants. We cannot get to a discussion of how best to do these tasks unless we have trained them in context and at RIVA, that requires a detailed Q&A forum around creating study purpose and intended outcomes.

RIVA faculty members are continually amazed that, at this point in the twenty-first century, the concept of context is still something new to our students. We know they work in companies that require study briefing documents and fill in the blank templates that have the phrase "study objectives" right at the top of the page, but they see those memos and templates as task driven checklists where study objective has the same weight as something like respondent specifications. Perhaps it reflects the quality in our society which has us race off to do a task well before we know the reason for the task. In our haste to get it done, we leave little time for truly understanding how the results will fit into the larger picture.

The RIVA Training Institute faculty sees a big "a-ha!" moment for many students when they realize that setting context for their future studies is going to result in a much better study design and a much clearer moderator's guide to help them achieve the study objective on that in-house memo.

One of the secrets of successful focus groups is becoming crystal clear about the context so that the screener, the moderator's guide, group activities, and the outline for the final report are all congruent and that any content that is developed fits into the frame created by the context.

The Magic of Eight

> *Not too big, not too small, but just right! This doesn't just apply to Goldilocks and the three bears. Come here to learn more about how you can find the focus group size that is just right!*

Qualitative research moderators often prefer to work with a specific number of respondents, for reasons of interviewing comfort and for how group size affects the research objectives. This article outlines some issues related to focus group size and desired research outcomes, since the size of the group (i.e. the number of respondents) affects the skilled moderator's ability to get below top-of-mind comments.

Group size and research objectives are closely aligned. The "right" group size is often a function of a client's need for specific results to support long-range decision making. For example, a client may request a group size of four to six respondents when a few, but very important issues need to be discussed in detail. A group size of twelve may be right when the study is a one-hour "Ad-labs" designed to get a thumbs-up/thumbs-down reaction to the final three versions of a television spot.

Sometimes the right group size is a function of room size. Recently, a focus group held in a mall facility required the use of a room with a round table that would only accommodate six respondents and a moderator without extreme discomfort. When a pregnant respondent had to leave to use the restroom, everyone had to stand to let her pass by to get out the door! Clearly, room size dictated group size.

In focus group planning, research design is often a blend of moderator experience (knowing how to reach the study objectives) and an attempt to honor client requests. Over the years, I have heard these comments from my qualitative research colleagues as they identify personal rules about group size:

- *"I insist on no more than six, because that size lets me get a lot of answers from everyone."*
- *"It is okay with me to take ten or twelve in a group because I know then that at least eight or nine of them will talk enough to get all the data—and I hate to turn people away who have been invited to a focus group."*
- *"For me, seven is the perfect number. I like it when it is an uneven number of people because then I as the moderator become the eighth person."*
- *"I know that conducting triads is the best research tool sometimes. However I just HATE them because I have to work much harder as the moderator to keep the creative juices flowing!"*

For each of the above moderator types, there is a rationale for a group size that works, and it is from that base that moderators lobby for a specific group size within the confines of good qualitative research design. Sometimes, clients have belief categories about group size:

- *"More is better"*
- *"Corporate policy"*
- *"Feels right"*

When More Is Not Better

When I can negotiate research design elements with clients, I first have to break the "more is better" rule. To that end, I have devised a formula to share with clients so they can see that **having more bodies in the room actually hampers the collection of data rather than promotes it.**

Method for Calculating Research Value by Group Size

- If twelve people present = this allows 1.66 min. per issue per person
- If ten people = 2 min. per issue per person
- If eight people = 2.5 min. per issue per person
- If six people = 3.3 min. per issue per person

In the bulleted list above, it is clear that the more people in the room, the less time there is available for actually getting respondent opinions! The trick is to find the mix of people and talking time that best helps meet study objectives.

When the group size shrinks to below six respondents, a different group dynamic occurs. Smaller groups sometimes become shy when given a lot of time to present an opinion. Different moderator skills are needed to maximize the time. The session is usually shorter than two hours since topics can be covered in-depth more quickly.

Communication Time in Focus Groups

Baseline Data:

- About one hundred minutes of research time is available in a standard two-hour group
- Five key issues to cover (standard flow for a two-hour focus group)
- If evenly divided, that would be about twenty minutes per issue

100 Minutes				
Issue A 20 min.	Issue B 20 min	Issue C 20 min	Issue D 20 min	Issue E 20 min

- Issue A: Baseline/background information (Purchase patterns of syrup, etc.)
- Issue B: Brand image (How does generic brand differ from brand labels?)
- Issue C: Reactions to concept ("Now syrup can be heated right in the glass bottle!")
- Issue D: Review of product names ("Hot Spout" vs. "Heat 'n Pour")
- Issue E: Advice to syrup manufacturer (What to do, what to avoid)

Not all of the 120 minutes of clock time is research-oriented. Some is administrative time (e.g. passing out and collecting papers), and some is logistics (e.g. moving people in and out of a room).

Corporate Policy on Group Size Dictated by Non-Moderators

Some clients insist that a specific group size is "corporate policy," and the demand seems to include a whisper of "we have always done it that way." RIVA's concern is that the policy is often stated or upheld by individuals who have never led a focus group. **I have never understood the rationale that would have a client set a policy about group size without the personal experience of how**

group size affects group dynamics and the ability to collect full and rich data from participants.

When Feeling Right Feels Wrong

Group size is sometimes determined by a client who indicates that *"six feels about right"* for this project. Feelings are the domain of focus group conversations between the moderator and respondents, and not an appropriate mechanism for determining research parameters. The moderator's experience in knowing which group size best matches the research tasks is a better gauge than client observers' expectations of which group size will produce desired outcomes.

The Magic of Eight

In the RIVA method of conducting focus group research, we believe in the "magic of eight" for traditional focus groups. The group can act as an octet, two pairs of four or a quartet of pairs. Assuming that all participants speak equally on each of the issues—eight people will each speak two and a half minutes per issue or about twelve minutes over the course of a two-hour group session.

When compared to television news sound bites, each lasting about thirty seconds, twelve minutes is a long time to allow a respondent to have the floor!

As it turns out, individuals in focus group do not speak equally! On one topic, two to three participants speak more than others, and on another, a different set of four to five respondents will lead the discussion.

Since there is insufficient time for each person to answer every question, the RIVA method aims for the "2/3rds" rule. If 2/3rds of the group members have answered the question under discussion, the moderator asks if there are any different points of view. If not, then the group moves on to the new topic. Under this rule, we do not expect every person to answer every question on every issue—just those who have a point to make or a point to contradict or echo what has already been said.

We have found that a group of eight allows for the following to naturally occur:

- Respondents do not have to wait too long for a turn to speak.
- There is no chance for a respondent to hide out in a group of eight.
- Everyone can be easily seen around a conference table.
- There is enough variation in eight respondents for participants to find someone else who thinks the way they do.

- There is enough conversation to promote an opportunity for diverse opinions and natural give-and-take.

Having eight respondents in the room also seems to allow for a level of comfort among respondents. The table seems full without being crowded, and there is sufficient room to allow for the Western cultural need for about three feet of space between people in groups. Respondents can see the faces of most of the other participants easily and can make eye contact with a peer (one who shares the same opinions). When the group is divided for a task (e.g. two teams sorting pictures to create brand image), it is easy to form quartets without anyone having to change seats—simply working across the table in a group of four at either end of the table. If the group is divided into sharing pairs, the even number of participants makes that an easy task and the moderator can give instructions and have them followed quickly. If the session is being visually-recorded, it is easy to structure the seatings, so that it looks natural and allows every face to be captured on the behind-the-mirror camera.

Although a traditional focus group takes place in a time slot of two hours, there are actually only about one hundred minutes of true research time since the remaining twenty minutes are generally spent getting respondents seated, introduced to the topic, and then excused and escorted from the room. In addition, time is lost when the group is a little late or when the discussion veers off topic briefly, when instructions are given, or when respondents are working silently and independently. Those one hundred minutes of research time need to be used wisely. Having a manageable group size that promotes the inclusion of respondents on every topic and allows time to go beyond top-of-mind responses mean that group size has to be carefully planned.

Win-Win-Win

Blending group size with moderator comfort and client research needs is tricky. For traditional focus group projects primarily aimed at testing respondent perceptions, opinions, beliefs, and attitudes, RIVA moderators have found that the "magic of eight" promoted a win-win-win situation for moderator, client, and respondent. Facilities are asked to recruit ten to eleven respondents to guarantee a show rate of eight. The facility wins as well by having a project that is manageable—not only in the recruiting process, but in the waiting room as well.

Codicil for 2010 and Beyond

When this article first appeared in the 1990s, eight was seen as a desirable number for a group discussion. Today, clients want to dive more deeply into topics, and sometimes eight people is too many. For some clients and types of group discussions, six is becoming the new eight. However, researchers are cautioned that group dynamics shift when there are fewer people in the room, and a different kind of moderator vigilance is required.

Turning Red Lights Green

> *Green means GO! Learn as much as you can from the lessons learned from leading over 5,000 focus groups. Avoid the frustrations and the slowing effect of unnecessary red lights on the research highway.*

A recent email contained a list of bits of wisdom gathered from a variety of sources such as the Dalai Lama and Tony Robbins. One stood out: *"When you lose, do not lose the lesson."*

In looking back over my last four decades in research, with thirty years being qualitative focused, I have certainly "lost" in the market research game a few times. When I think about it, those were the times when I learned the most! When projects go smoothly, the whole process feels effortless, like the lights turning green just as you hit each intersection, all the way from your house to the airport.

To continue the metaphor, when the red lights stopped me in qualitative research, each one was always a surprise—I was not looking to learn a lesson at the time. **This article points to six key lessons I learned on the long journey from my first group of respondents, to the one I led last week.**

Lesson One: Trust Your Own Judgment

My first focus group was a disaster. The client recruited and kept all sixteen respondents who showed. The respondents knew each other—all being members of a corporate after-hours bowling league. The topic was both sensitive and volatile. I moderated the session in the client's boardroom while the client listened through a wall by holding a glass to his ear. In my haste to get this first project, I suspended all my good judgment and ceded to the client's wishes, even though I knew those decisions were not in the interest of good research. The result: I learned lessons in spades.

As my group tally has increased over the years, I have never again surrendered my good judgment as a qualitative researcher. I clearly explain to clients that I am the research instrument and that, ultimately, the success or failure of qualitative project rests solely with me. Some examples of trusting myself and not being a "research lackey" included doing the following over the years:

- I threatened to walk out when a client wanted me to wear an earpiece so they could coach my questioning of respondents in real time.
- I refused to continue moderating a group when the client asked me to sell the product while moderating.
- I terminated a project mid-stream upon discovery that the client was using the process to pre-qualify prospects for future sales calls.
- I cried along with a group of widows who were thrown back into grief mode while talking about insurance payments they received when their husbands died. I could have terminated the group discussion because of high emotions, but I learned that I could cry and still ask effective questions.
- I included a blind respondent in a television advertisement test rather than dismissing her since she technically "watched television" with her family, and blindness was not a specific "do not recruit" screener item.

Lesson Two: Put Everything in Writing

A moderator colleague of mine told me a harrowing story. She booked a facility, using the central location for a national chain since the study took place in three cities and they had offices in all three. She paid the deposit, went to the first city in the series, led the groups, and on her way out, she said: *"I'll take the audio tapes with me now."* The hostess said: *"You never said you wanted the groups taped—we do not have that request in your papers."* The moderator was floored by the comment, expecting that every room rental at every facility in America included as a minimum: table, chairs, a mirror, and audio recording. She has learned to put it all in writing, no longer making assumptions about even the most obvious details. RIVA makes phone calls to clients and facilities and follows up with e-mails, recapping key points. The written materials keep all the team players apprised of all elements of the study and provide a paper trail to handle issues that may arise as the project unfolds.

Lesson Three: No One Remembers the Last Group You Led

This lesson has been the most difficult. Like most moderators, I am always comparing my current work to my past work and judging myself on how well I am doing. I am giving myself a "grade" for my work, and I am often looking for ways to streamline efforts, work more efficiently, keep research techniques fresh, and provide my clients with high quality services.

I remember the great group last week in Milwaukee, where my questions were stellar and I finished the group right on time. It is hard to remember that this week's clients, in a small New Jersey suburb, were not at the groups last week and have no resident history with my exceptional group in the Midwest on a different topic. I am at both events, even though the rooms look similar! I have to continually remember that I am only as good as my next group and that I cannot coast on good work done in the past.

Lesson Four: Maintain Research Rigor, Not Rigidity

This one took me a number of years to learn. As a former quantitative researcher, it had been drummed into me to ask questions the same way every time and to be crystal clear on what hypotheses were being tested, as well as to never forget the dependent and independent variables in the study. Qualitative research is more exploratory in nature, and a true question is one to which you do not already know the answer. It is similar to being on a high wire without a net.

It has taken a bit of time, but now I have learned to live without a sense of closure from group to group, knowing the final report is the first place to seek that closure. I now know that the guide I write will not have all the questions asked or answered in every focus group in the series. I also know that it is more important to follow the energy in the room when a gold mine is uncovered rather than asking people to hold their thoughts for the part in the guide where those questions were planned. I no longer get upset when a group does not start on time—just as long as I end it on time. I know it takes flexibility and resilience to do what is right, not what is easy, to create a good qualitative research experience for me, the respondents, and the client.

Lesson Five: Laugh Early—It Will All Be Funny Later

Some quick examples of "laughing on the inside" since I started qualitative research in the 1970s:

- Winning a lowest bidder award because I made an $8,000 mistake in

- arithmetic in the proposal and could not apply for an adjustment
- Leaving my only copy of the guide in the seat pocket on a plane just two hours before the group started
- Throwing up in a waste basket in the hallway outside the focus group room because of food poisoning and only having perfume to rinse out my mouth afterwards
- Hallucinating in the focus group room and believing the room had sixteen rather than eight respondents because my temperature was 104º
- Using God's name and a swear word together in a focus group with nuns when I dropped a book on my sore toe
- Losing all of a forty-seven-page report when I failed to regularly save to the hard drive, which then crashed when a power outage occurred in my hotel room

I think either Nietzsche or Conan the Barbarian said: *"What doesn't kill you makes you stronger."* I believe that what is stressful now is going to be funny later when I tell the story, so I have learned to start laughing early.

Lesson Six: Learning to Expect and Embrace Change

Since I travel much of the business week, I am often calling my research director to ask about project updates, and I have learned to start with this question: *"What has changed?"* I know that advertising agencies are changing stimuli right up to the first group and that the copy I had at the moderator guide development stage is probably not going to be what I am actually testing. I know the specs we worked on for the screener may not play out 100% in the humans who show up and that the study purpose may shift from what was true two weeks earlier. I know the client may forget the audio tape of the commercial and ask me to sing the jingle for the storyboard.

There have been true moments of levity in my work as a moderator across the years, and the final unnumbered lesson to report here is: *"Remember that working with people in qualitative sessions is really a lot of fun."* Here is a short list of humorous highlights across more than 5,000 focus groups:

- Hiding a smile when a young man said he did not worry about STDs because he practiced mahogany (he did not know how to say monogamy) and when the housewife said she did not like genetic brands (meaning generic brands)
- Suppressing laughter when a young woman who was totally bald due to coloring and relaxing her hair in the same treatment swore her hair was

- growing back, due to the use of the client's mousse
- Pretending to cough when the transvestite said the reason he liked control top pantyhose was because *"it holds up my stuff"*
- Laughing out loud when the client fell through the one-way mirror because he tripped
- Pretending to sneeze when the seven-year-old, who was asked to name some items on a tray that included typical medicines found in a family medicine cabinet, said ExLax was *"Jewish chocolate"*

After leading so many groups, I have had many more green lights on my research journey than red ones. I have learned how to turn the red lights green before I hit the critical research intersections on projects through planning and experience. I thank the Dalai Lama and Tony Robbins for reminding me not to lose the lesson when I think I have lost in an experience.

Problems & Solutions in Focus Groups: Three Tigers to Be Tamed

> *There will never be a qualitative research project without glitches. However, a number of traps and pitfalls can be avoided if three of the classic problems are caught early and solved. Like a tiger, these problems can be caged and tamed, so that project energy can be expended in a constructive way.*

As a seasoned moderator [having led more than six thousand focus groups in the last three decades], I have certainly seen my share of problems in focus group environments. I would like to address three that still crop up from time to time and some solutions I have put into place to minimize them, reducing my stress levels. I call these problems "tigers" because they can bite! I have seen skilled animal trainers tame tigers in such a way that they can perform for an audience. I have taken three of my "tigers" and indicate how I am taming them.

All three of my "tigers" can be classified in the "Too Many/Too Much" category. Before presenting these problems/solutions under this classification, I want to address the condition that leads to this problematic category.

A Contextual Condition

Clients are tasked with a need for qualitative research to inform decision making. A focus group allows a deep dive into perceptions, opinions, beliefs, and attitudes (POBAs) around a number of dimensions that affect products, services, and advertising.

When the opportunity emerges to put ideas in front of consumers or a specific target market, clients get excited about what could be learned and who should be in on that learning! Sometimes budgets allow for only one round of qualitative research, so the "salad bowl" plan comes to the forefront with everything thrown into the lettuce: chick peas, tomatoes, baby corn, onions, peppers, olives, cheese, cucumbers, chicken, shrimp, steak, and radishes. That is a whole lot of flavors in one bowl! The back room might have three or four different types of listeners from brand managers, to the research and development (R & D) staff, to observers from the advertising agency, along with project managers and staff from the market research division and every now and then, someone from the legal division.

Sometimes the best salad is a simple one of greens, one other item, and a delicious dressing. However, simple usually gets thrown out the window and the "all you can eat" salad bowl is the only thing on the menu. This often leads to stimulus overload for respondents, for observers, and for the moderator.

Tiger # 1:

Too many concepts to test in a focus group [also applies to too many positioning statements, prototypes, advertisement strategies, etc.].

Solution # 1:

In order to tame this tiger, the moderator must **manage client expectations and direct research activities, rather than be an 'order taker' trying to fit in all requests to "make the client happy."** It is the job of the moderator to hold the line and provide research rigor, to ensure that qualitative research is used as an appropriate tool.

The right number of "things" to test [concepts, prototypes, advertisement strategies, or ideas, etc.], should not exceed six. If more are desired, then it is best to pick a core set of four that are seen by every group and rotate in a different satellite set in varying groups. The four that always get tested will get a good "read" by respondents and some insights can be gleaned from those not seen by everyone. The end result of this process might mean more research, but that is better than a "once over lightly" approach across multiple stimuli without sufficient time for a deep dive understanding.

Tiger # 2:

Too many varied tasks [package graphics, prototype products, desire for an ideal spokesperson, and new advertisement strategies – all in the same group].

Solution # 2:

When there are too many tasks and activities occurring in a two hour time frame, it is similar to having one teaspoon of each dish at a gourmet restaurant and no chance for the palate to really evaluate any one item. Or it may even feel like trying to do all the rides at Disneyland in three hours instead of three days. It is overwhelming for respondents, exhausting for moderators, and clients get snippets of information rather than in-depth conversations.

The goal should be to determine the priorities of all that is desired and devote the lion's share of group time to the top two activities related to the study purpose. It might mean working with the client team to outline all the desired parameters and then crafting a series of projects, so that all goals can be met. If budget is the driver, then only the topmost priorities can be considered and moderators should resist being bullied into trying to fit everything in as if everything asked for is totally necessary for decision making.

Again, it is the job of the moderator to be the captain of the research process, directing resources where they can do the most good. A good military captain would not send a squad of men in six different directions hoping that an enemy artillery position can be disabled by that decision. A good captain would concentrate the squad to fight in such a way that every move is an advance until the high ground is taken.

Tiger # 3:

Too many "research partners" on the study with competing needs. This might include: brand group staff, R&D members, advertising agency staff, members from market research, staff from the package design company, and sometimes folks from the legal division.

On a project for a product company, the market research director's wife attended because she wanted to see what her husband was doing when he said: *"I'll be late honey – I'm going to watch focus groups tonight."* She sent in a question for the moderator because she was curious about what the group would say. Her husband allowed her to do that even though her question was not relevant to the research itself. Rather, it focused on an artifact of group dynamics. However, when the question came into the room as a written note, the "author" had not signed her name, so the moderator did not know who sent in the question or the reason for the question. As a result, time was wasted on setting up the question and gathering respondent POBAs to something that did not even relate to the study, serving only the ego of an observer.

In another case, in a project commissioned by a cosmetics company, they invited their advertising agency as guests so all could hear unfiltered respondent comments about two different advertising strategies. Since the agency knew it was in danger of being replaced, they had a vested interested in getting some "buy in" on the strategies being tested and wanted to have some influence on the questions to be asked of respondents. They lobbied heavily for specific questions to be asked that were tangential to the research purpose because their "political issue" took precedence in their minds. As the moderator, it took every bit of dignity and grace to keep repeating that the purpose of the study was "x" not "y," and keep tempers cool.

Solution # 3:

When there are too many "research partners" on a project, some should be limited to the true role of "observers"—adding nothing to process other than just watching—they do not contribute any questions for the guide and they do not send any questions into the research room during the process – they just watch. Of course it never plays out that way – there is a sense of entitlement as an observer – *"I'm watching and I have an investment in the outcome."*

The "True Clients" are the ones who get to provide input into the research process: before, during, and after the event. However, as stated above, everyone behind the mirror has an investment and everyone wants a good return, so each individual aims to get their questions asked by the moderator.

Compare this process to passengers flying on an airplane. They buy a ticket, ride the flight from NYC to LA, and they have an investment in getting there. However, they do not get to pick the route, determine the speed of the aircraft, or determine the exit or arrival gates. In this case the "True Client" is the one in the co-pilot seat. The one flying the plane [pilot] is the moderator. The co-pilot serves as the navigator, giving direction to the pilot.

The moderator's role is to make sure the passengers are clear on the destination, clear on the departure and arrival times, and clear about the weather patterns. Other than that, they are told to wear their seatbelts, sit back, and enjoy the ride.

This would be ideal in the research field, but instead, the "passengers" want to come up to the flight deck and have conversations with the pilot and co-pilot. Therefore, it is the job of the moderator to make sure the door to the flight deck is kept locked throughout the whole flight!

On a practical level, I have learned to appoint a back room spokesperson (also known as a single point of contact or SPOC) who collects observers' questions. This spokesperson is the only one talking to the moderator. I no longer go behind the mirror to ask the backroom anything I meet the client spokesperson in the hallway ten minutes before the end of the group, and he/she tells me what is wanted in the time remaining. I also ask that no written questions are sent into the room until at least the forty minute mark, so that I have created deep rapport with respondents before having any interruptions.

Summary

While the solutions above are ones that work for me, I do not presume they will work for every moderator. Part of the reason they work for me may be due, in part, to the following:

a. I am secure in my role and responsibility as a moderator
b. I stay firmly focused on the purpose of the project and if what is requested is "off purpose," I can say *"No"* to clients with certainty
c. Being "liked" by the client is not my first priority, being respected is
d. I am willing to do what is right, not what is easy – holding a flag for research rigor

Even as a seasoned moderator, these three "tigers" still crop up from time to time when working with clients and I am quick to put my solutions into practice, so that projects move forward and expectations can be met. I have tamed these tigers, but still run the risk of snake bites from other problems that sinuously twine themselves around my body and squeeze the life from me while I am moderating! I will be working on snake charmer solutions as my career moves forward.

The Invisible Focus Groups in a Qualitative Research Project

> *There is more to a focus group than the actual focus group! Learn a holistic approach that values the importance of the invisible focus groups that bookmark the process—the focus group is never complete without the pre-focus group and post-focus group!*

When a client calls for qualitative research, the reasons are myriad and may range from a desire to know what and how target markets are thinking, to how they are making purchase decisions. Clients may be looking for insights underneath the impact of advertising or wanting more insights about what elements in a line extension have staying power. Or they may want exploratory research to uncover missing needs and gaps. The range of qualitative research is as wide as the diverse thinking of clients.

The job then, for the qualitative researcher working to meet client needs, is to be crystal clear on the study purpose and write the appropriate questions to discover the information needed from consumers. Over the years, I have learned that a focus group project is not just the four, six, eight, or ten plus groups that a client requests within the budget set aside for the study. There are some invisible groups that are not part of the final group count, but have a strong impact on planning the project and supporting the analysis. I am calling one a "pre-focus group" before the project starts and the other a "post-focus group" at the end of each day of the study and for sure on the last night in the last city. These "invisible" groups are not part of the planned number for the study, but can be a critical factor in the success of the study.

The "pre-focus group" is the conference call or meeting that sets up the study parameters. The moderator's job is to determine, usually from a group of diverse decision makers, across several teams or content areas of interest, what they want and the best way to help them get their desired outcomes. A set of three key questions form the planks in the platform of that "pre-focus group:"

- If the session were just one minute long, what key insights would you want to take away?
- What do you **not** want to hear about in the sessions—what data is of little interest to the team?
- What is going to happen after the study is completed—how will the data be used?

Of course, these are not the only questions to ask in the strategy planning session I am calling the "pre-focus group." Questions about city sites, regional issues, recruiting specs, budgets, timelines, number of observers, stipends, prototypes, concept/position statements, travel policies, and so on, are also a part of that session. The three questions above are simply the frame for getting the best data out of the research part of the visible qualitative sessions to ensure critical time is spent on getting the key data wanted, not just some answers to some questions.

Questions within the qualitative research session have their own separate life, and the best moderator guides go from general to specific across the face of the whole guide, echoing that strategy within each specific topic area of the guide. One way to picture the line of questions across the group is to see a triangular coffee filter and imagine that all the questions are ground beans. The moderator is the hot water pouring over the beans, and the resulting flow of coffee coming out the end of the filter is the answers from respondents! Across the whole scope of the session, each of the topic areas are smaller filters with different kinds of coffee beans— some are strong French roast beans; some are mild Mocha Java, and some are decaf.

Skilled moderators know that these rules work best to get respondents talking freely:

- Write true questions—ones to which the moderator does not know the answer—let respondents take the moderator into their universe.
- Write questions that do not put respondents on the defensive— but let them answer fully and freely.

- Write probing questions that allow respondents to open up. Know that "what else?" is a probe to get divergent answers, while "anything else?" is a probe that shuts down a line of answers in a group discussion.
- Write a variety of probes—not just the same two or three standard ones that start with "Tell me more about that."
- Write short questions that promote long answers (SQLA)
- Write questions that do not have part of the answer in the question (POAIQ). (For example: *"What are some reasons you grocery shop after 11:00 p.m.?—Is it because the store is less crowded or because they are restocking items?"*—The moderator should have stopped the question at 11:00 p.m. since what follows helps the respondent and shuts down their ability to express their own self-generated reasons).
- Write questions that flow logically along the path of how consumers think—not how researchers or clients think—that means sometimes asking context type questions to set an environment before diving into key issues.
- Write questions that create "rolls"—the group talking across the table to each other (one at a time) discussing the topic—not serial questions where the moderator asks and a respondent tells the moderator what he or she thinks, over and over in random order.

There are many other rules that also apply to writing effective guides, and this list is only intended to point to critical areas that should be considered when writing guides. If the reader can pull up a recent guide and use the above as a checklist, it would be ideal if at least seven items are checked off as present throughout the whole guide as an indicator to the quality of the questions posed to consumers.

The post-focus group session occurs at the end of each day the project is on the road and for certain on the last night in the last city. A good moderator has been listening intently throughout the focus group sessions and answering these internal questions along the way:

- Do I have enough data to analyze this topic area for this group in the report?
- Have I heard from at least two-thirds of the room on this topic?
- Are the answers I am getting helping to fulfill the study purpose?
- Did I lead respondents to what I wanted to hear or did I let them take me to their world?

Ideally, at the end of the day (and the end of the project), pull the clients from the back room into the focus group room and conduct the post-focus group, asking them these key questions:

- What did you hear tonight that was an "a-ha!" or "surprise"— something you did not expect?
- What did you hear tonight that was a confirmation—you expected to hear it and you did?
- What new thoughts were generated by observing tonight's groups (and at the end of the project)—across all groups?
- In what ways, if at all, did you hear any opportunity to meet new needs?
- How will the insights from these qualitative sessions fit into next phase of strategy planning?

If this session is also audio recorded, a transcript can be quickly and easily made and combined with any flip charts made in that post-focus group session and any "hot notes" made by the moderator across the series. Then a topline report, will be easy to write with all key points covered.

The power of the "invisible" focus groups before and after the study make the best use of the moderator's skill set: providing opportunities for a group of people to provide insights. On the front end, the session with the clients in the planning phase allows the development of a good cohesive plan with everyone's issues included or excluded by agreement. On the back end of the study, the post-focus group session makes sure that all walk away with a clear understanding that everyone heard the same key take-away points.

By seeing these two events—pre/post-focus groups that bookend the actual focus group sessions—as extensions of the focus group process, we can make the whole study congruent and balanced. This process enhances the benefits that qualitative research can provide by helping clients get the best out of this tool.

PART II: FOCUS GROUPS: TOOLS, TIPS, & TECHNIQUES

SECTION I: WORKING EFFECTIVELY WITH RESPONDENTS

Let Respondents Be Stars 185

The spotlight is on. It is time for the respondents to shine—and it is your job to help them! Learn different ways to dialogue with respondents, enriching your focus group data and making your work more fulfilling at the same time!

Diving Below Top-of-Mind 189

Learn from a Master Moderator™ how to get below easy top-of-mind answers and uncover what really makes consumers tick!

Best Practices for Testing Ads 195

How do you know if an advertising campaign is selling your product or service? You need a wide range of consumer insights to find your way to the campaign that is right for you. Come here for tips and techniques to guide your marketing future!

The BRUM Test: Going Beyond Likes/Dislikes When Testing Advertising
.... 199

How far apart are the worlds of advertising and of qualitative research? Learn how your work can help advertisers to understand the effect their ads have on consumers in terms of four vital elements: believability, relevance, uniqueness, and motivation.

Do Not Ask Me Why 207

Why?—Heavens! Do not ask it! Learn how to ask better questions by simple avoidance of a single word, expanding your vocabulary of questioning beyond "why" so that you can really elicit the responses you need.

Cross the Bridge—Enter the Respondent's World 213

"Hello, my name is… now tell me all about your perceptions, opinions, beliefs, and attitudes?" This may not be the perfect way to draw out good data from a focus group! Learn how to cross the great divide and step into the respondent's world.

Let Respondents Be Stars

> *The spotlight is on. It is time for the respondents to shine—and it is your job to help them! Learn different ways to dialogue with respondents, enriching your focus group data and making your work more fulfilling at the same time!*

In an intriguing conversation over wine and cheese at a friend's home in the late 1980s, I heard about a course called neuro-linguistic programming (NLP). As a trial lawyer, my friend told me that his firm was always looking for an edge to help win cases. He mentioned that a number of his firm's trial lawyers took NLP to help them better present cases to jurors. I noted the comments, but did not feel obliged to follow up on NLP, especially because the founders were from California: a known hotbed of weird workshops in my view, particularly at that time.

A few months later, I ran into my legal buddy again. He raved about the success his colleagues had when working with jurors, and he relayed that his firm obtained spectacular settlements out of a pair of trials. I wondered: what could those lawyers have done to acquire such results? Using my best moderator questions, I found the answers—and they were surprising. He told me that by carefully watching the jurors as data was revealed to them in case summaries or during opening/closing statements, the lawyers could predict with some accuracy how jurors would debate points. He mentioned that his colleagues could not read minds, but they could read faces. That skill gave them some advantages in deciding how to present case points.

Now I was intrigued. I researched when and where the course was offered, and I signed up for the six-month training: one long weekend seminar per month, from Thursday night to Monday night. It was by far one of the hardest courses I have ever taken—not just the content, but also jettisoning my rock-hard beliefs about how the mind works and the true key influences of behavior. I learned a whole set of jargon such as "representational sets" and "eye-accessing cues," and I unlearned a whole set of behaviors (no longer useful) such as reading body language.

One of the basic techniques I acquired in the course, which I apply daily as a moderator, is "pacing and leading." The premise is that when two or more people are engaged in a dialogue, one person leads and the other follows—and the roles can change in a flash.

In a therapeutic model, a good therapist lets the patient set the tone or pace for the session's first part by asking a question such as, *"How's it going since we last met?"* The patient begins to talk, establishing the pace for the amount and type of information revealed. After a short time, the therapist subtly directs the conversation—via a line of questions—so that the therapist is in control, leading the patient to talk about other areas. (This is not always visible to the patient.) Pacing and leading is the primary tool for advancing the session and resolving the patient's long-term problems.

Subtle Maneuvers

In focus groups, the best way to employ pacing and leading is with two steps. The result is a more dynamic session and more opportunities to get below "top-of-mind" responses.

Enter the world of respondents, and let them set the original pace of discussion. During these early moments of "rapport and reconnaissance," group norms are established, and the moderator learns how individual respondents venture forth to offer opinions.

For example, in talking with sexually-active teen girls about preventing pregnancy, it is not a wise idea to ask the obvious blunt questions: *"How do you prevent pregnancy?"* It makes more sense to ask a question that is wholly relevant to the topic, but from their viewpoint. For example, *"What are some of the names you use in your friendship network when you're talking about having sex with your boyfriend?"* The group usually laughs, then provides terms ranging from "doin' it" to "doing the nasty." They set the discussion's pace for a few moments, and an adept moderator uses one of those terms to introduce the next line of questions. *"When you are 'doing the nasty', but do not want the result to be a baby, what are some things you can do to prevent the outcome?"* And bingo, the moderator is leading them to the next round of data gathering.

Shift from Pacing to Leading as Smoothly as Possible

The trick is to think of the progression as the compartments of an ice cube tray. All the squares are the same size, and when you pour water in one end, you can fill the tray just by slightly tipping it; as the water from the tap hits the elevated end, it flows to all compartments. A good moderator makes moderating look like a dialogue when in fact it is a one-way conversation: "I ask, you answer, and I do not put opinions in the room." In the early part of any pacing and leading incident, the moderator arranges the environment to let respondents make the first of many wide-ranging comments, and then settles on one to lead the conversation where she wants it to go.

Let us suppose the moderator asks: *"What data does the Census Bureau collect every ten years?"* The answers might be number of rooms, number of bathrooms, number of adults and children, number of books read, amount of liquor consumed, type of exterior, and square footage in a household. Some of this is inaccurate (data about books and liquor). An adroit question by the moderator would seamlessly lead respondents to provide more specific information: *"How did you find out that the Census Bureau collects data on the number of books you read and the amount of liquor you drink?"*

In the ebb and flow of a session, a gifted moderator moves the water of discussion elements from one compartment to another—sometimes pacing, sometimes leading. The desired outcome is extracting respondent perceptions, opinions, beliefs, and attitudes. This helps clients understand how respondents think and feel about products, services, advertising, and ideas.

A Careful Introduction

I firmly believe that pacing and leading works best when the moderator has no "ego investment" in looking good or serving as entertainment for the back room. Sometimes the most effective leading is done with a set of questions making the moderator look a bit like an intellectual novice. For example: *"I know a lot about shampoos and conditioners, but I do not know how mousse works—can someone tell me about that product?"* or *"It has always been a mystery to me how a restaurant can serve one burger rare and one well-done and they both come out hot—how does that work?"* In this way respondents are the stars of the session.

If a moderator is invested in ensuring that her advanced degree is known and honored (*"Hello, I am Dr. Hairston, and I am leading the group tonight"*), then many respondents might unconsciously abdicate to a thinking premise of: *"I do not have a PhD, so I'll just wait until Dr. Hairston calls on me."*

Success means investing more in conducting good research than in looking good. A better opening would be: *"Hi, I am interested in hearing your thoughts on our topic tonight. I am good at asking questions but I do not know much about how XYZ works in your world. I am going to need your help to understand how you feel about tonight's topic, so I can accurately present your views to decision makers."* This opening asks for assistance and honors the group's ability to be smart about what it knows.

A skilled moderator asks questions in a way that lets respondents tell her what she might already know—and she never reveals how much she knows. That means packing the ego in a metaphorical suitcase, and checking it at the door.

Talking Points

After years of using pacing and leading techniques with respondents, I have gained several insights:

- I do not have to work so hard to obtain the data I want.
- Groups are more likely to fully answer any question I ask.
- Sessions are livelier and less apt to get bogged down with uncomfortable silences.
- Respondents usually will engage in more "ping-pong" dialogues with themselves than one-to-one responses with me.

I saw my lawyer friend at a social event earlier this year, and I again thanked him for his NLP recommendation twenty-five years ago. He asked, *"You still find that course useful?"* It was easy to answer yes. And then I paced and led him into a conversation that allowed him to share about his newest grandchild. As we parted, he said, *"It is always interesting to talk with you."* And I just smiled.

Diving Below Top-of-Mind

> *Learn from a Master Moderator™ how to get below easy top-of-mind answers and uncover what really makes consumers tick!*

Clients in qualitative research want to know what makes consumers tick, in terms of purchase decisions; sorting through options; and forming opinions about products, services, ideas, and advertising. They do not want to hear from consumers that they "like it" or "always buy name brands." These are obvious answers and do not provide much in the way of insights.

However, respondents are not accustomed to thinking deeply about their rationales for buying/not buying or liking/not liking products, services, or advertising. They can be great at answering direct questions such as, *"How often do you shop for dog food?"* But they tend to clam up when the questions are more abstract: *"What is the philosophy behind your decision about what to feed your dog to extend his life?"*

So qualitative researchers have developed ways to get below "top-of-mind" and help respondents access the drivers of their own unconscious behaviors. In the process, they are helping clients understand consumers so they can create better products, better services, and more effective advertising. It takes a few tools and techniques to help respondents access what is below their first rational thought about an issue of topic in a focus group discussion. The most basic element in this process is using ways that allow respondents to talk about inner thoughts without feeling like they are on the witness stand as a defendant or at the police station undergoing an inquisition.

The most common techniques rely on the simple process of projection. This means letting respondents talk about something internal as if it were outside of them. Many realize that in doing so, they are accessing core or internal thinking, but many are just relieved they do not have to say "I think" or "I feel" when reporting on actions that may be difficult to talk about. They are reassured that they do not have to self-reference or take responsibility for the impact on others of what they say.

In a focus group that included a review of a brochure on sexually transmitted disease prevention, it was necessary to get respondents to talk about how to get a partner to use protection. The subject population, age 18–24, was a group just coming to grips with their own sexuality. And although they had no trouble having sex, they did have trouble talking about it comfortably with people at a conference table.

The moderator used a scenario device to allow respondents to talk about the issue without revealing their own life experiences in the group discussion. They were presented with a short scenario about a fictional couple named Tracy and Dana, who were at the third date stage and contemplating consensual sex. Once the story was read, the ending was left unfinished and respondents were asked to tell the group what Dana would ask Tracy about wearing a condom and how Tracy might respond. A very lively discussion ensued, with respondents providing insights, and it was clear they were basing their advice on their own experiences. They laughed and joked about the mythical couple and, in doing so, revealed their attitudes.

In another example, respondents were asked to report on what "people in your ZIP code" might do if quarantined for a smallpox epidemic created by terrorists. At no time did the moderator ask, *"What would you do?"* Instead, she asked, *"How many people live in your ZIP code—best guess?"* Then she set up the scenario with a series of rapid-fire questions to get them thinking: *"Now think about those who live in a four-block radius of where you live and tell me about those people. How many are in apartments, how many are in houses, how many have cars, and how many take the bus to work?"* She created an opportunity for them to talk about their communities and allowed them to paint a picture that was broader than their own households, for the group to see where they have commonalities.

When respondents were asked to talk about 100 of those people and how they might react in a quarantine situation, some very interesting insights emerged. Those insights helped the client understand how people would circumvent a federal quarantine law and what their attitudes are about being restrained/constrained in the event of a terrorist disease-based action. This device also showed the client some issues it had not considered, such as the desire for individuals to be heroes when it comes to children and the elderly in their communities. A lot more data was garnered than could have been by directly asking, *"What would you do if…?"*

Sometimes projective techniques are simple, and sometimes they are more involved. The trick is to make sure the directions are clear so that respondents do not have to spend so much time understanding what they are to do. Rather, there should be quick and easy instructions, so the bulk of the time is spent doing the task quickly and then reporting about that task.

Qualitative researchers walk a fine line when using projective techniques because in some cases those techniques access information that is below the level of consciousness. And if they investigate too deeply, researchers run the risk of entering the area in the subconscious where trained therapists go to reach deep-seated issues.

The mark of an effective moderator is one who can ask questions that part the veil just enough to get at the core data of interest to clients. This means being able to gain an understanding of the drivers that are in place for specific behaviors, but staying shy of the Freudian overtones that might accompany those drivers.

An example of going just far enough presented itself in a recent research project. The client wanted to understand the drivers present when shopping for health and wellness items at a drugstore. The challenge was getting respondents to talk about the drivers and not the items they purchased.

The moderator asked respondents to bring a picture from a magazine that helped show how they felt when going to the store to buy items in the aisles stocked with health and wellness items, and to write a headline on the picture that captures that emotion.

It did not matter what was in the actual picture. What was important was hearing what respondents had to say about the picture and what it meant to them. Respondents were asked to show the group their picture, describe the picture, and then report the headlines they wrote to go with the picture. One respondent had a picture of tangled telephone wires bunched up in a pile and her headline was "Confusion and Twisted up in Knots." Another brought a picture of an angry woman yelling at another woman, and the headline was "I am So Mad that I Can't Find What I Want, I Could Spit."

This simple exercise works to get beyond top-of-mind because it focuses the respondents on feelings and emotions. The instructions were to bring a picture that shows how they feel when shopping for health and wellness items in a drugstore. They did not call for respondents to bring a picture that shows what they are thinking when they are buying that category of products.

This distinction between feeling and thinking is one of the critical factors in the game of projective techniques. Thinking is in the rational area, whereas feelings are in the emotional arena, and anything that helps access emotion or behavior is automatically below top-of-mind.

Sometimes it is tricky to get respondents to go to the emotional because that area is often "private" in the circle of communication. If you draw three concentric circles and label the outer one "Things I Would Tell Anyone," the middle circle "Things I Would Tell Someone I Trust," and the innermost circle "Things I Would Not Tell Anyone," the outermost circle can be seen as the rational/logical arena, the middle circle as the emotional, and the inner circle as where therapy sessions thrive.

Figure 3: *Circle of Communication*

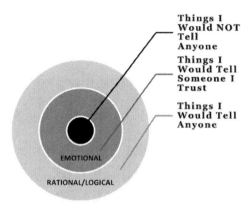

If the middle circle is to be accessed, respondents must first feel that they can trust the person or persons with whom they are sharing the information. In a QRE, the moderator must build up that trust at the rapport stage, reinforced early and often with comments from the moderator along these lines: *"Thanks for that insight—that's just the answer I am looking for."* Or, *"A-ha! I see—now I know how important it is to get a parking space near the door when you go to the 24-hour drugstore, to get something at 1:00 a.m."*

Trust is created when these factors are in place in a group discussion:

- Respondents are listened to, but not judged.
- All respondents are treated equally by the moderator.
- The moderator does not allow judgmental comments to be made by one respondent to another.
- From time to time, respondents are acknowledged for contributing with a "thanks," "I see," or "interesting, I never thought of it that way."

However, just because moderators ask how a respondent feels about the President not being elected for a second term does not mean that the answer they get accesses feelings. The moderator is just as likely to get a response such as: *"I think the President should have been reelected."* It is then up to the moderator to probe to get at the feelings by asking: *"What did you say to yourself when you found out he wasn't reelected?"* Then one can hope to get an answer such as: *"It is a crying shame he did not—he could have turned this country around in a second term."* This gives the moderator an open door to feelings by a third probe: *"You say it is a crying shame, tell me more about that feeling."* And bingo! The moderator is below the rational circle and into the emotional circle with a respondent.

In qualitative research, what counts is what cannot be counted, and that means asking questions that access feelings. These questions also should allow clients to see how consumers make decisions and sort options. When respondents invite you to visit them in their worlds and allow you to probe that area below top-of-mind, it is important to respect the privilege given and to honor that invitation with dignity.

Good qualitative researchers have developed ways to get below top-of-mind and help respondents access the drivers of their own unconscious behaviors. Master Moderators™ do that with ease—similar to an Olympic skater who nails that triple-triple combination and lands going backward, yet still has the presence of mind to smile.

Best Practices for Testing Ads

> *How do you know if an advertising campaign is selling your product or service? You need a wide range of consumer insights to find your way to the campaign that is right for you. Come here for tips and techniques to guide your marketing future!*

"Is this advertising campaign working? Will it sell the product or service?" These are the two key questions that advertising agencies have when they use qualitative research to help understand how a campaign resonates with consumers. Qualitative researchers, both the ones In-house and the vendors who serve advertising agencies, must walk the thin tightrope that allows them to test a campaign and, at the same time, avoid leading the consumers to a particular viewpoint. This ensures agencies have the best data to make decisions about the content and the best method for advertising.

What gets tested in qualitative research, either in IDIs, mini-groups, or full groups under the header "communication checks," can be any of the following stimuli: concepts, position statements, storyboards, marker comps, swipe art, mood boards, rough-cut television spots, final spots for radio or television, head shots, tag lines, headlines, jingles, spokespersons, product shots, and scripts. Sometimes, during a qualitative project, new or additional campaigns are thrown into the mix for testing or current ones are changed with white-out and sticky tape, so new ideas can be tested right on the spot.

The request for advertising research is sometimes on shorter timelines than for other research because the need to get it tested is driven by pressing demands from the agency's client to "get the word out about our new item" and start making sales. It is not unusual for researchers to get a call with this request: *"We have two campaigns and three strategies to test for each one… can we get into the field early next week?"*

While the request makes everyone from the moderator to the field service feel a little rushed, we know the special demands of advertising agencies. A good team springs into action to help the agency and their product/service client to get the voice of the consumer into the advertising development process to check the resonance of advertisements.

Advertising Research Challenges

Once the sites are chosen and the recruiting specs defined, the challenge becomes what to test and what the research needs to provide for decision making. What makes it a challenge for the researcher? We do not usually get to see what we are going to be testing too much in advance. It is typical for an advertising agency to work on stimuli to show to consumers, right up to the hours before the first interview. Sometimes it is because they do not get sign-off from their client until the eleventh hour, and sometimes it is because they are struggling with how to make the advertisements stand out from the clutter of all the other advertisements and specifically from the advertisements for the competition. There also are philosophical points of view to be ironed out between the art director, the copywriter, and the account executives (not to mention senior agency staff) that are ultimately responsible for any advertisement created.

Over the years, I have developed some ways to test advertising even when I do not see the elements until just before the first time they are presented to consumers. My plan includes getting a broad overview from the client on what will be tested and what might be tested. That way I have questions and strategies for all eventualities. For example, the client may say, *"We want to have the rough cut video ready for testing, but we may have just to show the storyboards."* I tell the facility to have video players on standby for me in case I have a video format to show. As well, I ask them to assign me to the room with a display rail in case I have to show storyboards and also to have an audio player on tap in case clients want me to play recorded voice-overs of advertising agency staff reading text or singing jingles.

Another part of my plan is to get to the facility a full two hours before the first interview to meet with and get a briefing from the developers of the materials to be tested. That way I am clear on what the advertisement elements are and what research questions need to be asked.

The last part of my plan is to resist the desire to whine and complain about how much uncertainty or requests for changes are present in the study. Instead I embrace the positive dynamism of having a chance to test materials that will be seen by millions of consumers. Sometimes, I am at home watching a TV show and see an advertisement in final form that I presented months before in a research environment. I see how the client has taken the voice of the consumer (VOC) and fine-tuned the advertisement to hit the key points, and I excitedly tell my husband: *"Look—here's my ad!"* Seeing those advertisements in my living room often makes all the headaches along the way worth it!

Tips and Techniques

The trick to getting the widest range of insights includes finding ways to avoid a thought leader driving the discussion about elements of an advertisement. I use some simple worksheets to capture private thoughts before the open forum discussion and then compare those worksheets against the transcript to make sure what they wrote down privately is congruent with the ensuing discussion.

Another technique is to make sure that, where possible, each person has a copy of what is being evaluated—the concept, a mini-version of the storyboard, or the tag line. When respondents hold the item under discussion in their hands, they become invested in it, and the conversation about it is richer. When they do tasks with the item (e.g. circle key words or put question marks on it or underline elements), they pay closer attention and go deeper into thinking about what they are looking at. When they fill out short worksheets that allow them to think privately before talking aloud, they have a chance to think quietly the way they would at home and bring that "private viewing" experience into the research discussion.

I have developed some question categories that tend to work regardless of what is being tested in the way of stimuli—shifting the discussion to get in these questions that are of key interest to the client:

- What is this advertisement all about?
- Who is it talking to—you or someone else?
- What are the key messages?
- What is the single most important message?
- What, if anything, is unclear?
- What, if anything, is missing?
- What do you find appealing?
- What turns you off?
- In what ways, if at all, does it make sense?
- In what ways, if at all, is it plausible?
- What is your view: standard, fare, or unique?
- What, if any questions, are raised in your mind?
- Which is true: a call to action, a reason to consider, or neither?

Over the years, I have learned not to ask, *"Based on what you see here, would you buy this product or service?"* On the surface, it seems to be a good question—a way to prove the advertisement is effective. However, in the climate of qualitative research, the answer cannot be trusted because it asks the consumer to comment on an act that will take place outside the room and in the future. A researcher can ask the degree to which the advertisement has "stopping power" or the ability to create interest (pull) or disinterest (push) and this pull/push element is of more value to an advertising agency than: *"I might buy XYZ based on this advertisement."*

The pull/push factor or stopping power of an advertisement can be checked right in the research room, making the responses more relevant for the advertising agency. Respondents can also be asked to comment on what would enhance the advertisement for them or what improvements would solve some of the problems they felt the advertisement might have.

The last area of key importance in advertising research is to respect what the consumer has to say. Forty years ago, TV advertising was new, and magazine advertisements were fewer. Now, the consumer is very savvy about subliminal messages and images, the power of tag lines, the influence of spokespersons, and the way advertisements are targeted culturally. They even have the terminology that was once only heard at agencies: *"Aren't you worried you might cannibalize your parent product with this line extension?"* says the systems engineer from Houston!

Good researchers learn to honor what consumers have to say because they know what makes them pay attention when an advertisement leaps out of the clutter. Good researchers also understand the power of keeping consumers in the living room during a commercial, as well as appealing to their higher senses or their primal emotions. Consumers watch carefully to see how ethnic groups are treated in advertisements, and they listen carefully to see if the advertisement has a putdown in it—real or implied. A good advertising agency listens to consumer viewpoints and embraces those elements that help the agency craft an advertisement that really speaks to consumers and invites them to try a product or service.

I am privileged to have been the researcher on a number of advertisements that have since become icons in American advertising. For example, at Kentucky Fried Chicken, I was at the group discussion where the respondent said the statement that led to: *"We do chicken right."* I also tested landmark advertisements for Miller beer as well as the headshots that led to the new look for Aunt Jemima products. I credit the success of those advertisements to crafting research that let the advertising agency hear from consumers directly, without filters.

The net/net of advertising research is that it is always challenging and infinitely interesting. Those who walk this tightrope best are flexible, open, and creative to meet the demands of agencies and provide them with quality input via the VOC.

The BRUM Test: Going Beyond Likes/Dislikes When Testing Advertising

How far apart are the worlds of advertising and of qualitative research? Learn how your work can help advertisers to understand the effect their ads have on consumers in terms of four vital elements: believability, relevance, uniqueness, and motivation.

    Years of watching TV advertisements; reading advertisements in magazines and newspapers; and seeing billboards and advertisements shown with the previews in movies, have trained Americans how to watch advertisements, what to listen for, and when to be charmed or annoyed by what they see. They know when the spokesperson is authentic and when he/she has been paid to tout a product or service. They know how before-and-after pictures have been retouched to make a case, and they know what promises are likely to be fulfilled when they buy a product/service and when they are buying "hope."

    With the plethora of advertisements aimed at consumers and the innumerable different media types, we all see advertisements aimed for us and for targeted groups as we move through our lives. Consumers know to tune out when an advertisement for skateboards is shown on the Disney channel as they prepare dinner for the family. They know when to pay attention when an advertisement is shown during the nightly news that reports the tax-free shopping day will be the following Friday. They understand the concept of targeted advertisements by being the focus of some advertisements and not the focus of others.

    Advertisers are challenged to present advertisements that engage and interest consumers through the clutter of other advertisements to make their product/service one that consumers remember, so it is purchased the next time that product/

service category presents itself in the marketplace. **Smart advertisers know it is wise to test advertising concepts, strategies, and executions before deciding on which advertisement to run widely for consumers to see. That is where qualitative research can play a key role in helping advertisers understand the effect advertise**-ments have on consumers.

It is up to the qualitative research consultant to devise questions and activities that get below top-of-mind reactions from consumers. The researcher must also determine what emotions are generated in the minds of consumers, which message is remembered, and what image of the product/service/manufacturer is left when the advertisement has been viewed. It is of little importance in the scheme of advertising review if consumers like or dislike an advertisement. One past pundit said it well: *"It doesn't matter what they say about you in the press as long as they spell your name right."* Some of the most remembered advertisements are those that are unpleasant, loud, or brash. Not only is the advertisement remembered, but the product/service as well.

A good example of this is an advertisement from the 1960s for a record store that sold albums of pop music in the Washington, D.C.; Maryland; and Virginia area. The name of the record store was Kemp Mill Records, named after a local geographic site. The ad started with an annoying announcer saying, *"Kemp Mill breaks the records!"* followed by the sound of a hammer hitting and breaking a stack of records. The advertisement was loud and annoying and every teenager in the tri-state area knew the record store. While there were many other stores selling the same record, many teens made the trip out to Kemp Mill Records because they knew they could get a good discount and the records would always be in stock. They were one of the largest sellers of records for years. Talk to any baby boomer today who grew up in that area and mention the name Kemp Mill Records. Most likely they all will remember the tag line. That is a pretty powerful advertising memory for a store that is now out of business.

The annoying old lady who repeated *"Where's the Beef"* or *"I have fallen and I can't get up"* are other examples of how an advertisement can go against the grain and make itself memorable using the "annoyance factor."

In a focus group or IDI, respondents are shown an advertisement (e.g. on a monitor, via storyboard or marker comp, or they listen to a radio spot) and asked to review it and make comments. Sometimes they see an advertisement at the draft stage, and sometimes closer to being finished.

We can measure what is important to advertisers in four dimensions:

- Believability
- Relevance
- Uniqueness

- Motivation

Before diving into these areas, it is good to get reactions to the advertisement overall and progress from the general to the specific down a logical path in order to understand the impact of the advertisement and the message it leaves behind.

A good way to get below top-of-mind and into the thinking of respondents is to start with questions such as these:

- *"What is this advertisement about?"*
- *"What is the story told by this advertisement?"*
- *"Thinking back, what elements of the advertisement stand out in your memory?"*
- *"Tell me what you would tell a friend or family member about anything you saw/remembered in this advertisement."*

This approach lets the researcher see if respondents can report on the context of the advertisement and the single overarching theme. For example, respondents see an advertisement for dog food. In this advertisement, a puppy with a red bow around his neck plays with a ten-year-old boy. As the boy throws a stick and the dog chases it, the voiceover says: *"Feed your puppy XX, and he'll grow up to be strong."* After viewing the advertisement, one would expect to hear this story reported by respondents: *"This advertisement is about a little boy who has gotten a puppy for his birthday. If he wants the puppy to grow up strong, so he can always bring back the stick, you should feed him XX brand of food."*

That would be a "clear read" and all the insight one would need about the "message" of the advertisement. It is not as effective to ask: *"What is the message of this advertisement?"* because consumers do not think about messages. They think about stories.

After understanding the story and the message of the advertisement, now it is up to the researcher to perform the BRUM test on the advertisement shown to consumers to get beyond the message.

B: Believability

The "B" of the BRUM test is meant to see if the advertisement makes sense, supports the notion of "willing suspension of disbelief," and hangs together as the story unfolds. The key questions to ask respondents to uncover the degree of believability include the following:

- "*In what ways, if at all, does this advertisement make sense?*" (The probe to follow up is: "*Where is it going?*")
- "*To what degree, if at all, can you believe what is promised in this advertisement or not?*"
- "*How, if at all, does this advertisement hang together and move logically from point to point, from beginning to end?*"

When advertisements do not make sense to consumers, they feel frustrated or stupid. They translate that discomfort into not liking the product/service and the company that presents it. When an advertisement makes sense, consumers feel empowered and knowledgeable. They tend to think well of the product/service, even if they are not the desired target for the product. This carryover benefit reaches not only the targeted consumer but makes the non-targeted consumer one to carry "word-of-mouth" praise when the subject around that product/service comes up in conversation.

For example, a non-mother works in an office environment with a newly pregnant mother-to-be who works on her team. The non-mother watches TV on a regular basis and sees advertisements for diapers but pays little attention to them. When a conversation occurs at the office about the benefits of cloth diapers over disposables during a team lunch, the non-mother has the opportunity to say something such as: "*I saw this advertisement for XX diapers, and it said they were softer than cloth and prevented diaper rash because they wicked wetness away from the baby's skin, and cloth diapers hold the wetness next to the skin.*" This non-targeted consumer is now an advocate for the XX brand of diapers because she found the advertisement believable, and she alerts the mother-to-be about a brand to put into her consideration set as she becomes a heavy user of the category after the birth of the baby.

R: Relevance

The R in the BRUM test stands for relevance and refers to those to whom the advertisement should speak. For example, an advertisement for vacation travel to Disneyland is aimed primarily at parents and kids, while an advertisement for a new day spa site is primarily aimed towards women. The questions to ask respondents around this issue are: "*In what ways, if at all, is this advertisement talking to you or someone else— and if you, what is it promising? If it is talking to someone else, who is that person, and how are they different from you?*"

Most researchers know, when they hear the dreaded comment of "*Oh, it would be good for seniors*" for a product aimed at teens, that the relevance factor is way off. If some respondents say that it is talking to them and others say it is not, it is fertile ground to explore in discussion to tease out the dichotomy.

The degree to which an advertisement "talks" to the intended targeted consumer is an important factor of how well that advertisement may work in the marketplace.

U: Uniqueness

The next area in the BRUM test is the "U" for uniqueness. There are three aspects to uniqueness. One refers to how the advertisement is different from other advertisements in the category. Another aspect measures how "wacky/way out" is this advertisement? The third factor focuses on whether the product itself is unique in some way. The trick is to first discover which unique aspect is the advertisement promoting as a primary impact and move forward to see if it is communicating any other uniqueness aspects.

Questions to ask if it is the same/different than other advertisements in this category:

- *"Could I replace the name of the product/service in this advertisement with a competitor, and would the advertisement still work?"*
- *"Does this advertisement make a promise that no competitor can ever hope to beat?"*
- *"Does this advertisement make you think about this product/service in a new way or the classic way you have always thought about it?"*

Questions to ask if the advertisement is "wacky/way out" in the unique factor:

- *"Does the fact that this advertisement is very different hurt or harm the level of information about the product/service being offered?"*
- *"Is the level of 'wacky/way out' style helping to make the product information memorable or not?*
- *"What will people say when they talk about this advertisement—the clever wacky/way out style or the product/service being sold?"*

Questions to ask if the uniqueness of the product is a factor:

- *"Is the product or some feature of the product different from others in the same category?"*
- *"What makes this product stand apart (above or below) from others in the category?"*

- *"Is there anything about the product that distinguishes it from similar items and makes it memorable in your mind?"*

It is interesting to note that many advertisements are not unique when it comes to presenting information. For example, take Chevy and Ford Trucks. Past campaigns for one have the tagline *"Chevy Trucks: Like a Rock,"* the other says *"Built Ford Tough."* That is essentially the same message, and the advertisements could be exchanged, so that one could read: *"Ford Trucks: Like a Rock"* and the other could say *"Built Chevy Tough."* What made each advertisement stand out was not the uniqueness of the taglines or the presentation of information, but rather, over time, the way each car company created a story around their slogans with images that resonated in the minds of viewers. A Ford truck dropped from a one-story building is never confused with a Chevy truck on top of an Arizona mesa.

At the time the concepts for both were first tested, neither would have gotten a "unique" score. But now, consumers remember both as "different/unique" because of the story that has been woven around them.

M: Motivation

The last area of the BRUM test is a dicey one: the "M" factor for motivation. Some clients want moderators to ask respondents: *"Will you buy the product/service you have been seeing advertisements for?"* On the surface that seems benign, but in reality any response given at that point in time is unreliable since the buying behavior will be in the future and outside of what is being discussed in the research setting where the question was posed.

Of more value to clients is to ask respondents about motivations now that they have seen the advertisements. By asking questions such as the following, a researcher can uncover the drivers that make for a particular set of motivations now held by the consumer:

- *"What did you hear/see in the advertisements that make you want to know more about the product/service?"*
- *"What, if anything, did you hear/see that pulls you toward this product/service?"*
- *"What, if anything, did you hear/see that pushes you away from this product/service?"*

Exploring the pull/push factor with respondents generates a lot of information about elements of the advertisement that create interest/appeal (pull) or confusion/dislike (push). From that understanding, advertisers can move along a dimension from tweaking to replacing elements creating a final advertisement that is consistent with strategy, helps them stand out from the clutter of other advertisements and, hopefully, drives increased sales.

In analyzing the BRUM scores for advertisements or concepts tested, it is lovely when an advertisement pulls a 4.0 for all four factors, winning with consumers. But a score of three out of four that is mentioned for one advertisement or concept is a good thing as well.

If one were to review 100 advertisements currently running on TV now, they would find that many score well on "B," "R," and "M" factors, and only a rare few also get the "U" score. Three out of four is wonderful when testing advertisements!

When considering questions to ask respondents, either in IDIs or group settings about advertising, try some of the ideas expressed in this article. Hopefully researchers can move beyond *"What did you like/dislike about this advertisement?"* or *"What changes would you make to this advertisement to make it more appealing?"* and help their clients get below top-of-mind with consumers.

Do Not Ask Me Why

> *Why?—Heavens! Do not ask it! Learn how to ask better questions by simple avoidance of a single word, expanding your vocabulary of questioning beyond "why" so that you can really elicit the responses you need.*

It is not at all unusual for journalists to ask celebrities questions like this in an interview: *"Why did you take that role in your last movie?"* or *"Why did you divorce him after only three weeks of marriage?"* or *"Why did you not want to sign the prenuptial agreement from the millionaire boyfriend?"*

Typically, interviewees answer those type of questions, sometimes openly and sometimes in a more guarded way, simply because they are celebrities. Americans are accustomed to those kinds of questions when they watch TV interviews or read them in a magazine. They know that a journalistic interview is a thinly disguised "grill session" to roast the interviewee over the coals in the hope they will let down their guard and say something provocative. In our non-celebrity lives we also ask and answer a great many "why" questions in the course of the day, and we do not think much about the word itself.

The use of the word "why" is debated among qualitative researchers, and it inspires strong controversy. At a recent industry association speech, in which alternatives to "why" as a question were discussed, a participant raised her hand and said: *"I think if you use a soft inflection and do not sound judgmental, I do not see any reason you can't use this simple one-word question—it is already in common use everywhere."* The room started to buzz, and then the room split down the middle with those feeling strongly that "why" was a poor phrase and wasteful of discussion time in interviews, and those who thought: *"I use it all the time… works for me—what's the big deal?"* Yes, the word works in that it can produce an answer from a respondent, but is that answer deep or useful?

The Case Against "Why" as a Qualitative Question

All of qualitative market research is based on the "why premise." Our goal is to understand why customers do or do not buy something, why they like/do not like an advertisement, why they have not changed their style of eye-makeup since 1957, etc. We want to know the reasons why, but using the actual word "why" does not get us there. It almost seems that if that word is used, the game is lost. In practicality what happens is that when a "why" question is asked, a probe is needed to follow up and get the reasons for the answer given. Some examples:

- **Q:** *"Why do you buy Cool Gel toothpaste?"*
- **A:** *"Because it tastes great and it is fun to use."*
- **Probe:** *"What makes Cool Gel fun?"*

- **Q:** *"Why haven't you registered to vote in the last thirty years?"*
- **A:** *"I do not think we have a real democracy in America so why should I vote?"*
- **Probe:** *"What makes you think we do not have a democracy?"*

- **Q:** *"Why have you continued to use the same brand of paper towels for the last ten years?"*
- **A:** *"Because that brand is what I am used to."*
- **Probe:** *"How did you get used to the brand over the years?"*

This simple test proves the "weakness" of a "why" question. The probe is a better question than the why question! See how easy it would be to just ask the probe without wasting time on a "why" question that does not allow the respondent to go deep enough in responding? Each of the questions above supply an answer, but is that answer rich enough to write up a research finding after it is asked across four groups? No, it is not, but the probe could lead us there. Look what happens when the "why" is gone, the rational "because" defense answer disappears, and the category question is phrased to get below top-of-mind:

- **Q:** *"What are some of the reasons you buy Cool Gel toothpaste?"*
- **A:** *"I prefer a gel to paste—makes my teeth feel cleaner and the taste of gel seems to be more pepperminty than toothpaste. Also there is something whimsical and fun seeing that stripe on my toothbrush—makes it more like something fun to do to brush my teeth… not some boring ritual I do because I want to have strong teeth and fresh breath."*

- **Q:** *"You mentioned you haven't registered to vote in the last thirty years—what led to that decision?"*
- **A:** *"I am almost embarrassed to answer because I know people died so I could vote… but people also died because I did vote. Votes like mine put John Kennedy into office, and he supported Martin Luther King, and he put his brother in place as Attorney General, and all of them were killed, and that's because we voted John Kennedy into office. Those murders proved to me that there are forces in this country that make the fact that we are a democracy a lie. We might vote someone in, but if the dark forces do not like those choices, they just 'remove' people by assassination and put their puppets into place. So I do not vote anymore because I do not think my vote really makes any difference."*

- **Q:** *"What has made you loyal to the same brand of paper towels for the last ten years?"*
- **A:** *"You know, it is funny that you ask. I do not consider myself 'loyal' as much as I consider myself having made a smart choice of Deltina brand ten years ago, and they have always delivered what I want in a paper towel."*
- **Probe:** *"And what do you want in a paper towel?"*
- **A:** *"Plenty on the roll, easy to get on the rod in the kitchen, a choice of sizes in one sheet—either full or half, and always a chance to buy with a coupon."*

Just look at the depth of information when the word "why" is not used. "Why" questions by their very nature ask for a rational answer.

- **Q:** *"Why do you drive a stick shift car?"*
- **A:** *"Because it means I have more control."*

The next natural probe would be: *"What is the benefit to you of having more control?"*

- **A:** *"I can feel the road. I can react quickly to situations without using the brakes, and it keeps me involved in the driving process."*

"Why" questions force short, rational answers that require further probes. Those secondary probes break up the internal dialogue the moderator wants to elicit without respondents editing themselves. If "why" had been asked differently, the probe would not have been needed and the respondent would have gone beyond the top-of-mind level more quickly.

- **Q:** *"What are some factors leading you to drive a stick shift car?"*
- **A:** *"I have got more control. It lets me feel the road. I am more involved in the act of driving. It makes me feel cool, and it gives me options in bad weather."*

The word "factors" supports the respondent in answering with a list and gives him less reason to edit his thoughts. Further, he does not feel like he has to defend himself against the "attack" of a "why" question.

Many of RIVA's students believe that adjusting their tone of voice so they do not sound judgmental makes "'why" acceptable. It seems, on first blush, that it might work, but the "why" question is too imbedded in Western society. It is often used by authority figures to put people on the spot. No matter how warmly "why" is posed, it feels like a loaded question in the mind of the person asked. "Why" evokes the defense "because," which does not tell us very much. The moderator has lost the chance to get a rich response without a separate probe. Better to go for the probe without "why" first.

During an exercise in a recent class, the trainer asked for a volunteer to answer some questions about what led to his enrolling in the class. All the trainer did was thoughtfully ask a series of "why" questions, and when they answered the first one they were asked the "why" for that answer. By the fourth "why" question asked in a warm tone with a smile by the trainer, the student had crossed his legs and arms in a "ward off" pose and started to get a bit red in the face and breathe more quickly. When asked later how it felt to answer those "why" questions, he also reported an increase in heart rate and feeling hot and feverish. He also reported he felt like a child or an employee getting grilled by a parent or a boss. Is that how we want respondents to feel? Probably not. What, then, are some alternatives to asking "why?" Questions like these have proved useful to RIVA moderators over the past thirty years:

- *"What are some reasons that…?"*
- *"How did you form that viewpoint?"*
- *"What drives your thinking about…?"*
- *"Tell me about the situation that led up to your thinking this way."*
- *"What makes you do 'x' instead of 'z' in that situation?"*
- *"When you do 'x', what do you say to yourself about it?"*

I remember asking my husband a few years back: *"Why are you late for dinner?"* when he got home an hour later than promised. His first response was to yell back: *"Why are you nagging me?"* and that set off a tit for tat shouting match that went several rounds between them. It became very clear that the source of the shouting match was standing on that simple word "why?"

In later years of that same marriage, I learned to frame questions to avoid unpleasant debates such as that and create more productive dialogues.

"Why are you late?" turned into *"What happened today that caused you to be late to dinner?"* And the answer sounded more like this: *"You won't believe the domino effect that led to my being late! It started with having the wrong fax number for the client and repeated efforts to send a fax with no hope of it going through. So I left later than planned and ran into that one-lane part of the Beltway just off Georgia Avenue where they are still doing construction. I know we moved fewer than one hundred feet every twenty minutes. I hate when that happens, and you just have to creep along until you get to an exit to get off and take surface roads."*

So after many years of avoiding "why" in research settings, I also avoid it in my personal life! Both areas work much more smoothly now, and I am convinced that better questions than "why" ones result in better customer service, longer answers in research, and more compassionate dialogues in social settings. All by taking out one simple word—"why"—and finding better ways to get deeper answers to critical questions of interest.

Cross the Bridge—Enter the Respondent's World

> *"Hello, my name is… now tell me all about your perceptions, opinions, beliefs, and attitudes?" This may not be the perfect way to draw out good data from a focus group! Learn how to cross the great divide and step into the respondent's world.*

When I get a contract to conduct focus groups, mini-groups, or in-depth interviews (IDIs), my attention is on getting the answers that the client needs for the next round of decision making. My clients may ask me to find out what respondents think of the advertising campaign variations, what they like or dislike about the new package design, or how the client might use the new line extension for dusting cloths to help consumers do a better job of housekeeping.

Clients want to garner perceptions, opinions, beliefs, and attitudes (POBAs) from respondents so they can craft new products or services or sell their existing services in a better way. They all want a window into the thinking of their target markets so they can move forward on strategic plans. It is my job to help them get the data to do that.

Once we agree on the research model (e.g. mini-groups of friendship networks, focus groups of strangers, or IDIs with mothers of handicapped children), the next step is crafting a guide to ask the right questions.

Respondents are recruited and invited to *"participate in an individual or group discussion about_____topic."* Not too much is revealed prior to the discussion so respondents' comments can be spontaneous. Sometimes we give them homework to jump-start their creative thinking. For example, they might be asked to bring pictures of how they have decorated their bathrooms or a collage that shows how they think about their pets. However, most come to talk about "X" for a fixed period of time for a fixed stipend amount and know only that they will be giving their opinions about a specific topic.

At the end of some groups, I ask respondents some of the reasons they came to the group or individual interviews beyond the chance to get paid for their opinion. Here are some sample responses I have gotten over the years:

- *"I was curious and wanted to know what other people thought about _____."*
- *"I wanted my voice to be heard. I feel strongly about _____ and wanted my viewpoint to be on record."*
- *"I have been having problems with_____, and I thought by coming to this group discussion, I might learn something that would help me."*
- *"I thought it would be fun."*
- *"I wanted to make a difference in the future of_____. By coming to this session, I felt I might be able to shape the outcome."*
- *"I heard about focus groups, and I thought it would be interesting to see research in action."*
- *"I thought I might get some advance information before _____ is seen by the general public."*

It is important to realize that respondents do not share the same reason for participating as clients! Respondents do not care about line extensions, more shelf space, or the true benefits of a royal blue vs. a teal blue box for the product. They do not really care about the pricing difference between the regular and the plus-size product, and they do not really care how the new logo looks for that famous bank.

What they do care about includes making sure they have been heard, that their opinions are respected, that it is safe to say what they really think, and that they are valued as customers or potential customers.

They also care about having a say in what products or services are being sold in their country.

What Young Mothers Know

When I write the guide for a qualitative research session, it seems to work best to enter the conversation where the respondent is—not where the client is. Starting in the respondent's world makes more sense to them and creates a sense of safety. Later, when I invite them to come over to my world, they hardly notice the bridge they have to walk over.

I learned this lesson from an early group discussion with unwed teen mothers at the start of my career as a moderator. My client wanted to get their opinions on ways to prevent teen pregnancy so a federal agency could produce posters and brochures for use by junior high and high school counselors. As a young moderator in the 1970s I waded into the deep end of the pool first, and in my first group I started the session with these questions:

- *"What have you learned about being pregnant as a teen?"*
- *"What advice would you give to one hundred teen girls if they wanted to avoid pregnancy?"*

The room shut down almost immediately, and many of them looked like I had just slapped them. These fifteen and sixteen-year-old girls thought that I was judging them and using them as guinea pigs for some big experiment.

For the next group, I entered their world first before asking questions from the client world. These questions opened the group discussion and opened the respondents as well:

- *"When is your baby due?"*
- *"What are you having: a boy or a girl?"*
- *"What names are you considering for a boy/for a girl?"*
- *"Had a baby shower yet? If so, what did you get?"*
- *"If not, what are you looking forward to as gifts?"*
- *"Have you taken any classes or read anything to get ready for the baby?"*
- *"Who's going to be with you when you deliver?"*
- *"Who has been giving you advice while you are pregnant?"*
- *"What are you looking forward to when the baby comes?"*
- *"What worries you about the process of being a mother?"*

With this line of questions, I entered their world, and they could not wait to tell me about their thoughts, concerns, and dreams. They gave me the natural bridge to cross to ask about the choice to have or not have the baby, the role of the father in the process of parenting, and how it would affect their lives. They had great advice for how to avoid getting pregnant, and they made me laugh with all the new names for sex that teens use beyond "doing it."

The findings from this round of focus groups produced a line of public service announcements on preventing teen pregnancy that won the Ad Council's highest award that year. Those young women in that study taught me a valuable lesson that I have never forgotten, and the client got a whole lot more than they expected.

Ever since that early study, I have written questions from the respondent point of view by asking myself, **what would respondents naturally want to talk about first on the topic of "X"?**

The Client-Respondent Divide

My biggest battle has been with clients who want to write the guide and hand it to me as if it were a script for a Broadway play. They want to control what questions are asked, and they almost never write the guide from the respondent's viewpoint.

I have one client who has argued with me for years about the questions he wants asked to open every one of his groups: *"What do you think about the state of the U.S. economy these days?"*

Now, the topic he wants me to address in most of his focus groups is always something political such as: *"Should women be sent into combat zones in wartime?"* or *"Should taxes fund local charter school programs?"* But he likes to start his groups with large global questions before he dives into the key political issue, so he can see how the group handles an abstract question.

This client still wants his global question to kick off the group, but now he allows me to ask one that more closely aligns with the lives of the participants: *"What worries you most these days about living in America?"*

Usually one of the answers from the respondents is tenuously related to the topic at hand. When they get near, I hook onto this by asking, *"Carole mentioned that she worries about her kids getting a good education. Where are the rest of you on this topic?"* And then I am off and running down the political path to the line of issues that interest my client. He gets his global abstract question, and I get an invitation into the world of the respondent.

Another client does not like me to spend time on the introductions or the easy rapport-building questions. It took me a long time to convince her that I need an emotional handshake with respondents before I ask them to share their POBAs freely with me. I have convinced her that the early rapport questions let me enter their world, and it is the way I pay my dues to their sorority or fraternity of opinions.

Because she still sees those early questions as "time-wasters," we have agreed that she should come to the 6 p.m. group at 6:15 p.m. when the first "pay dirt" questions are being asked. For the 8 p.m. group she goes out to the lobby to check her voicemails and comes back at 8:15 or 8:20 p.m. That way she does not have to watch me gain entry to the world of the respondents where they let down the plank over the moat and invite me into their castle. She just rides into the courtyard when she is ready!

I have found writing the guide from the respondent viewpoint constitutes a type of logic that respondents can sense and that often they answer the next set of logical questions before I have even asked them. This "organic" approach to conducting qualitative research sessions seems to make them feel that they are in charge of the discussion to some degree rather than being led like a cow with a ring in the nose.

Respondents are courageous to come out alone to a qualitative research session or to talk on the telephone to someone they will never meet. We have asked for permission to get their opinions, and they are not sure that we are going to be nice in the process. Many of their fears can be allayed just by starting the interview in the comfort zone of their experience, where they can answer easy questions and realize the moderator/researcher is not there to shoot them down.

Just one word of warning for researchers—it is sometimes dark in the world of the respondent, so be sure to bring a light to find your way back.

SECTION II: TOOLBOX: "POWER TOOLS"

Powerful Guide Development: Seven Protocols 221

Writing a guide is not just getting some questions down on paper. It is a process that builds from a clear purpose statement and an awareness of the dynamics of interviewing. Here are seven protocols to help get the job done.

The Power of Rapport 227

It is you alone with a room of strangers—and you're the one who has to get them to talk! Learn important lessons from a Master Moderator™ so that you too can build the rapport bridge to put respondents at ease so they will give you the data you request.

The Power of a True Question 233

People may think it is easy to lead a focus group: "Just ask a few questions— how hard could that be?" But what makes a question a good question? It is not just the use of a question mark! Learn the real importance of asking the right sorts of questions!

The Power of Probing 239

A Master Moderator™ knows the primary secret of success: probing! Learn the importance of probes and variations, from proactive, reactive, and spontaneous, to elaboration, definition, word association, clarification, comparison, classification, and even silent probes!

The Power of Silence 243

Tired of uncomfortable silences? Hate those moments when everyone stares at the floor and refuses to talk? Learn the real power of silence, how to use it to great advantage in client meetings and in focus groups, and bid awkward silences farewell!

Creating Powerful Focus Group Questions 249

Questions, questions, questions! Each question should take the researcher on the path toward achieving the client's objective. Learn more about creating effective questions through two very helpful question-asking scenarios.

Power Up In-Depth Interviews 255

What are the right tools to get the job done properly? How and when do you use them? Here are practical lessons for understanding in-depth qualitative interviews: how they work and what tools you'll need to take from your toolkit!

Powerful Guide Development: Seven Protocols

> *Writing a guide is not just getting some questions down on paper. It is a process that builds from a clear purpose statement and an awareness of the dynamics of interviewing. Here are seven protocols to help get the job done.*

I have had the opportunity to attend a number of plays and seen some really great movies with friends and family over the years. I have also had the chance to see improv comedy shows, both on TV and live in clubs. Thanks to client requests, I have also had the opportunity to write hundreds of moderator guides. You may be asking, *"So, what do these things have in common?"* Answer: All require some pre-planning and writing before execution.

After one comedy improv event, I had the opportunity to chat with some of those who had been on stage and ask: *"What, if anything, do you write down as you are planning your performance?"* Some answered, *"I write a general frame and then wing it once I'm on stage."* Others said, *"I have more success if I write out how I think it might go and then review my language and delivery before I go onstage, but I don't try to remember what I wrote down – I just work on the timing."* Still another replied: *"I just get a theme in my head and then riff on that theme until my time on stage is up."*

Having seen many plays and movies, I am guessing that playwrights and script writers write and rewrite dialogue and scene information that actors use, but at the last minute, some improvisation occurs and if it is consistent with what the director wants in the scene, it stays.

The world of writing guides for QREs [qualitative research events such as focus groups, IDIs, ethnographies, etc.] is not based on a firm or exact science. QREs could be seen as "structured improvisation" and there is no one "right way" to craft a guide or work with respondents who participate in the qualitative interview.

Some moderators write in an **outline format** and keep it to one page. What the reader sees is a row of bullet points and maybe a subhead or two. Another moderator might draw a **mind map** that swirls out from a nucleus with the study purpose in the middle and five to six radiating lines with key topics to be explored. In this scenario, respondents from each QRE in the study are asked a family of questions pertaining to every one of the key topics outlined in the moderator's mind map. However, in this approach the moderator is not concerned with ensuring each QRE is presented with every question or category of questions in the same order/way.

Yet another group of moderators uses **file cards** with a topic header on each and three to five key questions they want to explore on that topic. They shuffle the cards as they moderate. This technique requires the moderator to be constantly vigilant to make sure that core questions are asked in every group conducted, so data can be analyzed across the series of QREs that make up a study.

Still another set of moderators writes what is called a **"Universal Guide,"** so named because it can be picked up and followed by another moderator who can then see the logic path intended by the author. This type of guide has respondent instructions for all tasks and instructions for the moderator, so that time spent in a QRE is focused on collecting data, not formulating the strategy to collect the data. This is often the approach when a team of moderators is working on a project together.

As a trainer of moderators, I have had many opportunities to look at guides from a broad spectrum of companies across America and from a variety of moderators ranging from novice to seasoned. As well, the RIVA Research Division has had the opportunity to work on teams with other moderators in contracted research projects, observing different models for guides and the varied methods in which qualitative data can be collected.

The more guides I see, the more I realize that there is no "one size fits all" and that guide development is more a function of individual moderator personalities and style than a set of templates.

Over the years, RIVA has developed some protocols for writing guides that work for how we relate to our clients. While refinements are always being made, these protocols have been in place for almost three decades. The basis for most of the protocols finds its roots in the pain/pleasure principle: it is painful to rewrite or rework a guide more than twice. So, we learned how to get it right for the client as quickly as possible, to keep rewrites to a minimum, allowing the data collected to become immediately useful for strategic decision making.

While every guide ever written by RIVA is not in our corporate archives, a number of them are and once in a while, we will pull one out to look at a line of questioning or an intervention that worked in one product category that might work in another. What we have discovered is that it is impossible to reuse a guide even when working in the same product category, with the same client, even with only six months between assignments. The simple reason: the study purpose is different for every study and since this is the platform on which the guide is positioned, every guide becomes a unique document, just like a fingerprint. While family members might have a similar whorl of lines on a thumbprint, even identical twins do not have the same print. **Guides are unique, one time only documents, and seasoned moderators are very skilled at writing just the right guide for the study at hand.**

Below is a summary of the RIVA protocols for writing an effective guide:

Protocol 1: Be clear on the study purpose: developed as a result of answering these questions:

A. What is the desired objective?
B. What will be done with the data that is collected?
C. Who is the ideal respondent?
D. What are respondents going to talk about?
E. What stimuli [if any] will be shown to respondents?
F. If the QRE is only one minute long – what key question must be answered by the research process?

Protocol 2: How long is the QRE?

A guide for a two hour focus group should look nothing like the guide for a thirty minute IDI.

How many individuals will be answering questions? In a focus group of eight respondents – the industry standard is to make sure that two-thirds of the room answers the question before the next question is asked. This means that the moderator cannot have seventy-five questions to ask in the two hour session, as there will not be time to ask them all. Conversely in an IDI, since only one person is answering questions, the guide has to be written with ancillary probes depending on what the respondent may answer.

Protocol 3: What stimuli will be shown and what activities are planned?

For guide development it is critical to manage the timeline. Doing exercises and activities to get below top-of-mind are great, as long as it is kept in mind that they have time price tags, leaving less time for direct question and answer options. So, knowing what stimuli or activities are planned will direct the flow of guide development.

Protocol 4: Leaving time for "Gold Mines" and unforeseen events

If every minute of the QRE is scheduled, there is little room to explore new territories [gold mines that respondents open by their answers that are directly and critically related to the study purpose] and unforeseen events [such as respondent meltdowns; arguments; resistance; long stories or answers that are rich with information; unplanned collaborations by respondents who are able to create something right on the spot; etc.]. Experience shows that too many planned questions can "kill" the energy that a QRE can generate and limit access to the desired deeper insights.

Protocol 5: Leaving time at the end for client input

No guide should be so jam packed with questions that there is not time to fit in two or three last minute questions from the client at the end of the QRE (after they have heard from respondents). Sometimes questions asked as the clock is running out help clients get closure on a key point or just the right "consumer language" for something they are working on understanding.

Protocol 6: Write the guide to flow from general to specific

Imagine a funnel. Early questions are broad and general as the questions move down the funnel toward the narrow end, they become more focused and specific. This model works with the notion of building trust early in the session and offering opportunities for respondents to invite researchers into their world as the questions become more specific.

Protocol 7: Write questions that match the flow of the natural dynamics of a QRE

There are four stages to a QRE, regardless of length of time or methodology:

Stage One: Introduction
Stage Two: Rapport and Reconnaissance
Stage Three: In-Depth Investigation
Stage Four: Closure

The questions in Stage One are baseline questions that create an environment for respondents to settle into the qualitative inquiry process and are useful for the moderator to calibrate group dynamics. Stage Two includes "cannot fail" questions, usually related to past history, baseline beliefs, product usage or awareness, familiarity of competitive set, or advertising. Stage Three questions dive down into respondent thinking and are where the study purpose is supposed to be realized. This is where interventions have great usefulness, allowing clients to see what shapes understanding and behaviors. Stage Four serves respondents "wrap up" questions that close down the environment. The lion's share of questions is asked in Stage Three, with the other stages playing supporting, yet necessary roles.

Writing a guide is not just getting some questions down on paper to obtain sign-off from a client. It is a process that builds from a clear purpose statement and an awareness of the dynamics of interviewing. RIVA favors the "universal guide" approach, so that all the hard thinking and planning are done in a non-sweaty place without hot lights. That way, when the lights are on, the microphones are running, and the client is peering intently through the mirror, the questions roll out easily. While it might look like an improv performance, it is really an Academy Award winning screenplay that sets the tone for the actors [respondents] to turn in their best performance, leaving room for improvisation as the quirks and vagaries of interviewing unfold in mirrored facilities.

The Power of Rapport

> *It is you alone with a room of strangers—and you're the one who has to get them to talk! Learn important lessons from a Master Moderator™ so that you too can build the rapport bridge to put respondents at ease so they will give you the data you request.*

My mother used to tease me by saying that I could talk to a rock and get it to talk back. As a child I would go up to strangers and start asking questions, and more likely than not, they would stop and answer them.

When I finished college, my first job in research included door-to-door interviews about government-sponsored school programs. My respondents lived in substandard housing in a remote rural community deep in the southwest corner of Virginia. The town looked as if nothing had changed since the Civil War. Among those of us assigned as interviewers, I had the highest rate of access—actually getting them to answer the door and letting me in to do the interview. These interviews predated today's rules of never going alone to someone's house and never eating the food or drinking beverages once inside. On that project I drank a lot of "doublesweet" Kool-Aid from mason jars and ate a lot of boxed sugar cookies and Fig Newtons in the homes of the respondents. In looking back, I realize all those activities related to rapport building.

I never much thought about what techniques I used to gain their trust so they would let me in the house. I used the same "script" as my colleagues: *"Hi, I am Naomi, and I am doing a project for the Department of Health, Education, and Welfare in Washington, D.C., and I would like to ask you some questions as part of a survey."* In looking back, I realized I did not start with that phrase! I did say it, but not first thing.

Here is what I did. I tapped on the door—a polite, not imperious, knock, and when it opened, I said *"Hi."* and I smiled. I waited until I got a smile back, and I kept eye contact until I did. I said, *"Can I come in and talk to you for about 15 minutes? I am not a salesman—I am Naomi and I…"* That is when I said the words in the script. Most of the time, I got into a house and when I did not, the rejection came fast, through a door only opened a crack—I heard only a voice saying *"go away—we do not want any of whatever you are selling!"* I did not see any eyes and the next thing I did see included a really close look at a closed wooden door. Thankfully, that did not happen too often. In looking back I can see that it is the small elements that contributed to my success rate: *"Hi,"* plus smile, plus *"I am Naomi,"* plus a timeline. Small elements that added up to open doors and long interviews—not to mention refreshments!

Just recently, while teaching a fundamentals class about the art and science of moderating, a student asked: *"Does it take a long time to establish rapport, and won't it take time away from the research?"* I forgave her double-barreled question and instead I smiled and said, **"Rapport can take a few seconds or a few minutes, and if you do not take the time to create it, the quality of the comments and interactions is reduced. Without strong rapport, the research interview can often be just a long series of boring 'I ask/you answer' events.** It reduces the effectiveness of the wonderful tool that qualitative research can be to increase the client's knowledge about respondent perceptions, opinions, beliefs and attitudes (POBAs)".

The rest of the three day class gave me ample time to demonstrate that fact via mock interviews with the class and with recruited respondents. At the end of the course, she said, **"I get it—rapport is the key to the game—if you take time to make that relationship with respondents— they will just about tell you anything you want to know."** I praised her perspicacity, and I knew that she had learned the rapport lesson well.

As I continue to lead focus groups, one-on-ones, and in-home ethnographic interviews, I have found, over the years, that rapport is a multilayered process, and while it does not take long to establish it, it is not composed of just one activity. It reminds me of the act of walking, not something I think about when I am doing it, but when you break it down, it is composed of many different activities that encompass the whole body—head, shoulders, arms, quads, knees, calves, and ankles, and not just the feet.

The research definition of rapport is to be in close or sympathetic relationship: in harmony. Shaking hands with someone in a social setting creates this harmony. **In many respects, rapport is an "emotional handshake."**

Once created, the focus group reaches an unspoken agreement to engage in conversation. The moderator has created a safe space for respondents to answer a wide variety of questions and has demonstrated a nonjudgmental listening style, and respondents step up to answer because they know that they will be listened to and respected. Moderators know they will obtain responses because they have established guidelines for behavior and they have also demonstrated an open manner and attentive attitude.

Rapport building in groups or in an IDI should begin the instant the moderator enters the research room or, indeed, before. As I move about the facility and see respondents on their way in or waiting, I do not hesitate to greet them cheerily with *"Hello"* or *"Welcome."* There is no need to stop and make formal introductions, but a friendly gesture will be remembered in the focus group or the IDI, and it gives me an easy start. Conversely, an averted gaze and no greeting can give an instant impression of unfriendliness that may take a while to wear off once the group begins.

There are differing opinions on whether the moderator should already be in the room to greet the respondents, walk in with them, or walk in after they are seated. Each choice has its advantages and is generally a matter of personal style, although each sets up a slightly different kind of rapport:

- Being in the room first allows me to welcome respondents into the space and establishes the fact that it is a group discussion. The chitchat around the last football game for their home team or the sudden weather shift as they are taking seats contributes to rapport building. It has the same tone and mood as those times when I welcome guests to my home for dinner.
- Walking in with the respondents can put me into physical relationship with them and gets them thinking of me more as a co-participant than as an expert, a teacher, or a host.
- Walking in after they are seated tends to set me up in the role of leader or expert. When I enter like that, I sometimes look like an actress coming in to start the action in a play, and that is a different kind of rapport with the "audience."

Establishing Rapport—Some Tools, Tips, and Techniques

- Smile as soon as you see respondents, and be sure it is genuine.
- During ground rules and each respondent self-introduction, make eye contact lasting at least twenty seconds with each participant to form a bond or connection in a group. In those twenty seconds, no one is in the room except the moderator and that one respondent. Group reactions and interactions will come later in the interview.

- Imagine that you are making a physical connection with each participant during introductions similar to a handshake when you meet someone. As you greet them and say hello, picture handing them one end of a silk thread while you hold all the other ends in your hand. Asking a follow-up question to their introduction or referencing a similarity in your life (e.g. *"I have a dog too"*) is when they accept their end of the silken thread, via dialogue. During the session, keep checking the threads to make sure none have gone slack. At the end, picture taking the threads back for closure.
- Make an extra effort to respond warmly to each respondent when round-robin introductions are made. Make comments such as: *"Welcome!"*; *"Glad you could make it!"*; *"Thank you for coming!"*. This reinforces the value of their presence in a group.
- Think of the conference table as a clock with one person at approximately each hour. Make sure to check in regularly with the hours, to "sweep" the room like a second hand in a group. In an IDI, think of the respondent as your "newest best friend" that you are going to enjoy talking to and unpeeling the layers of very interesting onions.
- If some participants have problems or concerns as they arrive at the group—such as parking, worries about getting out later than told, a headache, worries about the session and their role, or a soda spilled on a dress—address these issues, either on your own or by enlisting facility staff help, before starting the group itself. People will appreciate your concern for them and on behalf of others and will reciprocate by doing their best to help you, creating powerful rapport. In an IDI, judge the situation and see if this question can be asked: *"Is there anything that would keep you from completing this process in the next____minutes."* If their answer is *"yes,"* set up a time for another interview. If no, their response to your question is the deepest level of commitment they can make. Use the time with them well!
- Include logistics with your introductory statements. Mention food and drink, where bathrooms are located, and ask if everyone is comfortable with the temperature. All these add to the group's impression of you as a caring person, not just a taker of information. In an IDI ask questions like these to build rapport: *"I can hear you clearly, can you hear me?"*; *"Do you want water or something to sip on in case you get thirsty?"*
- Strong rapport is not fragile. In any qualitative session, even the most experienced moderator makes some kind of mistake that briefly breaks rapport with an individual or the group. Effective rapport building early in the session will ensure that the uncomfortable moment passes

quickly and is both forgiven by the individual or group and forgotten. Make sure to come to complete closure at the end of your qualitative session. Even if the comments are brief, make them final. There are times when rapport is so strong that the group does not want to leave, or individuals want to stay in touch beyond the research setting. Learn to say a firm goodbye. Do not leave people hanging. A good way to bring closure in a focus group is to stand up, go to the room exit, and say, "*I'll shake your hand on your way out.*" In an IDI, the best way may be to say, "*I have asked all my questions, and I see our time is about up. I am going to walk you out and say goodbye unless there is something more you want to say.*"

- Find a way to be fully sincere in the actions suggested. If you remain authentic and appropriate without phoniness or lies, you set the example and imply that the same behavior is desired from the respondents.

I have learned that it is during the first three minutes of a group that participants form their first opinions about me and that is where the platform for rapport is built. Without rapport, discussion can take place, but will invariably lack the richness of groups where it is present and may well affect the level of candor achieved. I know it is my job, as a moderator, to establish and manage rapport as early as I can, and be willing to rebuild rapport at any stage of the group as needed.

Yes, I probably can talk to a rock and get an answer, as my mother has often said. However, now I know that ability is a well-honed skill called building rapport.

The Power of a True Question

> *People may think it is easy to lead a focus group: "Just ask a few questions— how hard could that be?" But what makes a question a good question? It is not just the use of a question mark! Learn the real importance of asking the right sorts of questions!*

One secret to successful focus groups is becoming crystal clear about the context—so that the screener, moderator's guide, group activities, and outline for the final report are all congruent, and any content that is developed fits into the frame created by the context.

The focus of this article centers on the power of "true questions" in focus groups and how they can lead to stellar focus groups. Once the base (purpose) is established, what is next is a highway of good questions.

Veteran moderators have often heard respondents, back room observers, and others make this comment: *"You have an easy job; all you have to do is ask some questions and sit back and let participants talk— sure wish I had a job like that!"* Experienced moderators know that the easier we make it look, the more comments like that will surface and the more the truth about what moderators do will be obscured. Like the duck we see gliding across the pond with seeming ease, no one sees those feet paddling madly under the water.

Comparing the work of good moderators to competitive ice skaters, illuminates this illusion. The better a skater gets at triple jumps and artistic spins, the easier it looks. They have great costumes, inspiring music, and they land most jumps while gliding backwards coupled with a big smile. *"How easy they make it look!"* the viewer says. The difference is this: everyone knows that to learn to do triple jumps with ease, there are years of practices, lots of falls and injuries along the way.

Since no one sees the research rigor that moderators undergo to master their craft, it just looks like something anyone could do. *"Just ask a few questions—how hard could that be?"*

The secret rests in the words "a few questions." That is where the secret power of successful focus groups lives: in the questions. Here are a few interesting facts about questions:

1. A true question is one to which you do not already know the answer.
2. All internal dialogue humans have in their heads is in Q&A form.
3. Questions reveal something about the person who is asking them.
4. The one who asks questions in a dialogue is holding all the power.

Elements 1 and 4 are of particular interest to moderators who ask hundreds of questions every evening on focus group projects running between 6:00 and 10:00 p.m., and so it would make sense to have a very clear understanding of both elements 1 and 4 above to create more effective focus groups.

A true question is one to which you do not already know the answer. This implies that the one asking the question needs to really hold an open mind with no judgments about the answers that might bounce back once the question is asked. If there is any thought in the mind of the asker about what the respondent might say, that will color what the listener hears and color the probe that follows. Questions which do not meet the "true question" rule often tend to fall into either the "leading" or "judging" category. As well, they are weak questions that require multiple follow up probes to get at the true issue to be discussed. It is hard to craft those questions on the spot—they require some advance planning and some practice in asking.

For example, a moderator doing a series of questions for the makers of Buick cars might say: *"You like Buicks, right?"* since respondents were recruited for not being opposed to buying a Buick in the future.

Not only is this not a "true question," it is a leading one—the most deadly kind for qualitative researchers. To make a question about Buicks non-leading and more of a "true" question, a moderator might consider one of the following:

- *"What do you like about Buicks?"*
- *"What do not you like about Buicks?"*
- *"Where, if at all, would Buicks fall into your 'consideration set' for purchase?"*

The moderator has honored the rule of splitting the question, so it is not double-barreled, and they meet the SQLA rule: ask short questions to get long answers.

At first blush, it would appear that either of the two like/dislike questions is non-leading and moving toward a "true" question, since the listener would not know what kind of answers a respondent might make. In fact, question pairs like the two above are classic questions in nightly focus groups somewhere in America. However, each one assumes that a respondent has a firm "like" or "dislike" for Buicks and is willing to share either or both in the focus group room.

To make the question a "true" question, the moderator would have to "unload" the question, so there are no assumptions. In addition, there must be very limited data about what the one asking is thinking to create the opportunity for the respondent to surprise the moderator with an insight. Furthermore, no part of the desired answer can be in the question—the third question above moves in that direction.

Now, how do we ask a question about Buicks that moves it to the realm of a "true" question? It might look like questions along this continuum:

- *"What have you seen, read, heard or thought about Buicks over the past several years?"* (This allows for a broad range of answers including "nothing" as a response.)
- *"What can you tell me about any impressions you have of a car called Buick?"* (Again, a broad range of answers can be presented to the moderator including one where the respondent states— *"I haven't formed any impressions… I just have an interest in American cars in general and would prefer an American-made car to one made overseas."*)

It takes more time to craft a set of questions that are "true" questions. It requires thorough, strong, and solid clarity about the client purpose and desired outcomes for the research. Most importantly it means getting the moderator's belief system out of the way at the question design stage. It means thinking about questions for a long time, not just jotting something down on a file card or in a mind-map format and winging it in the focus group.

If a moderator already believes something is true, that will, of course, color the direction that questions take on that topic or issue. So, in addition to crafting good questions to help the client reach the study purpose, the moderator has to question him or herself:

- *"What do I believe?"*
- *"How might that get in the way of writing my questions?"*

- *"Am I asking questions that really move the group discussion along, or am I just dashing off questions that I have used before that I know respondents can answer?"*
- *"What if my questions lead respondents to say so many negative things about the client product, service or idea that the conversation bogs down into a gripe fest?"*

Since qualitative research is already subjective, there is a high risk that poor questions can slide into mushy thinking on the part of moderators and mushy answers from respondents. When questions are not "true" questions, there is high probability that a poor question will be illuminated in the harsh deadly glare of focus group rooms where a question falls flat with no response from respondents, or that it will result in that deadly phrase from the respondent at the end of the table who asks: *"What was your question again—what do you want to know?"*

It might be useful to consider this internal set of moderator questions for each respondent-oriented question crafted for the moderator's guide:

- *"Is this a true question—one to which I do not know the answer?"*
- *"Can this question be answered by respondents, and will that answer forward the discussion along some topic line?"*
- *"What does this question reveal about myself as a moderator?"*

The second area that warrants mention here is element four from the original list early in this article: the one who asks questions in a dialogue is holding all the power.

In the focus group room there is a dynamic of power that continually shifts, and if it could be photographed, one would see waves of energy flowing from the moderator to the respondents and back in a rebound, along with energy between respondents, and waves of energy from the client through the mirror to the room as a whole. To harness all that power, a moderator needs to know that whoever asks the questions holds the reins to the power in the room. Mastery occurs when the moderator knows when to loosen the reins and when to tighten them.

It follows that if the one asking the questions has all the power, that person should have a mighty fine set of questions to ask, and the more "true" the questions are, the more effective the focus group.

If those that look at the role of moderators could see the paragraph above that asks the moderator a set of internal questions, they would not be so quick to say: *"I would love your job!"* or *"What an easy job you have, you just have to ask a few questions and then sit back. How hard could that be?"* They would begin to see the rigor that moderating takes, and they would begin to honor the invisible set of skills that sets a good moderator apart from a moderator who has mastered key techniques for leading effective focus groups. And what sets a "Master Moderator™" apart from good moderators is the ability to ask "true" questions, group after group, night after night, letting respondents illuminate key insights for clients.

The Power of Probing

> *A Master Moderator™ knows the primary secret of success: probing! How should we ask questions? Learn the importance of probes and variations, from proactive, reactive, and spontaneous, to elaboration, definition, word association, clarification, comparison, classification, and even silent probes!*

Regardless of the qualitative research event (QRE) being conducted—such as a focus group, an in-depth interview, or an in-home interview—questions will emerge that will require a probe by the qualitative researcher, so that clarity and full understanding is gleaned.

Some researchers think about possible probes ahead of time and write them in their guide. Others just pause after a question and ask the probes naturally, as the responses are made in the room. Some type the phrase "why/why not" after every question they plan to probe.

I have seen that "why/why not" phrase in old moderator guides left in facility back rooms, in student guides brought to the RIVA Training Institute for classes—as well as in client guides, written as drafts for moderators to use. It has always seemed odd to me that this probe is so common, when it often proves useless—or worse. Here is an example of a question/probe duo I saw on a guide: *"How long does a smallpox vaccination last? Why/why not?"* The probe does not even fit the question! A much more effective question/probe duet might be one of these:

- *"What have you seen, read, or heard about smallpox vaccinations?"*
- *"Are there booster shots for smallpox vaccinations like there are for tetanus?"*
- *"Raise your hand if you have had a smallpox vaccination. How long ago did you get it?"* Probe: *"And are you still protected?"*

Those kinds of probes will get the qualitative researcher into an arena where information will emerge on whether respondents are clueless or "clued in," regarding the amount of time the vaccination will keep you safe.

Powerful probes will advance a discussion quickly away from top-of-mind responses and seat-of-the-pants answers and access deeper information, allowing insight into the baseline thinking that drives behavior.

Three Areas

Probes fall into three distinct areas: proactive, reactive, and spontaneous. The last one is also called a "natural probe," since it just pops up instantly in the mind of a researcher who knows that deeper insights need to be expressed. For example, a respondent says: *"I get upset when the line is too long at checkout."* A natural probe has to be: *"What upsets you?"*

By contrast, a proactive probe is one that can be planned ahead of time and might look like the following:

The original question might be: *"What were some key factors of importance to you when buying your last car?"* And the proactive probe might be: *"In reviewing those key factors in your mind, which one stands out as critical to your buying decision?"*

A proactive probing series can be planned ahead of time to lead the discussion to fertile areas for discussion, aimed at reaching the study purpose. And from time to time, a family of proactive probes might have a visitor from the "natural" probe family as well.

Reactive probes are almost like natural probes, except they are more "knee-jerk" in character. The most common ones are: *"What makes you say that?"* Or: *"What is the basis for that belief on your part?"* Those kinds of probes question the baseline thinking of a respondent, rather than relying on a report of behavior.

A Variety of Distinctions

Within these three types of probes, there are seven distinctions between probing strategies. They are listed here with some examples of the phrasing used, when they are chosen:

- **Request for elaboration:** *"Tell me more about that."*; *"Give me an example of…"*
- **Request for definition:** *"What do you mean by…?"*; *"What does the term_____mean to you?"*
- **Request for word associations:** *"What other word(s) do you link with__*

_____"; *"Give me synonyms that also describe____."*
- **Request for clarification:** *"How does that differ from…?"; "In what circumstances do you…?"*
- **Request for comparison:** *"How is ____ similar to ____?"; "Which costs more, X or Y?"*
- **Request for classification:** *"Where does _fit?"; "What else is in the category of?"*
- **"Silent" probe:** a non-verbal gesture characterized by such actions as raised eyebrows or hand gestures such as moving the right hand in a rolling motion that signifies "Tell me more."

Nuances of Probing

Probing Element	Examples
Comprehension or Interpretation	What does the term outpatient mean to you? How do you refer to yourself—as a patient or as an outpatient?
Paraphrasing	Can you repeat the question I just asked you in your own words?
Confidence or Judgment	How sure are you that your health insurance covers drug as well as alcohol treatment?
Recall	How many times did you brush your teeth yesterday? Follow-up probe: What were the reasons for each brushing? How many times did you go to the bank to make a deposit in person in June? Follow-up probes: Is June typical or not? If so, in what ways; if not, what are the reasons?
Accessing self talk	You hesitated before answering… what was going on in your head in the pause?
Accessing values/beliefs	What makes you think that cancer is America's most serious health problem?

Final Considerations

There is one more refinement to the categorizing of probes. And while the names of these refinements seem benign, the reader is encouraged to look deeper at what is possible when any one of them is used in a QRE. They include probes for comprehension or interpretation, probes that ask for paraphrasing, confidence or judgment probes, probes for recall, probes for accessing self-talk, and finally, probes for accessing values and beliefs.

Lately I have seen the value of a recall probe (which asks for detailed specifics in recent memory) as a richer avenue than what is typically gleaned from this type of request: *"Tell me about brushing your teeth."* A recall probe asked specifically: *"Tell me about brushing your teeth this morning—how was it typical or atypical for you?"*

I have seen a long volley of back-and-forth responses in a group, when a confidence probe was asked. And when self-talk is accessed, there is a whole bed of hot lava in a volcano of discussion, which starts to bubble up to the surface when people talk about what they were thinking when they did not answer the question asked.

Not every question has to be probed or mined for more information. But a great probe—a powerful probe? Now, that is a beautiful thing to see—when the respondents take the bit like a horse and run full out in a gallop of words—helping the client see the world of the target consumer fully and completely.

The Power of Silence

> *Tired of uncomfortable silences? Hate those moments when everyone stares at the floor and refuses to talk? Learn the real power of silence, how to use it to great advantage in client meetings and in focus groups, and bid awkward silences farewell!*

Interstices. Interstitial. Interesting terms. What do they mean? If you had some, what would they look like? Interstices are spaces between things. Like the space between two bricks in the façade of a house. Since stacking bricks without mortar between them will result in a house that falls down, the interstitial space between the bricks becomes important. Filling this space in with mortar usually solves the problem.

In qualitative research, the interstitial space between events in a timeframe can be as critical as mortar. It can be seen in a client meeting, a focus group, an in-depth interview (IDI) or the time between final billing and receipt of final payment when you are a freelancer. Interstitial space can be bigger than the elements it is wedged between in terms of importance.

Silence in Client Meetings

In a client meeting, a seemingly simple question such as *"What is the purpose of this research?"* or *"How will the research be used?"* should be followed quickly by someone stating a phrase or thought fragment with stems such as: *"So that we can_____"* or *"In order to learn more about _____"* or *"To get reactions to this new product idea related to_____."*

When the space between the questions grows into an uncomfortable silence, with looks across the table between team members, or eyes looking up at the ceiling or inspecting cuticles, it is a clear signal about something. An astute researcher will note that gap in time, before replies are made, and might form this opinion: *"The objectives for this study are not clearcut, and I'd better listen to what is not being said, as well as what is."* Attending to the space is more valuable than the actual words that follow.

Suppose a client asks the qualitative researcher: *"What is your moderating fee for a study of twelve, ninety-minute, in-depth interviews with terminally ill patients in a hospice?"* and there is a long pause before the moderator responds. The silence provides a lot of information to the client, who is mentally filling that quiet space with a different set of thoughts than the researcher may be having.

Silence in Focus Groups

In a focus group, some moderators are reluctant to let silence fill the space after a question is asked. Every minute in a group is precious since there are more questions planned that can be asked and answered in one-hundred-and-twenty minutes. **So, silence, or the space between words spoken by respondents, after hearing a question, can cause anxiety for the moderator and for the observers. However, this space of silence is exactly what is needed and wanted to allow respondents to answer more fully, more deeply, and more below top-of-mind.**

Topics that the moderator and the client team have been grappling with for weeks are fresh and new to the ears of the respondents. The concept statement for the new product idea has been worked and reworked and is crystal clear to the moderator and the back room. But the respondents are seeing a new idea for dog food for the first time. The very notion of frozen dog food meals shaped like hot dogs takes a little thinking about.

They need the space of silence to look in the file drawers of the mind, find the folder with the data inside that reflects their beliefs and attitudes. They have to pull the mental file card for that topic and look to see what is printed there that reflects their current opinions and perceptions. If the moderator fills the space while they are in that mental file drawer with another question or chit-chat, the respondents quickly learn to shoot off a phrase so the discomfort in the room is lessened. That top-of-mind comment fills the space, but it is usually like thin and watery gruel rather than a substantive soup.

Good moderators have learned techniques for managing the silence so it becomes a powerful tool. Here are a few different ways to manage that silence, borrowed from RIVA Training Institute classes:

- Slowly count to ten before asking the question again or reframing the question on the table.

- After the count of ten, ask: *"What were you saying to yourself as you thought about my question?"*
- Throw the question out to the room like a grenade and metaphorically expect the shrapnel to hit a respondent, and focus your eyes on someone who has been talkative in the past as an inspiration to get them to answer.
- After waiting, ask an incomplete question: *"And the answer is…"* and smile.
- After the ten counts are up, make a fun statement such as: *"Well… do not all talk at once,"* and smile at someone to encourage a response.
- Learn from experience that the respondents are more uncomfortable with the silence than the moderator, and someone usually gets the ball rolling, giving others permission to piggyback.

One of these techniques usually jumpstarts the group after a ten-beat silence and gives respondents time to think about the question and frame a thoughtful reply. **The way to powerful responses in a group is to harness the power of silence so that it works to provide deeper answers.**

Silence in In-Depth Interviews (IDIs)

In IDIs, the space between the moderator's question and the response is actually a part of the analysis. Imagine being a respondent, sitting in a room with a big mirror, a moderator who looks prepared with papers and stimuli and a microphone or tape recorder in easy view. Imagine being told that this session is being audio-recorded, videotaped, and observers are present, and that you are an important part of the learning process for this project. No pressure to respond, right? Imagine answering a few easy questions like your age and family composition and what TV shows you enjoy watching and what magazines you like to read.

Then imagine being shown a TV spot and asked: *"What's the main message here?"* If the spot is for a car, and it is clear that the advertisement is talking about how safe the car is, it is easy to answer. But what if the advertisement is about a consumer directed prescription pharmaceutical product that does not state the ailment for which is it intended? Compound that with using imagery of a dandelion puff followed by a man flying above a freeway with a big smile on his face while wearing a hospital gown, to communicate something about health (or the hallucinogenic properties of the product, maybe?). The advertisement ends with, *"Ask your doctor about Traplex,"* and you have no idea what the product is or what ailment it is meant to address. There is likely to be a long silence after the moderator's initial question of *"What's the main message here?"*

In the silence that follows, respondents may be thinking thoughts such as the following:

- *"Oh my! I wonder how many of them are staring at me through that mirror and if they know I do not have a single clue what this advertisement is about?"*
- *"Is this a trick question—is there some hidden message I am supposed to find?"*
- *"I do not know what to say, so I am not saying anything."*

A good moderator will wait to the count of ten, restate or reframe the question or use one of the other RIVA Training Institute techniques outlined above. For subsequent IDIs, the moderator will keep track of whether the initial question of *"What's the main message?"* produces a long silence when asked about Traplex and begin to sort through a set of possible explanations like:

a. "What's the main message" is a lousy question.
b. The advertisement is too vague or murky to have a main message than can be articulated by respondents.
c. Other factors are affecting the interview.

By staying alert to the silence between the question and the response, the moderator is working to find out if a, b, or c above is at work. If the moderator does three interviews, and the long silence happens every time, one way to check if a, b, or c is at work is to change the question to *"What is this advertisement all about?"*

If the next four respondents quickly answer either with a story about what they think it means, then "What's the main message" was a lousy question. If the same next four respondents answer *"I do not know"* with almost no silence, the new question was a better question and cues the moderator that the message in the Traplex advertisement was vague or murky, a point that can be confirmed by additional probing.

In either event, the amount of silence is a clue to the value of the question asked, a powerful indicator for the qualitative researcher, and a way to provide clarity in the analysis.

Speed Versus Silence

The world of business values: speed, efficiency, and results. Technology that supports these elements is also valued. Just a short look back on the evolution of business communications that relied heavily on the phone as a primary communication tool will show the jump to fax machines, personal computers at home and office, laptops, PDAs and wireless options for phones and networks. Speed, speed, speed with very little time for thoughtful silence. Music and noise blares from TVs, earphones, car radios, shopping malls, elevators, and even waiting rooms in hospitals.

What we do not have is silence. We go faster and faster through life and through tasks. We do not sit and meditate, looking inward and listening to ourselves. No wonder it is difficult to allow for it as an observer of focus groups, as a leader of focus groups, and as a participant. We are wasting this powerful tool of silence in research.

Harnessing the Power of Silence in Qualitative Research

What if research were deeper, richer, more valuable—if we waited in silence for respondents to reach into the file drawers of their mind and give a thoughtful answer rather than one that relieves the discomfort of silence? It might look like these two ends of a continuum:

No-Silence Model

Moderator Question: *"What comes to mind when you think about shopping at Home Depot?"*
Rapid-fire answers from several respondents:

- *"Parking so far from the door"*
- *"Waiting in long lines"*
- *"Walking through aisle after aisle, looking for what I need"*
- *"Shopping late at night when it is not crowded in the 24-hour stores"*
- *"Looking for bargains"*
- *"Finding lots of choices"*

Allowing for Silence Model

Moderator Question: *"Think back to the last time you went to Home Depot. Think about your state of mind and the reasons you were there. What can you tell me about the experience?"*

Moderator allows 10–15 seconds of silence. Answers from respondents:

- *"I look forward to going to Home Depot—it is like being in a waking dream—I can see how the finished product looks, like when I went to buy bathroom faucets, and I thought I wanted silver ones until I saw the new bronze kind… changed my whole outlook on faucets and got me to thinking how I could easily change the look of my bathroom from cool and practical to warm and homey with just the faucets."*
- *"Home Depot was a little scary for me. I just got divorced, and I was in there looking at things that my ex-husband used to buy, and now I had to figure out what I needed to change the knobs on my kitchen cabinet. But I wasn't willing to use a handyman service, so there I was at Home Depot, buying new hardware for my cabinets, and the guy that sold them to me carefully explained how to do it and let me practice with one before I bought them. That's more than my ex-husband would do."*

In looking at the two models above, the first type of question does not allow for silence, and the comments are quick but "thin." In the second model, one that allows for silence, respondents have a chance to go back into the file drawer of the mind, and pull out a complete experience, and share the richness—full of imagery and details. You can almost see the advertising agency bubbling with ideas for a TV spot from insights gleaned in the second response.

Final Thoughts on Silence

Kermit the Frog says *"It isn't easy being green"* and we can borrow that to say *"it is not easy living with silence"*. However, one can learn and the wise moderator will find a way to incorporate it into qualitative research, so that he or she collects a richer body of data.

Creating Powerful Focus Group Questions

> *Questions, questions, questions! Each question should take the researcher on the path toward achieving the client's objective. Learn more about creating effective questions through two very helpful question-asking scenarios.*

Role and Purpose of Effective Questions

Traditional focus groups have four distinct stages: introduction, rapport building, in-depth investigation, and closure. One of the moderator's most important roles is to frame good questions that get below top-of-mind and help clients see and experience the world of consumers in each of those stages.

The role of any question in a focus group is to elicit information that helps reach the study objective, and every question should be on the path toward the primary objective. Consider a study about catalog shopping. In the introductory stage, the questions are meant to give a snapshot of the lives of respondents.

- *"Who lives at home with you?"*
- *"What are your hobbies or free-time activities?"*
- *"How many catalogs came in the mail this week so far?"*

When the moderator moves into the rapport-building stage, questions in this session should be easy to answer and allow respondents a chance to flex their answering muscles.

- *"What factors make you keep a catalog to look at again later?"*
- *"Catalogs come in small formats (such as the size of 'Reader's Digest') or larger (the size of a 'Time magazine'). Which size is your preference?"*

When the session moves into the in-depth investigation stage, the questions tend to become more precise and specific. In this stage, each question should clearly support the study objectives and ideally build on the other questions.

- *"What items are missing from the catalogs you like?"*
- *"What do you think of this new fold-out page format?"*

There are no readily available, pre-formed answers for any of the questions above. As long as the questions support the study objectives and can be answered, they are appropriate. The degree to which each question produces a rich body of data that can be analyzed is the measure of the value of that question.

Questions for the closure stage are typically general in nature and are meant to close down the conversation:

- *"What advice would you give companies who regularly send catalogs to consumers?"*
- *"What insights about catalog shopping are you taking away from the discussion today?"*

Drawbacks of Poor Questions

Poor questions exact a price, sometimes a very dear one, and the research can suffer in a number of ways:

- Study objectives are not realized.
- Respondents do not have enough opportunities to deliver perceptions, opinions, beliefs, and attitudes.
- Respondents get bored.
- Respondents talk, but do not really answer the questions.
- Client sends in lots of notes in an attempt to focus the lines of questions.
- Moderator under a lot of stress and must "pull teeth" to get data out of respondents.
- Clients feel their needs are not being met.
- Qualitative research gets a bad name, pushing clients to rely only on quantitative measures.

So what is the best way to ensure that none of the items on the above list appear in traditional focus groups? The moderator primarily avoids difficulties by carefully crafting questions. Moderators need to be like neurosurgeons cutting

Creating Powerful Focus Group Questions 251

into the brain—they need to know exactly what area of the grey matter they are working on when they ask questions and manage group dynamics.

The Importance of Questions

Effective focus group research requires several key elements:

- A clear purpose statement
- The right respondents
- A trained moderator
- An appropriate research setting (a safe place for communication)
- The right questions

Of all five areas above, the last one has the most impact on the success of the session.

Two Scenarios to Demonstrate the Power of Effective Questions

In the soft brightness of fluorescent lights, eight respondents wait earnestly for the focus group session on catalog shopping to begin. Each of the eight receives more than ten catalogs and spends more than $100 each month on items from catalogs. The moderator gives a clear statement of purpose: *"We are here tonight to talk about catalog shopping and to look at an idea for a new catalog format."* General guidelines for participation are given, and disclosures are made about taping and the one-way mirror. Respondents introduce themselves, and the moderator easily builds a genial, warm rapport with the respondents. **(Note: In these scenarios, the moderator's questions are in italics.)**

Scenario One

> The moderator asks the first research question:
>
> *"Why do you shop from catalogs?"*
> - One participant answers, "Because it is convenient."
>
> *"How is it convenient?"*
> - "It saves time—time you would spend driving to the mall."
> - Another respondent says, "Because there are more choices."
>
> *"More choices than what?"*
> - "Than what you can find in the mall or in department stores."
> - "I just like the idea of having the world's goods just a phone call away and the books themselves are fun to look at!"
>
> *"Fun, how?"*
> - "You know, you get a cup of good coffee, look at your catalogs,— that's a form of entertainment."

On the surface, the question and follow-up probes produce responses that may help achieve the study purpose. Sometimes respondents add on comments to ones made by another participant. It certainly sounds like a focus group discussion. In addition, the original questions meet qualitative research standards of asking easy, non-threatening questions at the outset of a focus group.

However, if the moderator continues down this path of questioning, what evolves can set a "tone of inquisition," and the focus group will soon fall into an "I ask, you answer" pattern, rather than one that allows respondents to interact more spontaneously. The hallmark of a good focus group is respondents regularly talking to each other and not just responding to the moderator.

Scenario Two

> The scenario would develop differently if the moderator began by asking:
>
> *"What role do catalogs and catalog shopping play in your life?"*
>
> - "I can't wait to get home to see what new ones have come, I love looking at all the items and marking the pages. For me it is a wish book that I can use to make my wishes come true."
> - Another respondent takes off on a tangent: "While I like catalogs, I am feeling inundated these days. If you order something, they put your name on other lists, and then you get these strange catalogs with items you would probably never buy."
> - Yet another respondent takes a different tack: "Yeah, but sometimes you get to see some catalogs for things that you would never see otherwise."
> - The respondent who first spoke up says, "That's the thing about catalogs. They are convenient, and you get all these wonderful options, but sometimes you can have too much of a good thing."
> - Another respondent says, "They are an important part of my life. Talk about convenient! I can't get out to the malls as easily as I used to. With two kids under six, catalogs are my salvation. I can give great gifts that take only minutes to choose, and I get some unusual things that you can't find at the mall."

From one short question, the responses continued like a tennis match with comments lobbing back and forth across the table—a true interactive qualitative research process.

Analyzing the depth of the answers to the initial questions in the two scenarios, it is clear that the Scenario One questions elicited a paucity of responses and the Scenario Two questions produced a waterfall, with many opportunities for respondents to provide rich detail for clients. The secret is in the use/non-use of the word "why." "Why" questions invite rational, not behavioral, answers, ones that often begin the response with "because." A question that starts "What is the role of…" allows respondents to enter the "answer arena" from a number of different directions.

Given the constraints of focus group research (two-hour time frames, the need for relatively equal air time for respondents, and multiple client issues to cover), it is critical that every question in a focus group be an effective question. The challenge for researchers is crafting every question carefully so the best use is made of qualitative research tools.

Power Up In-Depth Interviews

> *What are the right tools to get the job done properly? How and when do you use them? Here are practical lessons for understanding in-depth qualitative interviews: how they work and what tools you'll need to take from your toolkit!*

As a little girl, I often helped my dad when he worked around the house. He answered all my questions, never missing an opportunity to teach me practical life lessons related to the chores. One lesson that works as well today as it did in the 1950s is this: *use the right tool to get the job done correctly.* The first practical lesson that accompanied this sage wisdom related to screwdrivers. Dad patiently explained the difference between screws with one slot and screws with two slots that form a cross. He told me that the flathead screws were fine for regular carpentry when many were used to anchor one piece of wood to another. However, when you wanted to make sure that the two pieces were held tightly or there was not space for more than one or two screws, then a Phillips screw served best, primarily because the extra slot allowed the carpenter to really tighten down the screw. Two different screwdrivers were needed: a flathead screwdriver with a squared off tip for regular one-slot screws and a Phillips screwdriver that had a tip that looked like an axe. He demonstrated how difficult it would be to use the wrong tool to set and tighten a specific screw. Later on, he taught the same lesson regarding slip-joint pliers and needle-nose pliers. (To this day, I reach for the right tool to get my chores done around my own house, bringing that analogy to research tools used for qualitative research interviews.)

Five main categories comprise the bulk of qualitative research studies: Focus Groups, Mini-Groups, Triads, Dyads, and In-Depth Interviews (IDIs). In past years, IDIs were also called one-on-ones, but as the technique improved, it got a much better name! In IDI sessions, the moderator has a guide and a planned flow to the questions. Comments from respondents can move away from the planned path and take the interaction in different directions. For example, a respondent is asked which of three package designs is most appealing. While answering, he digresses to talk about the wastefulness of American packaging, and that tangent might be briefly explored before returning to the planned line of questions. Or, a respondent may answer in such a way that a later planned question is answered before it is even asked! This is the very nature of IDIs—while there is a plan, the moderator does not rigidly follow it as long as the questions asked keep leading to achieving the study purpose of finding out respondents' perceptions, opinions, beliefs, and attitudes (POBAs).

IDIs are the exception in qualitative research in that it looks like a survey experience with one interviewer and one research subject. The difference is in the setup of the interviewing experience and in the way questions are asked. **Survey research relies heavily on closed-ended questions, while IDIs rely on open-ended questions.** This key difference is important, not only in the interviewing process, but in the analysis as well. Moderators have to stay vigilant in IDIs to avoid cookie-cutter interviewing across a series. Rather, they have to become inventive in finding ways to streamline questions, so that the respondents have the widest range of answers as they share POBAs. **This is the challenge of IDIs: keeping the research rigor that puts this technique squarely in the qualitative arena and avoiding the pitfalls of sliding into quantitative scorings in an attempt to categorize data from a string of individuals interviewed one at a time.** A survey can be completed by a trained interviewer, while an IDI is best handled by someone who has mastered a key set of qualitative research skills.

Qualities of a Proficient IDI Researcher

A proficient researcher, skilled in IDIs, must stand on a good platform of qualitative research. Experience as a moderator is a good training ground, as is related work in anthropology, sociology, and psychology. However, specific academic degrees do not necessarily confer competence in this area. For example: A professor of psychology with two books to his credit had a contract to complete a series of IDIs on a study related to a social issue. He could not create genuine rapport (he thought a hearty laugh and a back slap were sufficient); nor did he demonstrate any listening skills by asking questions on issues that had already been answered earlier as part of other questions. He also showed clear examples of disdain for the lifestyles of the respondents through snide and sarcastic remarks during the interview. When he got tired of the interviewing process, he convinced his client that he had enough proof to write the report, and he cut the project short.

By contrast, a telephone interviewer with only six months of experience as a researcher did a credible job in a pinch when a moderator became ill with food poisoning. She respected the respondents, had a pleasant and genuine manner, and really listened! A husband-and-wife research team interviewed gender-matched respondents, and one had better skills than the other although both had received the same training. Each spent twenty-five minutes with the respondent, and while respondents gave wide, expansive answers, the other moderator had respondents who answered in short sentences, requiring repeated probes, even on simple questions. Observing this pair illustrated how important it is to watch for bias in research, not only in data collection, but skill level bias as it relates to interviewers.

Between these extremes are a set of skills that frame the key qualities of effective in-depth interviewers, and they include the following:

- Good interviewing skills (e.g. listening without judging, asking clear questions, etc.)
- Right mix of intelligence and good common sense
- Good voice tone, pacing, pitch, and volume
- Appropriate combination of critical reasoning and imaginative thinking
- Eye for detail and ability to hold big picture at the same time
- Able to appear genuinely interested (as a person) and truly detached (as a researcher)
- Appropriate blend of empathy and neutrality in word and deed
- Able to think analytically and live without a sense of closure

Appropriate Applications of IDIs

While focus groups may be conducted more often, from time to time, the right tool is to conduct IDIs. These single person sessions, with a moderator, can last as little as fifteen minutes or as long as two hours or more, depending on the topic and rationale for use. Some classic applications for IDIs include:

- Communication checks (review of print, radio or TV advertisements or other written materials)
- Sensory evaluations (e.g. reactions to varied deodorant formulations, viscosity of hand lotions, sniff tests for new perfumes, or taste tests for a new frosting, etc.)
- Exploratory research (to help define baseline understanding of products, services, or ideas)
- New product development—prototype stage

- Packaging or usage research (IDI research is used when clients want to mirror personal experience and obtain key language descriptors)

This is not a comprehensive list of the applications, just the most common ones. RIVA has been asked to test recordings of talent for radio and TV stations in IDIs to help broadcast clients tease out insights about the image of on-air personalities. We have conducted individual interviews with terminally ill patients about plans they are making for their families now and for the year following their certain death. We talked to liquor store owners about a controversial issue regarding liquor consumption.

In past years, moderators commonly used IDIs for sensitive topics such as feminine hygiene, AIDS treatment, incontinence, sexually transmit-ted diseases, or hemorrhoids. These days, with an increase in support groups, these topics and others are no longer kept quiet or private, and respondents are motivated to tell their stories and be heard in a research setting with others who share the same condition. While sensitive issues can still be explored in IDIs, the tool has been expanded to cover communication checks, sensory testing, and to mirror situations of individual use of products or services, as well as for traditional applications (e.g. exploratory research, new products, and packaging studies).

IDI Benefits and Drawbacks

Returning to the screwdriver analogy, it could be said that focus groups require a flathead screwdriver because the interaction between respondents outweighs the risk of thought leaders who might sway others in the group. A moderator just needs to make sure each screw is tight enough to hold the wood in place. By contrast, IDIs need a Phillips screwdriver because insights from each respondent have to be locked in tight to ensure a clear understanding of key research issues.

Elements Typically Present in IDI Research

A number of key factors or elements are present in an IDI study, and they include having a trained researcher, a qualified respondent, and an appropriate setting for the interview. In addition, there are payments to respondents, a guide for the discussion, and a subjective report of findings across the series of interviews conducted. Interviews are usually recorded. Digital files or DVDs are made if there is a requirement for a historical record of the interviews or if there are many instances of show-and-tell events in the interview.

Sometimes, clients make a request for IDIs thinking they will have better research if there is no group influence on the conversation. Sometimes, clients make the choice because they are heirs to previous bad research techniques where a poor moderator failed to allow for individual distinctions or let a "thought leader" run away with the discussion. In group settings, a good moderator can mitigate the influence of thought leaders with such techniques as private writing before public disclosure so that respondents can anchor their viewpoint first. Another technique is to spend a moment at the ground-rules phase and let respondents know that you value a difference of opinions rather than consensus. **When clients choose IDIs to avoid focus group problems, it is the wrong application of this powerful research tool.**

Trained Researcher

The training models for in-depth interviewers can range from learned techniques in the social sciences (ethnographic research skills learned in anthropology courses, interviewing techniques from sociology and psychology) to specific course work in corporate workshops, seminars and training programs. Some graduate programs in colleges and universities also have course work in group dynamics and interviewing. Regardless of the basis of the training, it should teach interviewers to incorporate the following factors:

How to:

- Write effective questions
- Probe for clarity
- Establish and maintain authentic rapport with respondent
- Pace the interviewing session
- Use interventions and projective techniques appropriately
- Analyze data to support client objectives

Recruiting Respondents

All the same rules are in place in recruiting qualified respondents for IDIs as exist for focus groups. An appropriate screener is used to find respondents who match research specifications, and respondents are paid for the time they spend answering questions. Rescreening is also completed when they first arrive at the facility. In IDI research, there is a need to ensure there is always a respondent waiting for the next interview, rather than hoping each respondent will show up on time. Facilities are asked to have a floater recruited for each set of four interviews to be conducted. For example, if four thirty-minute interviews are planned between 9 a.m. and 12 p.m., one respondent is paid a higher fee than the standard stipend, to wait for that whole time period in case one of the four recruited is a no-show. That way, the moderator is never waiting for the next interview. The floater is given refreshments and reading materials (or they are encouraged to bring their own). I have even witnessed floaters watching TV or doing their knitting!

Setting

It is a good idea to set up the interviewing room to achieve as intimate a setting as possible. If all that is available is a traditional focus group room, with a big conference table, then it is best for the moderator to sit in one of these two positions:

- Traditional chair (moderator's back to the mirror) with the respondent on the right side, slightly facing the moderator and slightly facing the mirror.
- No one in the traditional chair. Moderator on left side of table (first chair) and respondent on right side of table (first chair).

In both models, it is critical to allow the client to see the respondent's face and to reach all materials easily.

If there is only a large conference table, create a small-table effect by placing something about five feet from the front of the table (like a set of books with bookends; a row of small plants; some decorative vases with flowers, a row of office supplies)—anything that creates a demarcation— showing the limits of the interviewing space. The intimacy of a smaller setting is more conducive to the intimacy of an IDI. In newer facilities, special and smaller IDI rooms have been constructed to physically create that intimacy. Chairs with wheels allow both moderator and respondent to wiggle around while talking or listening, adding to personal comfort levels that are a key factor in full communication.

Creating Relationship

Some moderators like to excuse a respondent at the end of the IDI and then wait for the facility hostess to bring in the next one. RIVA prefers to go out and get the next respondent and bring them to the room, chatting with them on the way and creating initial rapport, putting the respondent at ease. When timelines are short between interviews, RIVA moderators use the walk down the hall time to give guidelines and a context for the discussion: *"Sometimes these interviews are done in a group of eight people, but today we are talking to consumers one at a time to get personal reactions to (ads, products, ideas, etc.). I am really interested in your viewpoint and will be audio recording and videotaping (if true) this session so I can compare your comments with others and find out the trends and themes to put into my report. Your name won't be in the report. You get paid at the end of this session, and I want to say, right now, how happy I am you could fit this session into your schedule. There are no wrong answers today, just your opinions about X, Y, Z."*

After entering the room, point out where they will sit, reference any beverages available, and indicate the source of the microphone (and/or videotape camera). Indicate that observers are behind the mirror because *"they can't wait for the report, and they want to see the trends as they emerge, person to person, day-by-day"*. Recap any key guidelines, such as speak loudly, say what you believe, okay to change your mind, etc. Make sure the first question is an easy one. This gives them time to talk aloud and hear their own voice in the room, and it allows the moderator to demonstrate listening. Questions that seem to work best include the following:

- *"Tell me about…"*
- *"What is it like to…"*
- *"What have you seen, heard or been told about…"*
- *"When was the last time you did XYZ? What was that experience like?"*
- *"What are you looking forward to next year, etc…"*

These questions open the door to an interchange that gets the interview off to an involved start.

Conducting the Interview

Keeping a little clock to see the movement of time and pre-thinking the timing for each portion of the guide allows calibration in an effort to avoid rushing the respondent through the process. Give instructions for any procedures (e.g. *"Open the package, and tell me what you are doing at each stage,"* or *"Pick up each of the prototypes, feel them and be ready to tell me the benefits and drawbacks of each one before moving on to the next one"*). It is a good idea to write instructions down and give a copy to the respondent, so they are clear about what they are supposed to do and in what order.

When a respondent is made to feel like a research partner rather than a research subject, the benefit is a deeper level of communication and more fuel for the research furnace. Whenever possible, make sure that the respondent is never confused or murky about what they are supposed to do besides just answering the questions posed by the moderator.

When designing the interview process for IDIs, it is good to remember that efficient use of time and respect for respondents should be paramount. Here are some guidelines to consider:

- Respect respondents by being honest about generic topic content and time set aside for the discussion.
- Avoid rushing through the setup (i.e. disclosures about recording or mirrors and ground rules for participation). Allow time for respondents to settle into the research environment.
- Plan the discussion in a logical format so the respondent sees a pattern or evolution of the relationship of your questions and their answers. In interviews longer than thirty minutes, it is a good idea to provide a generic roadmap of key items for respondents to explore. For example: *"Today we'll talk for a few minutes about products, then I'll show you some materials and then ask you to pick a favorite."*
- Let the respondent know they are doing a good job by occasional praise statements, eye contact, or a smile.
- Encourage participants to say big thoughts and small thoughts equally and to avoid editing comments because they feel either the answer is obvious (in their minds) or they feel it is not worthy of comment.
- Allow enough time for respondents to think before responding, especially in the later interviews when the moderator is now "smart" about the kind of answers that emerge.
- Telegraph (by word or deed) that the interview is coming to a close, so that the respondent can volunteer additional information they may have held on to waiting for a question to give them an opportunity to comment.
- At the end of the session, thank the respondent for his or her contribution to the research study and for the difference they made by participating.

Organizing Materials

This function is what separates the successful IDIs from the poor ones. Typically an IDI process has manipulative—i.e. physical—items that can be moved about by either the moderator or the respondent. They may include checklists or items housed in clear plastic sleeves (e.g. brand names of soap powder). Items, such as prototypes of products or pictures or architectural drawings of the gas station of the future, might be shown. Actual product items such as six brands of cat food might be displayed. The moderator could present visual items, such as storyboards for TV spots or sample brochure pages or a rough edit of a TV advertisement and show boxes of pasta or incentives intended as giveaways for buying the two liter size of a popular beverage.

Usually, it is prudent to keep these items hidden or covered until the appropriate time in the interview. If there are multiple manipulatives and very short lead times between respondents, the organization of materials becomes critical to saving time and presenting items in a neat and orderly way. If items are thrown in a box and the moderator has to sort them out during the interview process, that takes up expensive time. If the moderator is showing three commercials on one recording, and there is insufficient time between advertisements to ensure that each advertisement gets full play with no cut-offs, it might be best to have each advertisement on a separate DVD. Paying that kind of attention to the organization of materials creates more successful IDIs.

RIVA has some procedures to help moderators when they are presenting lots of paper items. Using colored Xerox paper for each new item shown (e.g. checklist, brand names, worksheet, sample names for new hair coloring, etc.), creates visual interest for the respondent and RIVA moderators have a visual anchor when they set up the flow of the conversation and execute it. It is easy to see the yellow versus the green document and avoid rummaging through a stack of all white documents to make sure the moderator presents the right one in the correct order.

If we are showing tipped-in sample advertisements or existing advertisements in a magazine, the pages are pre-tabbed to help us find them easily. Respondents are less likely to become engaged in the other magazine content if they know exactly where to look. If the IDI includes showing recordings or DVDs or listening to tracks via audio equipment, the machine should be close enough to the moderator to play the recording without standing.

RIVA moderators find it useful to conduct several mock interviews with staff or family members to perfect the flow of the discussion and to test the manipulatives. Timing those mocks will also point to where streamlining is needed. It is not a good idea to use the first two actual interviews for this process because it creates tension for the moderator and dissatisfaction for the client who is excited about the IDIs at the outset.

Recording Data

Depending on the type of interview, moderators can create a cheat sheet to record a few key answers to support the analysis phase of the study. It is not a good idea to take expansive notes because it distracts from the intimacy process and takes on the look of a survey. The cheat sheet might be a chart to check off plus or minus features of a prototype, or it might be boxes for key words that describe a product, or it might be a subset of key questions from the guide, formatted to allow one or two inches of space between questions for jotting some quick notes.

When clear trend data can be easily collected over the series of IDIs, use an easel pad to mark columns or boxes in a pre-made chart with respondent order numbers down the side and options across the top. For example, if respondents are asked to choose a favorite among three options labeled P, Q, and R, mark an "X" in the row for the winning option as respondents are leaving the room, and then cover the chart so that incoming respondents cannot see the trends! Position the easel so that it can only be seen by observers. From time to time show the chart to the clients so they can see the trends emerge. Showing trend data like this helps keep the client focus on the key issues of the IDI.

Costing IDIs

There are two primary models for costing focus groups: the flat rate, all-in-one cost for all services related to conducting a series of focus groups, and the line-item method where individual costs are provided for each service (e.g. recruiting, room rental, moderating, analysis, travel, etc.). Costing IDIs is more difficult because more variables are at play. Focus groups are traditionally two hours long, and traditionally two occur on the same day. IDIs vary in length (fifteen minutes to two hours) and different numbers of them can be completed in a work day that may extend from 9:00 a.m. to 9:00 p.m.

In conversations with moderators about this issue, the following models for costing IDIs emerged:

- Type A Costing: per-head costs
- Type B Costing: per-day costs
- Type C Costing: focus group parameter costing

Costing IDIs is more a matter of personal accounting style than any prescribed industry standard. The figures given here are intentionally low so as to provide the mathematical thinking behind the costing approach, rather than a suggestion of actual costs.

Type A: Moderators who set fees based on a per-head model indicate that they set a fee for each interview, and that fee includes all the estimate costs expended to complete an interview and analyze the findings. For example, if they charge $10/head for each one hour interview, that $10 has to cover the costs of recruiting, room rental, interviewing, paying stipends, feeding clients, moderator travel and preparing a report. By having a per-head cost, an estimate can be prepared for client review, and project costs can be adjusted as budget constraints come into play.

Type B: Moderators who charge a per-day cost (for example $150/day) indicate that this flat day rate allows the client to choose any model they want (i.e. ten thirty-minute interviews or six forty-five-minute interviews or five one-hour interviews). The costs are calibrated to cover all the same costs from recruiting to final report. Moderators indicate that the benefit of this model is that they do not get into nickel-and-dime project costing.

Type C: Some moderators calibrate IDI fees based on the costs of doing focus group research since that costing approach is familiar to clients. By apportioning costs on a traditional research model for two focus groups in a day, a per-head rate is constructed. For example, if a moderator charges $1000 for a focus group (for all costs from recruiting to final report for that group) and divides that number by eight respondents (an ideal number for a focus group), the per-head cost would be $125 per person. If a moderator interviews eight respondents in a day in an IDI format, the same money is charged as if they had participated in a focus group.

Analyzing IDI Data

Moderators can write two types of reports based on insights gleaned from IDI research: <u>memo reports</u> recapping plus and minus aspects, or a <u>detailed report</u> indicating insights about broad themes across the series. When IDI sessions are short (i.e. fifteen minutes), a memo report is probably sufficient to capture the tops of the mountains. Longer sessions with more detailed activities may require a longer, more detailed report with illustrative quotes or with tables that compare options presented. Analytic text blocks to help the reader understand the results and what they mean, along with implications or recommendations, complete this type of report.

For the detailed report option, RIVA recommends the use of written transcripts to avoid the tendency to report head counts and to step away from selective memory of what happened. Since moderators conduct IDIs to illuminate nuances, those nuances need to be carefully reviewed and reported in a final document that is intended to support client understanding. As with focus-group reports, it is good to include, in the appendices, a copy of the guide and worksheets or descriptions of stimuli used in the interviews.

Summary

When used appropriately, IDIs can help clients get an insightful look into the thinking of their target market and the language used to describe usage and attitudes. In the hands of a skilled interviewer, who shows real respect for respondents and the research rigor to use interviewing time effectively, insights can be deep and rich.

Focus groups require flathead screws to hold in place a stable platform of ideas. Because there are more respondents in a series, the insights tend to be broader than in IDIs. On the other hand, IDIs are best held in place with Phillips screws due to the precision needed to lock down the research planks—a function of fewer people and deeper insights. Using the right tool to anchor those screws is important, just like my dad told me in the 1950s.

SECTION III: ANALZYING QUALITATIVE DATA & REPORTING RESULTS

"Hot Notes:" Capture What Shouts Loudest... 269

"We want results, and we want them now!" Timeliness is crucial in this business, but it can't just be quick—it has to be good too. Learn how to write your "hot notes," giving clients feedback in a swift but effective topline report!

A Practical Approach to Analyzing & Reporting Focus Group Studies: Lessons from Qualitative Market Research... 275

It is time to report the findings—the "easy" part of the project, right? It could be! Broaden your researching perspective with some practical tips to help you become an expert in reporting data from qualitative research— the last steps in a twelve-step process!

Tools, Tips, & Techniques for Qualitative Report Writing....................... 289

In a hurry? Need your feedback now and a rapid-fire guide to qualitative report writing? No need to panic—read this NOW! Take a copy with you at all times for those moments when an unexpected report needs to be written!

Qualitative Report Writing: Is Faster Better?.. 295

Slow down for a moment. Do you really need to work at the speed of light to be a master report writer? Take time to breathe and to think. Rest here for a while and learn some vital re-definitions for your topline reporting.

Adding Value When Reporting Qualitative Data to Clients 301

It is not just data—it needs to be interpreted or it won't really serve your client. Hear more about the frustrations, lessons, and unexpected learning from the first qualitative report of a Master Moderator™. Learn how to make every report valuable to your client!

"Hot Notes:" Capture What Shouts Loudest

"We want results, and we want them now!" Timeliness is crucial in this business, but it can't just be quick—it has to be good too. Learn how to write your "hot notes," giving clients feedback in a swift but effective topline report!

In a world where the pace of business has moved from a light jog to a full sprint, it seems that clients want the report before the recording clicks off after the last QRE (Qualitative Research Event). After a speedy debriefing following the last QRE, to align on key takeaway points, it is not uncommon to hear this request: *"When can we have that topline report?"*

This client request is not out of line. They need to move right away to strategy sessions and plan the next phase of a project in which the qualitative piece is only one corner of a big jigsaw puzzle. The quicker that corner is locked down, the faster the client can move on to other parts of the picture.

Qualitative researchers all have many ways to garner the key insights and wrap them into fast and cohesive toplines. This article is only going to address the RIVA method for accomplishing this task. The RIVA method for toplines is based on three premises:

- Write "hot notes" quickly when the day is done—before going to bed.
- Capture only what speaks the loudest.
- Go for broad brush strokes—the tops of mountains.

Write Quickly

Most qualitative researchers report they are usually "wired" at the end of a qualitative research day. Some drink a glass of wine to wind down, some have a meal or fruit, and still others just turn on a TV show or movie and let it do the talking. RIVA moderators use that wired energy to write "hot notes," using a unique format.

Type the headers from the moderator's guide into a quadrant grid format. Then ask yourself the following questions:

- What did I find out from respondents about elements in Section A, B, C, D, etc.?
- Did my discoveries match my expectations, and if so, for what reasons; and if not, for what reasons?
- What themes emerged across the course of the day of qualitative data collection (e.g. from ten IDIs, six triads, or two focus groups)?
- Was the study purpose realized in the majority of QREs done today?
- What analytic insights could I report just about today's QREs (or across the series if the "hot notes" are at the end of the data collection phase for the study)?

In the early days of RIVA, moderators experimented with talking these points into a tape recorder and typing them up later, but we all found that method spotty and incomplete, and we still had to type up the notes! We realized we could cut to the chase and just type up notes very close to the end of the QREs. Turns out, seeing it on paper forced us to fill in the gaps as we were writing, and the notes were a terrific platform for the second phase of analysis.

Making detailed written notes at the end of each day provides the advantage of capturing fresh memories and insights. It is frustrating how potentially good ideas and insights from QREs can fly away just a few hours later and move very far away by the next morning unless you are blessed with an eidetic memory.

Everything humans ever experience and think is filed and retained in the brain. However, accessing it once it is moved to long-term memory can be difficult, and it is nearly impossible to hold onto small, critical, and significant details once time enters the picture. Grabbing ideas via "hot notes" gets key information down on paper, making it easy to quickly analyze themes and create a finished document. Any elements that are not needed or do not fit the themes can be easily tossed out later, once a considered analysis is conducted.

What follows is an example of how a section of "hot notes" might look at the end of an evening of QREs.

"Hot Notes:" Capture What Shouts Loudest

Example of "Hot Notes"

These notes were made at the end of a pair of focus groups with dog owners who looked at ideas related to three potential TV advertisements ideas for dog food for puppies. These notes only relate to "users" of the client brand. Another set was created for non-users on another night in the study.

The items in bold are the subheads from the moderator's guide:

A. **Role of puppy in household**
B. **Advertisements recalled**
C. **Reaction to client advertisements**
D. **Respondent advice for client**

Notes

- There was no attempt to indicate which group provided the insight in the chart.
- Notice "notes to author of report" in the chart (indicated by the use of parentheses).

HOT NOTES—Users of Client Brand Name Dog Food
GROUPS 1 & 2 IN SEATTLE, August 7

A. Role of Puppy in Household	B. Advertisements Recalled
• Like a new baby—needs pampering	• Client company almost always mentioned first
• Takes a lot of time/attention	• High recall of advertisements from past year
• Fun to play with	• Spontaneous mention of "twists" in advertising campaigns
• (List other classic baby metaphors in a word chart)	• Key competitor comments focus on product attributes rather than what it could do for the dog (stress this in the report)
• (Give this section only 2–3 paragraphs in report)	

C. Reaction to Client Advertisements	D. Respondent Advice for Client
• All three advertisements got high ratings for believability and humor (stress in the report how unbelievable incident translates into product believability) • "Frisbee Toss" got highest ratings for communicating strategy the best (give lots of verbatim in report on this) • Other advertisements could be follow up advertisements to "Frisbee Toss" in the future • Request for more varied age groups in all advertisements • Request for music to be <u>less</u> loud in "Sidewalk Shuffle" • Coupon was of less interest for puppy owners: *"Only the best for my dog... at any price."*	• Keep tone of new advertisements consistent with strategy from past advertisements • Keep "twist" factor in play for all future advertisements to carry heritage factor • Work diversity factor into advertisements—not only age, but lifestyle and race as well • Consider a theme song for the advertisements... rather than just any music that fits, more than a jingle—something of substance • Couponing may not be needed for this puppy food since "dog is my child" syndrome and price is not a key factor in decision

Imagine making notes like the preceding grid for each of the subsequent groups, and you can see that both trends and anomalies can be quickly illuminated, making the next stage of analysis more rapid in producing a final report.

Capture What Is Shouting the Loudest

When writing "hot notes," start the findings by sitting down at the computer and typing thoughts and ideas that are "shouting the loudest". Do not worry about where they might fit in the report. And do not worry about missing something critical. "Hot notes" are all about speed— capturing data quickly.

If the moderator guide headings are used, type each "loud statement" or paragraph under the appropriate heading. Trust yourself to rely on recall and any flip chart sheets you made or worksheets respondents completed. Later, you will have time to sit and resonate with the data and do a thoughtful analysis on the second pass when you look over the whole set of "hot notes" across all QREs.

When recalling a respondent comment that strikes the right chord, use it as an illustrative quote that drives home the point, since you can still hear the conversations of the day resonating in your head. If you get a chance to later review transcripts, you can find that quote and report it accurately word for word.

Go for Broad Brush Strokes

It will take a bit of discipline to learn to write the "tops of the mountains" when making "hot notes"—this is not journaling or writing text— it is a technique that uses a four way grid to collect relevant thoughts quickly. The idea is just to fill in the grid for each set of QREs conducted in a day—not to do final analysis. The client is never going to see the individual grids, only the insights you glean and organize after reviewing all the grids made on the study.

One interesting note: the more QREs conducted, the fewer notes need to be made in the later sessions because of the iterative insights created. I sometimes write this note in a grid: "Same thesis as in groups 2, 3, and 4" and throw in an illustrative quote (if I have one) that drives home that point.

Summary

Early in my career, I found it daunting to look at pages of traditional handwritten notes when I got back to home base. Using RIVA's "hot notes" grids makes it so much more efficient to write the final document that summarizes key findings from the qualitative series just completed. In laying out the grids, I can visually see the themes pop!

This technique requires a bit of discipline at the outset. The idea of shutting off the lights and crawling into bed to watch a movie or late night talk show is very appealing after a long day of travel and work. However, if twenty minutes at the computer each night on the road saves you a whole Sunday of report writing, often it is definitely worth that twenty minutes each night.

A Practical Approach to Analyzing & Reporting Focus Group Studies:
Lessons from Qualitative Market Research

> *It is time to report the findings—the "easy" part of the project, right? It could be! Broaden your researching perspective with some practical tips to help you become an expert in reporting data from qualitative research— the last steps in a twelve-step process!*

Market research studies often have a purpose and focus quite different from qualitative health research studies. An appreciation of approaches, techniques for analysis and interpretation, and reporting can broaden the traditional researcher's perspective and may suggest new approaches. **This article provides some insights about ways a small and busy qualitative research company analyzes focus group data and prepares reports for clients.** Reports support clients in making key decisions that affect organizational programs and policies and the marketing and advertising of products and services.

Our company has been conducting focus groups for decades. As our clients need reports quickly, we do not have long lead times for analyses and report preparation.

The research projects at RIVA progress though twelve steps (see Figure 2, found within the article "Qualitative Research Projects: A Twelve-Step Process"):

- Step 1: Receive client request
- Step 2: Determine project purpose
- Step 3: Write proposal/provide cost estimate
- Step 4: Attend client meeting to review project elements

- Step 5: Determine key project logistics
- Step 6: Locate facility
- Step 7: Develop screener (questions that determine eligibility) and monitor recruiting
- Step 8: Write moderator's guide
- Step 9: Conduct QRE(s)
- Step 10: Transcribe and analyze recordings
- Step 11: Write report
- Step 12: Make client presentation

This article will focus on report writing and client presentations (steps 11 and 12) and will outline some of the procedures we use, the contextual framework that supports our writing process, and some lessons learned from others in the qualitative market research field.

Where Does the Analysis of Qualitative Data Begin?

Goldman and McDonald (1987) state that *"Qualitative analysis always begins during the group session itself since the moderator must remain continually alert to analytic implications if the group is to be guided successfully."* The implication here is that the lines of questions posed to respondents, along with the moderator's probes and follow-up questions to the responses, begin the process of analysis. Krueger (1988) suggests that the analytic process begins by considering the audience who will be using the results and by developing an overview for the project. Gordon and Langmaid (1988) indicate that *"one of the least visible parts of research projects is the ongoing process of interpretation. From the client's point of view, nothing seems to happen until the fieldwork is completed, after which the practitioner disappears for a time, emerging at the debrief with the findings, conclusions and recommendations."*

At first glance, it would seem logical to begin the analytical step immediately after the collection of data from the focus groups. However, that is too late in the process. The true start of the analytical process in qualitative research is at the outset of the twelve steps of a research project. **Plans for analysis begin when the study purpose is crafted.** When the study objectives are outlined, the seeds of analysis are planted. Questions cannot be created for the moderator's guide if there is not some sense of how the answers will be evaluated when analyzed for the final report.

If analysis and reporting were not primary concerns, the line of questions in the focus groups would be very different. For example, in a project on sexually transmitted diseases (STDs) to determine consumer reaction to a new brochure on STDs and the level of information in the brochure, the group discussion started with obtaining an understanding of the baseline knowledge of respondents about STDs and the source of their knowledge. Then they reviewed the draft brochure and commented on what they found of interest and what they skimmed over. The final portion of the discussion related to their suggestions for improvement. Throughout the development of the moderator's guide and the actual conduct of the focus groups, the moderators kept the following analysis concerns firmly in mind:

- Will this question support the study purpose?
- Will the answers to this question provide the moderator and the observers with a baseline of respondents' perceptions, opinions, beliefs, and attitudes (POBAs)?

Without the analytical boundaries posed by the two questions above, the focus group could have easily gotten off track with tangential discussions about the reasons for the increase in STDs in the United States, how hard the dating game is these days, and the negative attitudes of doctors who treat patients with STDs.

The Nature of Qualitative Analysis and Reporting

One of the students in our moderator training school commented that *"analyzing focus group data is like describing smoke in a bottle—you could say it was light grey or dark grey smoke and that it nearly or completely filled the bottle. However, once you have described the smoke, you have just stated the obvious."* That student is absolutely right! **The nature of qualitative analysis is that you state what appears to be obvious (to those who observe the groups) and then provide a context or rationale for understanding that obvious information.**

In an example of this procedure in a study of health insurance for senior citizens, it was no surprise to hear respondents say that it was difficult to obtain low-cost health or life insurance after age sixty-five. This is not a new finding and, in fact, it is information that was known by the observers, the moderators, and potential readers of the report. So, what is the point in stating it in the focus group report? The primary reason rests in one of the three reasons that qualitative reports are prepared:

1. To serve as a historical record of what occurred
2. To report findings and results
3. To provide an interpretation of findings to support decision making

By stating the obvious, that seniors indicate that it is difficult to find low-cost life and health insurance after the age of sixty-five, the writer has stated a context for the findings that is related to the first two reasons listed above. This statement provided a perfect natural opening for having seniors design an insurance program that was fairly priced for their age group. That all six groups interviewed were remarkably consistent in their "wish lists" is a clear indication of an unmet need in this population, and the program designed was a clear avenue for meeting this need. Thus, by stating the obvious and using it to segue to an interpretation of an extended theme, the analyst/writer has provided the reader with something much more substantive than a statement of the obvious and a historical record.

Types of Data Collected

The POBAs collected in focus groups are subjective. There is nothing objective in this data dimension. Gordon and Langmaid (1988) indicate that *"subjectivity is not a dirty word, but an inherent part of the qualitative process… qualitative practitioners have different backgrounds, both academic and experiential, which provides a conversion mechanism through which 'what respondents said' is converted into 'what respondents meant,' and furthermore, 'what conclusions or actions this indicates.'"* This subjective process is the heartbeat of qualitative report writing. The following list indicates some of the types of information that the moderator collects in a focus group and the analyst processes through his or her subjective experience:

- Statements made by respondents in response to moderator questions: *"It is hard to get insurance when you are over sixty-five."*
- Unsaid information—analyst states in the report: *"No one mentioned the low-cost insurance offered by AARP, even through all were eligible to be members."*
- Untrue statements stated as fact: *"There is a computer in Boulder, Colorado, that the Social Security Administration uses to keep track of insurance payments made to U.S. citizens."*
- Results of hand counts—question by moderator: *"How many of you paid more than $400 for prescriptions last year?"*—hand count: majority of nine respondents raised their hands.
- Nonverbal cues—body language, voice tonality, degree of emphasis.
- Freewheeling discussions—the discussions could include statements, facts, untruths, opinions, beliefs, questions, comments, asides, etc.
- Reactions—Respondents are presented with a brochure to review and asked to indicate likes and dislikes and suggestions for change.

- Voting among choices—after reviewing a number of options (e.g. three advertisements, four names for a new product, three candidates for a news anchor on TV, four types of coffee flavorings, etc.), respondents are asked to vote on and pick their favorite (providing the rationale for that choice.)

Analytic Tools for Interpreting Data

The primary resources for interpreting qualitative data include the experience of the analyst and the analytic thinking process. The actual hands-on tools include:

- Client-provided study objectives
- Moderator notes (written within twenty-four hours of last group)
- Adequate audio recordings
- Transcript of the sessions
- Framework or outline for reporting the data

If the audio quality is inadequate, the transcript will be compromised. If the transcript is not an accurate rendition of the words and flavor of the group, the analyst cannot fully analyze it. If there is no planned direction for the report, the reader gets lost.

Some report writers in the industry prefer to listen to audio recordings and take notes on key elements rather than pay for or rely on full transcripts. However, we have found this process insufficient for full and complete analysis. It is tiring to listen to audio recordings of focus groups because adequate note taking requires multiple rewinding and fast-forwarding procedures to get full statements. Not every moment in a focus group is productive. Listening to an audio recording in "analyst mode" when the group was first heard in "moderator mode" is ultimately boring and can lead to the skimming of data, biased listening to confirm an existing view, or missing key data buried in a long diatribe that is fast-forwarded to get back on track in the main discussion.

Scanning the transcript can guide the analyst to listen to selected portions (quickly found via transcript) to better understand the tone of the discussion (were respondents angry or laughing when they said: *"that idea really stinks"*?). Another value of guided listening to portions of the audio recordings is to discover if the point made was the result of a "thought leader" or a combined group discussion. That way, the report can accurately make such statements as: "*At first, the teen mother of three served as a strong thought leader and convinced the room that the second concept was the best of the lot, but a few polite but dissenting state-*

ments from others in that session suggest that it was not wholesale agreement." Having high-quality audio recordings for professional transcribers to prepare transcripts is important. However, preparation of transcripts adds to the time allotted for analysis and report writing.

Skills Needed for Interpreting and Reporting Qualitative Data

To adequately interpret data and write findings, a moderator needs the following skills:

- **Ability to organize disparate information into categories.** The data range from results of voting on choices to statements (true and untrue) made by respondents. This plethora of information needs to be organized before it can be analyzed. Some key methods used include the following:

    - **Copying the transcripts on colored copy paper** so that the color of the paper immediately signals the analyst as to the type of respondent. This might be yellow for users and green for nonusers, or pink for women and blue for men. It might be orange for Los Angeles residents, white for Baltimore participants, and lavender for Chicago respondents.
    - **Highlighting key points with a yellow marker** (e.g. every reference to package design), no matter where the discussion occurred in the six groups.
    - **Double underlining spontaneous references** (e.g. respondent fears or concerns about the product/services/concept) wherever they occur in the transcripts.
    - **Using astrices to call attention to specific quotes** that will illustrate key points to support analysis statements.

- **Ability to analyze key points** that will support decision making by clients

    - **Using the subject heads in the moderator's guide as the outline**, look for evidence in the transcripts to support each issue area.

- **Ability to detach self from the findings** and report negative findings as good data for decision making. Sometimes respondents are very negative or hostile to issues, ideas, concepts, products, services, advertisements, and so on presented in focus groups. Maintaining some distance from those negative viewpoints, we report the findings and insights in a way that allows us to serve as the voice of the respondent without accepting or endorsing the beliefs espoused by those respondents. We ask that the client not shoot the messenger for delivering bad news. Rather, we indicate that it is great for clients to hear, at this stage in their planning process, that there are some issues they should continue to explore or notions they should reevaluate because there was such a negative reaction in the groups.

Additionally, the study purpose serves as the guiding spirit for the report and ties each of the major analytical findings to that purpose. We take great pains to point out the source of the negative reactions— was it a thought leader that swayed the group at first? Was it the colors in the product samples or the cartoon style renderings on the storyboards? Was it the image of the federal agency that drove negative reactions to the new brochure on health issues? Or did they just hate the new product because they felt it was a useless idea? Perhaps they felt the concept was just a ploy by the company to rip off consumers by trading on their health fears, and respondents felt no compunction to sugarcoat their comments. **There is a quote that we sometimes share with clients: "Bad news from respondents is still good data! It is better to hear it now when there is time to fix things, than later when lots of money has been spent."**

Additional Skills Needed for Interpreting and Reporting Qualitative Data

Crisp writing skills. The best reports are crisply written in streamlined format for easy reading. The logical presentation assists the reader in understanding what happened in the focus groups and identifies implications for decision makers.

Good layout and formatting procedures, so that results are easy to read and understand. It is important to say what needs to be said crisply and efficiently and to present the information in a way that makes it easy for the client to see and grasp the salient points. **A clear table of contents, appropriate headers and subheads**, and the use of symbols, numbers, or bolding to separate key data points are the hallmarks of a useful report.

Gordon and Langmaid (1988) refer to a concept called **"interpretive reframing"**, which is finding a framework for reporting subjective information gleaned in focus groups. The moderator needs to reign in all that disparate data across the series of focus groups and report it in a logical fashion. It means reviewing the concrete data (e.g. the audio recording and the transcripts); meshing this concrete data with the thinner data such as voice tone, posture, dynamics of the group process, what was not said, and so forth; and then reframing the whole of the data into an interpretation of findings that supports the study purpose.

Report Writer Mindset

Report writing borrows one useful context from anthropology. Anthropologists are charged with not interfering in the lives of subjects other than to collect data. They are not supposed to change the customs, mores, or practices of a culture by intervening in that culture. For example, if they encounter a tribe that has not evolved to include what we consider modern technology, they are not to demonstrate that technology in an obvious way—e.g. whipping out a recording device! By the same token, we do not seek to change the data that was collected or force it to fit some preconceived hypotheses to make the client happy. Rather, we report the results obtained, indicate its relevance to the study purpose, and provide implications for the client to consider.

The overall moderator mindset in report writing is that our job is to serve the client with accurate information from the viewpoint of the respondent and marry that information with our expertise and history of related projects. The mindset of the analyst is similar to what Krueger (1988) states: *"The researcher is a detective looking for trends and patterns that occur across the various groups."* Goldman and McDonald (1987) state that the analyst is more like a prospector, mining for information: *"It is the moderator's responsibility to prospect for raw materials… and to mine those raw materials at their deepest level."* The moderator has a particularly difficult situation when he or she has to write a report in which the same questions were asked of different groups of respondents and no trend in the answers across the groups can be found. In cases like this, we write mini-reports on the findings from each group and an analytical summary that indicates some reasons for the wide disparity of answers from the groups.

Beginning and Completing the Writing Process Without Getting Bogged Down in Minutiae

As stated earlier, the report writing process begins at the purpose generation state with the development of a clear set of objectives agreed to by the client. A planned line of questioning in the guide, with opportunities for "Gold Mines" or unplanned conversations with respondents that allow the questions to go below top-of-mind responses, completes the process of generating the data to be analyzed. The headers for each section of the moderator's guide (e.g. Baseline Product Information, Reactions to New Product Idea, Creating Names, etc.) become the subheads for the sections for the final report. A table of contents for most full reports to clients includes the following:

- **Introduction**:
  Background
  Study purpose and objectives
  Methodology
  Statement of limitations
- **Executive summary** (implications or recommendations): 2–5 page summary of all key report findings
- **Detailed key findings**: For each subhead in the moderator's guide, detailed findings supported by analytic statements and illustrative quotes
- **Summary**: Review of key findings and suggestions for the next steps to be taken by the client
- **Appendices**: Copies of the moderator's guide, the screener used to recruit respondents, any worksheets or documents used during the course of the focus groups

The researcher can prepare the introduction and the appendices while waiting for the transcripts to be returned, and the outlines for the remaining chapters can be typed into the computer at this time as well. Right after the close of the focus groups, we recommend that moderators write a set of "hot notes" that capture their first thoughts on what themes or trends easily emerged from the series. These "hot notes" become the basis for the executive summary and are amplified when the transcripts are reviewed.

The single most effective writing process that analysts use in preparing focus group reports is that of selective analysis. It is somewhat similar to being let into a king's treasure room and told that you have fifteen minutes to select anything you want from the vast treasures stored there as long as you can carry it out in your pockets. Given that the room is filled with priceless sculpture, paintings, tapestries, crowns, coins, precious gems, jewelry, scepters, and furniture, the smart commoner will quickly look for the precious gems that are small and very valuable. That commoner will stuff his or her pockets with those diamonds, emeralds, and rubies and carry out enough in fifteen minutes to fund a rich life.

Data Issues: What Is Reported and What Is Left Out?

The small gems with high value are those data points that relate to the study purpose and that further the client's understanding of respondent POBAs. An example of what is reported and what is left out can be illustrated with the study that examined respondents' reactions to a brochure about STDs. In the first fifteen minutes of the focus group, after the ground rules and introductions, a very interesting discussion evolved about STDs from the point of view of a fictional couple (Tracy and Dale). Respondents were presented with a one-minute story about a couple who had recently met and now, on their third date were considering having sex for the first time. Respondents were asked to indicate what questions Tracy would ask Dale and vice versa that related to the other person's sexual history and how they would handle the issue of practicing safe sex.

Very interesting responses emerged in this section of the focus group, and the client was very surprised at the differences in the two sets of responses from the all-male and the all-female groups. However, in the final report, this section and its findings got less than a half page of commentary and no quotes because, although the discussion was interesting, it was only a technique used to make it easier for respondents to talk later about their reactions to the brochure. What was reported in detail were information, points about the content, tone, layout, level of information, graphics, and color choices of the brochure, because that was the point of the research!

Moderators and analysts in the qualitative research arena grapple with what to do with data that is clearly wrong or inaccurate when it arises in a focus group. **The first rule is to not change that information or tell respondents that they are incorrect. The second rule is this: if a respondent feels that something is true, then in their universe it is true, even if the moderator and the observers know that it is pure baloney. It is imperative that the report writer communicate this baloney in the context in which it occurred, indicating the depth of feeling about the POBAs expressed and the degree to which there was agreement or support for the viewpoint in the focus group, because that is the nature of qualitative data collection—the analyst does not have to believe, like, or agree with what was said—he or she just needs to report it in context.** A respondent's belief in the baloney is the place where manufacturers, advertising specialists, and decision makers enter the world of the respondent. Knowing the mental geography of the consumer illuminates the nature of the solution to reaching that kind of consumer and shifting that attitude or belief. It is not appropriate to leave out the baloney when it reflects the beliefs of respondents when those beliefs are what drive perceptions and behaviors. (In health studies, the client and moderator can discuss inaccuracies and misperceptions after the session has ended.)

Formatting Reports

Report formats cover two distinct elements: appearance and sequence. Factors that affect how the report looks on the page include no indents for paragraphs, single-spaced text with double spaces between paragraphs, boldfaced and underlined subheads, main heads in 14-point type and text in 12-point type, and two tab indents for quotes, which always appear in italics. This type of formatting makes for easy reading, easy skimming, and improved comprehension.

The second type of formatting relates to the order in which information is presented. The report is generally formatted chronologically, starting with the study purpose and methodology and ending with a report summary. The exception is Chapter II, which is an executive summary or abstract of key findings. That chapter is presented out of order earlier in the report so that decision makers, who may only read the summary, can do so with ease. Another style of formatting is to give up chronological order and present information in the order of importance with the most important information present first.

Summary Strategies

Qualitative researchers have a number of directions they can take with regard to how the data are handled with regard to summaries, implications, and recommendations. If the report is primarily descriptive and the analyst has been charged with cleanly reporting what happened so that the client has a base for drawing his or her own conclusions, then a simple summary style executive summary can be written. A sample phrase in this chapter might read thus:

> *Summary*: After presenting respondents with three different graphic approaches for the brochure, the one style that garnered the most positive votes was version S, which had bold subheads and shaded areas. Respondents indicated that this style was easiest for them to read.

When the client is relying on the analyst to provide insights and advice for the next stage for research or implementation, the analyst can either provide the clients with implications and leave the final decision making up to the client, or make recommendations where the analyst takes a stand and makes clear suggestions about what to do next. Sample phrases in these styles might read like this:

> *Implications*: Respondents seem to like version "S" of the three brochures presented, stating that specific layout factors (bold subheads and shaded areas) made it easy to read. Given this strong preference, it seems that upcoming brochures by this federal agency on issues related to teen pregnancy and treatment of depression would benefit from a similar layout.

Recommendations: Given the strong positive reaction to version "S" of the brochure, due primarily to the bold subheads and the shaded areas, and the rapid increase in STDs in the United States, we recommend that the federal agency skip the pilot stage of brochure development and move immediately to the final printing of the brochures for distribution through the Pueblo, Colorado, mailing center.

How End-Users Use Qualitative Reports

Every analyst hopes that clients will read the entire report to garner the full impact of the findings so that decisions are made based on all the information available. However, analysts know that sometimes clients are busy with multiple responsibilities beyond the contracted qualitative study and that long-range decisions related to focus group research are often made right after the groups are over, without having the full benefit of analysis. In other cases, client staff members pore over the final report and look for nuances and trends to support their decision making. Sometimes those same clients ask for the original transcripts, so they can examine in detail some of the language used in the group discussions. Other clients want the transcripts to explore points that were not originally related to the key study purpose because those points relate to other projects.

In our experience, report reviews by clients seems to be someplace between skimming the executive summary prior to historical filing on one end of the continuum, and dissecting the report paragraph by paragraph on the other end. About one report in ten goes into historical files of a client firm or organization and is only reviewed in light of later research, if at all. Clients closely examine approximately two reports in ten under a microscope with requests for additional information. The remaining seven reports are read through, clipped or highlighted, and immediately used in the decision making process that typically follows focus group studies.

For qualitative research, unlike quantitative research, the report is often anticlimactic; the findings have been observed (although not analyzed) during the actual conduct of the sessions. When no observers are present or observers are present for only one session, the report takes on greater importance for confirmation of insights and for documentation.

An Optional Approach to Report Writing

To respond to the need of some clients for immediate reports, we also have provided reports prepared via an accelerated process. Examples of such situation have been:

- When qualitative research is used as a "disaster check" to determine which advertising strategy has the most merit, a report is needed immediately because rollout will occur within a few days.
- When a company or organization wants to be responsive to a new trend or opportunity brought about through means other than their planned marketing strategy (e.g. the advent of a vaccine for chicken pox just approved by the FDA, a new piece of computer software, trendy advertisements for children's toys, and so on), an immediate report is needed to support decision makers in moving quickly to capitalize on that opportunity.

When those situations occur, we provide a "rapid report," a written report on key findings that is prepared and delivered within forty-eight hours of the last focus group. To provide a full report in this short time frame, these elements need to be in place:

- Two moderators are traveling together who have worked together for at least two years. (Both need to be skilled in all aspects of moderating and analysis and familiar with each other's moderating styles and key techniques.)
- Moderator A serves as the data gatherer and conducts the focus groups after both have developed the guide, and both are crystal clear on the study purpose.
- Moderator B serves as the data analyst behind the mirror and takes concurrent notes during the focus group and analyzes trends as they occur, sorting and categorizing data while the groups are happening.
- With the support of a laptop computer and a travel printer or an all-night business center, the moderator pair prepares the draft report on the road and jointly amplifies key areas, coming to agreement on what was said and what it means with regard to implications for the client's study purpose and then sends the final report electronically within forty-eight hours.

Although this approach has a slightly increased research study price tag to cover the cost of two senior professionals traveling together, there are some inherent cost savings that offset some of those increased costs:

- No transcript fee because Moderator B takes notes during the groups
- Shorter time frame for analysis because it occurs in two business days rather than over the course of ten business days

Although there are important instances where the rapid report can support decision makers in time of critical need (Kinzey, 1993), our company (RIVA Market Research) does not recommend this approach for every study because the tight time frame precludes a more reflective analysis. In addition, it is a poor time use of two moderators, and it can quickly burn out researchers because it requires a heavy time commitment in a short time frame.

Summary

The purpose of this article was to provide some information about how a small, busy, qualitative market research firm analyzes focus group data and writes reports. In summary, here are ten tips from our analysis:

1. Write Chapter I and the skeleton of Chapter II within twenty-four hours of the last focus group.
2. Work only from transcripts to avoid selective perception and to get the full range of responses.
3. Use a standardized set of codes and cues to categorize data (e.g. blue paper for male groups and pink paper for female groups; asterisks in the transcript for key quotes that support analysis, etc.)
4. Establish formatting rules for how the document looks on the page and how the document is outlined.
5. Determine what style of reporting will comprise Chapter II: summary, implications, or recommendations.
6. Make sure that the report indicates how the findings relate to the study purpose.
7. Realize that the full report may not be read in detail by the client, and ensure that the executive summary has sufficient details.
8. Realize that analysis starts at the purpose development stage.
9. Work within the confines of subjective reporting and serve as the advocate for respondent viewpoint.
10. Avoid getting lost in reporting minutiae—report findings relevant to the study purpose and to support decision making. More is not necessarily better!

Tools, Tips, & Techniques for Qualitative Report Writing

In a hurry? Need your feedback now and a rapid-fire guide to qualitative report writing? No need to panic—read this NOW! Take a copy with you at all times for those moments when an unexpected report needs to be written!

This document is adapted from a RIVA webinar and is a series of easy-to-read bullet points!

Roadmap

- A. How QLMR reporting has changed in the last twenty-five years
- B. What do clients want in a QLMR report?
- C. Tools, tips, and techniques for giving clients what they want— effectively and efficiently

A. How QLMR Reporting Has Changed in the Last Twenty-Five Years

- Full reports of 40–100 pages for multiple city or site groups are no longer wanted.
- Clients want voice of the consumer ("VOC") but not a lot of quotes.
- They want net/net, quick/quick preferably within twenty-four hours or at the most within 5–10 business days.
- Some want the facts and what to do next.
- Some want the facts, and they will take it from there.

- Some want to be told what happened rather than to read what happened—i.e. a presentation rather than a document.
- Format (report type) has to fit "client culture"—some want Power Point, some want an executive summary, and some want a memo or a "stand and deliver" meeting. Some want it for the files and some want it for immediate use.
- Clients believe the moderator was listening and analyzing while moderating and therefore at the end of the evening has cogent thoughts they can provide to the back room.
- Some clients take the vendor report and repackage it as an "in-house" document—removing vendor name.
- Some clients "publish" reports (or excerpts) for stockholders or sales staff or strategic partners.
- Not every moderator writes his/her own report—sometimes contract writers or ghostwriters are used.
- Some report writers/analysts are behind the mirror when moderator is working, and they are the report writers.
- Not every study has a report request from a client.
- The term "report" has broadened from the twentieth-century meaning of text on pages—it might be a video report, an audio report, a storyboard, a presentation, a speech, etc.

B. What Do Clients Want in a QLMR Report?—Ten Tips

1. One that is easy to read—style and format
2. Record of key facts related to project (e.g. purpose, methodology and key issues explored)
3. Key findings—was the purpose achieved, and if so, how?
4. Detailed findings—what was discovered, and what does it mean?
5. The moderator's viewpoint—insights—"What did we get… did it help meet the client's needs?"
6. Sufficient substance for decision making
7. An "analytic path"—a way to find a theme/thread in myriad words across a series of QREs
8. Condensation of data—reduction of the plethora of information generated across multiple QRE events
9. All the news reported in a useful way (good news and bad news) — written all from an informational, non-judgmental base

10. Clear understanding of what happened, degree to which study objectives were/were not met, and either summary, insights, recommendations, or suggestions for next steps

C. Tools, Tips, and Techniques for Giving Clients What They Want

Some General Questions to Consider Before Writing a Single Word:

- When does analysis start?
- Does moderating style change depending on type of report required?
- Who sets format/style of the report?
- What questions should be asked of the client about the report, and when should those questions be asked?
- What can you provide?
- Summary
- Conclusions
- Insights
- Recommendations
- Suggestions
- Other

Key Questions Moderator Should Ask of Self:

- What questions must be answered by the research?
- What do *I believe is true* about the data gathered?
- Were the study objectives met—if so, how, if not… reasons?
- What was *not* a true finding of this research?
- Who are the key readers of this report?
- How is the report going to be used?
- How can this report create "added value" to the project?
- What should *not* go into this report?
- Is there anything I cannot (or should not) report on?
- Do I have an idea of the impact this report will have on the client's company? What decisions might get made when this report is read?

Some Questions to Consider Asking the Client:

- When do you need the findings at the earliest/latest?
- What kind of report are you expecting?
- Do you have a preferred format for QLMR reports?

- Do you want to see a lot of quotes or illustrative quotes?
- Who/what kind of reader will read this report?
- What has not worked with other QLMR reports you have received?

What Are Ten "Truths" About QLMR Analysis?

1. It is not easy.
2. There are multiple steps.
3. It is easy to get lost in the plethora of information.
4. Clients say they "want it all"—but they do not want to read a lot.
5. It is a process with definable steps.
6. Clients want reports fast—forgetting that analysis is a task that takes thought and reflection.
7. The "soft" nature of QLMR can hinder analysis (e.g. what about reporting on "non-verbals?").
8. How can I make my report compelling to read and not just a data dump?
9. The entire process is subjective—how do I handle all that bias?
10. How can I know for sure what to include and what to leave out?

Some "A-ha!" Moments RIVA Has Experienced over the Last Three Decades

- **A-ha! #1:** It is impossible to analyze until you have reported the "facts."
- **A-ha! #2:** The most important factor in reporting/analyzing data may be the preparation phase.
- **A-ha! #3:** The report writer has to take a stand before writing one word of analysis.

What Is the Best Report Format (Depending on the End-User)?

- Bulleted memo report of key insights/findings (2–4 pages)
- Executive summary: some text/some bullets (4–6 pages)
- Topline report (6–10 pages)
- Full report (20–40+ pages)
- Video reports: clips and captions
- Presentation report (e.g. PowerPoint)

Open Forum Questions

Some questions sent to RIVA prior to the webinar:
- **Q:** How do I capture non-verbals in the report?
- **A:** This is very difficult to do without using a DVD or other video format and carefully looking for clues—it is best done when the camera is NOT fixed (give beer taste test example).

- **Q:** How can I improve the end product—the report the client sees?
- **A:** Make the reader want to read the report (i.e. formatting; white space; key news up front; major insights in bold; word charts; VOC via formatting, graphics, etc.)

- **Q:** When do I use multimedia clips and written quotes?
- **A:** RIVA suggests that anytime the VOC is direct—(e.g. a video clip) it has more power; however if no clips are present, an "illustrative quote" from respondents set into the report in a fixed format that lets the reader know this is VOC material, is just as effective. Always let the respondents tell the story whenever possible.

- **Q:** How do I effectively communicate insights in a clear manner and also let readers know that it is qualitative and therefore not projectable?
- **A:** RIVA believes that *"what counts cannot be counted,"* and that is the power of QLMR. However, client readers need a context, and that is the role of a caveat statement in the front of the report.

- **Q:** What are some tips to speed up the process for reporting?
- **A:** Write Chapter 1 before you leave on your trip; write "hot notes" on the road each night; prepare appendices before you leave; write outline of report before you start moderating; think in big themes; and keep track of how the themes are filling out (tip: subheads in your moderator guide).

- **Q:** What if the moderator did not follow the guide and you still have to report findings to client?
- **A:** This one is tricky: Did the moderator fail to get the data, or did he or she get the data, but it was "out of order?"

- **Q:** What are some effective reporting styles?
- **A:** Outline reports; left adjusted subhead reports; using Q&A format to report findings; reports with no quotes; use of word charts; PPT reports; use of interesting wingdings ($\triangle$, $\rightarrow$, etc.); use of photos/graphics to create interest.

- **Q:** How to keep the creative focus group energy going into the report writing and delivery of findings?
- **A:** Let the VOC be paramount coupled with innovative graphics.

Summary

Figure 4: *Twelve Key Factors in QLMR Reports*

1. Clear purpose statement
2. Clear understanding of what client wants in the report
3. Analysis begins when moderator guide is written
4. Data reduction permits streamlined reports
5. A clear "analyst stance"—what do I believe is true?
6. Judicious use of verbatim comments
7. All key tools needed for analysis (notes, guides, stimuli, transcripts, outlines, etc.)
8. Ability to organize disparate information into categories for analysis
9. Able to detach self from findings and report only outcomes
10. Good baseline writing skills and ability to turn dry data into readable engaging reports
11. Willingness to accept client input for changes/corrections
12. Nurturing a positive attitude toward analysis and report writing

Qualitative Report Writing: Is Faster Better?

> *Slow down for a moment. Do you really need to work at the speed of light to be a master report writer? Take time to breathe and to think. Rest here for a while and learn some vital re-definitions for your topline reporting.*

Clients have recently made requests such as these:

- "Can you get me the final report on this quartet of groups within a week?"
- "Can I have a topline report on these Monday groups by Wednesday?"

From the client point of view, the request is reasonable. They need written reports to support or challenge their own thinking or provide a basis for decision making for the next phase of the project.

As a moderator, I have said "yes" to both questions, agreeing to support the request for documentation so the client team could start the next round of decision making. I have partly based my "yes" on a desire to serve the client and to be perceived as a qualitative consultant that delivers.

However, I think that neither the consultant nor the client takes into account the true role of the report and what it takes to fill a request for a full report versus a topline report. The remainder of this article addresses the two types of qualitative reports and the issues that surround the speed at which each report is generated. There's also a request made of clients at the end of this article.

Top-of-Mind, Not Topline

A topline report is really top-of-mind. The original word "topline" was borrowed from quantitative reporting and is an inaccurate term for qualitative research. "Topline" referred to the top banner in a set of statistics that reported findings from surveys. A true top-of-mind report is available within twenty-four, thirty-six, or forty-eight hours after the last qualitative research event (QRE), and it is usually based on what the moderator recalls. It is seldom based on listening to the tapes. There are not enough hours in the twenty-four-, thirty-six-, or forty-eight-hour time slot allowed to actually listen to what happened in the groups or IDIs make notes based on that listening, write a cogent report of the key findings, and travel back to home base. **The time allocated for top-of-mind reports only allows for what the moderator can remember and what stood out as the most salient points across the QREs.**

Conversations over the past few months with other moderators have supported this premise and underscored the desire to provide the best in the way of written results. Here are some sample comments from those conversations:

- *"I do not have time to listen to the recordings; I just jot down those elements that stood out in my memory and try to link them to the study objectives."*
- *"If I know the client wants a topline, I take more notes on the flip chart so I have something concrete to look at when I write my report—I do not have the time to listen to the recordings and do tasks on my other client contracts. This worries me somewhat because I change the way I lead the QREs—spending more time writing on the flip chart than at my seat probing answers."*
- *"I want to give my client the best of my thinking, and a topline only lets me give the thinking that I can remember. I do not think it is fair to the client, but it is all that the deadlines will allow."*

While a topline (top-of-mind) report does address the highlights that the moderator remembers, it does not allow for the considered judgment of the moderator. A moderator has a lot to juggle during a research session: hearing from all respondents; deflecting dominators and inspiring shy people; keeping the session on the content target; exposing ideas and materials in a timely manner; getting key information collected in the time set aside; and attempting to meet multiple objectives from the backroom observers. Listening, and remembering what happened in the QRE becomes difficult in the face of all the other tasks that a moderator is doing "live" and in the moment.

Full Report

The definition of a full report is one that covers, the methodology, procedures, findings, and analysis of the data obtained. This type of report may use illustrative quotes or multiple verbatim comments to support analysis.

In some respects, a full qualitative report is similar to a small master's thesis. It takes disparate data from a series of QREs, with different types of people, across different sites and weaves the comments, reactions, and events into a single report that documents something that is not easily measured: perceptions, opinions, beliefs, and attitudes (POBAs).

A master's thesis takes a long time to write because it takes a long time to collect the data, review it, form hypotheses, and then write about those findings in a clear and logical manner. By the same token, writing clear and logical findings about POBAs takes time—not as long as a master's thesis, but it does take time. Even though it does not take as long, it does use the same skills as those used for a thesis: sifting out what is not important, illuminating what is important, the reason it is important, and choosing a frame for reporting the data, so that the reader has the clearest insight possible.

Typically, moderators use one of the following methods to write up the results of QREs:

- Listening to the QREs via audio recordings and taking notes
- Having a transcript made and using it as the base for report writing
- Having an analyst take notes from behind the mirror and cowriting the report with the moderator

While there are variations on these themes (e.g. using a ghostwriter, writing from notes taken in the research room, etc.), the model still boils down to writing a report based on what happened in the QREs using notes or transcripts as the basis for analysis of data.

"Rapid Write" Versus "Rest & Write"

Some qualitative consultants like the notion of having a fast turn around for report writing, arguing that it is better to go into "crunch mode" and start writing right after the QREs are over so that the data is fresh and topical. Those writers tend to prefer working with a "behind the mirror" analyst partner and producing the draft report while still on the road or at most, a day or two later. These "rapid-write" moderators can easily fill the request of a client for fast turn around, and their clients are willing to pay the rush fee surcharge that accompanies the speed of reporting.

One moderator indicated that she had mastered the skills of producing the fast reports by using specific software and producing "word charts" that easily evolved into overheads for on-site client presentations a few days later. By working from notes and the recent memories of the QREs just conducted, she could offer her clients a finished professional document in a few short days. It must be noted, however, that this moderator stands on a base of thirty years in the advertising research industry!

Other qualitative consultants feel that they need time to carefully review the data from the groups, listening to recordings or reading transcripts and teasing out nuances, carefully separating the writer's subjective viewpoint from what was said or done in the QREs. The subjective viewpoint re-enters at the analysis stage, and the consultant reviews the findings and measures them against the study objectives. These authors could be called "rest and write," to distinguish them from the "rapid-write" authors.

Benefits/Drawbacks of "Rapid Write" Versus "Rest & Write"

One of the benefits of the "rapid-write" approach is that the reports are quickly done and the consultant is ready to move onto something new. The drawback is that the consultant cannot do back-to-back projects for a different client in a four-day period without paying a high cost in sleep loss. The consultant also risks the chance of missing key client contact opportunities for the second client of the week. They also cannot spend any time in marketing new opportunities because their attention must be centered on the work at hand.

The benefit of the "rest and write" method is that it allows for review and rewrite opportunities to look at the data generated and to report data across a broader band of issues. The drawback is that the "rest and write" method requires time—ideally ten business days from the date of the last QREs. These ten days are spent as follows: two days for preparation of transcripts or note taking via audio playback; five days for developing themes, outlines, and key analysis points; and three days for writing, editing, and production. The best writing courses indicate that it is advantageous to let writing "rest" a day or two before final edit, so that one brings "new eyes" to the reading and supports the development of the clarity that is needed to see it from the reader's viewpoint.

In the qualitative research arena, it has become standard for clients to request rapid turn around on reports, and the rationale given is that reports are needed for decision making. However, I question the request. If clients want data on which to base a decision, do they not want the best analysis possible, versus the fastest?

I have seen a number of situations with clients where project dates have slipped because more time was needed to revise a concept, or a sample product, or a new advertising campaign approach. Time was allowed for those changes, so that what was tested was appropriate. However, the qualitative researcher is asked to make up the lost up-front time by speeding up the research report or to provide a report that is "top-of-mind" rather than one that carefully considers the findings.

Open Request to Clients

I want to make an open request to clients and qualitative researchers to step back and ask: "Is faster better?" With the increasing support of technology, we have all seen an increase in the speed at which paper is moved through the American business world.

This article is a request to slow down and look at the original purpose of reports and to consider whether this area is one where speed should not have the power that it holds elsewhere. I would like to see clients resist the "top-of-mind" reports and allow qualitative researchers ten to fifteen days of time to truly review the findings and analyze the data from qualitative research. I am asking for the time to write reports that allow the benefits of objective viewpoints from non-vested researchers.

If a report has the power to support decision makers, should it be written mostly from memory by someone with little sleep and limited review opportunities?

Adding Value When Reporting Qualitative Data to Clients

> *It is not just data—it needs to be interpreted, or it won't really serve your client. Hear more about the frustrations, lessons, and unexpected learning from the first qualitative report of a Master Moderator™. Learn how to make every report valuable to your client!*

I remember my first qualitative report very well—in fact, my very first project is deeply embedded in my mind. The lessons learned from that first study have shaped the way I have done qualitative research since. It is a miracle that I ever went on to lead another group after that first one! Here are some highlights:

- Client recruited participants.
- Budget allowed for only one group.
- Participants all knew each other.
- Sixteen were recruited for ten to twelve to show.
- All showed up.
- Client afraid to turn any away, since they were members of an association.
- Sixteen participated—mostly women with a smattering of men.
- Client wrote the guide.
- One tape recorder without automatic reverse requiring moderator to be audio tech and remember to turn tapes on time.
- Session held without mirror—in board room of insurance company where some of the participants worked.

- Client listened to session with glass held to wall in the next room and slipped notes under the door to the moderator.
- Respondents hated all the client concepts presented.
- I wore a blue silk blouse, a black skirt, and three-inch heels and sweated like a pig, leaving big underarm sweat stains.
- It was 1978.
- I transcribed my own tapes.
- I spent thirty-six hours writing the report.

I have led over 5,000 groups since that first one and have never had a night like that since! Now, RIVA controls the qualitative research experience totally from recruiting to logistics to report. We fight for research rigor and push back when clients make demands we know are inappropriate. I also only wear cotton shirts and low-heeled shoes to lead groups now!

The report was difficult to write, since I was reporting bad news. Out of that experience came the first maxim for me with regard to reporting qualitative data: *"Bad news doesn't mean bad research—it means that respondents did not like what was presented."*

The point of that first report focused on participant reactions to three new concepts for members of an association and the topic related to new member benefits accruing to them as part of membership dues. The association had not been doing a good job serving members, and the concepts presented were seen as Band-Aids for a problem when major surgery, sutures, and a long recovery were what was needed and wanted.

The first part of the report flowed without incident: what participants saw as benefits of membership (primarily collegial networking), value of the annual conference (primarily collegial networking), and reasons to renew membership (primarily collegial networking). At least it was easy to report this trend data from sixteen respondents!

The problem came when reporting reactions to the concepts. While the concepts were well written and sufficiently distinct from one another, so that respondents could easily evaluate them, they were based on a flawed premise: the association believed they could "make nice" and offer palliative solutions to make members feel better.

Meantime, members were already standing on this belief system: *the only benefit to my membership is the chance to meet like-minded colleagues at meetings and conferences to share insights and get new information useful in day-to-day work.*

So a concept that promised discounts on books and materials for bringing in new members; another concept that promised a new and improved journal magazine; and a third one that offered regional workshops were met with stony viewpoints.

Even careful probing to get respondents to find something good in each concept build and expand each one to better meet their needs resulted in very few positive elements to report.

So, the task was to report the bad news in a way to help clients shape their long-range strategy with respect to how they might retain current members and even consider how they might attract new ones!

When I was working as a young moderator in the late 1970s, the term "qualitative consultant" had not even been invented. QRCA was just a budding idea. I had no industry standard to follow and few colleagues to call and thrash out my problem with this report. Working alone, at home, I might as well have been working on a moon of Jupiter.

Working in a service industry, I had been infused with the "how can I serve" mentality, and somehow, I just knew, intuitively, that just reporting what happened in the groups without some advice or recommendations for the client would not serve the client.

The term "value-added" was another term that had not yet emerged in American society, but I knew, again intuitively, that I had to give more than expected when submitting this report—as much to salvage a bad research design as to truly serve my client with some other eyes and ears on the membership issues top management was grappling with. Of course, the other driver was there as well: I was not going to get paid until I submitted the final report!

So, once I completed the first section on collegial networks, the section called "Reactions to Concepts" loomed like a tall mountain, slippery with ice and canyons.

I dove in and wrote from the classic approach first, presenting the concepts in a monodic fashion, finding whatever positive nuggets there were and reporting them first. The data was thin! Then I reported what did not work with the concepts—this was a much juicier segment.

Then, in fits and starts, I wrote the value-added section of the report. First I had to decide—was I writing recommendations, advice, insights, or conclusions? Was I just writing a summary of what happened and leaving the insights to those who worked at the association? I grappled with my fears:

- *"I do not work at this association, and I do not know their history."*
- *"I am a vendor—what advice can I bring them based on this one focus group?"*
- *"Who died and made me the expert on how to solve a problem their top management cannot solve?"*

Then it hit me! Wait a second, if I were senior management at this association, and had been listening only to staff and had a chance to hear from members, what types of things could I plan on changing, based on member input? I entered the world of the client, stood in their shoes for a moment.

The words flew from my fingers onto a correcting selectric typewriter—there were no PCs for small companies in the late 1970s. I wrote from the heart—providing insights that I would want to read if I were on the management team at the association. I drew on my years of experience as a member in my associations. I drew on results from quantitative studies I had done for other clients in the 1960s and early 1970s. I drew on articles and books I had read and case studies I had reviewed in other disciplines.

The section of the report was called "Advice for Senior Management at XYZ Association." I presented the data first in a word chart with these headings:

- Reactions to Concepts
- Positives and Negatives
- What Members Say They Want

The next section listed, in bullet point format, some issues or areas that the association might consider as they continued with internal meetings around the theme: "How can we better serve our members?"

The last part of the value-added section was composed of two more word charts with these headers:

- What Members Say They Want
- Value to Association if Members Get What They Want
- Summary of Key Member Needs
- How to Meet Member Needs Now and In the Future

Having no template (since this was my first report), I had some trepidation about sending off my neatly retyped document in the white spiral binding and clear cover sheet where the title page was typed on letterhead. While the client had written the recruiting screener for the "in-house" recruit, and written my guide, they did not send a sample report for me to use as a template or given me any insights to help me meet their expectations. When I asked: *"What are you expecting in the report?"* they answered with: *"We'll leave that to your judgment."* Great! Now I fly blind into the sun.

I finished the report and sent it off via courier, then I called and said it was on the way. Neither e-mail nor office voicemail had yet been invented yet for small companies in 1978. When the courier came to pick it up, my black cat growled at him, and I slipped it through a thin opening in the door and signed the receipt.

I waited one day, two days, and by the third day had not yet heard if they liked or accepted my report. I called and talked to my key contact and was told: *"Yeah… you did a good job, can you make a couple of changes in the order of the sections, add some additional quotes in one section, and get us twenty-five final copies for the board meeting coming up? My boss really liked your advice, and we're going to discuss it at the board meeting."*

I said, *"No problem, when do you need the changes made—when is the board meeting?"* trying hard to sound dignified instead of letting him hear the silly giddy laughter of knowing I had made the right decision to write the value-added section.

I told my contact that my little copier could not handle making twenty-five copies, but that I would make the changes and get him a clean copy suitable for making a controlled number of copies at his shop by a staff member. He agreed and, to this day, I send final reports as one bound copy for the file and a master for the client to make a controlled number of copies for distribution—saving me the logistics of shipping out reports after the final invoice has been submitted and giving my clients total power on who gets copies of their report inside their organization and among their partners outside the organization (e.g. advertising agencies, design firms, other consultants, etc.).

In the intervening years since 1978, I have written hundreds of reports. Early in the analysis and reporting process I have made the decision of what to report to clients as "value-added." I talk with the client ahead of the report submission and determine which of these approaches best match client needs:

- A straight summary of what respondents said, leaving the conclusions up to the reader
- Conclusions—here is the data and here is what the data means
- Recommendations—given this data, here is what the client can consider doing next
- Moderator Insights—given this data, the moderator thinks that the client should do "xyz" next (this approach is used if the moderator thinks that additional research should be conducted before major decisions are made)

Sometimes the client gets a blend (e.g. summary and conclusions or conclusions and recommendations). The decision is made based on study purpose and client needs.

I have learned a lot from that first hot group of sixteen respondents in the board room of an insurance company. I have learned about the true role of a "qualitative consultant" not only in the act of moderating, but the process of analysis and reporting of qualitative data. Pundits have said that we are shaped by our experiences, and that was certainly true for me. I believe that Conan the Barbarian (played by Arnold Schwarzenegger) said: *"What doesn't kill you makes you stronger,"* and maybe he borrowed that phrase from Nietzsche.

I am a much stronger moderator and analyst since that first group, and I have learned to trust my intuition. I might not have learned the same lesson if respondents had liked any one of the three client concepts in that first group!

SECTION IV: THE CLIENT'S ROLE

Choosing a Moderator: How Do You Find the Right Match for Your Project? 309

Too bad there isn't a site called "www.matchthemoderator.com". That would make it so much easier for clients and moderators to find common ground for qualitative projects. What questions should a client ask a new moderator being considered for a project? What materials should be requested beyond references? How do you discover if the moderator's values match client needs? These questions and more provide a foundation for creating a happy marriage between moderators and clients.

Enjoy the View:
Client Ground Rules for Observing Focus Groups 315

There are rules for respondents to follow so the QLMR process will be effective. Moderators have rules to follow so that the data collected will be useful for end-users. Clients should have guidelines too—it is not just an opportunity for sanctioned voyeurism.

How Clients Can Get the Most From Qualitative Market Research .. 321

Four methods are presented to help clients maximize the information they receive from QRE projects. These methods include finding creative ways to keep the client in the loop when they cannot attend every one of the planned qualitative events that comprise their study. After all, one QRE does not a study make.

How Clients & Researchers Listen Differently to Focus Group Comments
.... 325

Clients are listening "for" something when viewing focus groups – for example to confirm or clarify data. Moderators are listening "to" clients to determine desired outcomes. As well they are listening "to" respondents to gather perceptions, opinions, beliefs, and attitudes (POBAs). That is two very different kinds of listening.

Minimizing Client Problems on Focus Group Projects 329

Learn how to serve as the perfect project manager—another of the hats of a Master Moderator™. Nip client-related problems in the bud for a rich focus group experience!

🔑 **Asking the Right Questions of Clients Will Create the Best Questions for Respondents** 337

It is impossible to ask respondents the "right" questions if the study purpose is murky or if the client team has more than one agenda. Look here for the four key questions to ask clients before screeners or guides are drafted in order to keep projects focused.

Author Note:
While these articles focus on focus groups, the lessons provided here will fit any QRE.

Choosing A Moderator—How Do You Find The Right Match For Your Project?

> *Too bad there isn't a site called "www.matchthemoderator.com". That would make it so much easier for clients and moderators to find common ground for qualitative projects. What questions should a client ask a new moderator being considered for a project? What materials should be requested beyond references? How do you discover if the moderator's values match client needs? These questions and more provide a foundation for creating a happy marriage between moderators and clients.*

When a client organization looks for a moderator—either as a vendor providing a service or an in-house staff member who can moderate, they want a candidate who is comfortable with the following conditions:

- Is willing to take client desires for research and turn them into an **organized set of questions** and activities to better understand target markets;
- Is okay with being stared at through a one-way mirror by people who write them a check;
- Able to work with strangers in front of that same mirror and create a safe environment where respondents feel comfortable talking about things they probably never talk about out loud with their own friends and family;
- Has an ability to synthesize insights from those strangers and write a defensible document that outlines perceptions, opinions, beliefs,

and attitudes (POBAs) in such a way that an organization can make strategic decisions.

What if the client was looking for a samurai warrior – where would they start the process – at a website called Samurai Central? If you wanted a lion tamer, where would you look? At least for moderators there are websites to start the process: One is www.QRCA.org. Click on the "Find a Researcher," button and after selecting some parameters, the site will support you with a list of names.

Some other resources:

1. American Marketing Association www.ama.org and their "Green Book" —for a listing of moderators visit: www.greenbook.org.
2. There are also directory listings found at Quirk's Marketing Research Media: www.quirks.com.
3. Check existing business networks by asking: *"Do you have a good moderator you can recommend?"* Be willing to step outside your company networks and ask colleagues in other fields.

However, websites and referrals cannot tell you if Mary or Martin Moderator is the best match for your project since qualitative inquiry is a delicate balance of personality, experience, and awareness of the nuances of group dynamics. Finding a moderator, on the part of a client, is also finding a balance between trusting the unknown and having faith.

The odds of getting a good match can be improved (once you have a list of names of potential candidates) by asking some pertinent questions and requesting some materials from the candidates.

Ideal Questions to Pose to a Potential Moderator:

1. *"I have provided my project brief [or study objectives] to you – what questions do you have about what skills we are looking for on this project?"*
2. *"How, if at all, is this project like others you have done in the past for other clients?"*
3. *"There are several methodologies to help us reach the study purpose – what suggestions do you have about the best method for doing so?"*
4. *"You know what we are looking for – in what ways, if at all, are your skills, history, and experience a good match for us?"*
5. *"We have been doing XYZ research projects on this topic for a number of months/years and will continue to do so in the future. What can you*

> tell us about your ability to keep the research fresh each time we conduct qualitative research studies?"

These are specific questions that will quickly help you weed out candidates who are not willing to "go a few rounds" with decision makers or who offer excuses rather than solutions. A creative researcher will see these questions as an opportunity to demonstrate their unique set of skills such as: probing for clarity, practicing unconditional positive regard (UPR), and asking questions that get below top-of-mind. **They will see the interview as a chance to demonstrate what they can do in a qualitative research environment.**

What Questions Should I be Asking of a Moderator's References?

It is always a good idea to ask for references and here are some recommendations about navigating the reference challenge:

A. Ask for four references from the moderator
B. Plan to call three of the four listed
C. Look for congruence in comments across all references
D. If in doubt, call the fourth reference to see if a theme can be established

Ten Questions to Ask References:

1. *"How did you find this moderator?"*
2. *"How many projects have they worked on for your firm?"*
3. *"In your eyes is he/she a 'niche' moderator [a specialist in a category] or a "generalist" [able to change categories]?"*
4. *"To what degree can he/she easily talk with different kinds of respondents or across different topic areas?'*
5. *"If you were to give this moderator a 'grade' for how well he/she satisfied your project needs on the last project they completed for you – what grade would you give and what is the reason for that grade?"*
6. *"How would you rate the 'flexibility' of this moderator, i.e., their ability to change and adapt as project elements change?"*
7. *"What would you say makes this moderator unique in your opinion?"*
8. *"What is this moderator's greatest:*
   a. Strength?
   b. Weakness?"
9. *"Would you hire this moderator again?"*
   a. "Yes…because: _____."

b. "No…because: _____."
10. "Is there anything I should know about this moderator before we consider them for our next project?"

While this is an extensive list of questions and the call to references may take ten to fifteen minutes each, the data collected will go a long way toward giving you an insight about how others see the potential candidate for your project. **The upside of time spent in this way is that when you do make your final choice of a new researcher, you may hire them for many projects over an extended time period.** Therefore, a few hours spent on questions, similar to the ones above, will save you having to repeat this process too many times in the future.

What Should You Ask the Moderator to Provide to You as Work Samples?

The last part of the process to finding a good moderator is to collect non-confidential work samples, so you can evaluate the scope of their experience. The list below is a good start:

Baseline Items Client Should Request:

1. Resume, Bio, or CV
2. Client List
3. Four Client References [See above section]
4. Sample Report [Should be redacted to maintain client confidentiality]
5. Sample Moderator's Guide for Unrelated Project [Redacted is best]

Additional Items That Might Be Valuable for Client to Request:

1. Sample DVD* exhibiting moderator style [See note that follows about what to look for on that DVD]
2. Articles written for industry trade journals
3. Essay entitled: *"My Philosophy on the Art/Science of Effective Moderating"*
4. Any "kudos" letters from clients commenting on the skill set of the moderator
5. List of professional organizations to which the moderator is a member and any information showing how they participate in that professional group [e.g., as a board member, a presenter, an author, etc.,]

*Note: What to look for on a researcher DVD:

A. Respect for respondents
B. Ownership of the room – clear demonstration of "invisible leadership"
C. Speaks clearly and loudly
D. Sets expectations for the group and gives all the industry disclosures
E. Asks short questions and actively listens
F. Moves things along without rushing and handles tangents adroitly
G. Avoids "serial interviewing"
H. Shows creativity and adaptability in the moment – varies the "I ask – you answer" model
I. Changes activities about every twenty minutes
J. Moves around from time to time – does not stay glued to the chair
K. Maintains an open body position – avoids clasped hands and folded arms
L. Moves from general to specific questions within a topic area
M. Creates safe opportunity for diverse opinions
N. Works along a logical path showing planning of questions and does not appear to be "winging it" with most questions or slavishly following a "script"
O. Handles thought leaders and shy respondents with ease so both can contribute
P. Misses no opportunity to probe for additional information.

This article presents the collected wisdom of leading over thirty years of QREs and working with thousands of students through RIVA's Training Institute. I hope it provides readers, who purchase qualitative research services, with some areas to consider when looking for someone new to conduct research using qualitative inquiry. It is also hoped that this article will provide freelancers with an arsenal of tools to provide to new clients who are looking for a moderator. Providing some of the above items, before they are asked for, will certainly make a new vendor prospect stand out from the mix of proposals a client might receive.

Now if you are looking for a lion tamer—please write to Naomi@liontamer.org. I will be looking for work in that arena right after I start collecting Social Security payments since "Samurai Central" is not an option.

Enjoy the View: Client Ground Rules for Observing Focus Groups

> *There are rules for respondents to follow so the QLMR process will be effective. Moderators have rules to follow so that the data collected will be useful for end-users. Clients should have guidelines too—it is not just an opportunity for sanctioned voyeurism.*

With clients pushing to cover as many different issues as time allows, researchers using traditional two-hour focus groups have to make every minute count. After allowing time for respondents to enter the room, get settled, listen to the study purpose, and introduce themselves, researchers only have one hundred minutes for questions! Setting up ground rules for respondents can help speed up the process and save valuable time. From the client point of view, the focus group or the in-depth interview is more than just watching respondents through one-way mirrors or remote video. It is "living research," and this article focuses on ground rules for observers to make the qualitative market research as rich as possible.

Get Focused

First of all, it is important to be clear on the purpose of research. What are the key reasons qualitative research is being conducted? Have you read the background file on the study of the research proposal? Is your agenda in line with the written study purpose? **Be sure to review the moderator's guide before the start of the first session** so you can become familiar with the key issues to be covered and the tasks to be completed.

Arrive at least forty-five minutes before the scheduled start of the session. Your early arrival cuts down on the chance of running into participants and heightening their anxiety about who the observers are. Then introduce yourself in a way that maintains corporate anonymity if the recruiting was blind. This phrase works well: *"Hello. My name is X and I am here as part of the moderator's team. Is she/he here yet?"* Avoid saying something like, *"Hello. I am the client and I am here to watch the focus group."*

A dramatic example of inappropriate client behavior occurred during a study for a radio station in New York City. The purpose of the research was to assess the image of that station among light and heavy listeners. The recruiting had been blind, so respondents did not know which radio station was paying for the project. An early topic intended for each group was: *"What's your impression of WKLT? What do you associate with this station?"* These questions were to be asked about three stations in the New York City area. It was critical to see what descriptive words were used about each station.

Fifteen minutes before the group was due to begin, two observers from the client radio station came into the suite, briefcases in hand, and marched up to the reception desk. One of them said, in a voice loud enough for everyone to hear: *"I am with the station manager for WKLT, and I am here to watch the groups."* The cat was out of the bag on several counts. Every respondent now knew which radio station was paying for the research and what they looked like. Any opportunity to get unbiased answers about the image of the station was lost.

This sorely compromised the research opportunity, and the advertising agency and the moderator jointly agreed the disclosure would adversely affect the research to be garnered. Therefore, the group of listeners were paid and sent home. That gaffe cost the radio station all the fees for that group and a lost opportunity.

Be Flexible

Both the moderator and the clients should be flexible. Moderators do not have to ask every question in the guide or ask the questions in the same language or order as the written guide. The qualitative process is not as rigid as a survey, and good moderators follow the energy in a discussion. Moderators also skip questions if respondents have already covered an area if time constraints exist.

Do not expect every minute of every group to be meaningful or every question to have an immediate payoff in providing important insights. Some questions, and their subsequent answers by respondents, are bridges to move from one topic to another or to close down an area. Respondents have to formulate an opinion, and sometimes they do that out loud rather than internally. Sometimes the moderator is "backtracking" or "future pacing," and the questions and their answers, on the surface, do not appear to be going anywhere.

You can also count on respondents to forget the ground rules occasionally. The group process is dynamic—the respondents feed and stimulate each other. In the excitement of a new idea, it is natural to blurt out comments and all talk at once. Fear and shyness about revealing one's thoughts or beliefs can make someone talk softly or want to share only with someone nearby and not to the group as a whole. Being the only one with a positive point of view in the face of negative reactions from others (or vice versa) can cause a respondent to lose his/her courage in the spotlight glare.

Listen and observe. Listen for more than a confirmation or a validation of your own point of view. Listen to what respondents are actually saying and see it from their perspective. Be willing to listen to misinformation and perhaps discover an insight into respondents' thinking. Be alert to the nuances of meaning and the language respondents use to present their perceptions, opinions, beliefs, and attitudes. Also, do not expect a consensus within or across groups. The degree of divergent thinking may be the trend that is reported.

Avoid Judging Respondents

Even though respondents are told they are being observed, they tend to forget because they cannot hear or see the observers. However, observers look at the respondents with no chance of making eye contact and can use that "fly on the wall" vantage point to gain an unobstructed view of individuals' perceptions, opinions, and attitudes. On the other hand, some observers experience embarrassment during the viewing opportunity because they are uncomfortable with the "sanctioned voyeurism" aspect of the mirror. Either type of client may fall prey to judging respondents. Respondents can be judged as not worthy to comment on the content under discussion because of their appearance or because they do not meet the observer's internal criteria or expectations.

Moderators have learned to work under a guideline called unconditional positive regard (UPR). This guideline enables them to interact with respondents, regardless of dislike of their looks, speech, or attitude so long as they are answering the questions posed and helping reach the intended purpose of the study. **It would be ideal if client observers could also master UPR and allow respondents to express themselves without being judged.**

Both moderators and clients should respect respondents and the information they bring along with their perceptions, opinions, beliefs, and attitudes (POBAs). And both **should honor respondents who have come alone to a re-**

search facility to meet with a group of strangers for a stipend to discuss a topic only vaguely outlined on the phone.

Watch Non-Verbal Behavior

Look for congruence between what is said and how the respondent looks. Do not label non-verbal behavior or attach external meanings. Example: a respondent crosses her arms over her chest and leans away from the table as other respondents talk about a sensitive issue. What does her non-verbal behavior mean? It could mean discomfort with the conversation or disapproval of the other respondent for having a different point of view or for speaking at all about the topic. It could mean an old back injury has flared up, and crossing the arms relieves some of the ache. Because several possible explanations exist, simply note the behavior and see if verbal comments are made that provide insights. If clients take notes during the discussion on non-verbal aspects of the discussion, they will be useful in the debriefing process since moderators do not take notes while moderating.

Set Up Agreements and Procedures in Advance

It is wise to remain in the observation room(s) during the full period of the interview. Repeated door openings remind respondents that the mirror is one-way. Also, treat the facility staff as professionals, not as servants. If you have a special food request, please ask for it in advance, not on site. Do not abuse the rental agreement the moderator has with the facility by arriving too early or staying beyond the allotted time without a prior agreement with the facility.
Meet with the moderator one hour before the group and work out agreements. This is the time to be sure the moderator is clear about any changes wanted since the last communication cycle. The moderator may ask for one person to serve as the single point of contact (SPOC) for the back room. The primary job of the SPOC is to serve as the focal point for any questions the backroom has for the moderator and to be the one voice that the moderator listens to if he/she has questions during the group. At this point, the moderator and SPOC should agree on how notes from the back room to the moderator should be handled, and in most cases, it is best to send no notes before forty-five minutes into the research room so the moderator has had a chance to establish rapport and trust with respondents. The SPOC is the person the moderator will meet, in the hallway, at the "False Close" to determine what, if any, areas need to be revisited or new areas to be explored before respondents are finished and paid.

Never ask a facility staff member to step into the room and say, *"Respondent Z, you have a phone call. Bring your coat, purse, or briefcase with you."* This lie is transparent and deeply harms the rapport process, because respondents will be waiting to see if their statement results in someone behind the mirror pushing the "eject" button on them. Send a note to the moderator with the name of the person you want excused and a brief reason, and the moderator will handle it appropriately without losing rapport or trust with the remaining respondents.

Establish the approximate time of "false close." The standard practice for the industry is to set the false close at about fifteen minutes before the scheduled end time of the sessions. To setup a false close, the moderator says, *"I have to step out for a moment. While I am gone, please do the following..."* The participants complete the assigned task while the moderator visits with the SPOC to obtain additional written questions observers want asked of respondents. The moderator then returns to the room and asks additional questions.

Tips to Remember

The one-way mirror in a wall is almost impossible to soundproof, so be careful when making any noise that respondents might hear. Also, remember that qualitative research is intended to provide clients with a variety of outcomes, such as a range of responses from varied groups of respondents, insights into the thinking of a person either in groups or individually, and detailed exploration of issues without full closure. It also helps researchers observe reactions after exposure to concepts, products, and advertisements. **When watching focus groups, do not expect to be entertained.** In fact, researchers can expect to encounter boredom, frustration, disappointment, enlightenment, confirmation, distraction, and confusion along with some really stellar insights.

Finally, keep in mind that qualitative research is not rocket science. It is real people providing their points of view about products, services, ideas, concepts, or advertising. Sometimes it is funny. Sometimes it is sad. It can be tiresome, enervating, exciting, or enlivening. However the process goes, it is always about people. You have a window into the lives of respondents. Enjoy the view!

Note:
See Client "Groundrules" found in Appendix B.

How Clients Can Get The Most From Qualitative Market Research

> *Four methods are presented to help clients maximize the information they receive from QRE projects. These methods include finding creative ways to keep the client in the loop when they cannot attend every one of the planned qualitative events that comprise their study. After all, one QRE does not a study make.*

On the personal side of the business equation as a freelance moderator, I long for the "good old days" when time and money were more plentiful. In those days the full client team was in on the whole process from creating the study purpose to attending the research presentation. Now, because of the pressures of the business world and the fragmentation of project assignments, not every client can be part of every step of the research process.

In the absence of returning to the past, I make it my personal mission to keep clients in the "learning loop" as quickly as I can, so that the best decisions can be made from the wonderful power of qualitative research – standing on this premise: *"If you know how your target market thinks, you have the best chance to inspire them to purchase your goods and services."*

When clients attended every Qualitative Research Event [QRE]conducted in a study, that meant watching all twelve in-depth interviews [IDIs]; every one of the nine dyads; and all six of the focus groups. However, with the press of other commitments and responsibilities, clients today cannot always attend every single QRE in a study. They come when they can and stay as long as they can. What then results is a "checkerboard experience" that does not mirror the experiences of observers who watched all the QREs. Additionally, it differs from the experience of the moderator who conducted all the QREs – the one person who sees and feels the themes and trends as they actually emerge.

The good news about seeing any part of the QRE experience is that a client at least gets a glimpse into the lives of the target market being interviewed. They can savor some of the mood and language of the target market as they respond to concepts, positioning statements, advertising elements, prototypes, etc., from whatever portion they happen to watch.

The primary drawback to seeing only a portion of the QRE process is that a client might walk away with a distorted image of the findings. For example, if a client watches two out of twelve IDIs; or one of the nine dyads; or seventy-five percent of one six o'clock group in the sextet of focus groups; they only have a slice of the research "apple pie". The difficulty is that they may have gotten: a bit of the pie without any nuts or raisins; the burned part; the soggy crust part; the part with very few apples; or the sweetest part of the pie. It is impossible to extrapolate what the whole pie was "like" from one slice. This is the downside of only seeing a little bit of the process in a qualitative research study.

To combat this situation, I ask myself this question for every project I work on: *"How do I help my client understand that they cannot project to the whole pie from the little slice they consumed?"*

Here are some methods that have worked for me:

1. Send the client an **"End of the QRE Day Memo"** each day the study is "on the road." In this memo I highlight the key insights gleaned that day from the data collected via "surprises" and "confirmations" format to highlight key information in an easy to read chart.
2. **Indicate any emerging trends** that are occurring as the field work rolls along – e.g., current winning concept; the newest ideas respondents are creating; or positive/negative reactions to advertising strategies; etc.
3. Caution that what they saw was a small **"slice of life"** and not a "holographic image" where the part represents the whole. One IDI does not a study make, nor does one focus group.
4. **Get a final report into the hands of the client as quickly as possible** that presents the whole story of the findings – the longer the gap between whatever part the client saw and what is written by the moderator, the more likely the client will default to what portion of the QRE(s) they saw.

At the end of the day, there is truly no way to control the thinking of clients – those who saw every QRE in the study or the ones who only got a taste of the process.

It is even possible for a client to see every one of the QREs in a study and via "selective perception" will only hold on to that information that supports their hypothesis – ignoring any element that does not. This is just as damaging as the client who saw a few of the QRE elements in the project and tries to extrapolate that experience as a proxy for the whole study!

Hopefully, the client who sees just a snapshot of the whole qualitative process can be supported by vendors or internal staff via clear memos and interim reports that keep them in the loop as the data comes in daily from QREs they did not personally experience.

How Clients & Researchers Listen Differently to Focus Group Comments

> *Clients are listening "for" something when viewing focus groups – for example to confirm or clarify data. Moderators are listening "to" clients to determine desired outcomes. As well they are listening "to" respondents to gather perceptions, opinions, beliefs, and attitudes (POBAs). That is two very different kinds of listening.*

A few minutes before the end of a focus group, it is my standard practice to leave the focus group room to talk to the client spokesperson to see what last minute items the client wants explored before the group is released. Some clients ask me to revisit an area explored earlier and recap an insight. Others want me to ask something new. Either way, it gives the backroom a chance to get a specific answer, to a specific question, before respondents are excused.

At the end of a research day, I conduct and record a fifteen minute "Aha/Confirm" debrief in the conference room with observers helping to fill in a chart with the same title. I ask them what they heard that was new, surprising, or an "aha," and what they heard that they expected to hear (which I call a "confirm"). The confirm side of the chart is always about one-third the length of the "aha" side, as qualitative research is seldom commissioned to confirm what is already known.

Recently, while doing this exercise, it dawned on me that clients and researchers are not listening to respondents in the same way. **Clients are listening "for" something and researchers are listening "to" something.**

What Are Clients Listening For?

Clients commission research because they want to find out something specific from respondents. For example:

- A **political consultant** may want to find out how his candidate is seen in the eyes of voters
- A **product manufacturer** may be listening for what respondents feel are compelling points of a new product and if the product will replace something they now use or be added to their consideration set
- A **television production company** is listening for insights as to whether the pilot show is something that grabs initial interest and will have viewers returning to see more of the show in future episodes
- An **advertising agency** is listening for what elements of the advertisement make it believable and move viewers to action

All these different clients are listening "for" information that will help them in their short and long term strategy decisions. Sometimes they are listening for specific words, such as adjectives they can use in a campaign; or are listening for how respondents describe emotions associated with stimuli presented. Ultimately, clients are listening for one of these two elements:

a. What they already believe to be true (i.e., seeking confirmation)
b. What they want to be true (using research to "check in" on those assumptions)

There is nothing wrong with clients listening for the two elements mentioned above. Where the problem lies is that this kind of listening can dismiss or delete comments that do not agree with a previously held hypothesis or belief on the part of the client. In some cases, clients will "play down" a comment they hear in a group discussion as being whimsical, frivolous, or mistaken when in fact, it is part of the thinking of a respondent as they look at the various stimuli presented in group settings or when they participate in spirited conversations. Yes, there are times when respondents say odd/bizarre things; or are completely confused by stimuli/the discussion. Sometimes, respondents just "don't get it." I am not referring to these instances. Some of the ways it becomes clear that the client is deleting what they are hearing is when they make comments such as this:

"With a hair-do like that—of course she doesn't like the idea."

"These people are not our target market —they are not at all what I expected to see tonight."

"They wouldn't know a good idea if it hit them in the head—they don't even have college degrees."

Phrases such as these are clues that the client is not honoring what is being said, in the event comments from respondents do not fit their expectations. By contrast, comments such as the ones below prove that a client is honoring respondent comments:

"Wow, we need to take into consideration some of the points they are making —glad we did this research."

"These folks are more savvy than we thought—we will need to make sure our RTB [Reason to Believe] holds water."

"Hmm…we didn't think they would react so strongly to that second concept…we almost didn't include it in the study—but at least we know what not to do."

What Are Researchers Listening To?

When tasked with discovering respondent perceptions, opinions, beliefs, and attitudes (POBAs) a skilled researcher has to set aside his/her own beliefs and assumptions in order to truly listen to what respondents are saying. Skilled researchers should ask **"true questions"** – those to which they do not know the answer. They are supposed to ask **neutral questions** that do not lead respondents to any particular point of view except the one they are standing upon. Furthermore, researchers should be listening to what respondents are saying and then probing for enough information to insure that they get **more than top-of-mind answers from respondents.**

An effective moderator guides progress from general questions that set a baseline understanding of the topic under discussion and then moves deeper into territory surrounding products, ideas, concepts, advertising, etc. In this way, clients can get a clear read on how consumers from the target market perceive what is being presented. Neutral, non-leading, true questions help set the stage for clients to hear respondent POBAs allowing clients to use those insights to shape the next phase of the project.

Skilled moderators are also listening to instances of misinformation. I remember a project for a company that makes veggie burgers where respondents were moms who had never tried or served a veggie burger, but were not opposed to doing so. Part of the study included asking what they thought were the key ingredients in a veggie burger. The moderator listed respondent responses on easel paper. Across eight groups of respondents, not one group mentioned a vegetable on the lists generated! They listed items such as tofu, whey, gluten, soy, spices, wheat, bulgur, and rice, but they did not mention beans, red pepper, lentils, peas, tomatoes, mushrooms, onions, corn, zucchini, or eggplant. If the moderator had been listening "for" vegetables on the list – rather than "to" what they were saying, the opportunity to discover what to play up in future advertising would have been lost.

The ability to listen "to" what is being said starts with the first interviews with the client when they start outlining what they want from qualitative research. If the moderator is listening "for" a research design, a specific methodology or "marching orders," it will be more difficult to meet client objectives. By listening "to" what the client is saying—i.e., concerns about the product prototype, difficulty with reaching agreement on the best concepts to test, or what new product names will help distinguish their product from competitors, then the moderator can help construct a clear study purpose, recommend a study design and methodology, as well as get a leg up on the design of the moderator's guide.

In the best of all possible worlds, it would be lovely if clients would work toward more listening "to" respondents and less listening "for" confirmations. Moderators would be wise to focus their research energies on listening "to" clients and respondents, so that both are served well.

Minimizing Client Problems on Focus Group Projects

> Learn how to serve as the perfect project manager—another of the hats of a Master Moderator™. Nip client-related problems in the bud for a rich focus group experience!

When the client-researcher relationship is more collegial than adversarial, the research purpose is more easily realized and the value of qualitative research techniques can be maximized. How does a researcher develop a mutually beneficial relationship with a client and minimize the problems?

Focus group projects pose a different set of problems than other types of research, and those problems often stem from the short duration of the projects. The ideal project would be one in which qualitative researchers had eight weeks to prepare for the project and six weeks to write the final report. Most focus group projects take less than eight weeks from client request to delivery of the final report.

The benefits of focus group research are fast turnaround time and having clients attend live sessions with target market consumers.

This article is intended to provide some remedies for minimizing the problems of working in a high-intensity, short-timeline environment with a variety of clients in the focus group process.

Minimizing Problems

Qualitative researchers have learned several techniques to minimize problems, some of which are practical and some philosophical: **determine the purpose of the project at the first meeting; communicate regularly with the client; tell the client the truth; take responsibility for the whole project.**

1. **Determine the purpose of the project at the first meeting.**

Many times the first client meeting is on the phone rather than in person. However, that initial contact is critical. The client is in the first flush of interest and is in close contact with the driving factors for choosing qualitative research at this phase.

Many project problems can be minimized right away by discussing these issues in the first meeting:

- Background: Where does this research fit in?
- Intended outcomes: How will the data be used to support client decision making?
- Vision: What is the client's picture of what the groups will look like, and what might they likely hear from respondents?

Once the researcher has the same picture of the research as the client, the clincher question can be asked: *"What is the purpose of the research?"*

Due to the timelines of qualitative market research, many clients have not taken the time to write down a clear statement of purpose. Rather, they have a working purpose that forms the base for conversations, and that working purpose often takes the form of assumptions.

Written Purpose

The technique that is most effective in preventing problems with clients is to address the assumptions in conversations with the client team, then to quickly formulate a written purpose, and have it approved by the client. This seems like such as simple step: just write down the reason for the research. However, in practice it is not so simple. It requires the distillation of many points of view from the client team, and there may be overt as well as covert agendas at work.

The difficulty in obtaining a clear purpose from a client team is a bit like asking a groom why he is getting married. There is not just one purpose, there are multiple purposes. The trick is to find out which purpose is the driving purpose.

To minimize researcher difficulties in writing a clear statement of purpose, I have found this question to be effective: *"If you could only ask one question of the respondents in the focus group, what would that question be?"*

Based on the response and careful listening to the overt and covert agendas in the client conversation, a good researcher can develop a workable written purpose that the client can read and own.

Below are some examples of purpose statements that we have developed using the afore mentioned question:

- Determine consumer interest in prepackaged telecommunications services
- Have target market members evaluate three different proposed print advertisements
- Explore concept of beauty products based on family folklore from women in rural America
- Obtain shopper reactions to new pantyhose display
- Determine image of imported beer versus domestic beer and occasions for use of each
- Compare taste of spicy versus non-spicy fried chicken, and discover what words convey those features to consumers who eat chicken from fast food establishments

Note the key words in these purpose statements: determine interest, evaluate, explore, obtain reactions, determine image, and compare taste. These "action words" are the clues to the driving purpose of the study. Within each purpose statement are other sub-purposes, but with the driving purpose clearly stated, the sub-purposes can be woven into the moderator's guide.

"So That" Phrase

However, in each of the purpose statements listed above, there is a missing phrase. That phrase would continue the sentence and start with "… so that…" It might end the sentence with "so that new advertising can be developed" or "… so that product sales can be increased." The "so that" phrase is never written, just implied. It is usually part of the hidden agenda that is involved in the discussion with the client team. The term "hidden" is not intended to be pejorative. Rather, it is a term to point to that part of the client-researcher conversation that never seems to come to light because it is in the daily fabric of the client's work.

The "driving force" is a bit like a laser beam; it burns a clean hole wherever it is aimed. Problems on projects often arise when new ideas for the focus group research pop up midstream. The source may be new players on the client team or a new set of ideas from the advertising agency. Regardless of the source, the study may start to stray away from the laser beam. When this happens, a researcher can ask the question: *"How does this new request relate to the purpose of the study?"*

If the response is "on track with the purpose," it is appropriate to include it in the study. If not, the researcher is within his/her rights to ask that the new ideas not be included.

2. Communicate regularly with the client.

The first communication with the client after the initial meeting should be a written letter proposal that contains the following information:

- Introduction: overview of the research project under contract
- Statement of purpose: clear, short statement
- Statement of intended outcomes: clear, short statement that indicates how the research will be used
- Study logistics: schedule, number of groups, recruiting specifications, study sites, and number of observers in each location
- Moderator qualifications: credentials, related experience
- Description of study tasks (with timeline for completion)
- Outline of what issues will be covered in the guide
- Product costs
- "Next steps" section: clear statement of what moderator will do and what client is expected to complete upon receipt of proposal
- Summary and closure

After the proposal has been accepted and the purpose agreed upon, it is recommended that the researcher stay in close contact with the client, and provide updates on the recruiting process as well as obtain reactions to the draft guide. On some projects this requires daily contact.

Our experience indicates that poor communication is a primary source of client-related problems. There is also a strong correlation between poor communication and the growth of assumptions. Regular communication (especially if there is bad news) reduces the possibility of a project going off-line and keeps all the parties moving along at the same pace with the same expectations.

A latter-day philosopher once indicated that an upset is composed of three elements: undelivered communications, thwarted intentions, and unrealized expectations. Researchers cannot do much about the latter two, but they can do a great deal about the first one. The ground rule is to communicate all the news and communicate it regularly.

3. Tell the client the truth.

This technique falls in both realms, the practical and the philosophical. Everyone's mother or grandmother has said at some point in the parenting process: *"Always tell the truth."* It is never more necessary than in client relationships. Philosophically speaking, the reasons for lying boil down to these elements:

- Desire to be well thought of or liked by another
- Desire to avoid looking stupid or foolish
- Response to fear
- Failure to deliver what was promised

How to avoid lying in relationships, client or otherwise, goes beyond the scope of this article. However, we can share one technique that keeps the door open to truth-telling with clients. Use this maxim: *"An informed client is a supportive client."* Without client support for a research project, problems are bound to multiply.

Recently, I worked on a project that involved focus groups with government decision makers. Phase I of the project was with individuals who worked in civil agencies. In Phase II we were supposed to recruit individuals who worked with a specific military agency. As the recruiting process got under way, recruiters had an unusually high refusal rate from qualified respondents. We tried every possible way to recruit respondents, but we kept hitting a stone wall. What we needed to do was tell the client the truth: *"We cannot deliver on our promise to recruit Phase II respondents, and we will not be able to conduct the research you want. We'll have to refund the deposit you have paid us, and we'll have to cancel the remainder of the study."*

Talk about difficult communication! It meant loss of face, loss of money, and failure to keep a promise. I stalled on making the phone call to the client as long as possible. But I remembered the maxim: *"An informed client is a supportive client."* When I called, the conversation was a lot shorter than I expected, and the client said: *"We had a lot of doubts about Phase II, and we're not surprised you've run into problems. I agree, let's cancel this phase. Just write up the results from Phase I, and we'll look at some other options to garner the opinions from the military."*

Yes, I had to return the deposit, and yes, we lost money on this contract. What we did win, however, was the respect of our client for telling the truth. They have referred us twice for other projects both within their division and outside.

4. Take responsibility for the whole project.

"Passing the buck" is an old game that many of us have played in one form or another. With the short deadlines and the fast turnarounds that qualitative research requires, it is a deadly game and one that can lead to a series of escalating problems with clients. Even though many qualitative researchers are consultants to the client team, not employees, the most effective role for us to play is as if we were the senior decision maker on the project, not just the implementer of the research phase.

When the moderator takes the position of being responsible for every portion of the study, not just the tasks and assignments outlined in the proposal, the project moves forward in the Gestalt Mode: in the whole, not the parts. When one works only on the parts, problems are sure to emerge in areas that are unknown.

A moderator's real role is that of project manager, managing the whole project and delegating tasks among all individuals working on the project. When the moderator holds this position, one can oversee all the tasks and the project functions.

Task delegation even comes down to telling the client what role they need to play in the research process. I can recall making statements such as the following to client decision makers:

- *"I'll need to have the issues memo by Friday, so I can keep your project on schedule."*
- *"My ground rules are not to accept any notes into the focus group for the first forty-five minutes. Does that pose a problem for you?"*
- *"There are too many disparate issue areas to cover in the two hours. If you want to have the taste test, what can I drop?"*
- *"The list of subscribers needs to be emailed no later than Thursday. Who on your staff will be responsible for doing that?"*
- *"I recommend that we have a conference call the week before the groups with the agency and the brand manager for an update on the issues that will be covered in the groups and to read aloud the concepts to be tested."*

If the moderator expects someone else to be responsible for the research tasks, we have abdicated our responsibility as researchers, then we become research lackeys for clients rather than consultants.

Check the List

It would be wrong to imply that RIVA does not have problems with clients. Sometimes we momentarily forget our own techniques in the swirl of multiple projects or run into a personality type that drives us up the wall. However, before the problem can torpedo a project, we mentally check our list and ask ourselves these questions:

1. *Are we clear on the purpose of the project?*
2. *Are we in regular communication with the client?*
3. *Have we told the truth to ourselves? To the client?*
4. *Have we "passed the buck?"*

If the answers are *"yes"* for questions 1, 2, 3 and *"no"* for question 4, and the problem still is not solved, we agree that the problem is bigger than all of us.

Statements like the above are good evidence of project management, not project doormat. While qualitative researchers are often told what to do, we do have the right to say, *"No, this will work better."*

Asking the Right Questions of Clients Will Create the Best Questions for Respondents

> *It is impossible to ask respondents the "right" questions if the study purpose is murky or if the client team has more than one agenda. Look here for the four key questions to ask clients before screeners or guides are drafted in order to keep projects focused.*

Questions for Qualitative Research Event [QRE] respondents are critical to helping clients understand the perceptions, opinions, beliefs, and attitudes [POBAs] of various target groups of consumers. QRE questions need to be open-ended and avoid leading respondents to some pre-ordained thought path. Powerful questions need to get participants to respond beyond top-of-mind answers. **However, a moderator may never get to those great questions, unless the <u>right</u> questions have been asked of the clients who commission the study.**

Questions are powerful tools to access a wide range of information from facts to beliefs and from behaviors to dreams and wishes. However, in the framed timelines of qualitative studies, it is best to focus the questions in the areas that are going to help clients with their strategic planning. This means the moderator needs to know what the client is "up to" in terms of the desired outcomes for the study and the eventual use of the final results.

RIVA has worked with clients on qualitative research projects since 1981, covering topics as diverse as bioterrorism and as practical as a new dog food for pet owners who have very small dogs. A candidate running for President sat behind the mirror on a RIVA project and listened to comments about his southern accent. Clients cried behind the mirror while listening to people dying of AIDS as they shared their concerns about trying to live everyday life with a deadly disease and provide for the children they were leaving behind. Everyone in the back room [including the moderator] laughed with a ten year-old boy when he saw a package design for a laxative and said *"My mom calls this stuff 'adult only' chocolate."*

These kinds of events do not "just happen"… they are the result of effective questions. Every one of those projects needed moderators to ask respondents questions that drilled down into client issues, so that decision making stood on a rich body of information.

Over the years, RIVA has formulated a set of key questions to ask clients early in the project planning process, so that guide formulation targets the key issues and raises the likelihood that the last sentence in a report reads as follows: *"The study objectives were realized in that this study provided insights about XYZ."*

This article highlights four key questions, from among the many that RIVA asks of clients, and provides a rationale for each one in the quartet.

Question 1: *If the QRE only lasted one minute, what must you know from respondents?*

This question forces clients to discard the "interesting to know" aspects of the project and focus in on the key element for conducting the study in the first place. When this question is posed to clients, there is often a moment of silence while they sort among myriad options to locate the "gold nugget" that defines the project purpose. Some responses heard over the years have included:

- *We really need to know if they prefer coupons over rebates for items costing more than $700*
- *It is critical to find out what impact viewing documents on-line vs. printed hard copy has on their purchase decision*
- *We need to know how much more they are willing to pay for pet food that is infused with vitamins, organic vegetables, and grains*
- *We need to find out the top reasons they stopped shopping at our stores*
- *We are looking at changing our marketing strategy to increase the conversion rate of inquiry to enrollment at this college – so we really need to know the reason they did not enroll after they attended the open house and took home an application packet*

The response to this question (when asked of the client team) becomes the "spine" on which the whole project sits and makes it much easier to write a screener, a guide, and a final report.

Question 2: *What baseline assumptions or hypotheses are already in place?*

Clients are usually already more than half way to having a strong hypothesis about the rationale behind something happening (or not) with their target market. By exploring this topic with them, a qualitative researcher becomes aware of the "listening filter" that clients will be using as they view the role qualitative research will play in illuminating their understanding.

The moderator's role in hearing the assumptions/hypotheses from the client is to use that information to craft the line of questions [from general to specific] that will help respondents clearly explain their POBAs, so clients can thoughtfully evaluate the qualitative elements that will help support or refute a particular hypothesis.

Question 3: *What might change as a result of conducting the QRE project? [Or what is going to happen once this data is collected and evaluated by the client team?]*

Moderators may well ask a very different set of questions once they know what might change as a result of gathering data from respondents for client decision making. For example, suppose the point of the qualitative research study is to determine the "most preferred advertising campaign approach from the three presented to respondents." If that is the case, the moderator knows that based on the results from six focus groups, a "winner" will be selected and given to the advertising agency to "run with." That means the kinds of questions to be asked of respondents will be different than if the purpose of the project is to see what elements in each of the three campaigns "resonate" with respondents in the area of aspirations.

Imagine a company is considering launching a new product (unless they hear something really serious as a barrier to product acceptance). In that case, the line of questioning has to address the issues of barriers along with acceptance in an even handed way.

Question 4: *What does the client NOT need information about – what would be a waste of time to explore in the QRE project?*

This point was driven home dramatically by its absence on a project early in my career as a moderator. I thought I had clear direction on the purpose of the study and the desired outcomes. I wrote a thoughtful guide with a fifteen minute section on current usage of the product category—a typical starting place for many focus group discussions.

In the phone call reviewing the draft guide I sent, my client said, *"Don't waste our time finding out about current usage—we already have tons of data on that in the files. We want you to confirm that they are heavy, light, or medium users and then show them the four new package designs right away."* She was not very polite in the use of the phrase *"Don't waste our time."* However, I got the lesson immediately and it is now a standard question in my first call with a client. I usually phrase my question like this: *"What information do you already have on the key topics?"* They might say *"We don't have much data—that's what we are looking to learn from this study"* but sometimes they say: *"So glad you asked…definitely don't spend any time on XYZ—we've already done that research."* This question fosters client confidence that I am committed to giving them what they need and not anything extraneous.

Summary

While the four questions outlined here are only a subset of a much longer list, they point to the need to start the qualitative research planning process with key questions for clients. This way, it is much more likely that effective questions for respondents will be generated and used in the QREs that follow.

PART III: CONCLUSION: MASTER MODERATOR™ MUSINGS

MASTER MODERATOR™ MUSINGS

New Is Not Always Better:
The Value of Tried-&-True QLMR Techniques 347

A shiny new pair of shoes may be lovely, but sometimes they pinch! Learn how to see through the lure of attractive new techniques to avoid falling into the trap of "tricks" or games to play on respondents. Have a balanced outlook on the new and the old!

Two Maxims for Moderators 355

Take your guide. Read it. Now ready... set... go... EAT IT! Eat the guide—burp the questions. Learn how to put your guide into action and how to be with people, not lost in paper! Practice really does make perfect.

What If? 359

Not all questions should be asked of focus group participants. There are questions that the qualitative researcher needs to consider too. Facing some important "what if?" challenges, follow this Master Moderator™ into the future of qualitative research!

Never Too Late to Learn a Good Lesson 363

Being a Master Moderator™ doesn't mean that learning stops. This lesson showed up after leading thousands of focus groups and it illustrates that it is never too late to learn something useful in the qualitative research arena.

New Is Not Always Better: The Value of Tried & True QLMR Techniques

> *A shiny new pair of shoes may be lovely, but sometimes they pinch! Learn how to see through the lure of attractive new techniques to avoid falling into the trap of "tricks" or games to play on respondents. Have a balanced outlook on the new and the old!*

Qualitative research tools have been around for centuries. Cavemen probably had a focus group to decide alternative uses of the wheel by asking: *"What is the value of a wheel, and how can we use it best?"* Caesar used a qualitative line of questioning when he asked his open-ended question: *"Et tu, Brutus?"* Through the speech of one of his heroines, Shakespeare basically asked: *"What is the quality of mercy?"* All these lines of questions lead to a discussion of POBAs (perceptions, opinions, beliefs, and attitudes) - the four pillars of qualitative research.

Focus groups, the premier research model in qualitative market research (QLMR), involve writing screeners, recruiting, booking facilities, moderating groups, and writing reports. All these tasks are twentieth-century innovations. Two of the founding fathers of the business, Dr. Ernst Dichter and Dr. Richard K. Merton, contributed greatly to the QLMR industry. Early focus groups in the U.S. were conducted in the late 1930s, and legend has it that the first client to buy the service was a soap manufacturer! Dr. Merton's book <u>The Focused Interview</u> was first released in the 1940s, and a revised edition was released in 1994 to update new insights.

Early research models for QLMR are still the standard and include these factors: two-hour time frame, one moderator with good skills, paid respondents, and a research setting conducive to promoting an interactive discussion.

New models such as large groups (more than twelve respondents), or mini-groups (between four and six respondents), or dyads and triads are used to collect data these days. These new group sizes have timelines that run from thirty minute sessions to all day events are custom tailored to fit an increasing set of client needs. Those needs may run the gamut from idea generation to package design to advertising evaluations, concept and storyboard tests, and sensory evaluations that cover food, health and beauty aids, and paint. Nevertheless, many truths still remain.

What is still true?

What is still true in all qualitative research is a line of questions designed to get respondents to open up and share their beliefs, their attitudes, their thinking, and their reactions to a wide range of client driven options about products, services and ideas.

What is still true of quantitative research is a desire to get the best data possible from respondents so that data can be accurately projected.

What is still true is researchers talking to real people and translating the findings into action reports so clients can make more informed decisions.

What is still true is that the imperfect science of asking questions of strangers helps clients understand more than top-of-mind behaviors of the very people who eventually buy or do not buy what clients have to offer.

There is a dazzling array of new technologies that are available for researchers. The business world is fueled by the speed of computers, software, cell phones, and presentation graphics. The research world experiments with hand-held devices for respondents to tally answers right in the group, online focus groups and faster and faster report cycles for clients who want the findings fast! With all this speed and technology, it is easy to keep thinking that the best research project is one that uses the newest tools.

One key point explored in this article: **the best research tools are not always the newest ones**. While the spotlight will be on focus groups, the reader can make applications to the other QLMR models in use today.

Here are some examples from everyday living where simple is still the best:

- **Making bread**: There are new machines, new types of flour, fresher butter, and pure sugars; and yet any simple bread made by a mother in any culture is best loved by her children— whether it is made in a skillet, on a rock, over an open fire, in a wood burning oven, or in a modern electric or gas stove— simple bread is still the best.
- **Brewing coffee**: There are new beans, new machines, and new techniques for roasting, yet the best coffee is still fresh roasted beans, freshly

ground and brewed with good water. Fancy machines do not make coffee taste any better than a treasured old coffee pot, although your attitude about the coffee may shift! This is a lesson that Starbucks has mastered well.

In qualitative research, there are nifty tools available to moderators like laddering and picture sorts and role playing opportunities. There are drawing exercises, projective techniques, sentence completions, and worksheets aimed at getting below top-of-mind responses.

There are other tools such as "sharing pairs" where respondents work in teams and look for solutions. There are collage exercises and the writing of product obituaries. Respondents can pretend to be members of an advisory board or a board of directors. They can use a light bulb or a magic marker or an ashtray as stimuli to see what those unrelated items could bring to a creative solution. They can use mind-mapping or hand-held recording devices to get private answers before public disclosures.

There is so much that a moderator can do that it is possible to use the full two hours of a traditional focus group in just setting up tasks, giving directions, and making sure respondents are doing what you asked!

It is very seductive to keep looking for more, better, and different tools to go deeper with respondents or to get them to confess early and often what they are really thinking or feeling. Sometimes moderators ask me: *"Do you know any tools or techniques that will help me get more information faster?"* Sometimes there is a nifty little tool or technique, but that is just what it is: a nifty little thing, like a band-aid. Maybe researchers really want to know if there is an MRI machine to look deep into the minds/hearts of respondents to get the needed data.

There is no QLMR MRI machine. What **is** available is the opportunity to build a moderator toolbox of simple, little, ordinary techniques that create the following environment:

- Trust between moderator and respondents
- Respect for what respondents have to say
- Steady pace to keep discussion moving along
- Variety of simple activities that keep interest
- Method of asking questions that do not lead the witness

Trust

The easiest way to create trust in focus groups is to meet the respondents as early as possible. One way is to go to the waiting room and simply say, *"I am*

the moderator for the group with the blue name cards. We are going to be starting in a few minutes—the hostess will let you know when. I promise you'll be out on time."
Next, greet them at the door with a handshake and a simple generic statement: *"Welcome to the discussion on cars"* (or cold medicines, or the next election). After all are seated, restate the purpose of the discussion, give all disclosures (mics, mirrors, observers, etc.) and clear, simple ground rules for participation. Ask quick, easy, self introduction questions, introduce yourself, and start the group with a question that anyone can answer.

Respect

One of the most seductive things in communication is to have a listener that really listens! An effective moderator or interviewer is one who asks a question and **really** listens (all while looking at the respondents). He/she gets a lot more data than one who asks a question and looks away while the respondents are talking! That is called a "listener interruptus," and like the phrase it copies, it is not very satisfying! When moderators or interviewers show true, active listening skills—listening without judging, respondents are motivated to say more, to divulge deeper and deeper levels of information. It is an addictive process; the more the moderator listens, the more respondents talk. The more respondents talk, the more they want to share beyond top-of-mind responses. The doorway into that respect is good, clear questions and good listening skills.

Steady Pace

A boring focus group is one that jerks along in fits and starts—some good questions and probes and some poor questions and limited probes. Another contributor to a poor focus group is a moderator who does not vary the pace of the discussion, doing only one model: *I ask… you answer.* An effective focus group has a slow build—from general to specific. The flow moves from easy to more difficult questions and from activities that are low-risk to those with a higher risk. A good ground rule for moderators is to vary the process about every twenty minutes. Since groups last about one hundred minutes out of a possible one hundred and twenty, that means just five changes of pace. One model to consider follows:

Figure 5: *Stages of a Standard Two-Hour Focus Group: Timing & Procedures*

Stage 1: Introduction (20 minutes)
  Tasks: Trust building and demonstration of non-judgmental listening via delivery of guidelines and context as well as self-intros

Stage 2: Rapport and Reconnaissance (20 minutes)
  Tasks: Easy, low involvement questions, and one exercise or process

Stage 3: In-Depth Discussion: Part I (20 minutes)
  Tasks: More detailed, complex questions and two quick exercises

Stage 4: In-Depth Discussion: Part II (20 minutes)
  Tasks: Deeper discussion, two exercises, and pointed specific open-ended questions

Stage 5: Moving Toward Closure: (20 minutes)
  Tasks: Summary-style questions; no exercises, or one that takes no more than one minute

Total Time Elapsed: 100 minutes

(Remaining 20 minutes is for transitions and people logistics)

Variety of Simple Activities That Keep Interest

The key obstacle in focus groups is using a sixty-plus-year-old model of a two-hour session and fitting in everything that a client wants! A 1937 client probably wanted to cover two or three key issues. A client today wants five or six issues covered! With the added charge of keeping the pace moving, keeping respondents interested, and getting the data, there is a need for simple activities to meet those client needs.

What follows is a sample of some that are quick and easy as well as support the process of discussion:

- Ask short questions to get long answers (SQLA).
- Occasionally stand and ask questions from a different place in the room to create a different atmosphere and to infuse energy into the room.
- Ask questions that access different models of listening on the part of respondents (those that process data visually and kinesthetically).
- Provide written instructions for worksheets or detailed activities.
- When asking for lists (e.g. *"What are the factors you consider when buying a car?"*) use ten-fingers and a verbal countdown method rather than charting on the easel.
- Use sleeved items or other show and tell items to make the abstract real (e.g. *"Here are some brands of dishwashers (show names). Which one is the gold medal standard for the industry?"*) Each brand (GE, Whirlpool, Maytag, Kitchen Aid, and Kenmore) is typed in forty-point type and inserted in a plastic sleeve).
- Use easel to draw graphics to forward the conversation… to act as stimuli to get below top-of-mind responses. Some easy ones include drawing a stick figure and asking respondents to "*Tell me about the heavy user of NutraSweet… what is that person like… a man or woman, over or under forty, works or stays at home, has what kinds of shoes in their closets, etc.*" Another one is to draw a circle with arrows leading to it with a key word or phrase in the middle, such as "old age," and ask questions like: *"What comes to mind when you think of this phrase?"*

Method of Asking Questions That Does Not Lead the Witness

Moderators and interviewers are always pressed for time, and an easy default is to drop into helping respondents or leading respondents by asking questions that lead them to the answer arena for which you need responses. Avoid putting part of the answer you want in the question you ask. For example, do not ask: *"What are some reasons you grocery shop on your way home… is it because it is convenient?"* Simply ask: *"When do you grocery shop, and what are some reasons for that time frame?"*

Some other classic questions that illustrate leading:

- **Question:** *You like sports utility vehicles, right?*
- **Alternate:** *What do you like about SUVs?*

- **Question:** *Do you ever go to the grocery in the middle of the night?*
- **Alternate:** *What time of day is your usual time for shopping?*
- **PROBE:** *What is the latest or earliest you have every shopped?*

- **Question:** *It is quieter in grocery stores late at night, isn't it?*
- **Alternate:** *How is late night grocery shopping different from daytime grocery shopping?*

Keep questions open and keep them true questions—defined as questions to which the asker does not already have the answer! The alternates above provide some solutions.

Summary

It is fine to use new techniques or approaches in QLMR, as long as those techniques are not "tricks" or games to play on respondents to stroke the ego of a moderator or to impress a client. New techniques that meet the following criteria are probably good candidates to make the grade as a new tool in a moderator's toolbox:

- Technique has a clear purpose and a defined outcome
- Task allows respondents to participate in a way that does not demean or belittle them or their experiences
- Is conducted by a trained and experienced moderator who has practiced the technique, before using in an actual group, and by a researcher who understands the principles on which the technique is built
- Moves understanding about consumer behavior to a new and deeper level

Some of the newer techniques have been borrowed from other disciplines and in the hands of inexperienced researchers, who lack knowledge about the fundamental principles or paradigms on which the technique is built, these techniques can "bomb." In the quest for "new, different, and better," qualitative researchers may erroneously place emphasis on the technique rather than the outcome produced.

Key Points Outlined in This Article:

- It is good to have a full toolbox of skills as a researchers, however, do not quest after the new tools, tips, or techniques thinking that they are better than the old.
- Master a set of easy, simple techniques that work in a broad variety of situations.

- Remember that the researcher is the data collection tool and that respondents have the answers you need—they do not have a copy of the guide. Keep the questions and instructions easy to understand.
- Work on creating your own set of techniques that allow you to:
    o Create trust between interviewer and respondents
    o Maintain respect for what respondents have to say
    o Develop a steady pace to keep discussion moving along
    o Execute a variety of simple activities that keep interest

Two Maxims for Moderators

> *Take your guide. Read it. Now ready... set... go... EAT IT! Eat the guide—burp the questions. Learn how to put your guide into action and how to be with people, not lost in paper! Practice really does make perfect.*

When you are in the room with respondents, at least fifty different activities may be going on that requires your attention. Chief among them are the following:

- Establishing rapport
- Maintaining rapport
- Maintaining eye contact
- Reading the room
- Using active listening skills
- Probing for clarity and clarification
- Watching the time/managing timelines for sections
- Making sure you hear from quiet respondents
- Managing dominant respondents
- Setting up/showing interventions
- Remembering what was said by using linking and logic tracking techniques
- Varying tasks every twenty minutes
- Managing the climate of the room
- Making sure questions are on target
- Practicing unconditional positive regard (UPR) for respondents
- Watching process and content patterns
- Managing own body needs (e.g. enough water)

- Allowing and living with silence

If your head is stuck in the guide, you cannot successful moderate or manage group dynamics. You must be sufficiently familiar with the guide to have no need to read it word for word. **Once you have started the group, the guide should function as a road map in the same manner as it does for a driver. A glance will give you directions, but you have to look up in order to drive.**

What Makes an Effective Guide?

- Should include questions that are double spaced
- Should begin with #1 for each section (this makes it easy to revise and renumber when changes are made)
- Should have short questions (ideally, questions should be one line long—with only a few wrapping to a second line of text)
- Should have clearly written probes and instructions
- Should have bolding, highlighting, boxed areas, etc. to catch the eye

RIVA uses a template for several sections of the guide:

- Template #1: Page one—changing only the topic, topic-specific questions for intros, and timelines for the scheduled events
- Template #2: Page two—Client Only page—includes roadmap
- Template #3: Spacing of questions, subheads, and probes so RIVA guides look the same to the moderator—so all the focus is on content, not format

An effective guide is also universal—anyone, even an untrained moderator, can pick up the guide, ask questions, and move respondents through tasks.

Eat the Guide

"Eating" your guide means knowing the guide so well that you have digested it thoroughly and it has become a part of you. When this has happened, you know the purpose of the study, the major issue areas and the lines of questioning so that you know where you are in the discussion at all times. By internalizing the guide, you will also know when to recognize "gold mines" or key new areas that can emerge in a discussion. In moderator training classes, we tell students to *"eat the guide"* and then *"burp the questions!"*

Keep in mind that the respondents do not know your guide. More often than not, respondents will get into important issue areas that do not follow the logic pattern and sequence of your guide. If you know your guide thoroughly, it will be easy to judge whether to move into this issue area now or put it on hold for later. If you have eaten your guide, you will always be on familiar ground. As well, if you have a written guide from their viewpoint, they will answer questions *before* you need to ask them.

A lot depends on your personal learning style. For example, if you are visually oriented and learn best by seeing words or pictures, you may want to read the guide over and over again until you can close your eyes and recall the printed page. Try taping your questions typed in large print over your bedroom mirror or office desk for several glances during the course of the days prior to leading the first group.

If you are an auditory learner and understand best by listening to words and sounds, you may want to use a voice recorder. Record yourself asking the questions and leave a pause for repetition of the question or possible answers. This way of preparing allows you to check your questions for clarity and answerability. You can play your recording almost anywhere, including the plane ride to the first research location.

If you are a kinesthetic learner and internalize information best by physical activity, you may wish to practice by rehearsing an imaginary group. Set up some chairs and run the whole group, complete with introductions and wrap-up, as if it were the real thing.

Practice Makes Perfect

It is essential that you practice your questions aloud. Reading and speaking are two completely different activities. Questions are almost never asked exactly as they are written in the guide because the group experience is a dance of "I ask/you answer," and that is done aloud. In practicing, you want to come as close to that conversational experience as possible. Ask your questions aloud as frequently as possible so that they feel comfortable coming from your lips. It should be easy to borrow some techniques from actors: they "run lines" over and over to ensure a flawless performance on the night of the play. The more time you allow for conditioning yourself, the more mentally and physically confident you will feel in the group.

Practice your questions on mock respondents. Nothing beats practicing your guide on willing people. Ask family members, neighbors, coworkers, or best friends. Ask them to answer questions for you as if they were the respondents. You can say: *"For these questions, pretend you are a car owner or pet owner or pantyhose wearer."* My husband became very adept at flipping into the mindset of a fifteen-year-old pregnant teenager one week and a construction worker drinking two six-packs of beer the next week—changing his voice each time.

Ask questions, and see what range of responses you get, but stay alert to certain elements. Make sure answers are in the right arena, and determine whether there are questions that should be more focused. Are you getting simple "yes" and "no" answers? If so, perhaps the questions should be more open-ended (do not include part of the answer in the question).

Keep asking yourself: is this question related to the study purpose or is it merely interesting? Your answer tells you if your questions will gather the data you need.

When your guide is clearly written and thoroughly "digested," you can put all your energy on being with respondents all around the table and reading all the cues they give as to what they are thinking. Then the group discussion can be all about the respondents and not focused on the person asking the questions. This will allow moderators to better serve clients by allowing the voice of the consumer really to come through.

What If?

> *Not all questions should be asked of focus group participants. There are questions that the qualitative researcher needs to consider too. Facing some important "what if?" challenges, follow this Master Moderator™ into the future of qualitative research!*

As the story goes, the first focus groups were conducted in the late 1930s. Sessions could be daytime groups with a deli tray for snacks or in the evenings, so Mom could have Dad watch the kids while she went out to talk about hand soap or lotion. Usually, two groups were scheduled, one at 5:00 p.m. or 6:00 p.m. and one at 7:00 p.m. or 8:00 p.m.. Each group lasted about two hours, with about ten people present.

The model of two hours per group, with four hours expended each night, is still the foundation of the qualitative research business. And the traditional evening group is still the most utilized model in the qualitative panoply and in market research texts. As well, these are the models that most clients request when doing classic qualitative research. Sure, there are groups at noon or 7 a.m. to catch specific populations. But, for the most part, qualitative research events (QREs) take place in the evening, when consumers are not at traditional jobs.

Holding two groups a night also has not varied much, although occasionally there is the dreaded trio of 4:00–6:00 p.m., 6:00–8:00 p.m., and 8:00–10:00 p.m. sessions—giving moderators the opportunity to demonstrate extraordinary bladder skills, combined with fasting! The model is the cornerstone of most facility rentals, and on any given night in thirty to fifty American cities you will find such offices containing focus groups in single or multiple suites.

A lot has changed, though. Very few focus groups include ten participants. The numbers have dropped and morphed into the more common eight-person model; smaller groups of six to seven people; mini-groups of four to five people; and even models that include only dyads, triads, and individual depth interviews (IDIs). There are also expanded models that have twelve or more people present for specific research events, where there is more "doing" and less talking.

In addition to the two-hour model, there are now one-hour or ninety-minute group sessions, IDIs of thirty to forty-five minutes, and half-day or full-day group events. With the advent of computer-based groups, such as online groups in real time, bulletin boards, or chat groups over time, the model is expanding even more. For some, the telephone focus group is exactly the right model for interviewing respondents. Each research model has specific applications, and through agreement between moderators and clients, one is selected with the hope that it will lead to a better understanding of key issues.

Reports provided to clients have also changed, with more clients requesting short memo reports rather than full, verbatim ones. Some only want qualitative market research reports in PowerPoint formats; others only want a presentation of findings, using a "deck" of documents as a framework. Timelines have also shortened, with clients asking for QREs ten to fourteen days after the initial request.

Look to the Future

Shifts have occurred all along the qualitative research continuum. Here are a series of questions I am planting for our industry to consider for moving deeper into the twenty-first century:

- *What if the "two groups in the evening" model were to change?*
- *What if the trend of cramming everything into a two-hour window were challenged?*
- *What if qualitative research consultants exercised more consulting to clients on project design, so group length and number of respondents were closely matched to study objectives—instead of historical precedents?*
- *What if more effort was made to video record participants in natural shopping modes and just capture the behaviors, without commentary? Later, the respondent and the interviewer could meet, review the recording, and tease out behaviors and the thinking behind them. In fact, one person could be video recorded, and several others could be invited to review the recording and comment on variations he or she might have pursued.*
- *What if clients co-moderated some sessions to get more of a hands-on feel for issues that consumers face?*

- *What if, the morning after the last focus group, the teams (clients and moderators) met for three hours in a detailed debriefing—rather than waiting for a written report?*
- *What if moderators met with key clients in January to look at research objectives for the year and plan qualitative needs commensurate with the scheduled rollout of products or services?*
- *What if there were more variations for conducting sessions in the time period from 5:30 p.m. to 10:00 p.m.? Here are some options to consider:*
  - *One long QRE, running from 6:00 p.m. to 9:30 p.m.. This would allow time for exploring issues and materials indepth, without worrying about forcing multiple concepts into a pair of two-hour sessions.*
  - *Four one-hour QRE. Here, each group would answer both a core set and a unique set of questions, to provide a broader variety of insights.*
  - *Eight thirty-minute sessions, with two to five people in each session. Some pre-work would be assigned here, so everyone is ready to roll when the session starts.*

With the exception of the long QRE, the setup and briefing for respondents in the other options would have to change, because there is scant time in the session to provide information about the mirror, the observers, and the rules for participation.

Furthermore, what if there were recordings that respondents could watch—ones that welcomed them to the sessions and thanked them for fitting the sessions into their schedules? The recordings could go on to provide the ground rules and other key information in the category of disclosures. The moderator would still have to establish rapport so that the group would be cohesive, but the standard disclosures and participation guidelines could be done on a recording. This format would be similar to what prospective jurors see, with a professional actor/actress providing the news needed by respondents.

By having participants also fill out short forms that can be reviewed by observers, prior to the start of the groups (while the respondents are waiting in the lobby), moderators could get the sessions started quickly. Those forms, along with the grids of key background information about respondents, could give the clients much of the crucial data needed to meet the respondent they are observing.

This process does not excuse the moderator from establishing the "emotional handshake" needed to bond the group into a cohesive research resource. Rather, it streamlines the effort so that more energy can be given to the content of the focus group, instead of the logistics. I would recommend that the moderator begin that emotional handshake by taking time—without looking rushed—to welcome the respondents and ask them to give brief self-introductions. This will allow the moderator to interact and make each person feel included and valued.

Richard Bandler and John Grinder, founders of Neuro-Linguistic Programming (NLP), indicate that rapport is not a lengthy process, but is a short and intense event lasting as few as twenty seconds and no longer than three minutes. True rapport between individuals is instantaneous, with the opportunity for both positive and negative balances to be created. An effective moderator should know how to build rapport that will ensure a smooth group quickly and efficiently without seeming abrupt—and at the same time, make respondents feel that their comments have value.

- What if we continued to explore new variations on the old "two groups a night," rather than using that model just because it is out there?
- What if we found ways to make qualitative research a more effective tool for our clients by bringing fresh thinking to the models that now exist?
- What if we got excited about making the ordinary more extraordinary, rather than just grinding through another set of respondents in another room without windows?
- What if we just thought about focus groups in a new way, seeing them through the eyes of a facility owner, respondent, or client—any eyes besides our own? What if?

Never Too Late to Learn a Good Lesson

> *Being a Master Moderator™ doesn't mean that learning stops. This lesson showed up after leading thousands of focus groups, and it illustrates that is never too late to learn something useful in the qualitative research arena.*

I had a big "a-ha!" moment a few months ago when I realized I have unknowingly been leading respondents for years with some of my questions. A spirited discussion at a client meeting tipped me off to what I had been doing.

The client had reviewed my guide and noted that a number of my questions were not neutral—i.e. stated in such a way that a respondent had a full range of possible responses from their point of view. Once the client pointed that out, I could see my errors over the years. I thought back to the hundreds of guides I have written over the years where I worked hard to be sure that question stems were varied and that the questions were short—completely missing the fact I led respondents, like a horse to water.

I knew I had been righteous about abstaining from asking "why" questions and making sure I was employing the "Teflon Method," by not answering any questions they posed to me related to content. To discover, in the third decade of my qualitative research career, that I have been leading respondents rather than letting them lead me, has been humbling.

I see that it is never too late to learn a good lesson, and I am happy to pass my learning on via this article.

The entire world of qualitative market research is predicated on a series of questions—original questions to get into a topic and probing questions to follow up. A "question stem" is the first several words that begin a question. See examples bolded that follow:

- *"**Can you tell me** where were you born?"*
- *"**Do you recall** the name of your high school?"*
- *"**Are you able to** define the term 'senior citizen'?"*

At first glance, these appear to be benign questions. I have certainly asked thousands of questions such as these over the years. Little did I know just how leading they were! **A leading question robs respondents of an opportunity to answer deeply and fully.** It forces the answer from the top-of-mind rather than from an emotional core closer to the heart. Some respondents feel they cannot contradict the group leader— so they answer *"yes"* to questions such as these to avoid conflict. **Additionally, leading questions serve as a tool to over-control the moderating process.** When they appear in a moderator's guide, the group does not flow as well as it could along the path of how respondents **really** think, feel, and believe.

Problems can emerge when questions lead the respondent to a specific place the asker wants them to go! Those questions usually have words such as these in the question stem:

Do you	Did you	Could you	Can you
Will you	Should you	Would you	Are you
Is this	Are they	Can't you	Won't you

Questions that start with these stems can result in these types of answers: *"Yes," "No," "Maybe,"* or *"I do not know,"* and will then require a probe to get more data. The following exemplifies what is possible when leading is not involved. These are just clean questions that put the respondent in charge:

- ***Where*** *were you born?*
- ***Who*** *is your high school named for?*
- ***What words fit into your definition of a "senior citizen?"***

The questions above are neutral in that they do not imply what response the question asker is looking for. Each question lets the respondent answer however they deem best.

More About Leading Questions

Leading questions are often directional: they might not indicate an answer, but they can close off alternatives and guide the person in a desired direction.

There are six kinds of leading questions:

- Assumptive
- Linked Statements
- Implications
- Asking for Agreement
- Tag Questions
- Coercive

Assumptive Questions

Leading questions can use the "Assumption Principle." For example, take this question: *"Do you think prices will go up next year?"*

This question leads the respondent towards the idea of prices going up—if they answer *"no"* then this may mean they believe prices will remain stable—however, the thought of prices going down may not have occurred to them. Better question: *"Where are you about prices for goods and services next year compared to this year?"*

Linked Statements

You can lead questions (using the "Association Principle") merely by comments you made previously and are still top-of-mind for the person being questioned (these comments will linger longer, if you put emotion into them). For example: *"I really hate this government!... What are your thoughts about the XX party?"*

As well, insidious thoughts can be lodged within the question: *"What do you think about John Richards? Many people are opposed to him, by the way."* (Note the social coercion in this statement.)

Implication Questions

Asking questions that get respondents to think of consequences or implications of current or past events links the past with the future in an inescapable chain of cause-and-effect. For example: *"If you go to the party tonight, what will happen when you take your examination tomorrow?"*

Asking for Agreement

A very direct leading question is one that is closed ended, clearly asking for agreement, making it easier for the other person to say *"yes"* than *"no."* For example: *"Do you agree that we need to save the whales?"*

Tag Questions

Tag questions are short questions that are tagged onto the end of statements. These questions effectively disguise a command to make it look like a question. These are short phrases and often include a negative element such as *"Isn't it?"*; *"Don't you?"*; *"Aren't you?"*; *"That's a good thing to do, isn't it?"*; or *"You'll come to dinner tonight, won't you?"*

Coercive Questions

Questions that force specific answers can include implicit or explicit coercion. Thus: *"You are coming tonight, aren't you? If you aren't, then there will be trouble"* or *"You do love me, don't you?"*

Implications for Moderators

One of the primary roles a moderator plays is to stay out of the pool of information generated by the respondents. Just as the Olympic-level swim coach does not jump in the pool of water with the swimmers he coaches, the Master Moderator™ must also stay out of the pool of commentary created by respondents. **The moderator's role is to present questions that let respondents provide perceptions, opinions, beliefs, and attitudes (POBAs) that they generate from their own experiences.**

If a moderator asks a leading question, these are the possible risks:

- Respondents will step out of personal experience and present something that is rational and may not be true.
- Respondents will go for the easy "yes/no" response, hoping the moderator will not probe for more information.
- The moderator is showing—by word and deed—that they do not trust respondents to share fully—the moderator feels he or she has to "help" respondents to the "right" answer—the one the moderator is looking for!

- The moderator wants to control the flow of information to fit an assumption base that he or she has already mentally created.
- Leading questions can result in short answers. The goal of a focus group is a spirited detailed discussion on the key points of interest to the client.

Moderators have an obligation to avoid leading questions, so that clients can hear (unfiltered) what respondents are thinking. It is this unsullied voice of the consumer that will more accurately help to guide client decision making.

One final point—I am finding it a good plan to take leading questions out of the non-research part of my life as well. That way, I do not carry over bad habits from my personal life to research I conduct for clients or the classes I teach to researchers. This old dog has learned a new trick.

GLOSSARY

GLOSSARY OF TERMS

1 on 1 - One-on-one interviews with one respondent and a qualitative researcher (QR) to collect independent reactions about products, services, ads, or concepts. Also known as "In-Depth Interviews" or "IDIs."

2/3rds Rule - A qualitative researcher's (QR) practice of hearing two-thirds of the respondents answer a line of questioning before moving on to the next line of questions. This is an industry standard.

4 Stages of a qualitative research event (QRE) - *Stage 1—Introduction*—The Qualitative Researcher's (QR) main goal in this stage is to establish a strong bond with respondents so that they feel safe in sharing their POBAs (perceptions, opinions, beliefs, and attitudes) with each other as well as the QR. This stage also sets the direction for the discussion and allows the QR to demonstrate openness to a variety of viewpoints. *Stage 2—Rapport/Reconnaissance*—This stage narrows the field of questioning, so as to gather a floor of understanding about basic issues being discussed and should include "can't fail questions" that any respondent can answer. *Stage 3—In-Depth Investigation*—This stage starts about one-third of the way into the research session and takes up the majority of time set aside for a qualitative research event (QRE). This is the area where the client's key issues are deeply explored. *Stage 4—Closure*—The QR brings the QRE to a close and provides respondents with a forum in which to express any thoughts on ideas previously discussed or last minute insights.

80/20 Rule - RIVA model in qualitative research events (QREs) where the percentage of qualitative researcher (QR) words in a group discussion decreases from 80% at the outset of the conversation (Intro, groundrules, etc.) to 20% for the remainder of the conversation – allowing respondents to speak 80% of the time during the interview.

Acknowledgement - Portion of the qualitative research event (QRE) where the qualitative researcher (QR) thanks the respondents for coming to provide their perceptions, opinions, beliefs, and attitudes (POBAs).

Active Listening - An effective qualitative researcher (QR) employs this technique during qualitative research event (QRE) sessions. This technique includes visual and verbal acknowledgement, paraphrasing appropriately (using respondent's own words as often as possible), listening for themes, recalling earlier comments, and linking. The three "A"s of active listening are: Alertness, Accuracy, and Acknowledgement.

Ad-labs - One-hour qualitative research event (QRE) sessions. Single purpose is to have consumers look at a series of ads and check relevance and communication issues. (Also referred to as "Disaster checks.")

"Aha" - RIVA term for an insight gleaned from respondents that can be shared in the post qualitative research event (QRE) debriefing with clients. These are the "surprises" that arise from QREs – and the main reason that qualitative research is such a powerful tool.

Annotated Guide - Any guide with extra notes to support the qualitative researcher (QR) in getting the best data from respondents. The annotations come from discussions with clients before and during qualitative research events (QREs).

Articulation Questions - Questions on a screener to determine if a potential respondent can be understood by the qualitative researcher (QR) and observers. These questions establish that the potential respondent is qualified enough to talk about the subject matter and is able to maintain "flow" in reporting answer without long gaps after a question is posed.

Associations - An intervention/projective technique used in qualitative research events (QREs) which offer respondents another means to discuss products, services, or ideas. Respondents are asked to either speak aloud or write down whatever comes to mind when a stimulus word or phrase is given.

Back Room - Refers to the location behind the one-way mirror in a typical research facility where observers (the client team) can observe, unseen, a qualitative research event (QRE) in progress. This allows observers the opportunity to hear participant responses firsthand and without filters to facilitate the decision making progress toward short and long term objectives.

"Be with people, not with paper." - RIVA Moderator Maxim to describe the necessity for qualitative researchers (QRs) to be present in the conversation with respondents rather than focusing on their moderator's guide and their pre-set questions. Successful qualitative research events (QREs) require the flexibility to follow the natural flow of conversation in the session—not being afraid to follow a tangent that could lead to deeper levels of data and understanding. This maxim is partnered with *"Eat your guide, burp your questions."*

Bid - Cost estimate that one receives for a project at hand (Examples: facility bid, vendor bid, etc.).

Blue Book - Directory published by the Marketing Research Association (MRA) listing market research companies/services as well as focus group facilities in the United States. This directory can be found online or a hard copy (published annually) may be purchased for a fee.

"Board of Directors" - An intervention/projective technique used in qualitative research events (QREs) which allows respondents to see an issue from a different point of view and provide a deeper range of answers. In this technique, each respondent is given a title – similar to what one would find in a company (CEO, Director of Marketing, CFO, etc.) and told to solve a "problem" from the point of view of their assigned "job title."

Bricolage - A term that refers to the deliberate mixing of qualitative methods and ways of thinking in order to address a specific issue or problem. (Example: A research design that starts with 6 focus groups, 12 in-home interviews, and leads to a 1,500 person quantitative survey.)

Bulletin Boards - These qualitative research events (QREs) are not conducted in real time. Instead, respondents are directed to a website where they respond to questions/stimuli the qualitative researcher (QR) has posted. Typically, these sessions are completed over several days and allow respondents to answer questions at a convenient time for them. This arrangement is particularly useful when respondents are geographically dispersed and perhaps operating on different time zones and work schedules. The QR reviews comments regularly and posts probes and/or new questions. These sessions can have more participants than online groups. The QR can decide to allow respondents to view or hide the replies from the other respondents.

Change of Scope Memo - Memo sent from the research vendor to the client in order to notate when conditions of a research project have changed from the original project sign-off. Example: Client requests final report (when they did not want one).

Children's Play Sessions - A research setting with three to seven children in limited age ranges (e.g., First Graders, Fifth Graders, etc.) who "play" with products, materials, or ideas. Data collection is primarily behavioral/visual rather than conversational. Sessions typically last no more than one hour in environments conducive to small children – e.g. not a conference table setup.

Clarification Question - A type of probe which elicits deeper levels of data. The qualitative researcher (QR) typically asks a respondent for clarification on a statement, phrase, or word they used during a qualitative research event (QRE). Example: *"What do you mean by the term disjointed?"*

Client - Refers to the entity that will use the research findings as part of a decision-making strategy. The client typically commissions the study, provides the resources to pay for the study, and signs off on all key study decisions. Also referred to as "End-User."

Client Spokesperson - Refers to the one individual selected to "speak" for the clients behind the mirror in a typical qualitative research event (QRE) setting. This technique ensures that the qualitative researcher (QR) is not inundated with client requests (both verbally and written) during a QRE session. During the "false close" the QR, typically, meets with the "client spokesperson" to see if there are any additional issue areas or questions the client would like to review with respondents before the session comes to a close. (Also referred to as a "Single Point of Contact" or SPOC).

Close-Ended Question - Type of question that narrows response options. While some close-ended questions are needed in qualitative market research (QLMR), there is a tendency for them to become leading questions, affecting the quality of data garnered in qualitative research events (QREs).

Closure - Refers to the fourth stage of a qualitative research event (QRE). In this stage the qualitative researcher (QR) brings the QRE to a close, summarizing key insights brought to light in the session. This stage also provides a space in which additional client questions can be discussed. This stage typically lasts five to eight minutes.

Coding - Refers to the practice of using different signs, symbols, colors, numbers, tabs, etc. to start the process of analyzing a set of transcripts facilitating the report writing process. Examples: photocopying each session transcript on its own unique colored paper; highlighting portions of transcripts relating to specific report topic in one color (i.e. blue); using "flags" to denote "voice of consumer" (VOC) to be included in the report (i.e. direct quotes); marking every reference to key client data, etc.

Collage - A type of intervention used in qualitative research events (QREs) to access deeper levels of data. This technique permits respondents to use pictures, words, and symbols to create a story about a product, service, or idea. This can also be assigned to respondents as "homework" to be completed before a QRE and brought with them for "show and tell" purposes.

Concept Statement - A type of intervention which provides respondents with one or more typed statements so that they have a clearer idea of the nuances related to a product, service, or idea.

Creativity Sessions - Qualitative research event (QRE) with a focus group room setting, fewer participants, more "doing" and less talking; respondents work on "problem solving" or stretching ideas beyond the ordinary. Useful at the concept or design stages. Respondents can grade or rate the concept.

Deliverables - Items promised to the client such as: screeners, moderator's guide, transcripts, report, etc. This can also refer to ads/concept statements reviewed during a qualitative research event (QRE).

Demographics - Term used to describe the listing of measurable characteristics of individuals within a market segment selected for participation in a qualitative research event (QRE), so as to create a descriptive framework of said individuals. These characteristics typically include: gender, age, ethnicity, employment status, occupation, residence, income, marital status, category usage, etc.

Devil's Advocate - Posing questions to respondents with the intent to emphasize the negative viewpoint so it may be discussed in depth. This technique is the opposite of "Angel's Advocate" which supports respondents in finding the positive elements.

Digital Recorder - A piece of recording equipment typically used during ethnographic interviews, shop-alongs, or non-traditional facility settings in order to record the interview for analysis purposes. They are also used in traditional qualitative research event (QRE) settings as "backup" recordings to ensure that data is not lost. The data can then be uploaded as digital sound files.

Disclosures - Refers to the point in the first stage of a qualitative research event (QRE) when a qualitative researcher (QR) informs respondents of environmental conditions (microphones, mirrors, observers, taping, etc.).

Dominators - Those respondents who "dominate" or monopolize conversation during a qualitative research event (QRE). They may have strong feelings on certain issues; have an agenda to push; or are simply used to leading in group settings. Some dominance by a few participants is natural in group discussion; typically "conversation crowders" are unaware of their dominance.

Double-Barreled Question - A question type that combines two questions in one sentence. These types of questions should be avoided in qualitative research events (QREs). Example: *"What car do you drive most often and how many miles per day do you drive it?"*

Dyads - A two respondent qualitative session with a qualitative researcher (QR). (For a total of three persons present in the room.)

"Eat your guide, burp your questions." - RIVA Moderator Maxim to remind researchers to know their guide "cold" [not memorized—but know the flow; areas where tangents might arise; and have a sense of the logic of questions in a section], so they can keep their attention on respondents and not on the guide. This maxim is partnered with *"Be with people, not with paper."*

"Echolalia" - As this term implies – the qualitative researcher (QR) act of "echoing" or repeating what a respondent says. This practice should be avoided as it does not affirm respondents nor clarify points. It is better to nod, smile, and ask another question.

End-User - See "Client".

Equal Air Time - Phrase used to describe the desire that each respondent speaks about the same amount (one person not sharing too much or too little). It is prudent to give this ground rule at the beginning of a qualitative research (QRE) event.

Ethnography - A term borrowed from cultural anthropology used to describe qualitative researchers going into the respondent's environment in order to observe and discuss behaviors, perceptions, opinions, beliefs, and attitudes (POBAs). Example: A qualitative researcher (QR) travels to a respondent's home in order to observe them bake cupcakes using a new boxed cupcake mix and discuss their impressions. Typically requires a team of 2-3 individuals, a video camera, a still camera, and a digital recorder. The team may include the QR, a client representative, and support staff member to manage the equipment. Note: in Market Research, this is not considered "true ethnography" but rather "ethnography lite" – using key tenets from the science of ethnography, but shortening the time spent with individuals in situ.

Eulogy - An intervention technique that can be used during a qualitative research event (QRE) in which a product or service has "died" and the respondents are asked to write what would be said about that product or service now that it is no longer in existence. The point of this exercise is to find only "good news" (speak well of the dead) and strong points about a product or service.

Executive Summary - A type of qualitative report that distills the essence of the qualitative experience and targets the key insights that relate to the study objectives. This report format is shorter in length than both a "Topline Report" and a "Full Report," usually ranging from two to three pages. Sometimes this Executive Summary is part of a larger report.

Expert Respondent - Refers to those respondents who are well informed (or believe they are) on a certain topic.

Extended Groups - Research sessions in which respondents are invited to attend sessions that last between two and a half to six hours or more, so as to delve deeper into the research topic. During these sessions, activities can include collages/storyboards (behavioral tasks); drawing stories/modeling clay (creative tasks); and even "field trips."

Facilitation - Sessions in which a "facilitator" guides discussions along a specific path, sometimes with planned activities and group management techniques. Group size can range from four to forty-four or more. A facilitated session can be as short as an hour and as long as a day or more. These sessions share similarities with traditional qualitative research events (QREs); however, the two should not be confused. The main difference between them being that facilitations look for consensus whereas QREs seek to gather all types of perceptions, opinions, beliefs, and attitudes (POBAs) concerning a topic (but not necessarily come to a consensus/result). Facilitated sessions sometimes provide concepts that are later explored in more depth in ideations, brainstorms, and/or QREs.

Facility - Refers to physical location where qualitative research events (QREs) are conducted (such as focus groups, in-depth interviews (IDIs), dyads, triads, ad-labs, etc.) Typically involves a room with a large one-way mirror, a back room for client viewing, audio/video capability and can include an easel, televisions, refreshments, etc.

Facility Bid - Bid from a facility listing costs for project specifics: hosting, recruiting, stipends, food, physical location, recording, etc.

Facility Contract - Also referred to as "Facility Letter" or "Project Confirmation". This written document includes project specifics (date/time/etc.), costing, room availability, and payment policy. This document is signed by representatives from both the facility and the client.

False Close - About ten minutes before the end of a qualitative research event (QRE) session respondents are given an exercise while the qualitative researcher (QR) talks to the client spokesperson about any additional questions to ask before respondents are excused.

"The Field" - Industry term used to describe the physical location in which research takes place. Example: Focus group facility, consumer's home/office, conference room, etc.

Flat Rate Estimate - One of two approaches for quoting costs to a client in a proposal. This method quotes costs in one flat rate (does not break down specific costs for client to see). Quotes can be provided per qualitative research event (QRE) or per project. (See: "Line-Item Estimate").

Flip Chart - The most popular intervention in qualitative market research (QLMR)! When used correctly [not turning the qualitative researcher (QR) into a scribe], it is an excellent tool to get respondents to provide more information during qualitative research events (QREs).

Floater - This industry term refers to a respondent typically recruited for a series of in-depth interviews (IDIs). In IDI research, there is a need to ensure there is always a respondent waiting for the next interview, rather than hoping each respondent will show up on time. Facilities are asked to recruit an extra respondent for each set of three to four interviews depending on the length of each interview to be conducted. For example, if four thirty-minute interviews are planned between nine am and noon, one respondent is paid a higher fee than the standard stipend, to wait for the whole time period in the event one of the four recruited respondents is a no-show. This ensures that a qualitative researcher (QR) is never waiting for the next interview. The floater is given refreshments and reading material (or encouraged to bring their own).

Focus Group - Led by a moderator, typically ninety minutes to two hours in length with six to eight respondents who fit screener criteria and meet only one time.

Focus Panels - All the same characteristics of a focus group, except the same group of respondents meet multiple times.

Follow-Up Questions - Sometimes called "probes," they are meant to elicit additional information on a topic and a way to meet the two-thirds rule in focus groups.

Full Report - A twenty to one-hundred page text report on key findings from a series of qualitative research events (QREs) that provides deep details on all aspects of the study and deep analysis: *"What happened and what does it mean?"* Analysis is based on verbatim respondent quotes.

Generalist - Industry term referring to qualitative researchers (QRs) who are not "niche moderators/QRs." These QRs work in a variety of arenas (consumer goods, finance, services, government, etc.).

"Getting Over the Wall" Technique - This RIVA technique is used to quickly access a variety of obstacles across the experience base of participants. See *"Qualitative Research Techniques: Taking the Best of the Past Into the Future"* in Part I, Section I of this book for instructions on how to set up this intervention.

"Gold Mines" - Phrase used to describe unexpected, rich comments from respondents during a qualitative research event (QRE). A qualitative researcher (QR) takes the time to explore this rich vein before moving on to the next topic for discussion. The benefit being that a QR never wants to miss the opportunity to go well beyond top-of-mind in the quest for key information facilitating decision making.

Graphic Guide - A guide that uses pictures and graphics rather than only text – not recommended for novice qualitative researchers (QRs).

Green Book - Directory published annually by The American Marketing Association (AMA) listing market research companies/services as well as focus group facilities worldwide. This directory can be found online or a hard copy may be purchased for a fee.

Grids - The summary page facility staff sends to the project manager to advise them about the status of the recruiting specifications for each respondent invited to a qualitative research event (QRE). Typically, includes these details: first name, age, gender, ethnicity, occupation, category usage, etc.

Ground Rules - Refers to a list of guidelines or behavioral expectations that a qualitative researcher (QR) delivers to respondents in the introductory stage of a qualitative research event (QRE). This list sets the "stage" for respondent participation, is important for ensuring respondent rapport/cooperation, and helps reduce issues related to speaking volume, equal air time, time management, etc.

Guide - The document that serves as a road map of discussion for the qualitative researcher (QR) of a qualitative research event (QRE). There are several types of guide styles varying in depth from a bulleted list of topic areas to a detailed list of questions and follow-up probes. Also referred to as a "Moderator's Guide".

Handout - A classic intervention, the purpose in a qualitative research event (QRE) is to accelerate respondent understanding while at the same time providing them with a concrete document to refer to during group discussion. Example: Concept Statement.

Hired Lips - Industry jargon for those situations where a qualitative researcher (QR) is hired only to moderate qualitative research session(s). They do not plan the study or select the research methodology. They do not write a report. They just moderate. For example, a study may have 14 groups of which 12 are with White respondents and two groups are being held with Hispanics, in Spanish. A Hispanic QR is hired to lead the 2 groups with Hispanic respondents, using the same guide used for the other 12 groups, and produce a transcript in English. The mainstream QR weaves these insights gleaned into the final report for all 14 groups.

"Historical Ally" Technique - This industry technique can be classified as both an intervention and a projective technique. It requires respondents to respond to a problem or an issue from the perspective of a historical personage. See *"Qualitative Research Techniques: Taking the Best of the Past Into the Future"* in Part I, Section I of this book for more details on how to set up this technique.

Homework Assignments - A qualitative researcher (QR) typically assigns pre-work or "homework" to respondents in order to maximize what little time they have in a qualitative research event (QRE). Homework affords respondents time to ponder a product, service, idea, personal experience, etc., **before** they come to the QRE, therefore prepping them to discuss said product, service, idea, experience, etc., in the session itself. Example: collages, journal of experience, digital photographs, etc.

Honorarium - Also referred to as "Stipend" or "Incentive." A one-time payment for participation in a qualitative research event (QRE). (Example: cash, check, gift cards, etc.).

"Hot Notes" - A RIVA term that describes qualitative researcher (QR) "mind-dump notes." This is a method which captures "what shouts the loudest" findings after a QR has completed a portion in a series of qualitative research events (QREs). This method relies on overall QR impressions and short-term memory.

Hybrid Moderator/QR - Qualitative researcher (QR) who can niche market in specific product or service areas, but also in race specifics, lifestyle preferences (gay and lesbian, religion, etc.), and life stages (children, teen, and mature market research).

Ideation/Idea Generation - Type of qualitative research which employs creative techniques to generate or develop new ideas for products, services, solutions to problems, etc. This methodology engages brainstorming techniques (focusing on quantity of ideas generated first, then moves toward "best ideas float to the top"). These qualitative research events (QREs) are usually larger in size (more respondents) and include a variety of activities to stimulate creative thinking in a non-judgmental environment.

IDI - Acronym for "In-Depth Interview" - involves one respondent and one qualitative researcher (QR) in order to collect independent reactions about products, services, advertisements, or concepts. Typically, anywhere from thirty to ninety minutes in length.

Image Test - A tool/technique used to determine how respondents see the "image" of a company, product, or service. For example, respondents might be asked a series of questions about how they see the brand image/reputation of a company that has released "recall" requests for cars that need to be repaired due to a problem with the fuel system.

Incentive - See "Honorarium."

In-Depth Interview - See "IDI."

In-Depth Investigation - Refers to the third stage of a qualitative research event (QRE). Nearly two-thirds of QRE time is spent here – the qualitative researcher (QR) directs the action of discussion during this stage without becoming part of the discussion and focuses on the "meat" of the study purpose using interventions, exercises, activities, and deep probes.

Initial Close - See "False Close."

In-Store Intercepts - Stopping respondents while they are shopping to ask several short questions about a product or about their shopping experience that delve deeper than questions one would find on a survey form (quantitative).

Instrument of Research - In qualitative market research (QLMR) the "Instrument of Research" is the qualitative researcher (QR). In quantitative market research (QTMR) the "Instrument of Research" is the actual survey document – requiring every interviewer to ask the questions in the same order and not to probe for answers or details. In QLMR qualitative research events (QREs), the QR has an effect on how respondents answer and has much more latitude with respondents than in survey research.

Intervention - A variety of activities (from simple to complex) that support the flow of conversation within a qualitative research event (QRE) and open new ideas for exploration. It is any activity that interrupts the two-way conversation between qualitative researcher (QR) and respondents for the purpose of enriching the discussion or focusing on a specific issue. There are two types of interventions: visual interventions and process interventions. Visual interventions require respondents to look at existing items and make comments (Example: Reviewing two different taglines). Process interventions require respondents to do something and then discuss what they did (Example: Product Sorts).

Introduction - Refers to the first stage of a qualitative research event (QRE), typically the first ten minutes, which includes a generic purpose statement for respondents, disclosures about the physical research environment (microphones, recording, observers, etc.), and self-introductions from the respondents. The qualitative researcher (QR) uses this time to begin creating a safe space for respondent participation and set the direction for the session.

Introductory Questions - Type of question used primarily in the second stage of a qualitative research event (QRE), "Rapport and Reconnaissance," to open discussion on an issue – establishing a base for deeper discussion. These low anxiety questions are easy to answer, creating a level of comfort among respondents, establish rapport, and provide insights on general perceptions and attitudes.

"Invisible Leadership" - The skill set a Master Moderator™ must display while leading a qualitative research event (QRE). The qualitative researcher (QR) is able to remain in charge of the session without dominating respondents, the practice of "leading from behind" - standing back and letting respondents explore the topic at hand - only stepping in to keep the conversation along the track defined by the purpose statement.

Issue Areas - Also called "Topic Areas" in a Moderator's Guide - these are the key themes that will be explored in a qualitative research event (QRE). They are often the subheads in a universal guide.

Judgment Words - Quick responses to respondent comments that imply judgment. Qualitative researchers (QRs) avoid using these words, so as to maintain neutrality within the qualitative research event (QRE). Examples: "Excellent," "Good," "Wow," are not appropriate.

Known/Friendship Pairs - Type of qualitative research events (QREs) where the interchange between a pair or pairs of respondents is explored. This can include: friendship pairs, married couples, mothers or fathers and their children, etc. Example: Watching a family play a new board game and talking aloud about how easy or hard the directions were to follow/understand.

Laddering - A qualitative market research interviewing technique adapted from psychology. This practice is based on Jonathan Gutman's "Means End Chain" Theory and seeks to flesh out consumer values as they relate to making choices about products/services. Through several rounds of questioning, the qualitative researcher (QR) isolates attributes of a product/service, benefits/consequences the consumer assigns to these attributes, and ultimately the values that the consumer associates with the benefits/consequences. Typically, this technique is used in one-on-one interviews or small groups due to the intensity of the practice and the duration of time it takes to complete. Results are typically depicted in a Hierarchical Value Map (HVM) and are used to establish and reinforce brand equity.

Leading Question - Type of question that directs or "leads" qualitative market research (QLMR) participants to an assumed response or in a certain direction. There are six types of leading questions: Assumptive, Linked Statements, Implications, Asking for Agreement, Tag Questions, and Coercive. These should be avoided in QLMR investigation.

Line Item Estimate - One of two approaches for quoting costs to a client in a cost memo or proposal. This method lists each cost element individually as a line item. Quotes are provided per qualitative research event (QRE) and then multiplied by the number of QREs in the project as a whole. (See also: "Flat Rate Estimate")

Linked Groups - See "Piggyback Groups."

Linking - When the qualitative researcher (QR) recalls what was said earlier in a qualitative research event (QRE) and connects or "links" it to current conversation. This technique allows for a deeper level of probing.

"Living with the Silence" - A RIVA moderator maxim which explains that: an effective qualitative researcher (QR) lets silence occur (about ten seconds) between questions asked and responses. This allows respondents time to form an opinion and then verbalize perceptions, opinions, beliefs, and attitudes (POBAs). The QR does not rush to fill the silence with chatter or constantly reframe the original question asked. Instead, they wait the ten seconds of silence before a response occurs or they reframe the question.

Logic Tracking - Ability of the qualitative researcher (QR) to maintain a logical path that follows respondent thinking and does not slavishly adhere to the pre-developed guide.

"Magnet Hands" - A RIVA term for qualitative researcher (QR) phenomenon: Imagine there are tiny magnets in each palm of a QR. She/he sits rigidly in their chair, hands tightly clasped – holding on for dear life – sending the message of "control, control, control" instead of sitting with their whole body open: hands in lap, or open - palms up or down on the table. This phenomenon should be avoided.

Manipulatives - Tools/tasks used during a qualitative research event (QRE) to forward discussion. Example: product sorts, worksheets, pictures, file cards, etc.

Market Segmentation - Marketing term which, when used in a qualitative market research context, refers to the breakdown of respondents into market segments based on similarities and differences affecting the recruiting process for a series of qualitative research events (QREs). Example: "Users" vs. "Non-users"; lifestyle segments ("working" vs. "non-working"); age; gender; etc.

Master Moderator™ - A RIVA term for those who have mastered the key skills and techniques leading to effective group interactions. They collect and analyze a rich body of oral information, and they report that data in appropriate ways to support the decision making needs of their clients. See *"Qualities of a Master Moderator™"* in Part I, Section I of this book for a listing of Master Moderator™ attributes.

Master Moderator™ Certificate Program™ - The RIVA Training Institute (based in the Washington D.C. metro area) awards the title of "Master Moderator™" to those qualitative researchers (QRs) who complete intensive training in a series of RIVA courses, workshops, and individual sessions with a trainer; exhibit mastery of qualitative market research theory (passing a written examination); as well as exemplify "Master Moderator™" qualities (through a practicum observed and reviewed by a panel of industry leaders).

Memo Report - Also referred to as an "outline report," this report format utilizes a short, bulleted style and is written from memory and/or qualitative researcher (QR) notes made after the qualitative research events (QREs) are complete (does not employ transcripts). Typically, this type of report is generated and delivered to the client within 24 hours of the last QRE.

Mind-Map - A graphic representation of information using boxes and radiating lines to quickly show information. This method can be used to draft a moderator's guide, a report, or a line of thinking in a qualitative research event (QRE). In some specific applications, this technique can also be used to collect information in a QRE.

Mini Groups - This term has two meanings:
1. Four to six respondents in a qualitative research event (QRE).
2. A focus group that may have six to eight participants, but only lasts one hour.

Mis-recruits - Refers to respondents recruited for a qualitative research event (QRE) that do not meet the project specifications. These respondents are excused from the group, but still paid for their time. (See also "Re-screen.")

Mock Juries - A research methodology that allows lawyers to try out two or three different approaches for presenting case points to a group of individuals who are proxies for the actual jurors who would try a real case. This type of qualitative research event (QRE) is also used when the outcome of a case depends on factors that verge on the emotional response of jurors, rather than clear-cut case points. Typically, they take place in two 8 hour sessions over a weekend.

Moderating Method - Refers to the planned approach to a particular qualitative research event (QRE) study. It includes consideration of the length of the group, number of participants, use of moderator's guide, and use of interventions. It also takes into account the use of a resource person who may demonstrate a product.

Moderating Style - Refers to the personal manner of the individual qualitative researcher (QR), whether enthusiastic or low-key, controlling or easy-going, directive or more open, etc.

Moderator/QR - Individual who leads a qualitative research event (QRE). They can also serve as the project manager/leader for the entire research project (working with client and facility). Preferably this person is trained in the "Art & Science of Qualitative Moderating". Also referred to as a "qualitative researcher" (QR).

Moderator's/QR's "Eyes Only" Guide - A private version of the guide for use by the qualitative researcher (QR) while conducting a qualitative research event (QRE) which allows them to "own" the project purpose and issue areas. It may be a more detailed guide than the one a client typically views, including such items as: probes, alternative lines of questioning for each issue, scripts for interventions, trigger words, bolded/starred items, items to omit should time shrink, etc.

Moderator's/QR's Fee - This refers to the fee a QR charges per qualitative research event (QRE) or over the whole research study. Several factors shape the pricing including: the level of experience of the QR, the length of the QRE, guide development, briefing/debriefing, calls, etc. This fee does not include screener development, report writing, recruiting, facility use, etc.

Moderator's/QR's Guide - See "Guide".

Mystery Shopper - A research methodology allowing businesses to evaluate the quality of the service they and their competitors provide to consumers. A researcher posing as a typical consumer assesses the nature and quality of the service they receive and reports this experience to the client (Example: Evaluation of an airline, cruise ship, hotel, hospital, fast food restaurant, dry cleaners, ATM experience, pet shop, etc.).

Neuro-Linguistic Programming - Also known as NLP, is the study of subjective experience. First developed by Richard Bandler and John Grinder in the late 1970s, it is defined as the way human beings generalize, distort, or delete their sensory experiences and how they act to produce a given result in themselves or others. NLP seeks to define or outline the things we do subconsciously or unconsciously and demystifies the outcomes that are created when we think or act. This is a useful body of knowledge for qualitative researchers (QRs), helping them "read the room" and know where to probe for more information.

Neutral Question - Refers to preferred question type in qualitative research events (QREs). This type of question leaves response choices open for the respondents and is essential in establishing a moderator's unconditional positive regard (UPR) in a qualitative research event (QRE) session. Author's Note: *"There is a big difference between having a neutral tone of voice that asks a leading question and asking a neutral question."*

Niche Moderator/QR - Refers to a qualitative researcher (QR) who works in only one or two defined areas to conduct qualitative research. They are often "specialists" in their field. (Examples: Pharmaceuticals, finance, advertising, research with kids/teens, IT, medical, etc.).

NLP - See "Neuro-Linguistic Programming" for definition.

Non-User When recruited for a qualitative research event (QRE), refers to a respondent that does not use the product, service, or brand, that will be discussed.

Non-Verbal Probes - A type of probe which elicits additional information without making a verbal request. Examples include: nodding, hand gestures, smiling, making eye contact, reacting to a comment with a puzzled expression, silence, etc.

Non-Vested Moderator/QR - Industry term used to describe a qualitative researcher (QR) who does not have a "vested" interest in the outcome of a qualitative research event (QRE). This QR does not work for the organization that is sponsoring the QRE and, as an "outsider," does not bring any content bias to the discussion.

ODC - Acronym for "Other Direct Costs." This acronym can be found in qualitative research project proposals and refers to any other fees associated with the cost of the project that do not have direct billable hours (such as shipping, client food, or equipment rental).

"Okay" - This term is one of the most popular "rejoinders" to a respondent who answers a question from a qualitative researcher (QR). A trained QR has a range of rejoinders to use with respondents. Since "okay" can mean anything from "I agree" to "whatever," it is the poorest rejoinder to use in qualitative research events (QREs) and is not recommended to be used at any time.

One-Way Mirror - Located in a typical research facility room for qualitative research events (QREs). This allows observers to view the QRE without being part of the process as they are physically located on the other side of the mirror.

Online Groups - Typically ninety-minutes in length, participants answer questions in real time via a virtual online facility portal. The qualitative researcher (QR) should be versed in the tenets of good moderating and very familiar with the technology that makes such a session possible.

Open-Ended Question - Type of question that leaves response options open for participants. This type of question is the preferred method of questioning in qualitative market research (QLMR), as it encourages a variety of responses with the most opportunity for "Gold Mines" in the research process.

"Open Frame" Technique - The simplest form of this RIVA technique/intervention is to draw a rectangle in the middle of a sheet of easel paper. Inside that rectangle, a word or short phrase is placed with ten or so lines radiating out from the edges of the rectangle. Respondents are asked either to provide a definition of the term or phrase or to give an example. This technique works best when the word or phrase is abstract in nature (Example: "Family Values").

Oral Report - Those times when a client wants a qualitative researcher (QR) to provide an in-person briefing of the key findings from a qualitative research event (QRE) study. It can include a PowerPoint presentation; however it can also be done solely from QR notes.

Outline Guide - This type of moderator's guide is extracted from a full guide and serves as an outline/roadmap for the qualitative researcher (QR) while leading a qualitative research event (QRE). It can take the form of a single piece of paper or a set of index cards with key questions or issues listed. This type of guide is not recommended for novice or emerging moderators.

Pacing - Refers to the rate or speed of a qualitative interview. In order to keep respondents engaged in a qualitative research event (QRE), it is important for the qualitative researcher (QR) to maintain a crisp pace, varying activities about every twenty minutes for a two hour interview.

"Periscoping" - While attentively listening to a respondent provide a POBA (perception, opinion, belief, or attitude), the qualitative researcher (QR) quickly scans the room to let others know he/she will be back to hear from them. This RIVA term stands on the same principle as the periscope in a submarine - rising just enough above the surface of the water to scan for other ships, but not risk being seen while doing so.

Picture Sort - A long respected intervention/projective technique that allows respondents to use pictures to access below top-of-mind responses. For example, respondents might be asked to find a picture from a deck that shows how they feel about an airline, corporation, or a service. The picture allows them to speak in-depth about the quality of the emotion they may be feeling.

Piggyback Groups - Also referred to as "Linked Groups." A set of linked sessions that take place one behind the other (For example one session takes place at 2:00 pm and the second session follows at 4:00 pm). What makes these sessions unique is that the respondents from the second group observe the first group. Their observation of the first group forms the basis of discussion in their own group. The primary benefit of this type of research is that the discussion is in the moment, not based on an old experience. Example: Group A – Dental Patients are interviewed while Group B – Dentists observe. Group A is then excused and Group B moves into the conference room to talk about what they heard from Group A.

Pilot Tests - This qualitative research event (QRE) format has respondents viewing samples of movies, TV shows, advertisement campaigns, or promotional ideas and reporting their reactions before the final editing phase or the decision to release or not is made.

POAIQ - RIVA acronym for "Part of Answer in Question" - when qualitative researcher (QR) provides respondents with "answers" to the question they just asked - thereby limiting the possibility of collecting a variety of answers. Example: *"What makes you shop after 11pm? Is it because the store is less crowded?"* (The better question is to stop after the first question mark!)

POBAs - A RIVA acronym to describe the main goal in qualitative market research: to gain an understanding of respondents' "Perceptions, Opinions, Beliefs, and Attitudes." Perception can be defined as a mental image or concept of something filtered through the experience of a consumer. Opinion can be described as a subjective judgment or appraisal formed in the mind of the consumer and on which he or she bases his or her reasons for feeling one way or another about a product, a service, or an idea. Belief is a state of mind in which trust or confidence is placed in a person or a thing based on evidence. Beliefs stand at the core of one's personality and are hard to shake, since they are formed early and reinforced on a regular basis. Attitude is the feeling or emotional or mental position that one holds about a fact or a statement.

Post-It Parade - A RIVA term referring to moderator guide writing styles. In this technique, questions are created before the guide is completed, writing one question per post-it. Then the post-it notes are moved around to determine a logical flow. Then, the guide is created based on that flow.

Probe - Term referring to a tactfully asked, pointed question which follows a respondent's response to a qualitative researcher's (QR's) initial question. These types of questions are designed to reveal more in-depth information or to clarify earlier statements and are essential to successful qualitative market research (QLMR) investigations. Example: Respondent: *"I think a good TV show requires a lot of action."* QR: *"What is your definition of 'action in a good TV show?'"*

Product Sort - Long time respected industry intervention/projective technique that asks respondents to sort a set of products into groups or "families" and talk about what qualities that group/family has in common. This technique is a good way to see where respondents place client product in competitive sets.

Project Manager - Individual who is in charge of all the research project pieces. Typically, independent qualitative researchers (QRs) are also project managers.

Projective Technique - A type of intervention which is a semi-structured, indirect method of investigating the private world of conscious and unconscious thinking.

Proposal - Written document defining research project objectives, methodology, timeline, costs, research qualifications, and delivered to the client.

Purpose Statement - Written purpose of the study which defines what the client wants to learn from the research project.

QLMR - RIVA acronym for "Qualitative Market Research" which includes: Focus Groups, In-Depth Interviews (IDIs), Ethnographies, Telephone Interviews, Dyads, Triads, etc. By its very nature, this discipline is "soft and flexible," although not lacking in rigor. The goal of qualitative market research is to gain as much insight as possible into a given issue or group without having a pre-ordained framework for the information.

QRE - RIVA acronym for "Qualitative Research Event" which can include: Focus Groups, Focus Panels, Triads, Dyads, In-Depth Interviews (IDIs), Mini-Groups, Extended Groups, Mock Juries, Children's Play Sessions, Telephone Interviews, etc. QREs are based on four cornerstones: Perceptions, Opinions, Beliefs, and Attitudes (POBAs).

QRs - Industry acronym for Qualitative Researchers, also known as moderators.

QTMR - RIVA acronym for Quantitative Market Research which includes survey research and mall intercepts. See "Quantitative Market Research."

Qualifier - Refers to responses to screener questions that qualify a potential respondent to participate in a qualitative research event (QRE).

Qualitative Research Quadrangle - RIVA phrase describing the four cornerstones for qualitative research events (QREs) also referred to as POBAs (Perceptions/Opinions/Beliefs/Attitudes).

Quantitative Market Research - The discipline of market research that focuses on collecting statistical data ("how many, how often, how much") through the use of surveys where responses can be analyzed to show patterns and facilitate projections for the future. See also "QTMR."

Question Stem - The first several words that begin a question. These are very important in the qualitative market research (QLMR) world - making the difference between a leading question and a neutral question - ultimately affecting the overall tone and success of the QLMR investigation. For a list of leading question stems see *"Never Too Late to Learn a Good Lesson"* in Part III of this book.

Quota - Refers to the minimum/maximum types of respondents needed to participate in a particular qualitative research event (QRE). It is tied into the screener and decrees how many people with which characteristics (age, place of residence, gender, education, profession, marital status, race, income, user/non-user, etc.) to include in a study.

Rapport - Refers to a qualitative researcher's (QR's) ability to form a bond with respondents in a qualitative research event (QRE) setting. It starts with the first eye contact a QR shares with a respondent.

"Reading the Room" - RIVA phrase describing the Qualitative Researcher (QR) technique of looking around the whole table regularly during a qualitative research event (QRE) in order to calibrate what is going on, such as: who is interested; who is not; what dynamics are in play in the session; as well as getting a sense of whether the pace of the session is working.

Recommendations - Included in the report phase of a research project. These are based on what respondents have said (direct quotes) during qualitative research events (QREs) concerning the purpose of the study.

Reconnaissance - A military term that qualitative market research (QLMR) has borrowed to define the territory in a qualitative research event (QRE) where the qualitative researcher (QR) seeks to collect baseline information. It is in this section that "can't fail" questions are asked of respondents to put them at ease.

Recruiting - The process of finding those individuals/consumers/etc. that fulfill the research specifications dictated by a research study. These specifications may include: Gender, Age, Geographical Location, Education, Income, Religion, Race, Occupation, User/Non-user of a product, service, etc. See also "Quota."

Release Form - The industry document respondents may sign before participating in a qualitative research event (QRE) stating that their ideas can be used to further research and that they will not receive further compensation. This form employs the "hold harmless" terms used in legal documents.

Repeaters - An industry term that is used to define those respondents who make it a practice of attending qualitative research events (QREs) in the city where they live as a way of earning income. They often falsify answers to "qualify" for QREs or misrepresent themselves to enhance their chances of attending a QRE (For example – using different names, multiple identification cards, saying they use a particular product/service, etc.). Often used in the following industry phrase, *"cheaters and repeaters."*

Report - The final stage of qualitative research event (QRE) process which compares data across similar/different QREs. There are several different types of reports requested in the qualitative market research (QLMR) industry ranging from 1 page in length to 100s of pages. However, every research report should include an overview of background information that led to the need for research, the purpose of the research, and how the research was conducted. Report formats include: Outline/Memo Report, Topline Report, Executive Summary, Full Report, etc.

Re-Screen - To re-phrase key questions from the screener to respondents when they arrive at a facility to ensure they are the correct respondent for the qualitative research event (QRE).

Research Analyst - Also known as a report writer, they report the findings of the qualitative research event (QRE) in a written report. The research analyst may be present behind the mirror during QRE(s) or may just review A/V recordings or transcripts of the QRE(s).

Research Methodology - Refers to the structure of qualitative research events (QREs). It includes the number of sessions, type of sessions, number of respondents to be recruited, length of sessions, and research location(s).

Research Rigor - A RIVA term that refers to the need to adhere to "best practices" and procedures in qualitative market research (QLMR) studies without becoming a slave to a pattern or a process that attempts to make every QRE the same in a study. It also requires *"holding a standard"* for collecting data so that biases are minimalized.

Researcher Neutrality - A good researcher does not have a vested interest in the outcome of the research other than collecting good data for decision-making. They are neutral to the content of the findings – putting a good deal of their attention on understanding respondent perceptions, opinions, beliefs, and attitudes (POBAs) about the elements the study is meant to uncover.

Researcher Source Book - Directory published by *Quirk's Marketing Research Review* listing market research companies/products/services as well as focus group facilities in more than 100 countries. This directory can be found online and a hard copy (published annually) is sent to subscribers.

Respondent - Term used to describe participants in a qualitative research event (QRE). They are also sometimes referred to as customers, voters, or employees.

RFI - Acronym for "Request For Information".

RFP - Acronym for "Request For Proposal".

RIVA - The qualitative market research company started by Naomi R. Henderson in 1981. The letters stand for "Research In Values and Attitudes." The company has two divisions: Research and Training and lives under the following banner: *"We do what we teach and we teach what we do."*

Role Playing - To take on the persona of someone other than oneself to project how that person might think or act. For example in a qualitative research event (QRE) a respondent might be asked to take on the role of a member of the board of directors of a toothpaste manufacturing company and describe what concerns that board member may have about the negative press related to fluoride.

Roll - Term used to describe phenomenon when questions produce ping/pong answers between respondents without the qualitative researcher (QR) having to ask any other questions or probes to elicit responses.

RTB - Industry acronym for *"Reason to Believe"* - the underlying principle in a concept or positioning statement that makes the product or service to be sold something plausible for the reader.

Sanctioned Voyeurism - A RIVA term that describes the role that observers take when watching qualitative research events (QREs) from behind a one way mirror.

Screener - List of questions that qualify an individual to be in a qualitative research event (QRE).

Scriberator - RIVA term used to describe a qualitative researcher (QR) who feels compelled to write word for word responses on flip chart/easel while moderating rather than engaging the group in a discussion based on responses - see *"Seduced by the easel."*

Security Question - This type of question is included in a research screener to ensure that the appropriate respondents are selected to participate in a qualitative research event (QRE). Primarily a question is asked to ensure that the following individuals are NOT recruited: work for a market research company or work in the field of the content discussion (e.g., respondents are asked to come and view a TV pilot – therefore, no one who works in the media or their family members should be invited as a participant).

"Seduced by the Easel" - RIVA phrase used to describe when the qualitative researcher (QR) writes most respondent responses on the easel - "scribing" rather than moderating - see "scriberator."

Self-Disclosures - Industry phrase used to describe the qualitative researcher (QR) technique of "closing the circle" during the Introduction Stage of a qualitative research event (QRE). After respondents have introduced themselves the QR shares some personal information as well. The QR community has debated the value of this technique. Some argue that this approach creates a "cozy environment" in which the QR is considered to be part of the group. Others argue that information about the QR can cause respondents to form negative/positive opinions and assumptions of the QR which may cause them to modify their responses.

Semi-Structured Method - One of the three moderating methods employed for a qualitative research study. This method uses a discussion guide outline with topic areas of discussion rather than a detailed discussion guide with specific questions. Unlike the "unstructured method", respondents <u>and</u> researchers share the responsibility for content during qualitative research events (QREs). This method oftentimes includes planned interventions in a flexible order. It is most useful at the creative development stage of research and is very popular in Europe.

Serial Interviewing - Industry phrase used to describe when a qualitative researcher (QR) asks respondents to answer in a pre-set order around the table; interviewing as if it was a set of one-on-one interviews rather than a group question. This practice should not be used in qualitative research events (QREs).

Shared Pairs - Type of intervention. Respondents work in teams of two for a short period of time (1-2 minutes) during a qualitative research event (QRE) to complete a task, answer a question, etc. They then report back their shared pair insights to the whole group.

Shopability Studies - Artificial or virtual setting of store shelving where consumers engage in "mock shopping," or a field trip to an actual site where consumers are asked to comment on how they choose items/products.

Shop-Alongs - A qualitative market research (QLMR) methodology that uses the elements of an ethnography or one-on-one interview while joining a respondent while he/she is on a typical shopping trip to buy specific items.

Skip Patterns - This is a quantitative market research (QTMR) term that relates to the flow of questions in a survey – if a person answers "no" to a specific question it does not make sense to ask the next two questions, so the researcher "skips" to the fourth question. Qualitative market research

(QLMR) borrows this practice for the screeners used to locate appropriate respondents for qualitative research events (QREs).

"Sneak a Peek" - RIVA phrase used to describe when a qualitative researcher (QR) repeatedly glances down at their guide while a respondent is still responding to a question and looking at the QR! This behavior gives the impression that the respondent's answer is of less value and/or the QR is not listening to their response, caring only how they are going to phrase the next question. It is rude, insensitive, and the mark of a poor QR. If a QR needs to look at the guide, it is best to say: *"Let me check where I am ..."* and then glance down on purpose, while no one is talking.

Sophisticated Naïveté - Qualitative researcher (QR) practice of demonstrating incomplete understanding during a qualitative research event (QRE) signaling a need for more detailed or in-depth information from respondents. It is important for the QR to avoid appearing phony or faking ignorance, rather he/she should express interest in new ideas regardless of their own level of expertise on the topic. Thus avoiding "leading" respondents or inserting QR's opinion into the flow of conversation.

SPOC- RIVA acronym for "single point of contact". Also referenced to as client spokesperson. See "client spokesperson" for full definition.

SQLA - RIVA acronym for "Short Questions/Long Answers" - the desired format for qualitative research events (QREs). Way to check for SQLA – the typewritten question on the guide does not wrap to a second line.

Statement of Limitations - This statement is typically included in qualitative market research reports to remind the client/reader that findings should not be projected to a larger group of individuals due to the nature of qualitative research (Example: *"Focus groups seek to develop insight and direction, rather than quantitatively precise measures. Due to the limited number of respondents and the restrictions of recruiting, this research must be considered in a qualitative frame of reference. The reader is reminded that this report is intended to clarify cloudy issues and point out the direction for future research. The data presented here cannot be projected to a universe of similar respondents. The value of focus groups lies in their ability to provide observers with unfiltered comments from a segment of the target population and for the decision makers to gain insight into the beliefs, attitudes, and perceptions of their consumer base."*).

Stipend - See "Honorarium."

Structured Method - One of the three moderating methods employed for a qualitative research study. This method uses a detailed, prepared discussion guide which includes predetermined issues to cover and specific probes in crucial areas of exploration. Due to its nature, this method ensures that information relevant to the project purpose is covered, thus minimizing respondent tangents and discussion of irrelevant issues. This method permits more confident comparison of results across QREs. It is very popular in the United States and most appropriate for the less experienced qualitative researcher (QR).

Study Objectives - What the client is looking to get out of research.

Study Purpose - Generalized statement of reasons for research.

Sugging - An industry term referring to the practice of "Selling Under the Guise of Research." This practice uses qualitative market research (QLMR) as a thin cover for selling respondents products or service rather than for its true use: collecting perceptions, opinions, beliefs, and attitudes (POBAs) from respondents for client decision making. Example: Respondents are recruited to discuss their long term health care insurance needs. A copy of their name and phone number is then given to a salesperson who is watching the qualitative research events (QREs) thru a one way mirror. A few days later, the respondent gets a call to hear a pitch about buying long term health care insurance. This is not a recommended practice and when done, and it damages the image of QLMR studies in the eyes of the public.

Synectics - A body of knowledge that stands on the Osborne-Parnes Model of creative problem solving. This methodology is most often used in facilitating meetings; it is seldom used in qualitative research events (QREs).

Taste Test/Usage Test - Respondents taste or use products and discuss their experience and reactions. This falls under a special branch of QLMR – sensory research.

TDIs - Industry acronym for telephone in-depth interviews – individual interviews conducted over the phone.

"Teflon Method" - RIVA phrase describing Qualitative researcher (QR) method employed to avoid providing any QR personal content or judgment in the space of the qualitative market research (QLMR) investigation. Oftentimes, QRs will respond to such inquiries with another question, thus deflecting the original question away from the QR and back to the group.

Teleconferencing - Audio or A/V interface with each respondent in a different location. A qualitative researcher (QR) with special expertise is required for these sessions.
Telephone Interviews - See "TDIs."
Terminates - This term refers to the responses on a screener that would exclude a potential respondent from being selected for a qualitative research event (QRE). Example: A product non-user when the QRE study requires product users.
"Top-of-Mind" - Industry phrase used to describe respondent responses that are quickly generated from first-level thinking, rather than responses that delve into deeper feelings and attitudes (second, or third-level responses- that are below obvious consciousness).
Topline - Refers to a type of report that relies on the qualitative researcher's (QR's) memory and notes following a series of qualitative research events (QREs). Typically this report format is 5 to 10 pages in length and is similar to an outline/memo report in format. This format does not utilize transcripts and typically has a 1 to 3 day turnaround time.
Trained Moderator/QR - Someone who has been through a formal external/ academic program or a rigorous in-house training procedure. It has been said that trained QRs bring a depth and dimension to moderating that someone who has not been trained cannot provide.
Transcripts - Refers to a transcript of qualitative research event (QRE) recordings. Highly skilled and experienced transcriptionists can customize transcriptions to fit the needs of the researcher/analyst. These are typically generated within one week from the date of the last QRE in a series. Transcripts range in format from verbatim, semi-verbatim, and edited.
Triads - Three respondent qualitative sessions with a qualitative researcher (QR). (For a total of four individuals present for the research process).
Triangle Method - A RIVA term referring to moderator/QR guide writing styles. This method is commonly used by qualitative researchers (QRs) with a very structured mode of internal thinking and by those with more experience writing moderator guides. This technique recognizes the funnel shaped structure of qualitative research events (QREs) where inquiry starts out broad and easy to answer working its way to more specific issue areas.
Universal Moderator's/QR's Guide - A detailed discussion guide for a qualitative research event (QRE) with specific questions and possible probes. This type of guide allows the qualitative researcher (QR) to spend time

managing QRE discussions rather than crafting questions "in the moment." It also ensures that another person can "lead" group in the case of QR absence.

Unstructured Method - One of the three moderating methods employed for a qualitative research study. This method uses a broad purpose statement rather than a discussion guide to conduct qualitative research events (QREs). Therefore, respondents determine most of the subject matter during a QRE. This method is most effective in the problem definition/exploratory stage of research and requires a high level of interpretive skills and experience for effective analysis. This method is more popular in Europe than in the United States.

UPR - Developed by Dr. Carl Rogers in the 1950s and now an industry acronym for "Unconditional Positive Regard" - allowing respondents to be "who they are" not what the qualitative researcher (QR) or client expects them to be or how the QR or client wants them to think. This skill includes presenting an empathetic yet neutral face and voice tone while hearing comments and responses that may range from dull to bizarre to exceptional.

User - When recruited for a qualitative research event (QRE), refers to a respondent that uses the product, service, or brand that will be discussed.

Vested Moderator/QR - Industry term used to describe a qualitative researcher (QR) who cares about the outcome of a project, beyond the research aspects. Also known as an "In-house QR." This QR typically works for/is part of the organization that is sponsoring the qualitative research event (QRE). There are benefits and drawbacks to being a vested QR. Example: A QR who feels strongly about the direction the company should take with respect to the product or service being evaluated in research may not be able to stay neutral when asking questions of respondents.

Videographer - In qualitative market research (QLMR) this term refers to the individual who operates the video camera and other audio-visual equipment which records a qualitative research event (QRE).

VOC - Industry acronym which stands for "Voice of the Consumer."

Why - While the qualitative market research industry is based on the "why premise," the actual questions posed to qualitative research event (QRE) respondents should not start with this term. In essence, "why" questions force short, rational answers that require further probes. In most instances, this evokes a defensive response, which can shut down further communication and ultimately make it harder for the qualitative researcher (QR) to access deeper levels of data. It is suggested that questions are reframed to exclude the term "why." To understand "why" someone does or does not do or believe something it is better to ask for their reasons or rationale, as a result, the answers will be much richer in response. See *"Do Not Ask Me Why"* in Part II, Section I of this book for further discussion on this premise.

"Wooden Delivery" - RIVA phrase used to describe qualitative researcher (QR) style - not "present" while delivering guidelines - more interested in checking off a mental checklist rather than inviting participants to help with research efforts. This practice should be avoided.

APPENDIX A:
Moderator Maxims – "Naomisms"

Moderator Maxims – "Naomisms"

Naomi R. Henderson started training moderators in 1982, standing on principles learned from mentors and honed in the fires of experience with thousands of respondents. These "Naomisms" are words of wisdom, and while these maxims may not be true for everyone – they are true for Naomi. They are listed here INPO – in no particular order.

- Watch what respondents do – not just what they say.

- Be with people – not with paper.

- Moderator should honor 80/20 rule – Respondents talk 80% of the time, moderator talks 20% of the time.

- Let respondents tell you what you already know – listen to their words.

- There is never enough time in focus groups to explore all the myriad avenues that could emerge – more is not better regarding group size. Group sizes from 6 to 8 participants are ideal.

- Respondents want to be with a moderator who cares and respects them as individuals – not with a set of perfect questions.

- "I ask – you answer" is a boring focus group – vary activities about every 15 to 20 minutes to keep the group engaged.

- The person who asks the questions has all the power.

- Ask only questions – make no statements. Exception: when giving instructions.

- Do not summarize or analyze comments from a respondent – it is like drinking and driving – it can be done, but it is not smart. Just ask questions – save summary and analysis statements for when the data collection phase is over.

- During the rapport building phase – provide the opportunity to have an "emotional handshake" with respondents.

- There is no "we" when moderating – you are all alone. Tonto is not coming.

- Let respondents do the work – do not "help" with leading questions or giving part of the desired answer in the question.

- What a moderator does has as strong of an impact as what the moderator says.

- Quantitative research asks the questions - qualitative research questions the answers.

- Keep questions short – because short questions lead to long answers. Definition of a short question: It does not wrap to second line of text.

- Eat the guide – burp the questions.

- Sometimes a detour can become the shortest route to new information.

- In quantitative research – the instrument is a written questionnaire. In qualitative research the instrument is a moderator whose voice, tone, pace, pitch, speed, diction, volume, demeanor, and personality all have an impact on respondents.

- What counts cannot be counted – i.e., there is no quantitative measure of perceptions, opinions, beliefs, and attitudes [POBAs] – drivers of human behavior.

- As a moderator - you are only as good as your next group.

- When a respondent is made to feel like a research partner rather than a research subject, the benefit is a deeper level of communication and more fuel for the research furnace.

- One QRE does not a study make. Qualitative insights are derived across a series of interviews.

- The moderator is not the "star" of a QRE – the respondent is.

- Trust yourself and your experience as a moderator when navigating a tough patch in a QRE.

APPENDIX B:
Supplements

BOILER PLATE OF A GUIDE

MODERATOR'S GUIDE

DATE: **April 9th**   TOPIC: "Green Fields"-Round 1

Group #	Date	Site	Type of Shopper	Time
1	4/9	Philadelphia, PA	Primary	5:30-7:30pm
2	4/9	Philadelphia, PA	Secondary	7:30-9:30pm
3	4/10	Philadelphia, PA	Primary	5:30-7:30pm
4	4/10	Philadelphia, PA	Secondary	7:30-9:30pm

Mix of M/F Primary food shopper – Low Income – live in Philadelphia City

A. **INTRO:** Hello. My name is XXXX. I am the Moderator for today's 2 hour group discussion. **The purpose today is to discuss issues related to local food stores.**

    Agenda: You will be doing several things: participating in a group discussion, occasionally doing some "private writing" and looking at some materials.

    This is a free flowing discussion and there are no wrong answers. I'm looking for different points of view.

    Mod.Info: I work for RIVA, a research firm in Rockville, Maryland and I have a contract to work on this project as a research consultant.

B. **ACKNOWLEDGE** Thanks for coming today and for fitting this session into your schedule.

C. **DISCLOSURES:**
  1. FACILITY SETTING: Mention mics, mirrors, observers, and recording
  2. The session is being recorded, so I can write an accurate report – "Not of who said what", but "What got said."

D. **PERMISSIONS:** At any time you can excuse yourself to go to the restroom or to get more food or beverages. Only one person should be up or out at a time.

E. **GUIDELINES:** In order to make this a research session, here are some guidelines:

1. Please talk **one at a time**
2. **Talk in a voice as loud as mine.**
3. **Avoid side conversation** with your neighbors.
4. Work for **equal "air time"** so that no one talks too little or too much
5. Allow for **different points of view.** There are no wrong answers
6. Say what **you believe**, whether or not anyone else agrees with you.
7. **Only one person up** or out of the room at one time

INTROS: PLEASE INTRODUCE YOURSELF TO THE GROUP AND TELL US:

First Name	Family Size	What you usually do in the daytime
Live in house or apartment	Personality word that describes you	One food you usually buy

Appendix B

CLIENT ONLY PAGE

Study Purpose: To garner POBAs [perceptions, opinions, beliefs, & attitudes] from respondents about issues related to the "Green Fields" image/brand, store experience, and competitive position

Intended Outcomes: To support short and long term strategy planning related to developing new marketing and communication plans aimed at increasing sales and enhancing customer loyalty.

Reminders for Observers:
1. Keep voices at whisper level, room is not truly "soundproof".
2. Every moment of every group is not productive...there are transition questions, bridges to new activities and sometimes respondents go off tangent as they talk.
3. The true value of focus groups is in the way it allows viewers to see and hear, first-hand, the perceptions, opinions, beliefs, and attitudes [POBAs] of respondents.
4. *Ten minutes before end of session, respondents will be given a task so that the Moderator can meet with **ONE CLIENT SPOKESPERSON** to collect any additional written questions to be asked of respondents.* <u>Please give any final questions you want asked to THE CLIENT SPOKESPERSON.</u>

ROADMAP OF ACTIVITIES PLANNED

Category of Information To Be Covered	Approx. Time Set Aside
Welcome/Groundrules/Self-Introductions	10 minutes
Issue A: Lifestyle Questions	10 minutes
Issue B: What's Important at a Food Store	25 minutes
Issue C: Competitive Set/Store Image	40 minutes
Issue D: All About "Green Fields" & Circulars	20 minutes
Issue E: Advice to "Green Fields"	10 minutes
Closure	5 minutes
TOTAL TIME ALLOTTED	120 minutes out of 120 possible

Planned Interventions:

[ ] Easel Work [ ] Visual Stimuli [ ] Team Discussions
[ ] Worksheets [ ] Dot Voting [ ] Media Habits – top five

- A. Lifestyle Questions
  [10 minutes]

- B. **What is Important at a Food Store?**
  [25 minutes]

- C. Competitive set/image of stores
  [40 minutes]

- D. All About "Green Grocer" (Links with Section E)
  [20 minutes]

- E. Advisory Committee to "Green Grocer"
  [10 minutes]

CLOSURE
[5 minutes]

I'm going to step out for moment – while I'm gone…I'm going to have ___ from the group serve as the GM [Guest Moderator] and work up here on the easel.

His/her job is to make a list of anything you learned tonight that was new.

"I LEARNED…"

Moderator will meet client in the hall and get additional Qs or revisit any area for more discussion.

Return and ask additional Qs and excuse the group.

Ten Client Guidelines for Observing Qualitative Research Events (QREs)

1. **Be clear on the purpose of the research.** What are the key reasons QREs are being conducted?

2. Prior to the start of each session, **review the Moderator's Guide** and become familiar with the intended flow of the QRE.

3. **Do not expect the Moderator to ask every question** on the guide or to ask the questions in the same language that is on the guide.

4. **Do not expect every question to have an immediate payoff** in "providing insight."

5. **Avoid "selective listening"** – i.e., paying attention to only those points that support an already established or preconceived point of view.

6. **Listen to what is NOT being said as well as what is being said.** Be alert to the nuances of meaning and the language respondents use to present their perceptions, opinions, beliefs, and attitudes (POBAs). Example: On a key question there is a long wait before someone responds and then they do so with – *"Hmm...let me think about that."*

7. **Watch non-verbal behavior** and look for congruence with what is spoken. Do not "label" non-verbal behavior or attach external meanings. Example: A respondent crosses his arms across his chest and leans away from the table as another respondent talks about a sensitive subject. What does this non-verbal behavior mean? Because of the wide range of "possible" explanations that exist, simply note that behavior and wait to see if verbal comments are made that provide an insight to the "stance" taken.

8. Remember that a **one-way mirror is not truly one way if you are wearing a white shirt or top...and a mirror in a wall is almost impossible to soundproof**, and the following sounds transfer easily to respondents:

- Clattering cutlery, plates, glasses
- Laughter, loud talking, tearing paper from pads, etc.
- Moving furniture (e.g., rocking back and forth in chairs, chair handles bumping into writing counter, etc.)
- Rhythmic tapping (e.g. foot against wall, pencil on countertop, etc.)

9. Please remember that the **facility is not a restaurant** – if you have a special food request, please ask for it in advance via email with the Moderator or the Moderator's Project Manager before arriving at the site [e.g., kosher food, allergy to shellfish, the desire for Coke vs. Pepsi products, etc.]

10. **Do not expect to be "entertained"** as an observer. The following range of emotions may occur during observation of QREs:

- Boredom
- Joy
- Frustration
- Enlightenment

- Excitement
- Sadness
- Creation
- Distraction

- Anger
- Enthusiasm
- Disappointment
- Attentiveness

Research Guidelines For Focus Groups

WELCOME!

Guidelines to make this discussion the most productive and enjoyable for everyone:

1. Please talk one at a time
   (Session is audio recorded)

2. Talk as loudly as the moderator
   (So that all may hear)

3. Avoid side conversations
   (All comments are important to research)

4. Work for "equal air time"
   (No one talks too much or too little)

5. Allow for different points of view
   (There are no wrong answers)

6. Say what YOU believe
   (Even if no one agrees with you)

7. One person up and out of the room at any one time
   (Keeps the session flowing and allows group to end on time)

Hot Notes

Users of Client Brand Name Dog Food
GROUPS 1 & 2 IN SEATTLE
August 7

A. Role of Puppy in Household	B. Advertisements Recalled
• Like a new baby—needs pampering • Takes a lot of time/attention • Fun to play with • (List other classic baby metaphors in a word chart) • (Give this section only 2–3 paragraphs in report)	• Client company almost always mentioned first • High recall of advertisements from past year • Spontaneous mention of "twists" in advertising campaigns • Key competitor comments focus on product attributes rather than what it could do for the dog (stress this in the report)
C. Reaction to Client Advertisements	**D. Respondent Advice for Client**
• All three advertisements received high ratings for believability and humor (stress in the report how unbelievable incident translates into product believability) • Frisbee Toss received highest ratings for communicating strategy the best (give lots of verbatim in report on this) • Other advertisements could be follow up advertisements to Frisbee Toss in the future • Request for more varied age groups in all advertisements • Request for music to be <u>less</u> loud in Sidewalk Shuffle • Coupon was of less interest for puppy owners: *"Only the best for my dog...at any price."*	• Keep tone of new advertisements consistent with strategy from past advertisements • Keep "twist" factor in play for all future advertisements to carry heritage factor • Work diversity factor into advertisements—not only age, but lifestyle and race as well • Consider a theme song for the advertisements...rather than just any music that fits, more than a jingle—something of substance • Couponing may not be needed for this puppy food since "dog is my child" syndrome and price is not a key factor in decision

NOTE: This set of "hot notes" was made one hour after the pair of groups was completed. The four parts of the quadrangle were based on the four subheads in the moderator's guide. "Notes to author of report" are indicated by the use of parentheses.

Suggested Readings

Suggested Reading

Books

American Marketing Association/New York Chapter. *The Focus Group Directory.* New York: Greenbook, 2010.

Bystedt, Lynn, & Potts. *Moderating to the Max.* Ithaca, NY: Paramount Marketing Publishing, 2003.

Chakrapani, Chuck. *Marketing Research: State-of-the-Art Perspectives.* Chicago, IL: American Marketing Association, 2000.

Crask, Melvin; Richard J. Fox & Roy G. Stout. *Marketing Research: Principles and Applications.* Englewood Cliffs, NJ: Prentice Hall, 1995.

Dilts, R. *Applications of Neuro-Linguistic Programming.* Cupertino, CA: Meta Publications, 1983.

Fiske, Marjorie; Kendall, Patricia L. & Merton, Robert K. *The Focused Interview: A Manual of Problems and Procedures.* The Free Press, New York, 1990.

Goldman, A.E. & McDonald, S.S. *The Group Depth Interview: Principles and Practice.* Englewood Cliffs, NJ: Prentice Hall Inc, 1987.

Gordon, Wendy. *Goodthinking: A Guide to Qualitative Research.* Oxfordshire, United Kingdom: Admap Publications, 1999.

Gordon, W. & Langmaid, R. *Qualitative Market Research: A Practitioner's and Buyer's Guide.* Aldershot, UK: Gower, 1988.

Greenbaum, T. L. *The Practical Handbook & Guide to Focus Group Research.* Lexington, MA: Lexington Books, 1988.

Grinder, J. & Bandler, R. *The Structure of Magic.* Palo Alto, CA: Science & Behaviour Books, 1976.

——— *Trance-Formations: Neuro-Linguistic Programming and the Structure of Hypnosis.* Moab, UT: Real People Press, 1981.

Krueger, R. A. *Focus Groups: A Practical Guide for Applied Research.* Newbury Park, CA: Sage Publications, 2000.

Langer, Judith. *The Mirrored Window: Focus Groups from a Moderator's Point of View.* Paramount Publications, 2001.

Mariampolski, Hy. *Qualitative Market Research: A Comprehensive Guide.* New York: Sage Publications, 2001.

——— *Ethnography for Marketers: A Guide to Consumer Immersion.* Thousand Oaks, CA: Sage Publications, 2006.

Merton, R. K. *The Focused Interview: A Manual of Problems & Procedures.* New York: The Free Press, 1990.
Morgan, David L., *Focus Groups as Qualitative Research.* Sage Publications Inc., Newbury Park, CA, 1988.
Patton, Michael Quinn. *Qualitative Evaluation and Research Methods* (2nd ed.). Newbury Park, CA: Sage Publications Inc., 1990.
Qualitative Research Online. Editors, Thomas W. Miller and Jeff Walkowski. Madison, WI; Research Publishers LLC, 2004.
Templeton, Jane Farley. *Focus Groups: A Guide for Marketing & Advertising Professionals* (Rev. ed.). Chicago, IL: Probus Publishing, 1994.
Richardson, Jerry. *The Magic of Rapport: How You Can Gain Personal Power In Any Situation.* Cupertino, CA: Meta Publications, 1981.
Rossman, G. B. & Rallis, S. F. *Learning in the Field: An Introduction to Qualitative Research*, Thousand Oaks, CA: Sage Publications, 1998.
Taylor, S.J & Bogdan, R. *Introduction to Qualitative Research Methods: The Search for Meanings* (2nd ed.). New York: John Wiley & Sons, 1984.

Periodicals

Atkinson, P., Delamont, S. & Hammersley, M. "Qualitative Research Traditions: A British Response to Jacob." *Review of Educational Research*, 1988: 58.
Bristol, Terry and Edward F. Fern. "Exploring the Atmosphere Created by Focus Group Interviews: Comparing Feelings Across Qualitative Techniques." *Journal of the Market Research Society*, April 1996: 185ff.
Bronson, Gail. "Focus Groups for Lawyers." *Forbes*, September 21, 1987: 48.
Carton, Michael. "Working Through Client Challenges: How to Avoid Problematic Projects." *ORCA Views*, Fall 2012.
Chakrapani, Chuck. "NLP & Its Applications to Marketing Research." *Canadian Journal of Marketing Research* 10: 1991.
Clowes, Rusty. "Making Storyboards Work for a Focus Group Facility." *Applied Marketing Review*, December 1993: 30ff.
Collis, Carla. "Confessions of a Telephone Focus Group Skeptic." *Quirks Marketing Research Review*, May 1996: 12ff.
Day, Rebecca H. "Moderating: When Gender Matters." *Quirk's Marketing Research Review*, December 1993: 18ff.
De Brauw, Chris. "Tips from the field to improve your yield." *Quirk's Marketing Research Media.*
Donovan, Michael. "When Ethnography Really Works." *ORCA Views*, Fall 2013.
Feder, Richard A. and Bryan Mattimore. "Rethinking Focus Group Reporting: Dynamic Debriefing." *Quirk's Marketing Research Review*, December 1996: 12ff.

Forcade, Karen M. "Focus Groups with Kids… Imagine." *Quirk's Marketing Research Review*, December 1996: 30ff.
Greenbaum, Thomas L. "The Focus Group Bill of Rights." *Quirk's Marketing Research Review*, October 1996: 62.
———"Who's Leading Your Focus Group?" *Bank Marketing*, March 1993: 31.
———"Answers to Moderator Problems Starts with Asking the Right Questions." *Marketing News*, May 27, 1991: 8ff.
Greenbaum, Thomas L. "Should You Do Your Own Focus Groups? The Answer Is No—and Here's Why." *Bank Marketing*, June 1991: 39ff.
Jacob, E. "Qualitative Research Traditions: A Review." *Review of Educational Research*, 1987: 51.
Kinzey, R. J. "Faster is better when writing qualitative reports", *Quirk's Marketing Research Review*, 1993 7(10): 12.
Langer, Judith. "Focus Groups." *American Demographics*, February 1991: 39ff.
Mariampolski, Hy. "Focus Groups on Sensitive Topics: How to Get Subjects to Open Up and Feel Good About Telling the Truth." *Applied Marketing Research*, Winter 1989: 6.
Rausch, Marilyn J. "Qualities of a Beginner Moderator." *Quirk's Marketing Research Review*, December 1996: 24.
Retinger, Charlotte and Lee Slurzberg. "A Review of Focus Groups for Advertising Agencies." *Quirk's Marketing Research Review*, March 1994: 10ff.
Robinson, Judith L. "Individual Versus Group Interviews: Is There a Difference?" *Quirk's Marketing Research Review*, December 1993: 28–29.
Schild, Rhoda. "So How Tall Do You Want Me to Be?" *Quirk's Marketing Research Review*, February 1995: 33ff.
Schindler, Robert M. "The Real Lesson of New Coke: The Value of Focus Groups for Prediction the effects of Social Influence." *Marketing Research: A Magazine of Management & Applications*, December 1992: 22ff.
Simon, Murray. "Physician Focus Groups Revisited." *Quirk's Marketing Research Review*, June/July 1996: 16ff.
Spanier, Jim. "Focus Group Listening and Hearing." *Quirk's Marketing Research Review*, December 1993: 33ff.
Whipple, Thomas W. "Mapping Focus Group Data." *Marketing Research: A Magazine of Management & Applications* 6(1): 16ff.
Yoffie, Amy J. and Marj Anzalone. "In Defense of On-line Focus Groups." *Quirk's Marketing Research Review*, June/July 1995: 24.

APPENDIX D:
Industry Resources

Industry Resources

> *This list is provided to readers as an additional resource for information about the market research industry. Inclusion in this list should not be seen as an endorsement of the policies or principles of any organization.*

Resource List in Alphabetical Order

American Marketing Association (AMA)
Council of American Survey Research Organizations (CASRO)
Creative Problem Solving Institute (CPSI)
European Society for Opinion Marketing Research (ESOMAR)
Green Book Directories (Division of NY AMA)
Market Research Association (MRA)
The Marketing Research and Intelligence Association (MRIA)
Online Moderator Training
Pharmaceutical Business Intelligence and Research Group (PBIRG)
Pharmaceutical Market Research Group (PMRG)
Qualitative Research Consultants Association (QRCA)
Quirk's Marketing Research Review
RIVA Market Research and Training Institute (RIVA)

Information about each organization follows along with contact information.

AMA: American Marketing Association

Professional association for individuals and worldwide organizations that are marketers.

Publications include: *Marketing News, AMA Magazines, AMA Journals, and AMA Newsletters*

311 South Wacker Drive, Suite 5800
Chicago, IL 60606-2266
Phone: 312.542.9000 or 800.AMA.1150 Fax: 312.542.9001
www.marketingpower.com

CASRO: Council of American Survey Research Organizations Professional organization for survey professionals offering members access to industry resources, training, and networking opportunities. Promotes industry ethics and advocates for the survey industry as a whole.

170 North Country Road, Suite 4 Port Jefferson, NY 11777
Phone: 631.928.6954
Fax: 631.928.6041
www.CASRO.org

CPSI: Creative Problem Solving Institute
(Part of the CEF: Creative Education Foundation)
Provides training in the Osborn/Parnes *Creative Problem Solving Method*.

48 North Pleasant Street, Suite 301
Amherst, MA 01002
Phone: 508.960.0000
Fax: 413.658.0046
www.creativeeducationfoundation.org
For information on CPSI events/trainings: www.CPSIconference.com

ESOMAR: European Society for Opinion Marketing Research International organization for market research professionals, end-users, and graduate students that provides members with networking and career development opportunities through conferences and publications. Publications include: *Research World* (monthly)

Eurocenter 2, 11th Floor Barbara Strozzilaan 384
1083 HN Amsterdam The Netherlands
Phone: +31 20 664 2141
Fax: +31 20 664 2922
www.ESOMAR.org

Green Book Directories
A subsidiary of the New York AMA publishes listings of market research companies, services, and facilities available across the United States. To be used as a resource when planning a market research event.

116 East 27th Street, 6th Floor New York, NY 10016
Phone: 212.849.2752 or 800.792.9202
Fax: 212.202.7920
www.GreenBook.org

MRA: Market Research Association
Professional association for market research facility owners that offers professional development and networking within the market research industry.

Publications include: *Blue Book, Alert! Magazine, E-Newsletters,* and *Advertisers Resource*

110 National Drive, 2nd Floor Glastonbury, CT 06033
Phone: 860.682.1000
Fax: 888.512.1050
www.MRA-net.org

MRIA: The Marketing Research and Intelligence Association
A Canadian, non-profit, professional association for market research practitioners, market research houses, and buyers of research services. MRIA's mission is to enhance the industry as a whole through education of its members; advocacy of public policy governing research services and consumer rights; and establishing professional ethical standards.

Publications include: *VUE Magazine, Canadian Journal of Marketing Research, Research Buyer's Guide,* and *MRIA PULSE (E-Newsletter).*
www.mria-arim.ca

Online Moderator Training
A comprehensive and experiential 5-day course detailing how to plan, supervise, and lead online focus groups and bulletin boards. This training takes place online.

EM: Trainers@onlinemoderator.com
www.onlinemoderator.com

PBIRG: Pharmaceutical Business Intelligence and Research Group A global, non-profit, industry association that seeks to advance global healthcare marketing research through the education/training of its members; provide a market research code of ethics; provide a communication portal for industry issues; and link members to other professional marketing industry associations.

EM: pbirg@pbirg.com Phone: 215.855.5255
Fax: 215.855.5622
www.PBIRG.com

PMRG: Pharmaceutical Market Research Group
Professional association for market researchers specializing in the pharmaceutical industry. This organization promotes professional development and networking, as well as advocacy for the pharmaceutical market research industry as a whole.

PO Box 1449
Minneola, FL 34755
www.PMRG.org

QRCA: Qualitative Research Consultants Association
Professional association for practicing qualitative research consultants who are in independent marketing or social research.

Publication: *QRCA Views* (quarterly publication)—please refer to the QRCA website for a complete listing of publications.

1000 Westgate Drive, Suite 252 St. Paul, MN 55114
Phone: 651.290.7491 or 888.674.7722
Fax: 651.290.2266
www.QRCA.org

Quirk's Marketing Research Review
An market research industry repository of information offering a variety of resources related to market research, including articles, job postings, glossary of market research terms, discussion forums, facility listings, moderator listings, calendar of market research related events, trainings, and more.

Publications include: Quirk's Marketing Research Review (print, monthly)

Quirk's Marketing Research Review E-Newsletter (electronic, monthly)

4662 Slater Road
Eagan, MN 55122
Phone: 651.379.6200
www.QUIRKS.com

RIVA Market Research and Training Institute
Conducts qualitative market research studies as well as hands on training in the art and science of qualitative market research. RIVA Training offers both public trainings as well as custom trainings to individuals and organizations. Clients include the federal/state government sector, public and private companies, and non-profit schools and organizations, as well as freelancers.

1700 Rockville Pike, Suite 260
Rockville, MD 20852
Phone: 301.770.6456
Fax: 301.770.5879
www.RIVAinc.com

INDEX:

INDEX

Symbols

2/3rds Rule 160, 371
80/20 Rule 14, 371

A

"Active Listening" 350, 371-372
ad-labs 27, 48, 53, 372
Assumption Principle 365

B

BRUM Test 199-205
bulletin board 53, 360, 373, 420

C

clients
  about 5, 6, 20, 22, 33, 35-36, 82
  evaluate moderator 309-313
  managing the backroom 10, 59-60, 318, 325
    seasoned moderator's tips for 59-60
    spokesperson (SPOC) 173, 318-319, 325, 374, 395
  post-focus 177-178
  pre-focus group 175-176
  the Client-Respondent Divide 216-217

D

disclosures 86, 89, 105, 110, 262, 350, 375, 382, 406

E

ethnographic research 39, 48-50, 259

extended groups 27, 48, 50-51, 144-145, 377, 390

F

facility 23, 377
false close 136, 318, 319, 374, 377-378, 381
focus group
  communication time in 159
  conducting a 132-137
  context of 151-155
  cost of 139-140
  elements of 41, 129-130
  group size 17, 38, 157-162, 348
  history of 37, 141, 347
  how to create trust in 42, 192, 349-350
  limitations of 138-139
  pre/post 175-178
  recruiting for 131
  role of moderator in 130
  stages of 147-150, 249-250, 351, 371
  uses of 138
  value of 139
  what is a 129

G

"Gold Mines" 11, 109, 224, 282, 379
ground rules
  delivery styles 147-148
  for clients 315-319
    examples of 406, 407, 409-410
  for respondents 69, 81, 105, 109, 147-149, 379
    examples of 411
  role of in QREs 69, 148-149, 150

what to cover 149
guide 176-177, 221-225, 277, 372, 379, 382, 384, 385, 388, 389
  example of 406-408

H

homework 35, 145, 374, 380
  examples of 213
"Hot Notes" 269-273, 380
  examples of 271-272, 412

I

In-depth interviews (IDIs) 195, 213, 245-246, 255-266, 371, 379, 381
  analyzing data from 265
  application of 257-258
  benefits and drawbacks of 258
  conducting interview 261-262
  costing of 264-265
  creating rapport in 260-261
  key qualities of IDI interviewers 256-257
  organizing materials for 262-263
  recording data from 263-264
  recruiting for 259-260
  reports for 265
  setting for 260
  training for 259
intervention 86, 381-382
  "Board of Directors" 373
  "collage" 374
  "Eulogy" 376-377
  "flipchart" 378
  "getting over the wall" 47, 379
  "historical ally" 47-48, 380
  list of 44-45
  "open frame" technique 46-47, 58, 387
  "picture sort" 388
  "product sort" 389
  seasoned moderator favorites 58-59
  shared pairs 59, 394
  visual vs. process 45-46

invisible leadership 12, 83,121, 313, 382

K

known pairs research 48, 50, 382

L

linked statements 365
linking 12, 13, 89, 105, 111, 136, 355, 372, 383
logic tracking 12, 13, 89, 108, 111, 355, 385

M

manipulatives 44, 384
mock juries 51-52, 385
moderator
  basic knowledge of 106
  "ego investment" of 187-188
  handling troublesome respondents 107, 134-135
  lessons of a master 101, 112-113, 163-167, 301-306
  managing stress of 121-126
  Master Moderator™ 9-15, 38, 97, 104, 237, 366, 382, 384
    tips from 55-60
  matching to respondents 91-97
  niche vs. generalist vs. hybrid 116-117, 379, 380, 386
  role of 5-7, 53, 130, 236, 306
  trained moderators 38, 77, 103-113, 251, 259, 397
  what makes a moderator unique 115-116
moderator's guide 176-177, 221-225, 277, 372, 379, 382, 385, 386, 388, 389
  annotated guide 372
  example of 406-408
  file cards 222
  graphic guide 379
  mind map 222, 384-385

outline guide 131-132, 144, 222, 388
protocols for writing 221-225
tips for questions in 176-177, 233-237
universal guide 144, 222, 225, 397-398
writing from the respondent's viewpoint 214-217

N

Neuro-Linguistic Programming (NLP) 41, 54, 56, 107, 185-186, 188, 386

O

on-line focus groups 38, 52-53
outline guide 131-132, 144, 222, 388

P

"Part Of Answer In Question" (POAIQ) 177, 389
Perceptions, Opinions, Beliefs, and Attitudes (POBAs) 19, 27-31, 34-35, 91, 213, 256, 278, 284, 327, 347, 389, 390, 403
    attitude 30
    belief 29-30
    creating environment for POBAs to emerge 105
    opinion 28-29
    perception 28
piggyback groups 51, 383, 388
probing 9, 58, 86, 87, 90, 105, 177, 239-242
    nuances of 241
    probe 28, 177, 193, 208, 209, 239-242, 378, 389
    distinctions of 240-241
    three areas of 240
projective techniques 59, 189-193
    scenario device 190
    thinking vs. feeling 191
proposal 334, 378, 383, 390
purpose statement 152, 155, 330-332, 390
    crafting a clear one 330-331
    role of in QREs 153, 331

Q

Qualitative Market Research (QLMR) 5-7, 19, 37-54, 91, 95-97, 140, 347-354, 381, 390, 396
    advertising research 195-198
    Pull/Push Factor 198, 204-205
    characteristics of 38-39
    history of 37-38, 347
    players in 5-7
    the "Why Premise" 207-211, 239-240, 252-254, 398-399
Qualitative Research Events (QREs) 5-7, 17-18, 21-25, 27-31, 33-36, 81-84, 85-86, 90, 104-106, 371, 373, 378, 381, 384, 385, 388, 390
    4 Stages of 39-40, 224-225, 351, 371
    closure 40, 86, 105, 150, 250, 351, 371, 374
    in-depth investigation 35, 40, 105, 150, 250, 351, 371, 381
    introduction 34, 40, 86, 105, 132, 147-149, 249, 351, 371, 382, 394
    rapport and reconnaissance 34, 40, 86, 105, 149-150, 186, 249, 351, 371, 382, 391
    major players 85
    pacing 43, 186-187, 188, 388
qualitative research projects 17-18, 19-25
invisible groups 175-178
questions
    alternatives to asking "why" 207-211
    creating powerful questions 249-254
    drawbacks of poor questions 250-251
    leading questions 352-353, 363-367, 374, 383
    neutral question 327
    POAIQ 177, 389
    question stem 363-364
    role and purpose of 249-250, 337-340

serial 177
SQLA 177, 235, 395
"true" questions 176, 233-237, 327, 353
"why" 77, 207-211, 398-399

R

rapport 391
  creating in IDIs 260-261
  ways to build with respondents 57, 132, 192, 227-231
recording 49, 133, 136, 258, 375
recruiting 131, 161, 259-260, 384, 391
reports 24, 137-138, 275-288, 289-294, 295-299, 301-306, 360, 392
  analysis of data for 292
  executive/topline 137, 269-273, 283, 285, 295-296
  format of 138
  full report 297
  key factors in 294
  oral 137, 388
  PowerPoint 137, 388
  tips for writing 276-288
  top-of-mind 295-296
research rigor 19, 79, 165, 392
respondents
  creating trust in 42, 192, 350
  "emotional handshake" with 216, 228-229, 361-362
  entering the world of 186, 213-217
  "floater" 259-260, 378
  getting below "top-of-mind" with 44-48, 50, 56, 58-59, 189-193, 244-246
  handling troublemakers 134-135
  maintaining interest of 43-44, 351-352
  pacing and leading of (NLP) 186-187
  respect of 42-43, 87-88, 124, 198, 214, 262, 317-318, 350
roll 177, 393

S

sanctioned voyeurism 393
Short Question, Long Answer (SQLA) 395, 403
silence 243-248, 383, 386-387
Single Point of Contact (SPOC)/Client Spokesperson 173, 318-319, 325, 374, 395
sophisticated naïveté 13, 75, 88, 109, 135, 395

T

"Teflon Method" 83-84, 363, 396

U

Unconditional Positive Regard (UPR) 11, 87-88, 107, 317, 386, 398
universal guide 144, 222, 225, 397-398

V

"Voice of the Consumer" (VOC) 197, 198, 367, 374, 398

W

Why
  argument against using 207-211, 239, 252-253, 398-399